I0469819

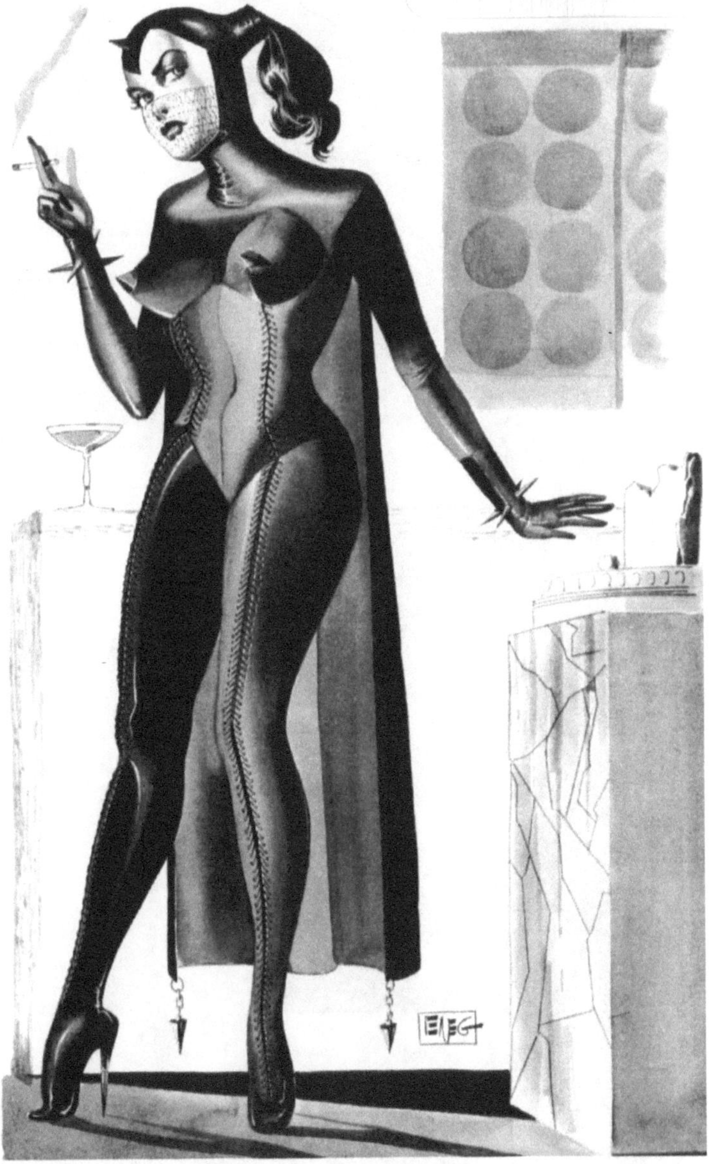

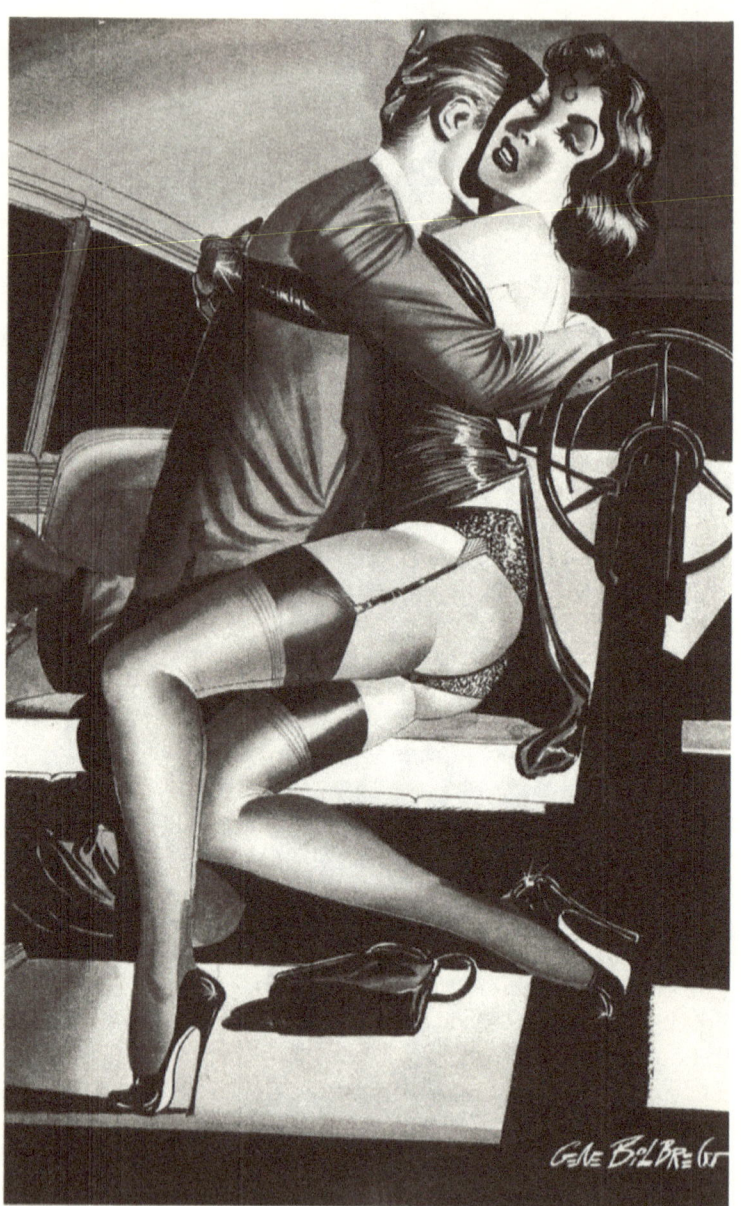

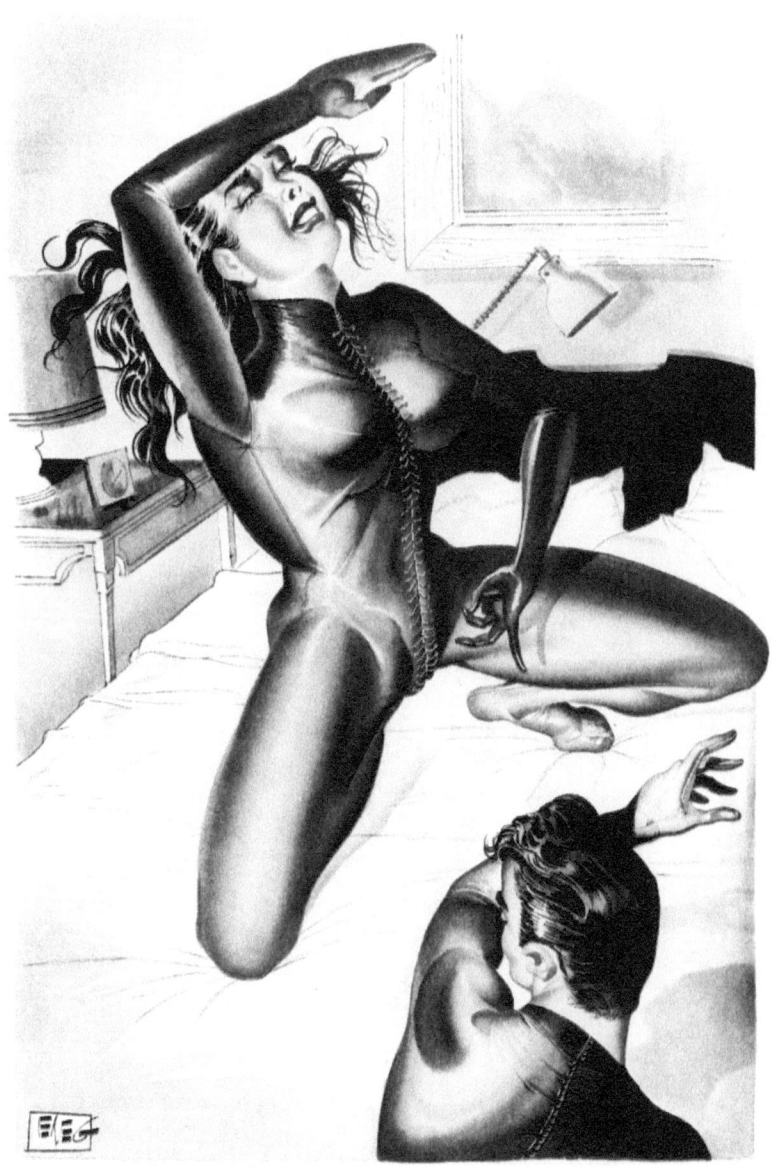

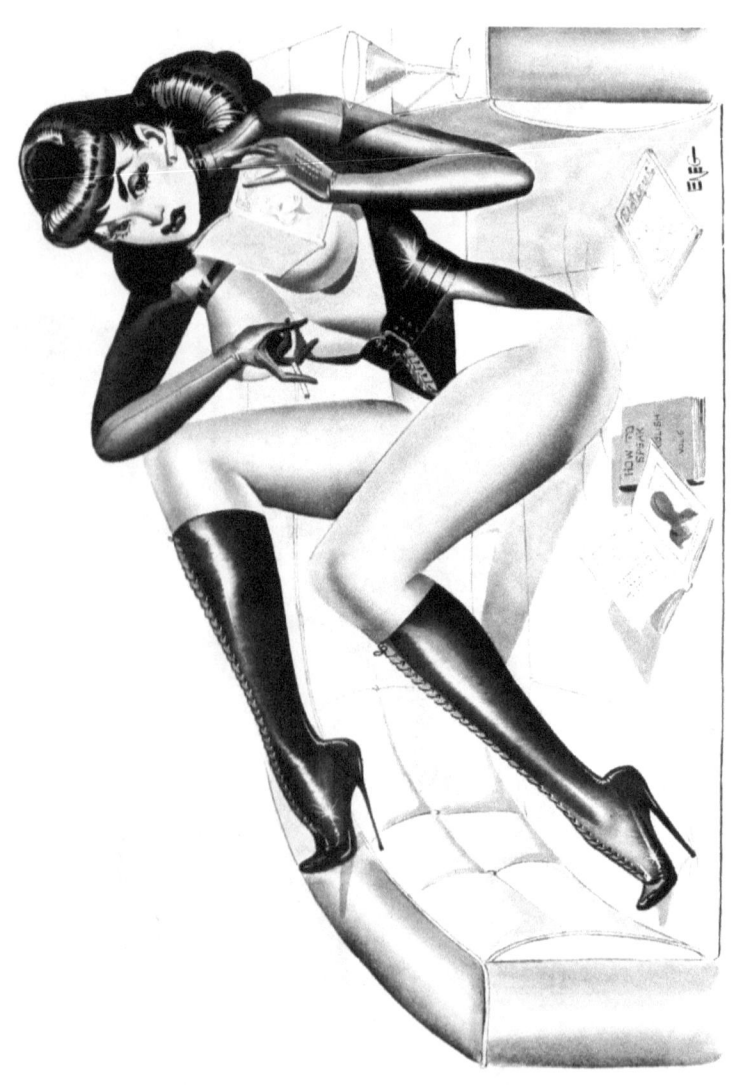

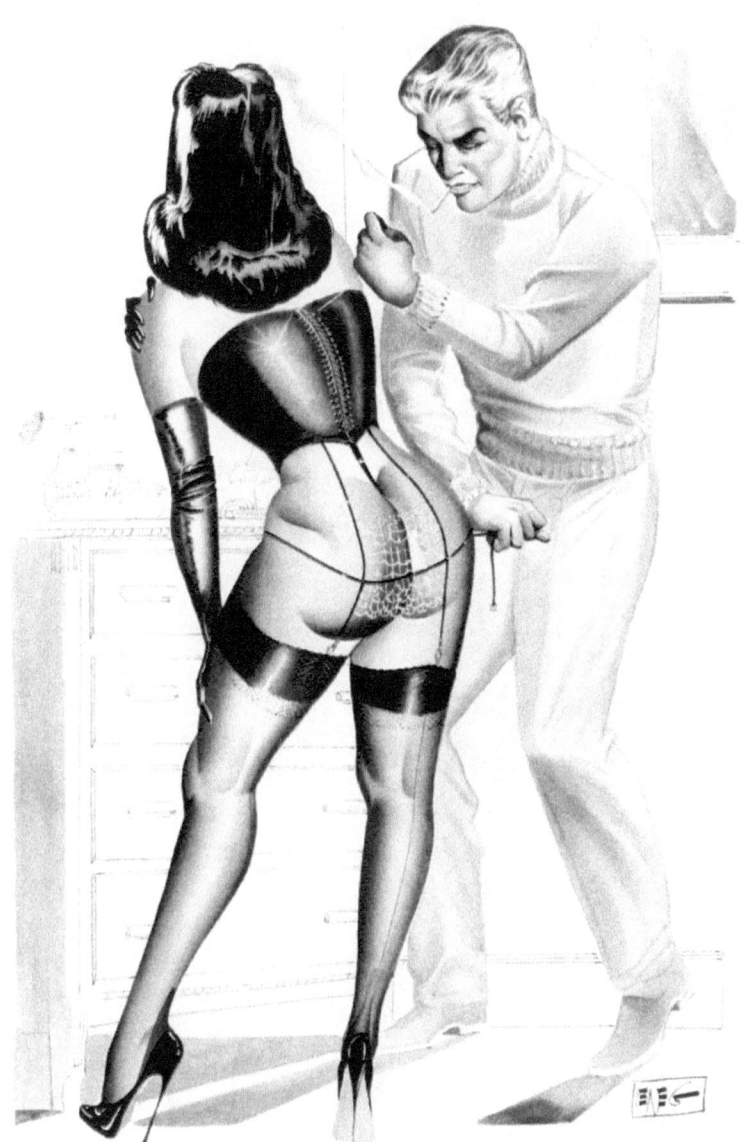

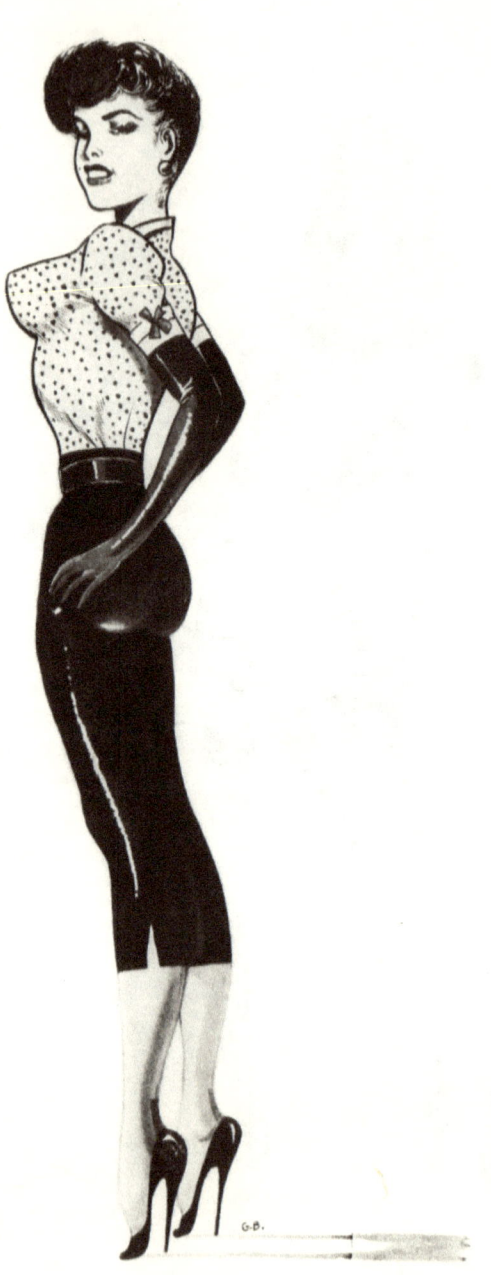

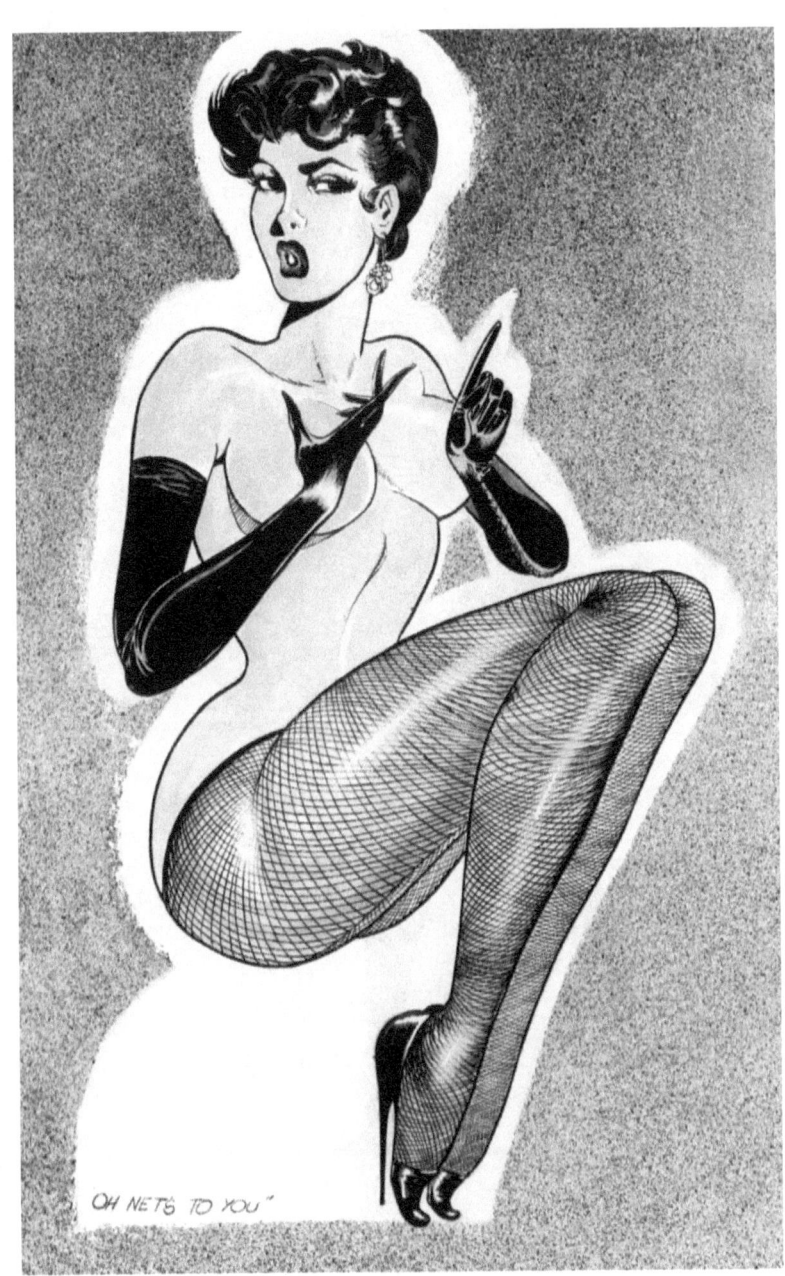

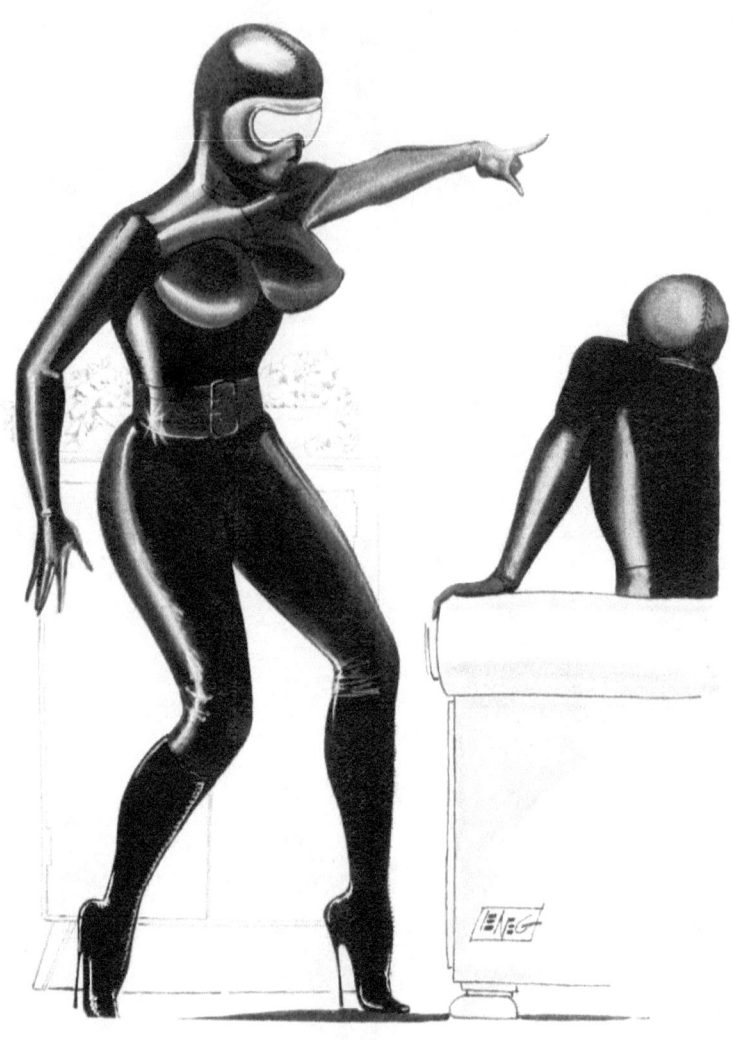

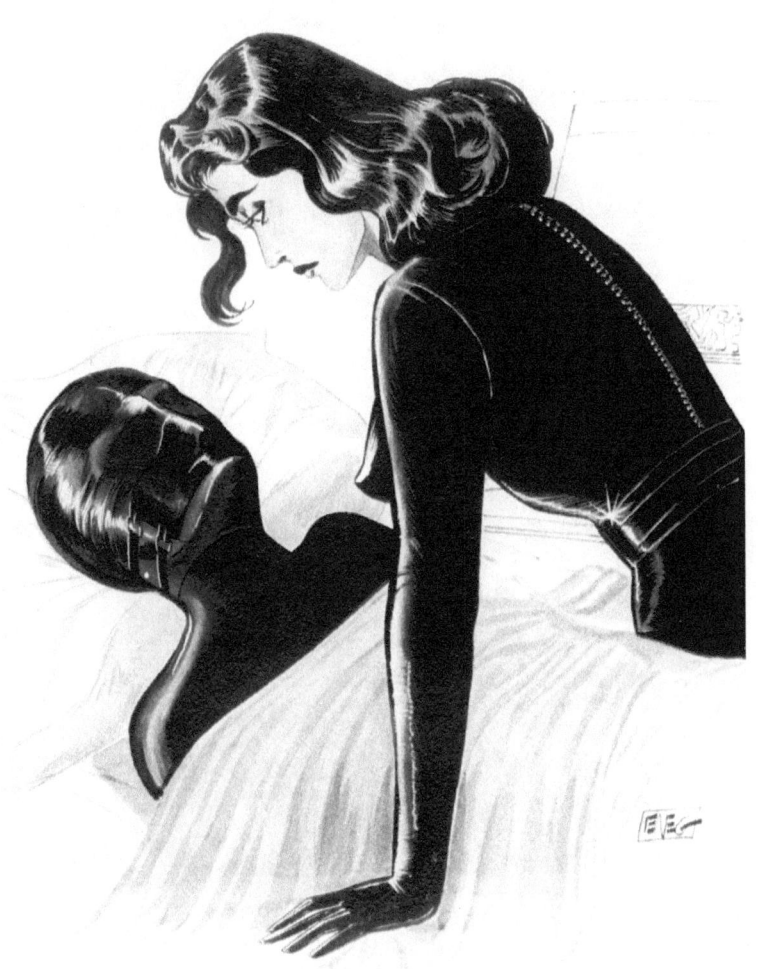

Eneg

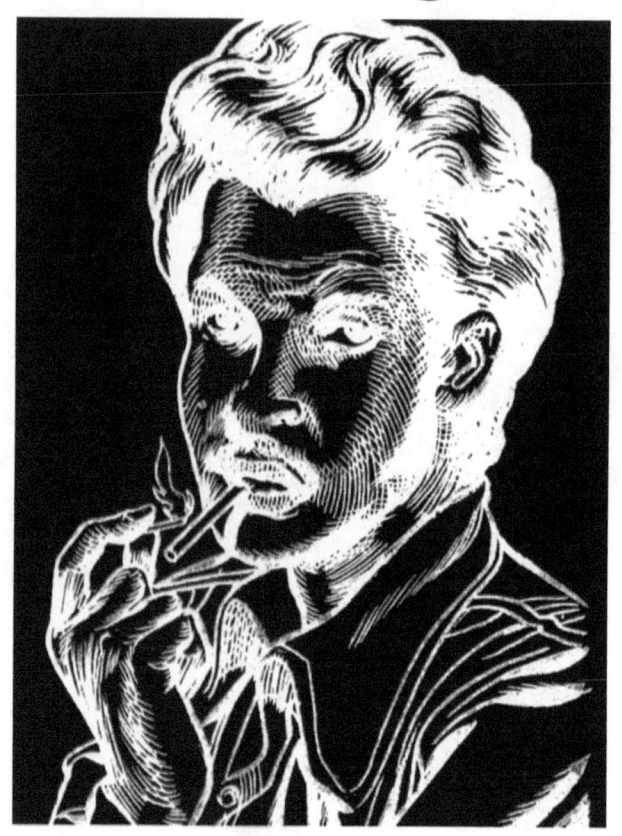

Revealed

Gene Bilbrew

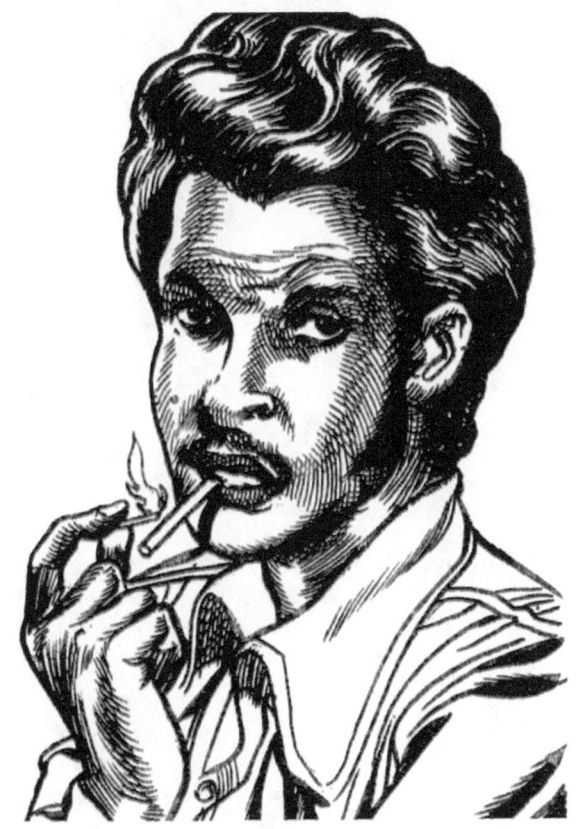

Revealed

by Richard Pérez Seves

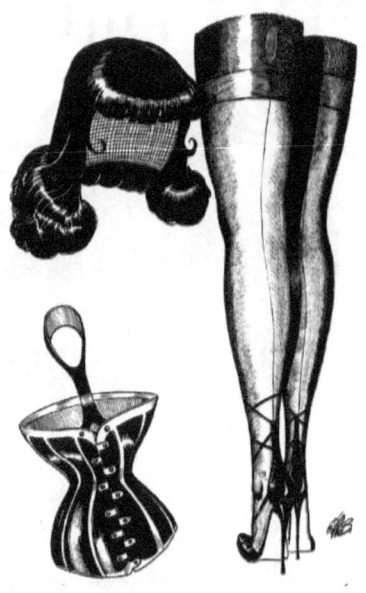

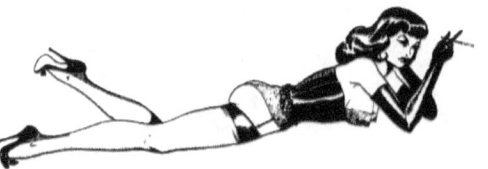

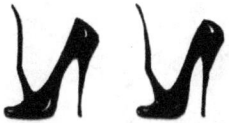

For Nicolas Winding Refn

(with thanks to Jimmy McDonough)

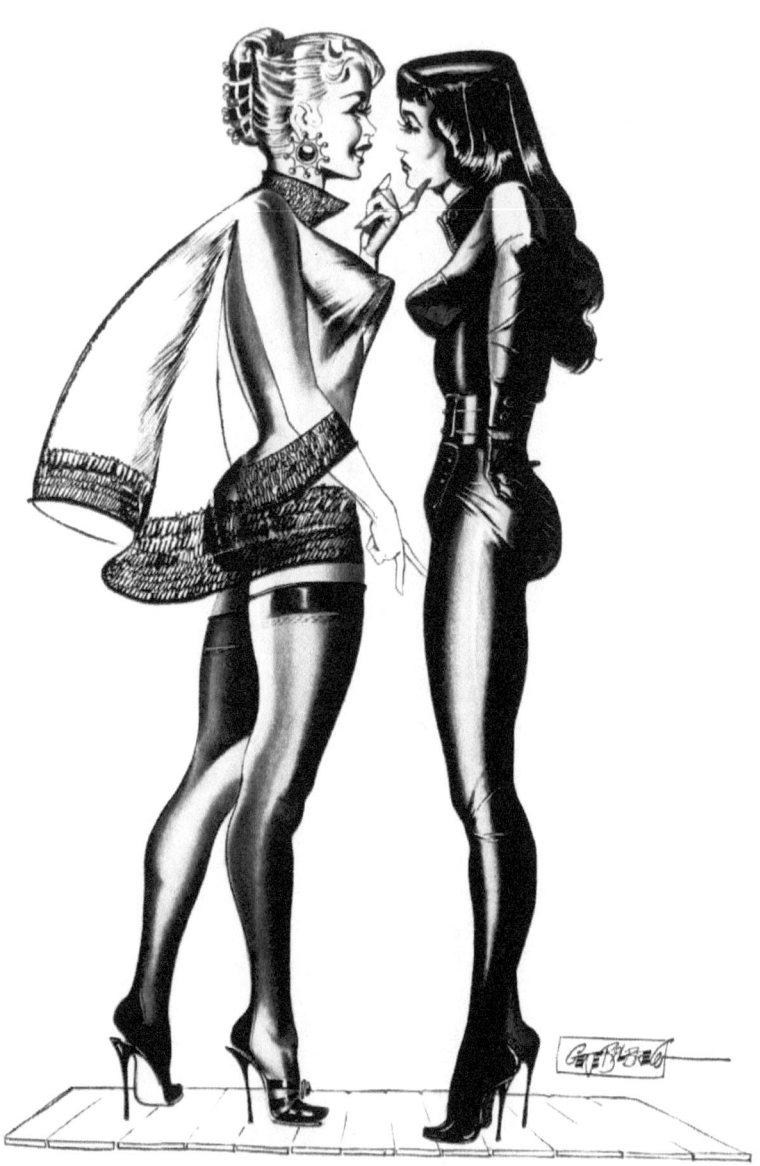

CONTENTS

Part One: Introduction to an Outsider Artist ... 1

Bilbrew's Childhood and Early Years ... 8

The Mellow Tones ... 13

Glory Days of The Basin Street Boys ... 18

The 5 Ebonaires & Rosita Davis ... 22

Part Two: Bilbrew Embraces an Art Career ... 29

Clifford & Will Eisner ... 30

Art School, Eric Stanton & Irving Klaw ... 32

Eneg for Klaw: Art Portfolio ... 39

Edward Mishkin & Bizarre Art ... 81

Leonard Burtman ... 122

Bilbrew for Burtman: Art Portfolio ... 127

Bilbrew in the 1960s ... 175

Peerless Sales & Fighting Women ... 190

Bilbrew's Unraveling ... 196

Bilbrew Sleaze: Art Portfolio ... 219

Bilbrew in the XXX '70s ... 233

Epilogue ... 244

Notes ... 270

PART ONE

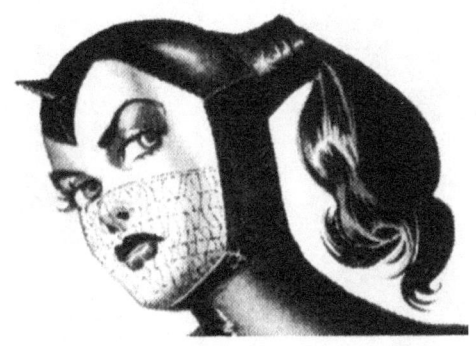

Of the great American outsider artists who gave shape and form to what today is known as "fetish art," perhaps the most neglected is Gene Bilbrew. Part of Bilbrew's obscurity is due to the shadowy culture in which he operated, a culture that prided itself—in line with the underworld element that funded it—on not keeping records. Part of it is due to the fact that Bilbrew was a black man in America—clearly, a black man who never got his due.

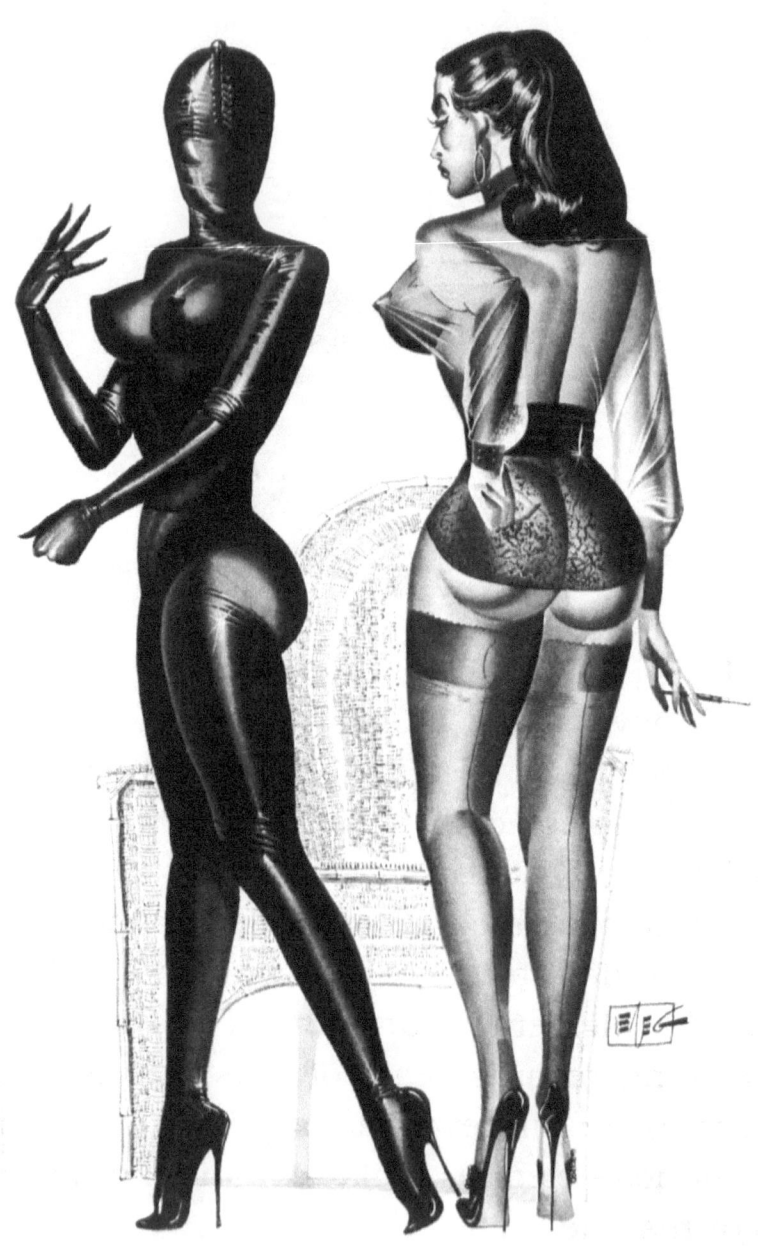

Extending to the present day—and even among art and comic historians of his own race—there is a peculiar ignorance or perhaps willful denial of Bilbrew's unconventional legacy, likely due to Bilbrew's material catering to a sexual minority. The *Encyclopedia of Black Comics*, compiled by an Eisner award-winning university professor and said to focus on "people of African descent who have published significant works in the United States or have worked across various aspects of the comics industry"[i] refutes or excludes any mention of Bilbrew's existence. Ironically, while Bilbrew's work has never been brought up in connection to an Eisner award, Bilbrew did work for Will Eisner in his lifetime, all the while choking down Eisner's portrayal of racial stereotypes, especially regarding African Americans.

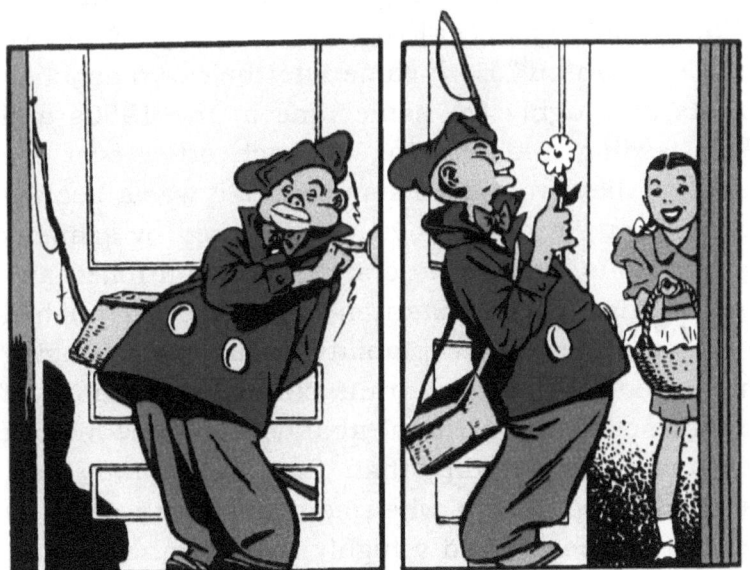

From Will Eisner's weekly comic, *The Spirit*

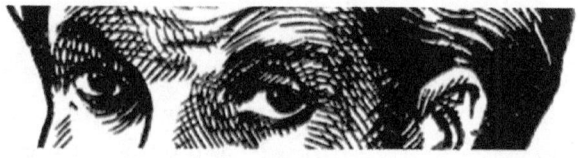

Was Bilbrew the first black career fetish artist in history? Yes. Was he the only black fetish artist operating in the 1950s or '60s? No. At one point, Bilbrew introduced fellow Angeleno and childhood friend William "Bill" Alexander to the genre, although Alexander only marginally became a fetish artist.[ii]

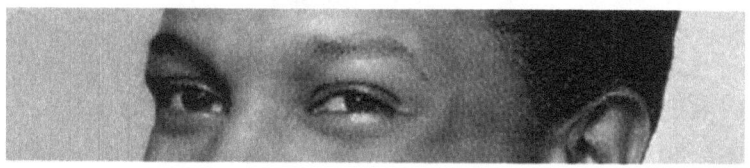

No telling of Bilbrew's story can leave out mention of fellow fetish art pioneer Ernest Stanten—better known as "Eric Stanton." Both came into their own as fetish artists at roughly the same time in the 1950s and '60s, feeding and reacting off each other over the years as they evolved. In some ways, it was a healthy competition; in other ways, not. Marked by a highly spontaneous, often erratic style—less controlled and precise than that of Stanton—Bilbrew's art pushed the boundaries of acceptability in his day, plunging into taboo narratives of trans culture and realms of sadomasochism with total abandon. Bilbrew's work contained more nudity than that of Stanton; also, more violence, which when combined with sexually deviant themes proved a highly risky combination in the legal landscape of the 1950s and '60s.

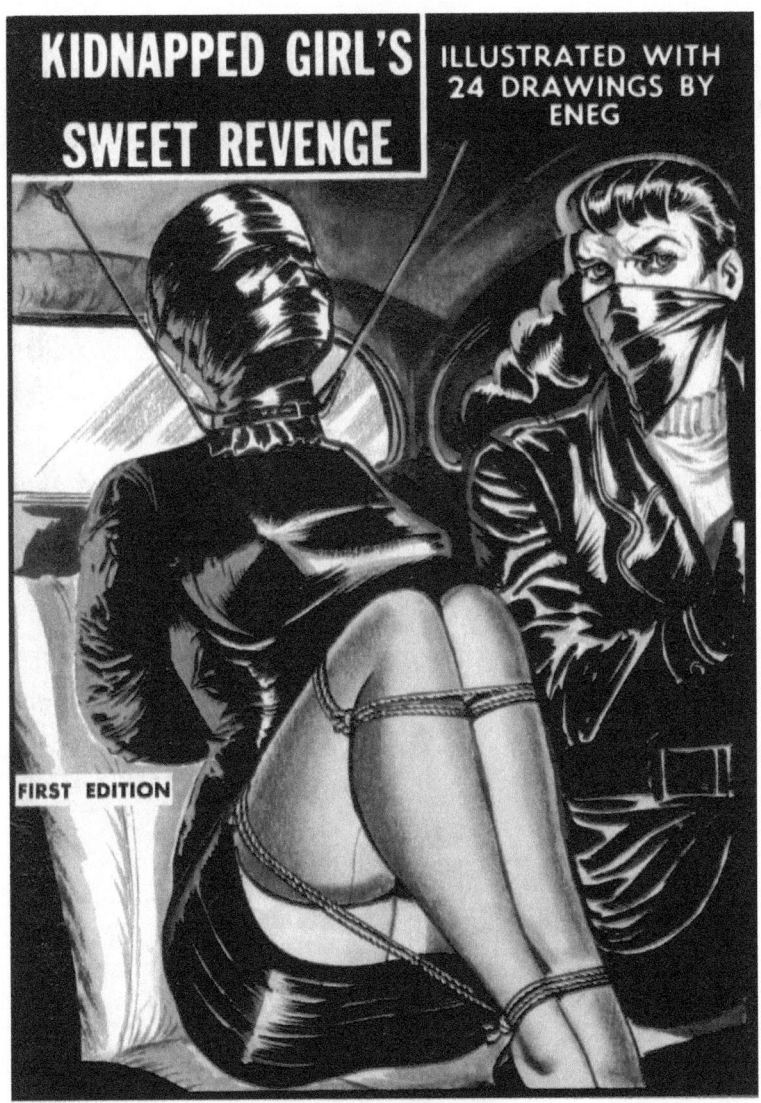

For Irving Klaw, 1959

In researching the life of Gene Bilbrew, there remains very little to draw on: Bilbrew gave no interviews in his lifetime, left no known family, and, other than his unique body of art, departed from this world without leaving a trace. As for what little is known of the artist, nearly all of it—widely paraphrased on the Internet—has come from the historical introductions written by fetish art publisher J.B. Rund, who reprinted seven volumes of Bilbrew's golden age work as part of the *Bizarre Comix* series in the 1970s and '80s. *Bizarre Comix*, as Rund informed me, was packaged through Star Distributors Inc., where Bill Alexander was art director for a number of years. This gave Rund an opportunity to ask Alexander about his longtime friend and one-time studio mate.

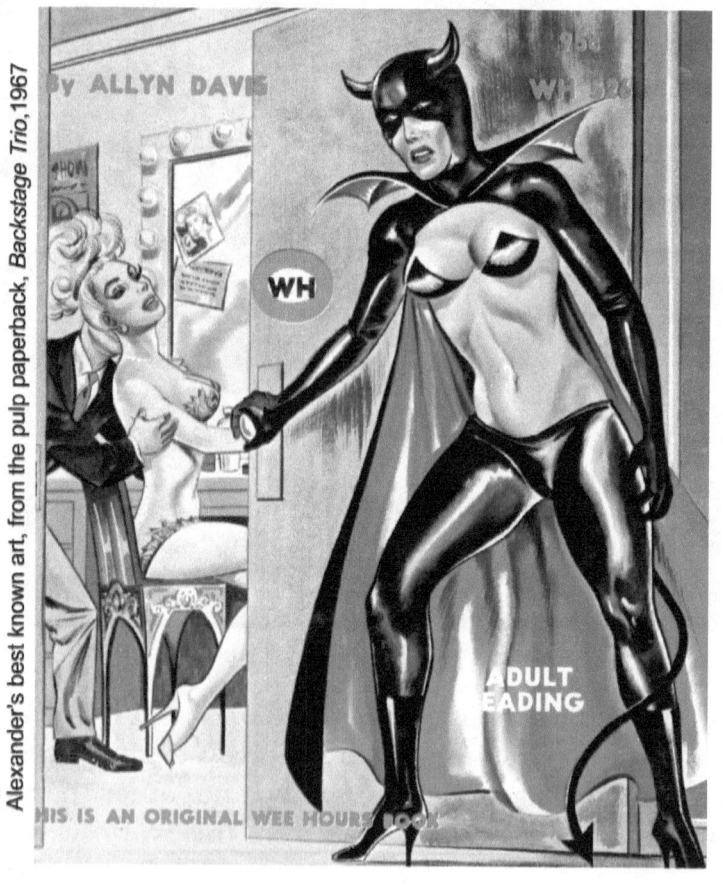

Alexander's best known art, from the pulp paperback, *Backstage Trio,* 1967

6

To the best of his memory, Alexander recalled that Bilbrew's first art-related project was in contributing the storyline for a comic Alexander illustrated—reputed to feature the first black superhero character—*The Bronze Bomber,* which ran in the African-American newspaper *Los Angeles Sentinel.* Later Bilbrew created a *Hercules* comic strip for a health (or fitness) magazine, according to Alexander.

The *Los Angeles Sentinel* (1934-2005) has been digitized and made available online. A careful search between the years 1934-1960 reveals no evidence of *The Bronze Bomber.* Though Alexander did contribute art to the *Sentinel;* both the line art style and the pseudonym ("Wm. Alex") is consistent with work he would later contribute to the Miltone record label.[iii]

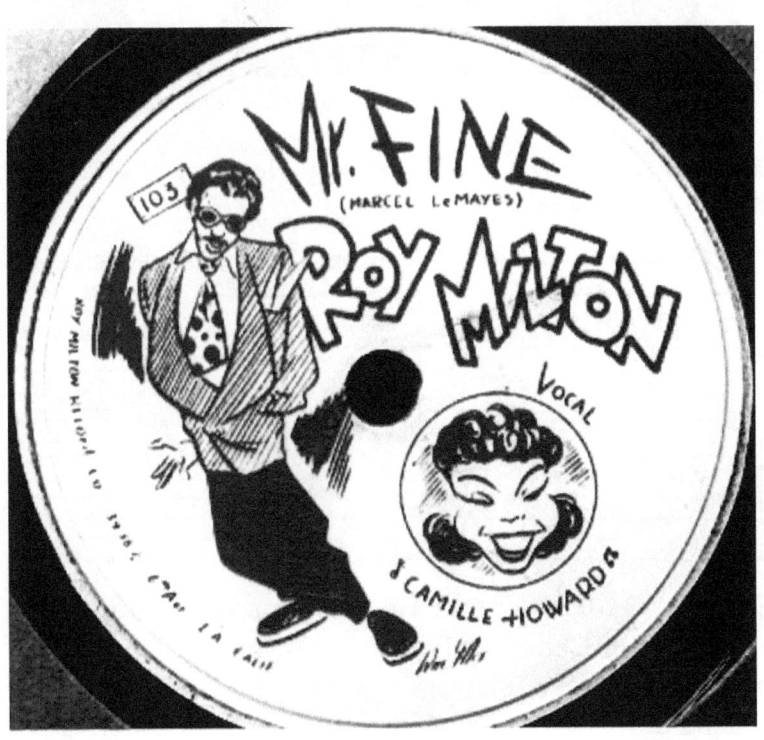

As it turns out, Alexander recalled the wrong newspaper. This discovery was made by artist Mildred Howard, who by sheer coincidence repurposed a 1943 section of the strip as the base layer of her collage *Millenials & XYZ #IV*. As we can see below, it was the *Los Angeles Tribune*. To be clear, Alexander was the artist of *The Bronze Bomber,* not Bilbrew (as appears in countless blogs). Is the character a superhero? It seems not. It's a man in a zoot suit.

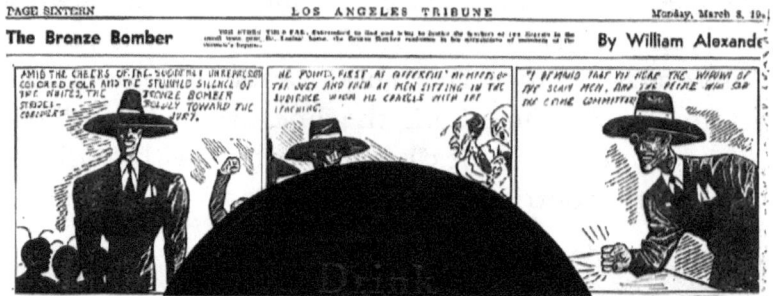

The Bronze Bomber by William "Bill" Alexander (dated March 8 1943)

But let's start from the beginning. Here are the facts of Gene Bilbrew's life:[iv]

Eugene "Gene" Webster Bilbrew was born June 29th, 1923 in the Central-Alameda area of Los Angeles—a neighborhood known for producing notable jazz musicians.[v]

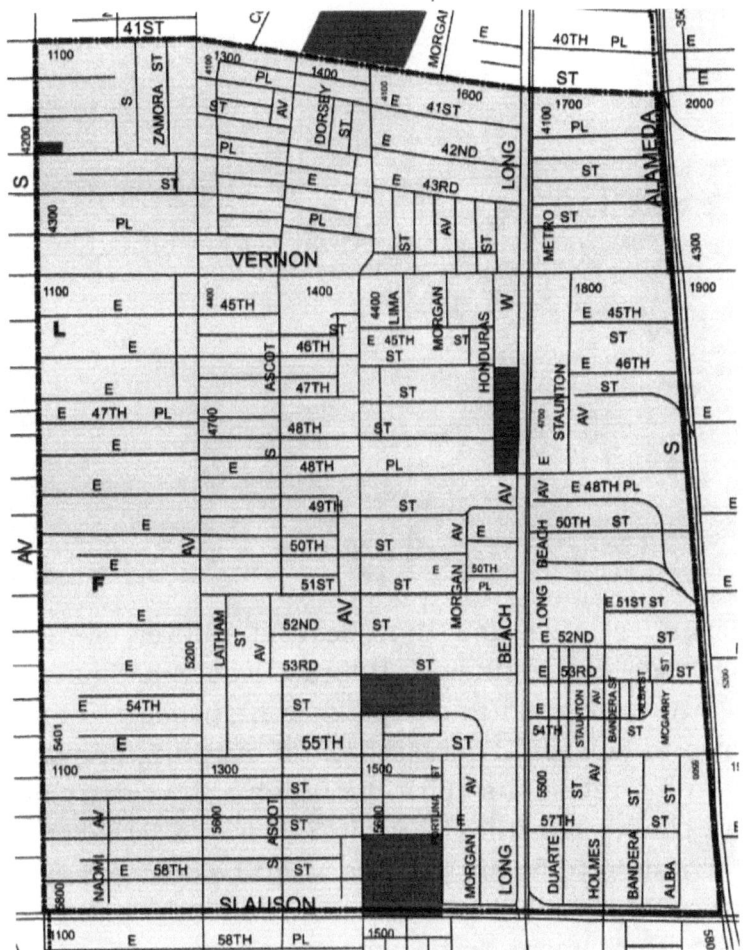

Bilbrew's hood: he lived on 47th and 52nd St. (see p. 270)

The middle child of three, his younger sister was named Ruth, and his older sister was named Frances Muriel. His parents were outsiders to that city. Omri Watson Bilbrew hailed from Texas, while Bilbrew's mother, Carrie, was from Oklahoma. They met and married in Los Angeles in 1914,[vi] with their first child, Frances, born in 1921. Omri supported his family through custodial work.[vii]

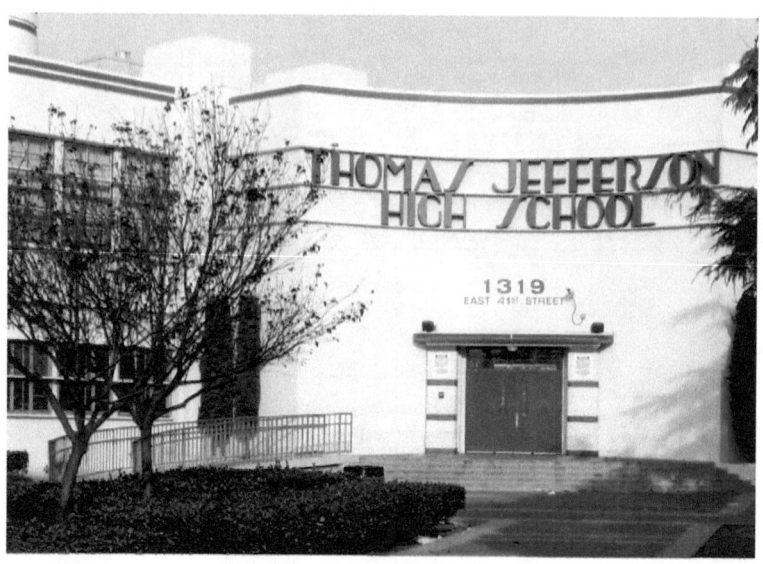

Alexander suggested that he and Bilbrew went to high school together.[viii] Bilbrew was smallish and slightly built, and to compensate he needed to make noise to be seen. Possessed of an outgoing personality and a rebellious spirit, he became the class clown and challenged rules—a trait that would be a source of irritation to future patrons when he emerged as an artist. While still a teen, Bilbrew evidently fathered a child from whom he became estranged.[ix] After three years of high school, he dropped out. In his young adult life, his one job was in the service industry, as a waiter.[x]

With World War II underway, it was a perilous time to be a young male, and in June 1942,[xi] as required by law, Bilbrew registered for Selective Service at his local board. As it happens, his military registration card—one of the few surviving personal artifacts of his life—provides significant details. On the back (below), height and weight; on the front (next page), a confirmation of his middle name "Webster," his home address, which he shared with his mother, and a notation made in the bottom left-hand corner "CDD Aug 27 1943," which indicates that Bilbrew was discharged from service for psychiatric reasons.[xii] [xiii]

REGISTRAR'S REPORT

DESCRIPTION OF REGISTRANT

RACE		HEIGHT (Approx.)	WEIGHT (Approx.)	COMPLEXION	
White		*5 5*	*1 3 5*	Sallow	
		EYES	HAIR	Light	
Negro	✓	Blue	Blonde	Ruddy	
		Gray	Red	Dark	
Oriental		Hazel ✓	Brown ✓	Freckled	
		Brown ✓	Black ✓	Light brown	✓
Indian		Black	Gray	Dark brown	
			Bald	Black	
Filipino					

Other obvious physical characteristics that will aid in identification...........

I certify that my answers are true; that the person registered has read or has had read to him his own answers; that I have witnessed his signature or mark and that all of his answers of which I have knowledge are true, except as follows:

(Signature of registrar)

Registrar for Local Board.... *2 1 5* .... *L. A. Calif.*

(Number)   (City or county)   (State)

Date of registration.... JUN 3 0 1942

Local Board No. 215   91

Los Angeles County   037

(STAMP OF LOCAL BOARD)

(The stamp of the Local Board having jurisdiction of the registrant shall be placed in the above space)

11

L B 215

REGISTRATION CARD—(Men born on or after January 1, 1922 and on or before June 30, 1924)

Bilbrew's draft card, front

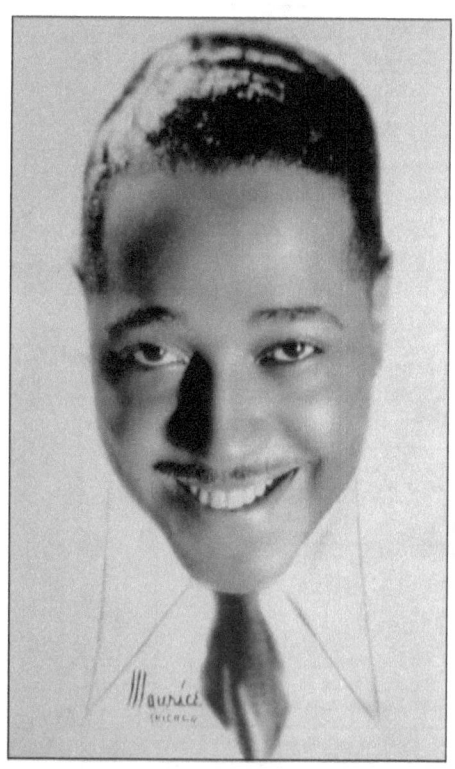

In their formative years, Bilbrew and Alexander bonded over their common love of jazz, and they attended live shows together. One outstanding event featured Duke Ellington (left), and it had a profound effect on Bilbrew, even inspiring a zoot suit style of dress.[xiv] According to Alexander, Bilbrew had little interest in drawing and art at this point and solely envisioned himself in the spotlight as an entertainer. It wasn't long before Bilbrew made this happen.

THE MELLOW TONES

Timed with his premature discharge from military duty, Bilbrew's first vocal group was formed in the summer of 1943, first spelled in print as "The Mellow Tones." A flattering review of the group appeared in the *California Eagle* that fall:

> May I take time and space here to give credit to this aggregation of scintillating rhythm whose talent speaks for itself. Ranging in ages between nineteen and twenty, these five young fellows Hal McEwen, Ruben Saunders, Gene Bilbrew, Walter Johnson, and accompanist Evon Morgan have definitely come a long way in the two short months they have been organized.[xv]

The Mellow Tones performed at jamboree hops, church and charity events, and opened for Earl "Fatha" Hines.[xvi][xvii] One individual taking notice was aspiring entertainer Ormonde Wilson Jr., a tenor in a notable swing choir named "The Plantation Boys."[xviii] Tall and suavely handsome, Ormonde Wilson had the look of a front man. By the time Wilson joined the Mellow Tones, circa 1945, only two original members remained: Reuben Sanders and first baritone Gene Bilbrew.[xix]

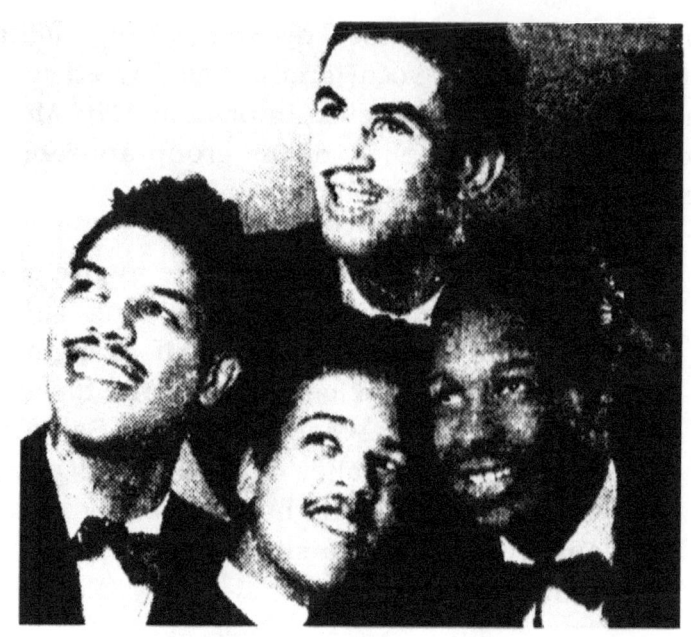

S. W. Tucker Presents
THE MELLOTONES
(Basin Street Boys)

Appearing with BENNY CARTER and his Orchestra at the Robinson Auditorium, Thursday Night, June 13th. Mantan Moreland and Nina Mae McKinney will help to make up the attraction.

NAME CHANGES

As it turned out, finding the right group name proved a challenge. Not only was the original name often misspelled in the press, more than one group had taken ownership of it.[xx] The "Basin Street Boys" moniker was attributed to notable musician Steve Gibson[xxi]—said to be the older stepbrother of Ormonde Wilson[xxii]—who had used it for his combo in the 1930s. Wilson would borrow it to give The Mellow Tones a more marketable handle. By 1946, the group's lineup included Wilson, Arthur Rainwater, son of an Indian chief—who later changed his name to "the more musician-like moniker of Artie Waters"[xxiii]— Reuben Sanders, and Gene Bilbrew.

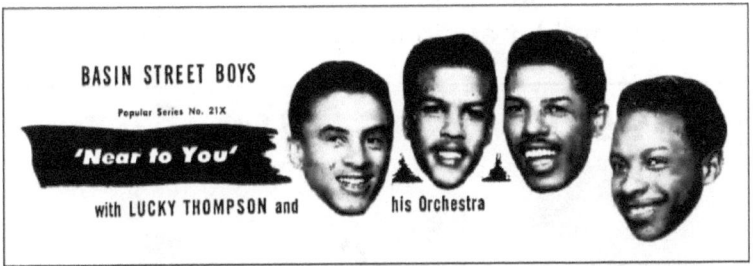

That year, Bilbrew adopted a name change of his own: to that of "Price"—the married name of his sister Frances.[xxiv] Aside from it being—as with Artie Waters—a "more musician-like moniker," we can speculate that a reason for Bilbrew's name change may have been that he was trying to distinguish or distance himself from his famous aunt[xxv]—an overtly religious singer, gospel group organizer, and radio personality at the time receiving considerable coverage in the press, A. C. Bilbrew.[xxvi] Although it might have been an easy step in launching or at least promoting his singing career, it's interesting that Gene never exploited this contact.[xxvii]

For the many who have wondered why they have

never seen photos of Bilbrew? As it turns out, they have—all over the Internet. Gene Price, founding member of the Basin Street Boys, is Gene Bilbrew.

In early 1946, at least for a short time, Price was still being identified as "Bilbrew." Examine the image that appeared in the trade publication *The Cash Box* (below). The magazine is dated 1947, but the group photo harked back to early 1946 in which Bilbrew is clearly identified by name ("Left to right..."). At about 5′ 5″ and slightly built, he was the smallest of the group, with Reuben Sanders a close second. Other physical details—eyebrows, impish smile—help us to identify him, once and for all, in other lineup photos.

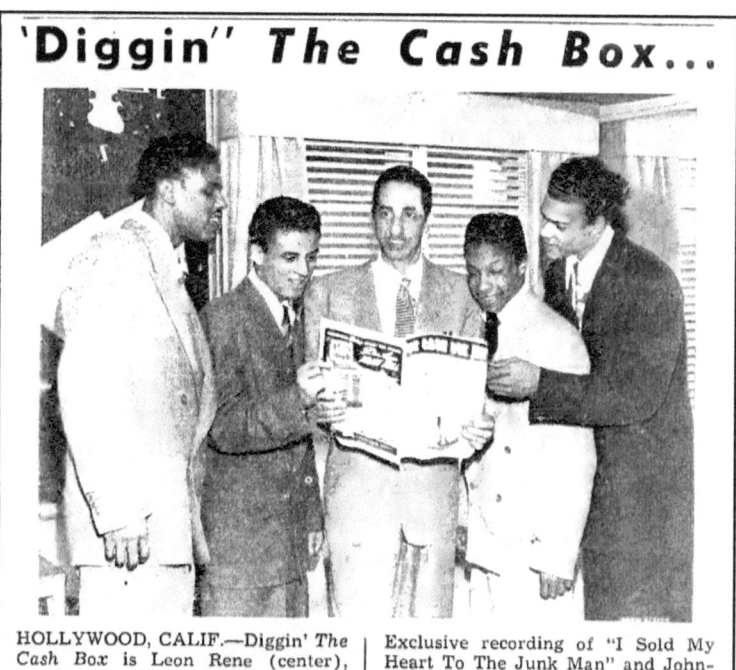

'Diggin'' The Cash Box...

HOLLYWOOD, CALIF.—Diggin' *The Cash Box* is Leon Rene (center), President of Exclusive Records, and the Basin Street Boys. Prexy Rene is justly proud of his artists' fine showing in *The Cash Box's* recent record poll. The Basin Street Boys were consistent favorites with their Exclusive recording of "I Sold My Heart To The Junk Man" and Johnny Moore and his Three Blazers placed first in their field in *The Cash Box's* annual awards for '46. Left to right: Ormand Wilson, Reuben Saunders, Leon Rene, Gene Bilbrew, Arthur Rainwater.

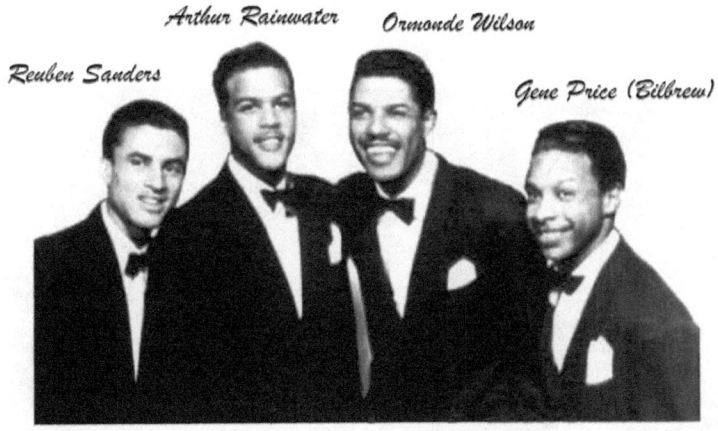

Reuben Sanders *Arthur Rainwater* *Ormonde Wilson* *Gene Price (Bilbrew)*

And so, long-time fans and collectors of his eccentric art now have reason to smile: Gene Bilbrew has a face.

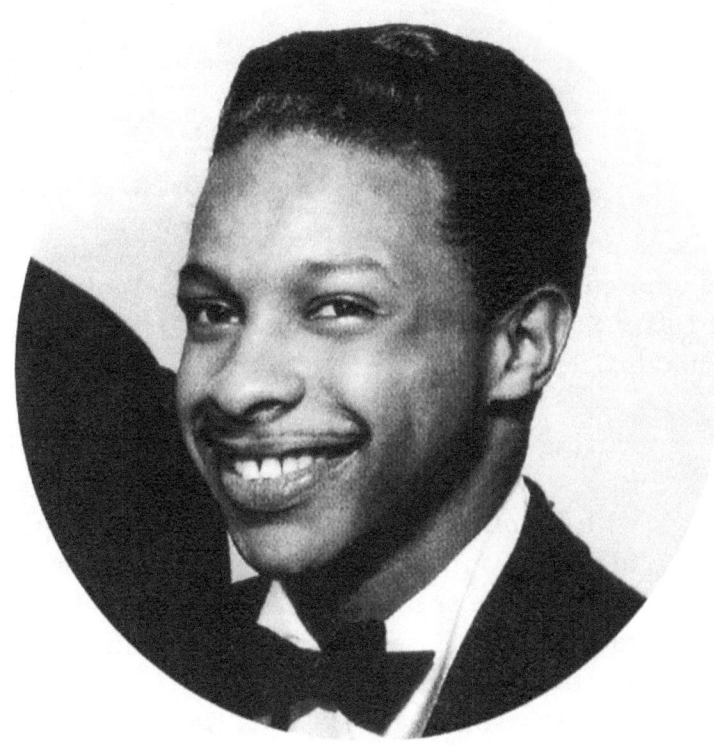

GLORY DAYS OF THE BASIN STREET BOYS

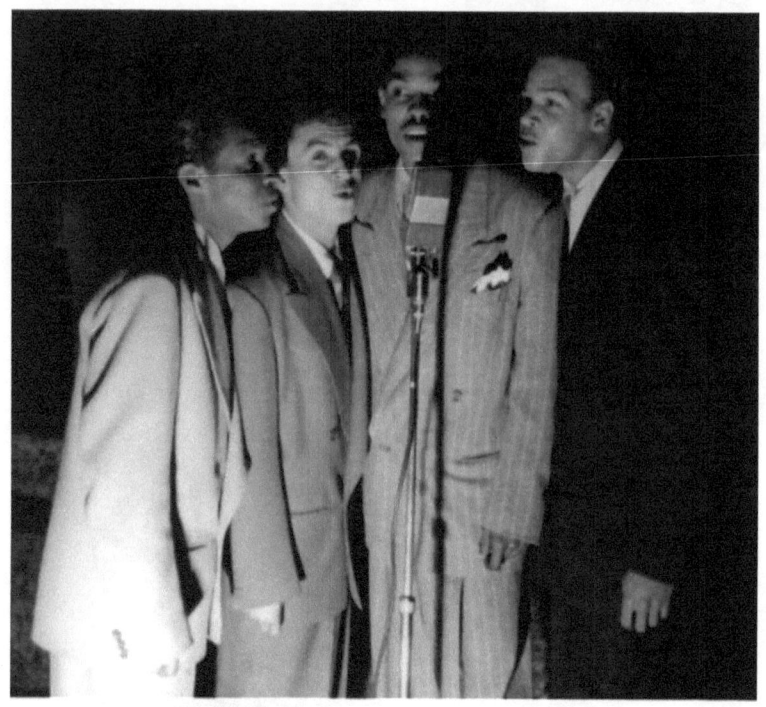

For a short time Bilbrew was living the dream. He had aspired to become a professional singer, and with the Basin Street Boys, he became one. An April 1946 tabloid article spelled it out:

> Having changed their name to the Basin Street Boys because of a similarity in name with another singing combination ... [the] talented young Hollywood singing quartet bid fair to prove one of the hits of Hollywood Gang revue which is embarking on a tour of the South this month...
>
> The Basin Street Boys ... have since been

featured with Earl Hines, Duke Ellington, and have played at the Apollo theatre and the El Grotto in Chicago. They have a unique and pleasant styling of swing tunes and ballads. Three of the boys are native sons of California and all have excellent musical backgrounds. Just recently they made several sides for Exclusive Records, one of them, "I Sold My Heart to the Junk Man," is expected to become a best seller.

Upon their return from the tour, they are tentatively signed to make a film short at a major movie studio.[xxviii]

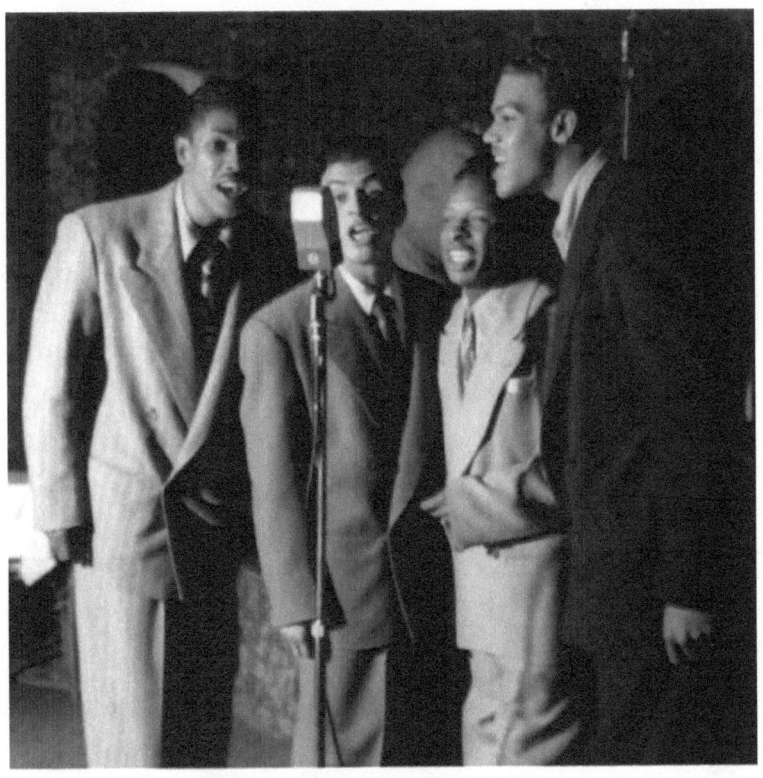

Bilbrew, second from the right

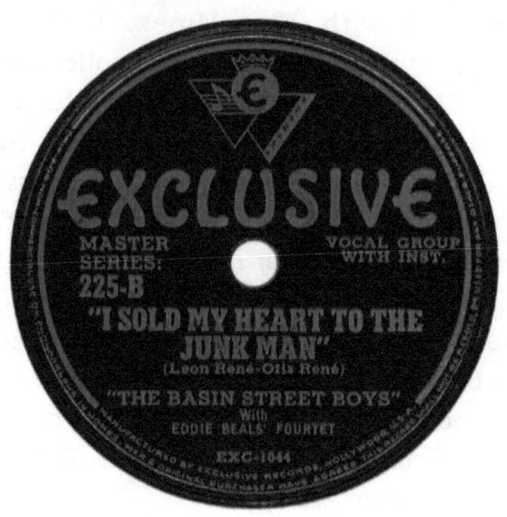

Although "I Sold My Heart to The Junkman" failed to burn up the pop charts, it was a long-running juke-box favorite and popular in live performance [xxix]— recognizable enough that it became a calling card in booking engagements.

Between 1946 and 1947, the peak years of the group, the Basin Street Boys appeared on radio, TV, recorded eight records (sixteen sides) for Leon René's Los Angeles-based Exclusive Records [xxx] and played club and theater circuits across the country, most heavily in New Jersey and Pennsylvania.

REALITY CHECK

"I Sold My Heart to The Junkman" was written by brothers Leon and Otis René, released on their label and, in truth, the Basin Street Boys were only hired hands. (Years later, the song would achieve greater fame as recorded by Patti LaBelle & The Bluebelles, among others. [xxxi]) In the end, Bilbrew and company saw little money, [xxxii] and the struggle to stay alive began. "Ain't Got No Loot," a song written by Bilbrew and Wilson in 1947, [xxxiii] would be accurate.

Ain't got no loot
My pocket's so dry
Feel like I want to cry...

Ain't got no loot
I'm busted out flat
What do you think of that

Ain't got no gold
That jive you hold
I'm just a bankrupted cat...

In 1947, flirting with changes and ways to freshen things up, the group briefly added an unnamed fifth member. [xxxiv]

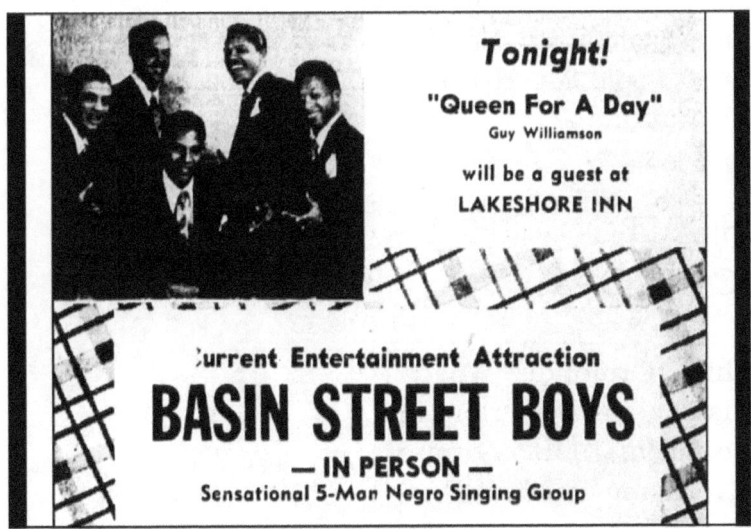

Tonight!
"Queen For A Day"
Guy Williamson
will be a guest at
LAKESHORE INN

Current Entertainment Attraction
BASIN STREET BOYS
— IN PERSON —
Sensational 5-Man Negro Singing Group

Gene Price Now Out On His Own As Featured Act

Gene Price is now singing with the Roy Porter band. Gene Price, in case you're not up on your entertainment history, is the singer whose golden voice skyrocketed the Basin Street Boys to the top of the musical ladder of fame.

Price, a local boy who made good in the sing-song profession, arrived home a fortnight ago and has decided to branch out on his own as a "single."

He handles the vocal chores with Porter's 15-piece swing band, in addition to being featured with his own special musical arrangements.

The Basin Street Boys disbanded several weeks ago.

Failing to find commercial success, the Basin Street Boys began to fracture in 1948 and finally disbanded that fall. By October, Bilbrew was singing with the Roy Porter orchestra (see left),[xxxv] but little was heard of "Gene Price" after that. Ormonde Wilson, not ready to throw in the towel, took a stab at reinventing the group with all new members. The *California Eagle* reported: "The Basin Street Boys, formerly a co-operative group, is now under the complete leadership of Ormonde Wilson...."[xxxvi] He renamed it "Ormonde Wilson and The Basin Street Boys."[xxxvii] The following year, Wilson and his new combo played in Delaware with the by-line: "Remember their hit tune 'I Sold My Heart to the Junkman?'"

THE 5 EBONAIRES & ROSITA DAVIS

While Ormonde Wilson was chasing past glory in the fall of 1949, a group advertising itself as "for-

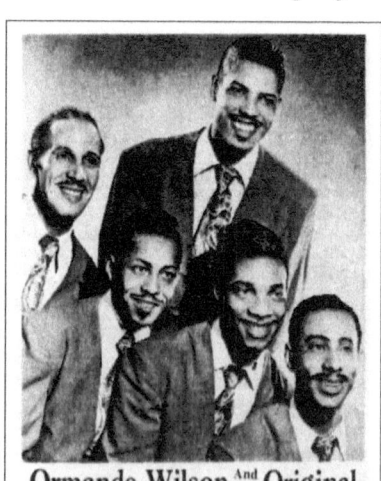

Ormande Wilson And His Original Basin Street Boys

merly the Basin Street Boys" [xxxviii] appeared simultaneously in Pennsylvania. This combo called itself "The 5 Ebonaires." Sharing the bill for an exclusive two week run in Hazleton, PA was Roszetta F. Davis, better known as "Rosita Davis," a Brooklynite who had previously toured with Duke Ellington. [xxxix]

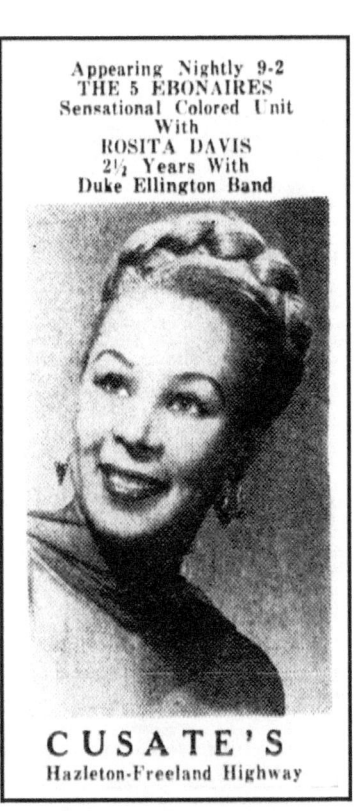

Appearing Nitely 9-2
Don't Miss Them
Sensational Colored
Quintette

The 5 Ebonaires

(Formerly Basin Street
Boys)
With

ROSITA DAVIS

(Lovely Blonde Vocalist
and Dancer. The Betty
Hutton Style, Formerly of
Duke Ellington's Band)

Vocals — Instrumentals

Comedy — Dancing
(Complete Production)

Cusate's

Hazleton-Freeland
Highway

Appearing Nightly 9-2
THE 5 EBONAIRES
Sensational Colored Unit
With
ROSITA DAVIS
2½ Years With
Duke Ellington Band

CUSATE'S
Hazleton-Freeland Highway

Was Bilbrew among the former Basin Street Boys making up The 5 Ebonaires? Evidence suggests that he was because, at the end of the booked two-week engagement, Bilbrew applied for a marriage license and on the 3rd of November 1949 married Rosita Davis. The surviving document (next page) even shows the officiating Reverend signing the document "Hazleton PA." Bilbrew listed his occupation as "entertainer," underscoring that he was still, at least marginally, in show business.

Application for Marriage License

Colored

Commonwealth of Pennsylvania) ss:
County of Luzerne

No. 4054 H

We, the undersigned, in accordance with the statements hereinafter contained, the facts set forth wherein we and each of us do solemnly swear are true and correct to the best of our knowledge and belief, do hereby make application to the Clerk of the Orphans' Court of Luzerne County, Pennsylvania, for a license to marry:

Gene H. Bilbrew
Rozetta F. Davis

Statement of Male:
Full name and surname ..... *Gene H. Bilbrew* ..... Color *Colored*
Occupation ..... *entertainer* ..... Birthplace *Los Angeles, Calif*
Residence ..... *Los Angeles, Calif* ..... Age *26* years
Previous marriage or marriages ..... *none* ..... Date of death or divorce
of former wife or wives
Is the applicant related by blood or marriage to the person whom he desires to marry? *no*
Is the applicant afflicted with any transmissible disease? ..... *no*
Name and surname of Father ..... *Orrin* ..... of Mother ..... *Carrie*
Maiden name of Mother ..... *Jefferson*
Residence of Father ..... *Los Angeles, Calif.* ..... of Mother ..... *same*
Color of Father ..... *Colored* ..... of Mother ..... *w.*
Occupation of Father ..... *Custodian* ..... of Mother ..... *H.W.*
Birthplace of Father ..... *Los Angeles, Calif.* ..... of Mother ..... *Oklahoma*
Is the applicant an imbecile, epileptic, of unsound mind or under guardianship as a person of unsound mind or under the influence of any intoxicating liquor or narcotic drug? ..... *no*
Has applicant, within five years been an inmate of any county asylum or home for indigent persons? ..... *no*
..... Is applicant physically able to support a family? ..... *yes*
Signature of applicant ..... *Gene H. Bilbrew*

Statement of Female:
Full name and surname ..... *Rozetta F. Davis* ..... Color *Colored*
Occupation ..... *Entertainer* ..... Birthplace *New York City*
Residence ..... *Brooklyn, N.Y.* ..... Age *24* years
Previous marriage or marriages ..... *none* ..... Date of death or divorce
of former husband or husbands
Is the applicant related by blood or marriage to the person whom she desires to marry? *no*
Is the applicant afflicted with any transmissible disease? ..... *no*
Name and surname of Father ..... *Hans* ..... of Mother ..... *Marion*
Maiden name of Mother ..... *Hook*
Residence of Father ..... *Deceased* ..... of Mother ..... *Brooklyn N.Y.*
Color of Father ..... *Black* ..... of Mother ..... *Black*
Occupation of Father .... of Mother ..... *H.W.*
Birthplace of Father ..... *Italy* ..... of Mother ..... *Boston, Mass*
Is the applicant an imbecile, epileptic, of unsound mind or under guardianship as a person of unsound mind or under the influence of any intoxicating liquor or narcotic drug? ..... *no*
Signature of applicant ..... *Rozetta F. Davis*
Sworn and subscribed before me this ..... *28th* day of ..... *October* ..... , A. D. 194 *9*
George Pierrs
Clerk of Orphans' Court

Asst. Clerk of Orphans' Court.

Marriage License Issued ..... **NOV 1 - 1949**
Married ..... *Nov. 3, 1949* ..... by *Rev Francis Alabrydria – Hazleton*

Commonwealth of Pennsylvania) ss:
County of Luzerne

CONSENT TO THE MARRIAGE OF CHILD OR WARD

I, ... residing at .....

Rosita Davis kept her name and without much of a honeymoon, on November 8th, was back on the road with the Ebonaires,[xl] which after various days, shedding members, morphed into "Three Ebonaires," then, lastly, "Jay Johnson and the Ebonaires,"[xli] with Davis still in tow; members of this last combination included Frank Smith, Max Cooper, Bill Arnold ... but no Gene Price—the only one in fact associated with the Basin Street Boys (Jay Johnson had been part of the original Mellow Tones). Following a final (December '49) engagement in Pennsylvania, Rosita Davis evidently put her performance career on hold.[xlii] By then, just as likely, Gene Bilbrew had renounced his.

And what of the marriage between Bilbrew and Davis? It seemed to survive, in one form or another, at least into the early '50s. In 1951 and '52, they shared an apartment and telephone number in the Bedford-Stuyvesant section of Brooklyn.[xliii]

In late 1952, Davis again picked up her singing career, which may have signified a tipping point in their relationship. According to one tabloid report:

> Roszetta Davis, former singer with the Duke Ellington aggregation, has signed an exclusive booking pact with the Shaw Artists Corporation, the agency announced on Monday...
>
> Roszetta, following her stint with Ellington, took over the mistress of ceremony duties at New York's Club Savannah in Greenwich Village, where she built an enviable reputation as a handler of the microphone.
>
> Returning to the singing end of show business, Roszetta has undergone an intensive six-month refresher period during which she studied with top vocal coaches.[xliv]

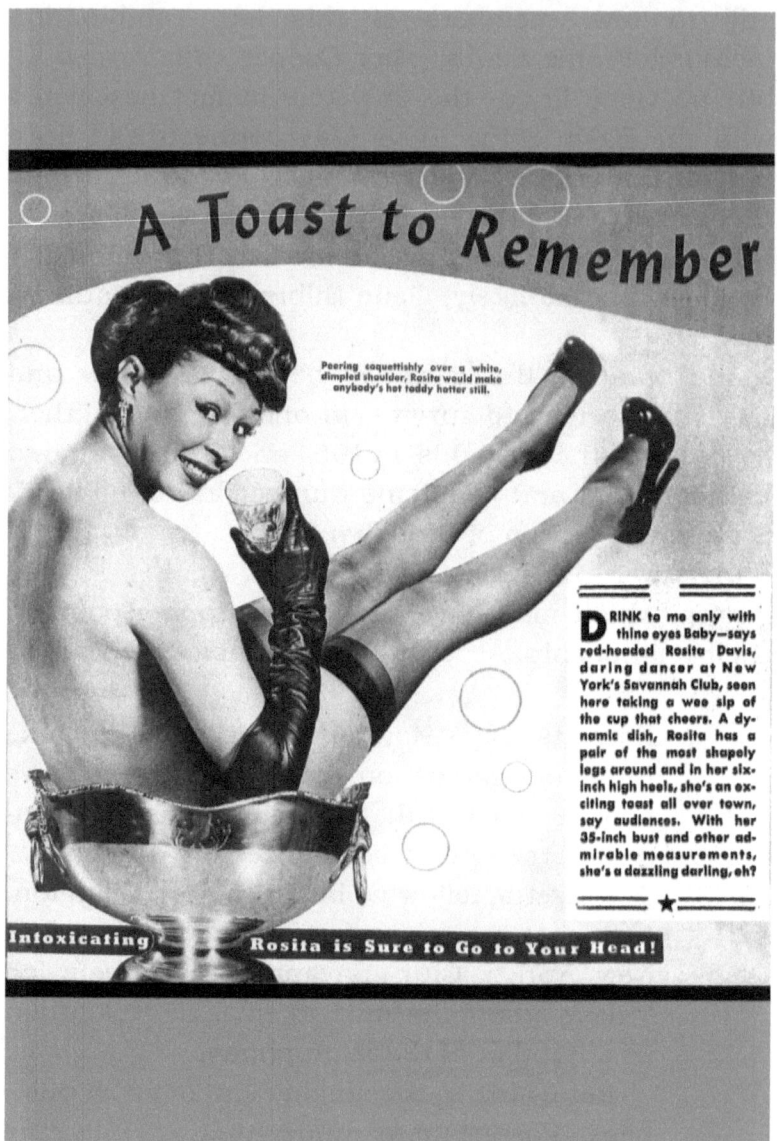

Rosita Davis, while at Club Savannah, in the pages of *Beauty Parade* magazine, published by Robert Harrison.

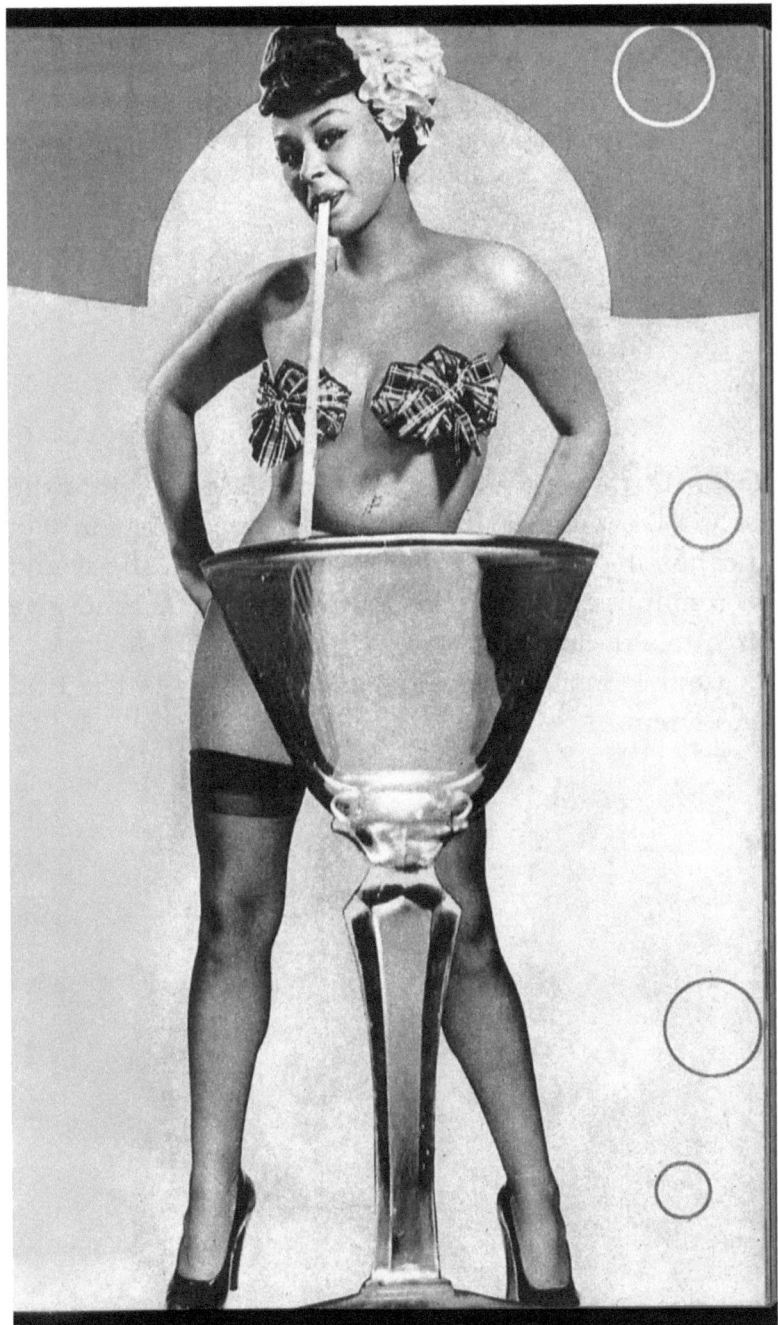

By 1953, Bilbrew was living in Manhattan within walking distance of Times Square and the subversive publishers who would play a big part in his life. [xlv]

Rosita Davis went on to have a minor career into the early '60s, singing in nightclubs, appearing on TV, and hosting an R&B radio show. In time, she would be romantically linked to Sammy Davis Jr. and give birth to a daughter.[xlvi]

Cue the Basin Street Boys B-side: "This Is The End Of A Dream."

PART TWO

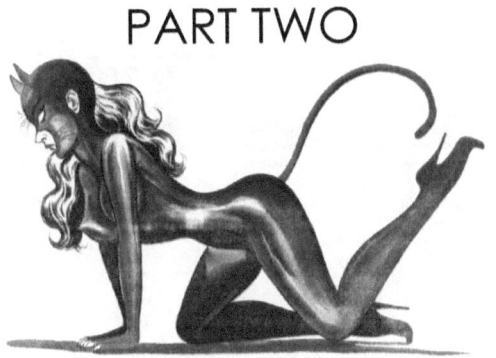

Whatever trauma Gene Bilbrew endured on the road with the Basin Street Boys—or with Rosita Davis—it was enough that he would never return to singing again. And this is where the real story of Bilbrew begins.

We might imagine Bilbrew contacting his old friend Alexander, bemoaning the end of his singing career. We might imagine Alexander suggesting, "Why not try art?"

Bilbrew *may have* contributed the storyline, as Alexander recalled, to one or more of *The Bronze Bomber* cartoon strips, and he *may have* contributed a Hercules comic,[xlvii] at some point, to a health or fitness magazine—one that remains to be discovered.

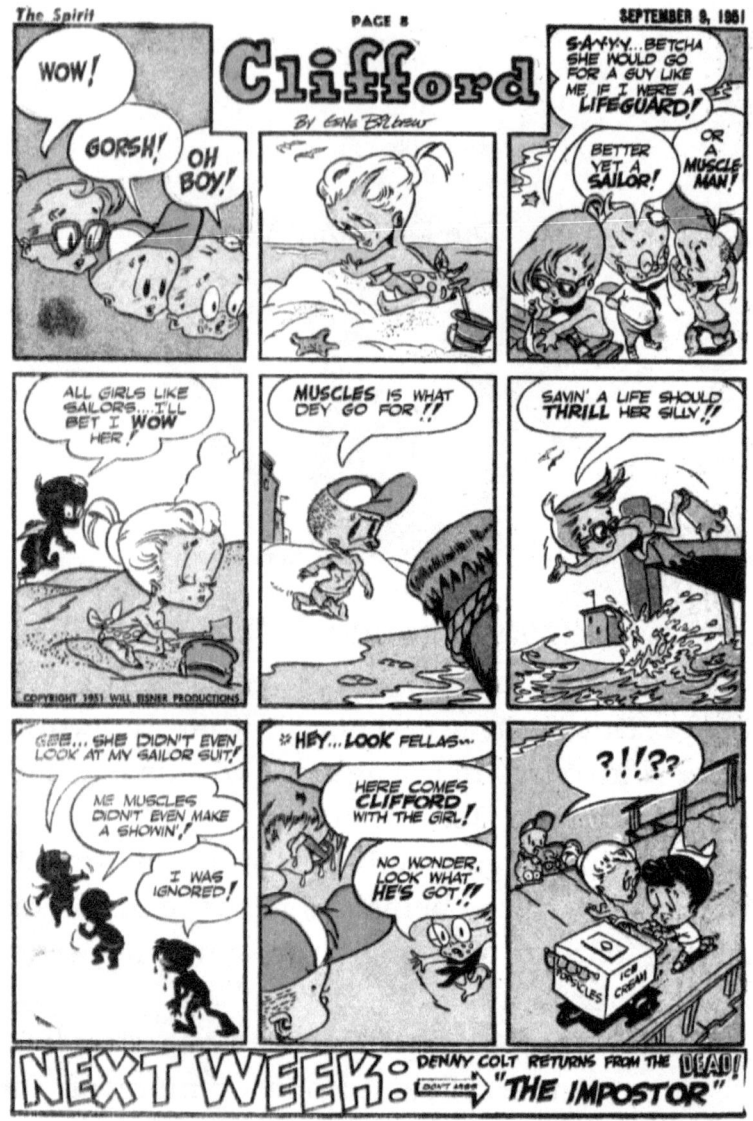

Clifford, a comic that ran on the back page of *The Spirit* section

As far as we can verify, Bilbrew's art career began in 1950, the same year he enrolled at Cartoonists & Illustrators school.[xlviii] Jules Feiffer, Pulitzer Prize-winning cartoonist and one time assistant to Will Eisner, recalled in a personal email:

> Bilbrew started with Eisner, if flawed memory is correct, as a troubleshooting background artist, called to help on dead-lines. Then when I was drafted in [January] 1951, Will had him take over *Clifford*. It's possible that I did the scripts for a couple of months, but no art. Gene and I got along well... He was young, eager, friendly, and I remember some good conversations, probably about comics. I had no further contact with him after my basic training in Fort Dix.[xlix]

Feiffer's final *Clifford* was published December 31, 1950. From this, we might gather that Bilbrew was with Eisner at least by the end of that year, as comics were drawn (according to Feiffer [l]) six to eight weeks in advance.

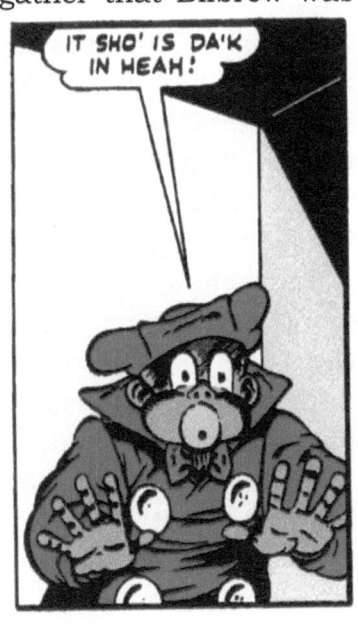

And how did he get the job? Bilbrew reportedly told Eisner that he empathized with the Spirit's black sidekick, Ebony White.[li] If this is true, Eisner may have hired Bilbrew out of white guilt, because the character was a hideous racial stereotype.

Notoriously cheap (even proud of it), Eisner paid Bilbrew what in his mind was the generous sum of $5.00 per each installment of *Clifford*,[lii] which ran until 1952 when Eisner abandoned the 8-page syndicated version of *The Spirit* altogether.[liii] [liv]

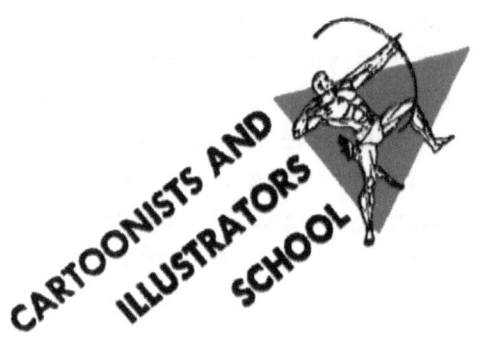

ART SCHOOL

Established in uptown Manhattan by co-founders Silas H. Rhodes and Burne Hogarth, Cartoonists and Illustrators School relocated to a four-story building on the corner of 23rd Street and Second Avenue in 1950,[lv] and it was here that Bilbrew enrolled, likely with government assistance.[lvi]

Instructors included cartoonists Marvin Stein (who worked on *Captain Valiant)*, Tom Gill (best known for the *Lone Ranger* comic book), Jerry Robinson (best known for his work on the *Batman* syndicated strip), and, of course, Burne Hogarth (best known for illustrating the syndicated strip, *Tarzan).*[lvii] Of all his instructors, it was the anatomy-obsessed Hogarth, for better or worse, who left the most enduring mark on Bilbrew's style.[lviii]

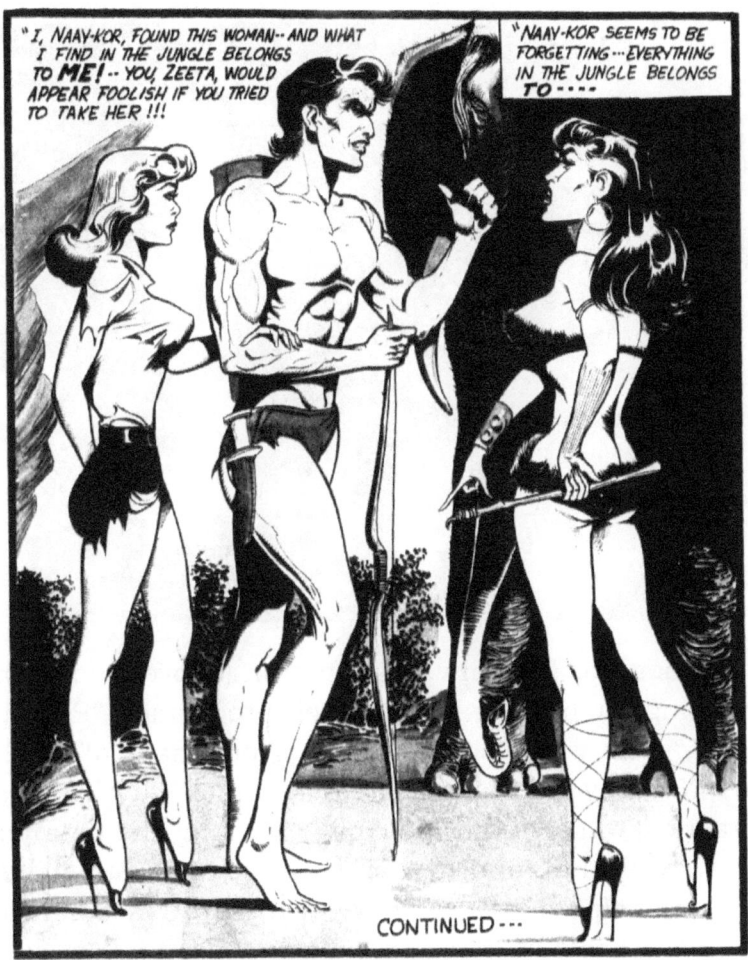

Bilbrew's Tarzan-like tribute to Hogarth in *Exotique*, c.1955

Sharing Jerry Robinson's cartooning class with Bilbrew by spring 1951 were Stephen John Ditko (a.k.a. Steve Ditko)[lix] and Eric Stanton (then known as "Ernie Stanten").[lx] One fateful day, as Stanton later recalled, he caught sight of an illustration on Bilbrew's desk that made him pause: it featured a full-blown bondage fantasy—and right away this proved an ice-breaker.[lxi]

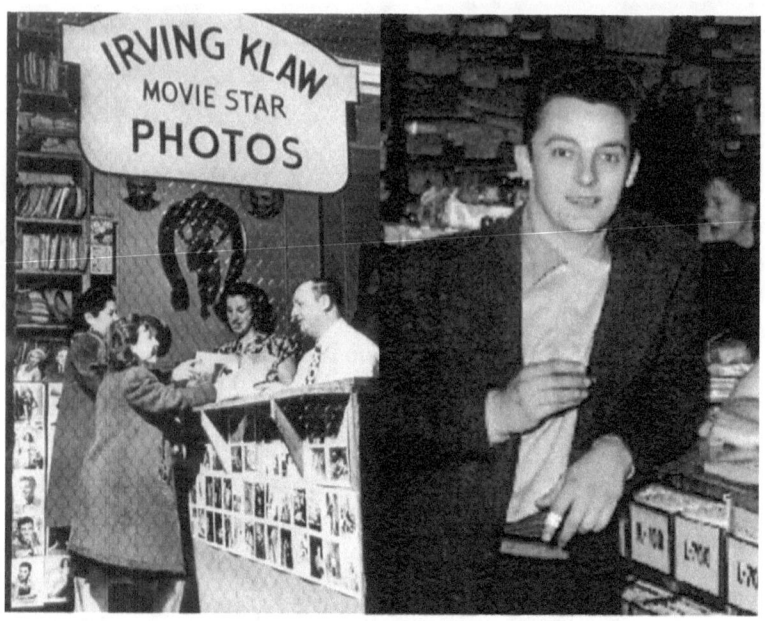

By then, for several years, Stanton (above) had been working for Irving Klaw, the self-proclaimed "Pin-Up King," who was also a pioneering merchant of fetish art. Not only did Stanton produce art for Klaw, he was practically his right-hand man, working the counter at Klaw's brick-and-mortar store on 14th Street, as well as helping out with Klaw's hush-hush bondage fantasy shoots on select weekends.[lxii]

No doubt Bilbrew mentioned Eisner to Stanton, and what he was being paid. No doubt Stanton mentioned that there were, perhaps, other creative opportunities available. Less conventional ones.

With a Klaw meeting arranged by Stanton, Bilbrew presented samples of his most "bizarre" art. Klaw's response was encouraging, and Bilbrew recognized his destiny: reinventing himself as a renegade artist known as "Eneg" ("Gene" spelled backward).

ENEG'S CHAPTER SERIALS

Chapter serials were unbound illustrated narratives printed on photo paper. They could be purchased in full or by single pages for the artwork. Pages were referred to as "chapters" or "episodes," in the manner of Saturday matinee serial installments. Often each episode was designed around a single creative objective: how to ensure that a damsel (or damsels) ended up in the most imaginative "predicament" possible. This was the challenge of a damsel-in-distress narrative. The best chapter serials (e.g., Stanton's *Duchess of the Bastille)* have single page narrative arcs (concluding in a predicament) that work within an overall (20/30 page) narrative arc.

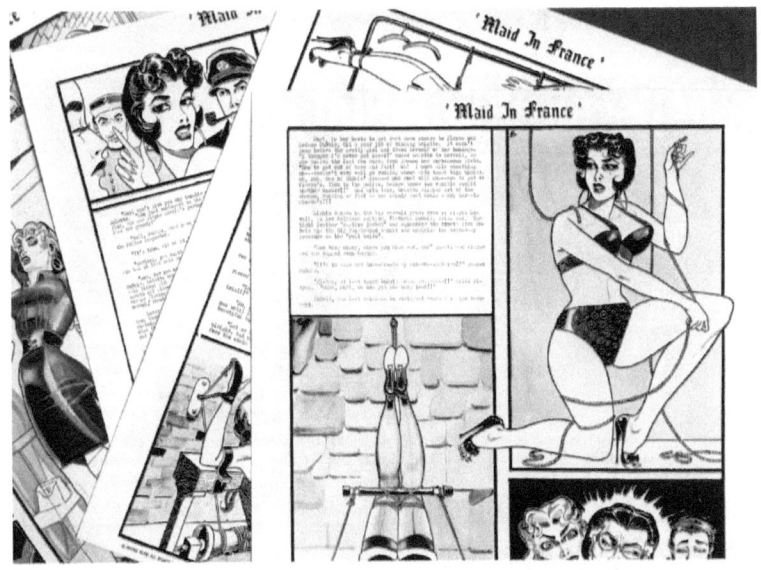

After his preliminary bondage fantasy sketches for Klaw, Bilbrew embarked on his first chapter serial with Kamikaze-like intensity, even going so far as to drop out of school.[lxiii] It was named *Princess Elaine's Terrible Fate* and set in Roman times. According to Stanton, Klaw was against the idea of Bilbrew doing a period piece, but Bilbrew proceeded with it anyway.[lxiv] The end result impressed Klaw as much as it horrified him. Klaw had imposed strict limitations on his artists—in keeping with obscenity standards: no nudity, no implied sex of any kind. And here was Bilbrew's first serial full of phallic symbolism! Cocks everywhere! Klaw's solution? Get Stanton to censor Bilbrew's work, which infuriated Bilbrew, while Stanton felt batted back and forth. In effect, Stanton had "discovered" Eneg, so Klaw made him Stanton's responsibility. Worst of all, it would not be the first time Klaw assigned such censorship/babysitting duties to Stanton, which of course made things uncomfortable for Stanton.[lxv]

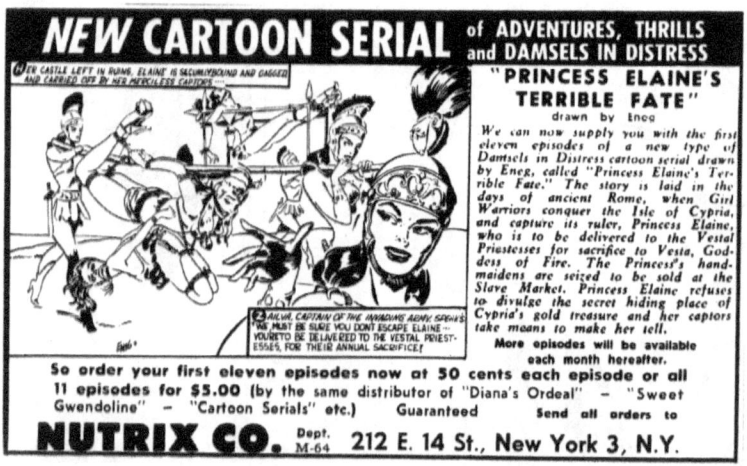

Princess Elaine's Terrible Fate, consisting of thirty episodes and likely produced between July and November of 1951,[lxvi] clearly demonstrated Bilbrew's natural talent and how quickly he developed as an artist (see below). While earlier pages of the work appear somewhat uncertain and amateurish, by midway point he was executing ideas like a seasoned pro. His confident inking deserves special mention. Not bad for a person who just several years earlier had a completely different career.

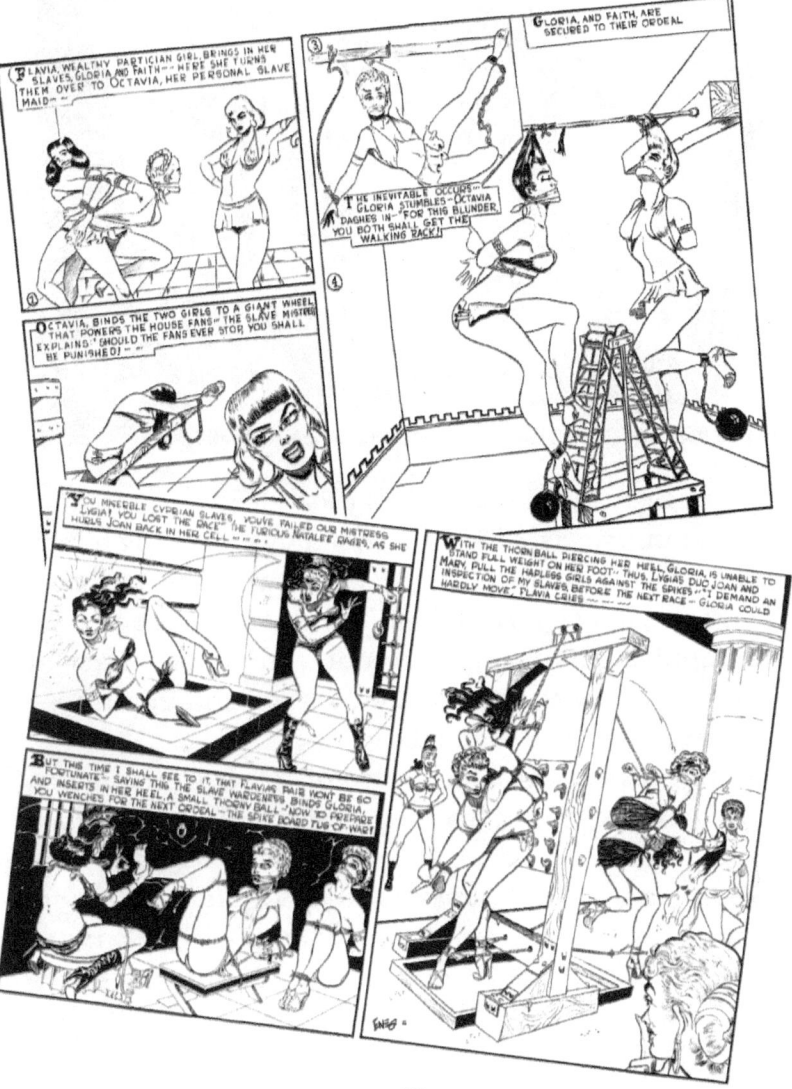

Despite having produced more Klaw chapter serials by then, [lxvii] Stanton was forthright about Bilbrew's advanced skill: "Listen, he was a better artist at the time than I was. Much better. Better craftsman." [lxviii] On some level, he must have been dismayed by how quickly Eneg overtook him.

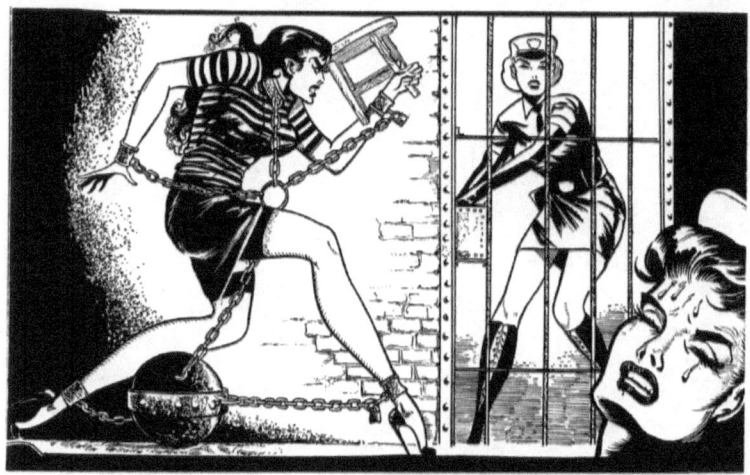

Conversely, Bilbrew could be careless as an artist: misspelling words, disproportionately extending torsos and legs of his female figures, and winging his page designs erratically. His art, in some ways, underscored his impulsive nature, yet no one could deny that—at least in the subculture of the bizarre underground— a major player had arrived.

Among Eneg's greatest hits for Klaw were: *Prison for Women* (1952), *Captives of Madame La Bondage* (1953), *Island of Captive Girls* (1953), *Sorority Girls* (1953), *Ladies in Rubber* (1954), *Captain Kidnapp, Lady Pirate* (1955), *Maid in France* (1955), *Bondage Society's Gala Slave Ball* (1959), and *Kidnapped Girl's Sweet Revenge* (1959 [lxix]).

ENEG

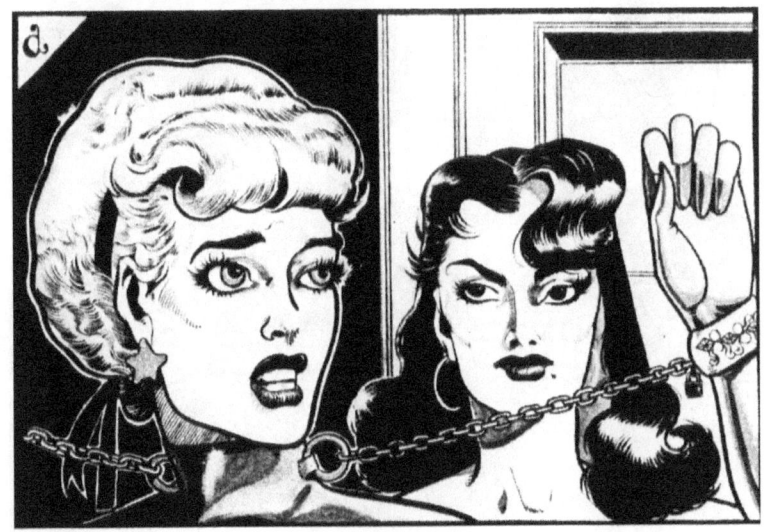

FOR

KLAW

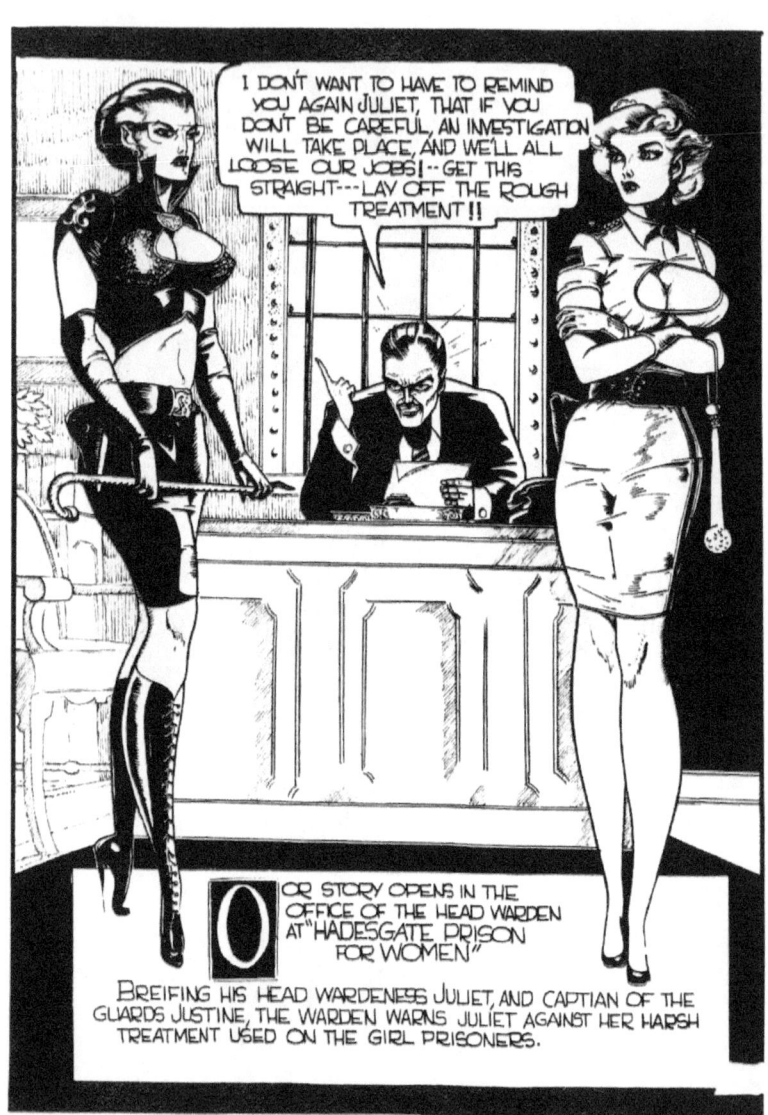

Prison for Women (1952)

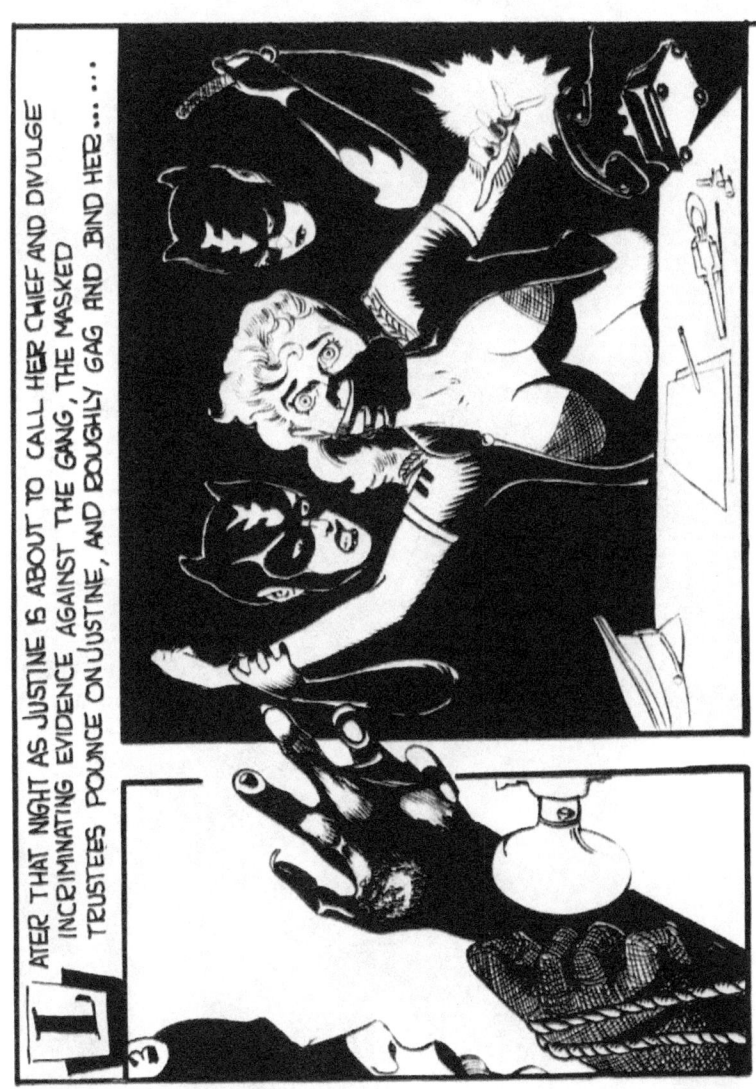

Prison for Women (1952)

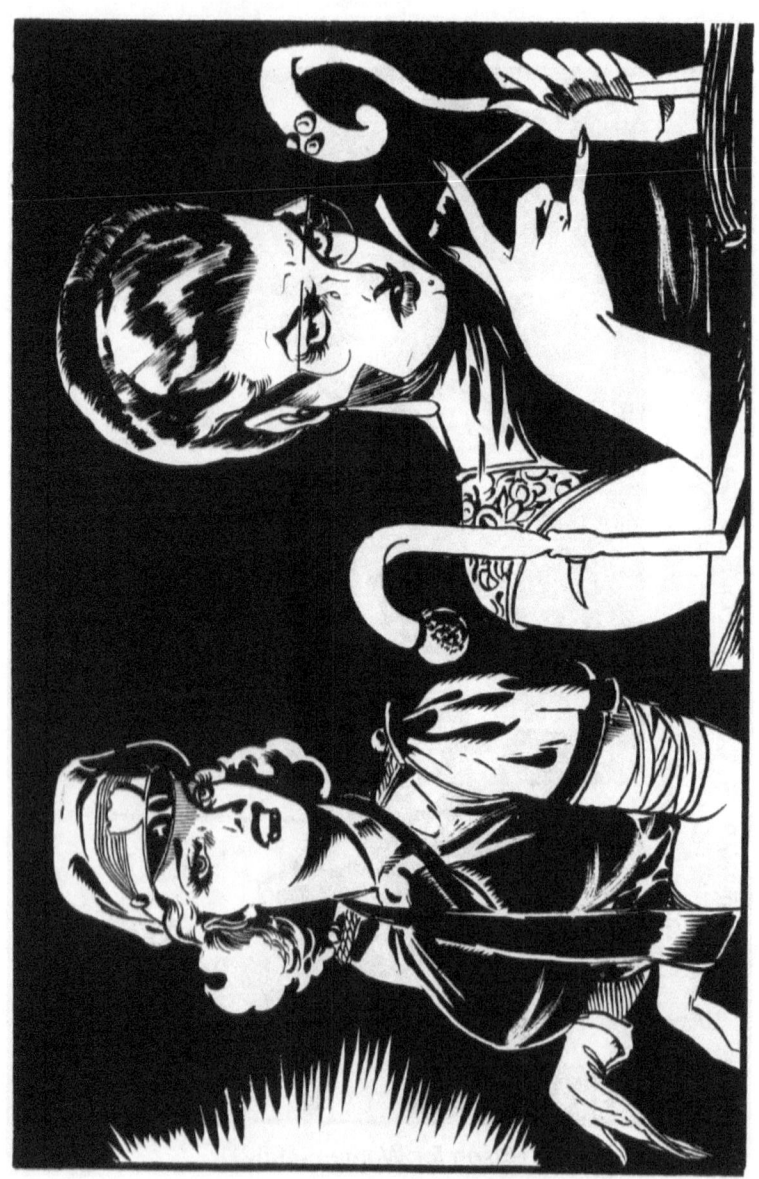

Prison for Women (1952)

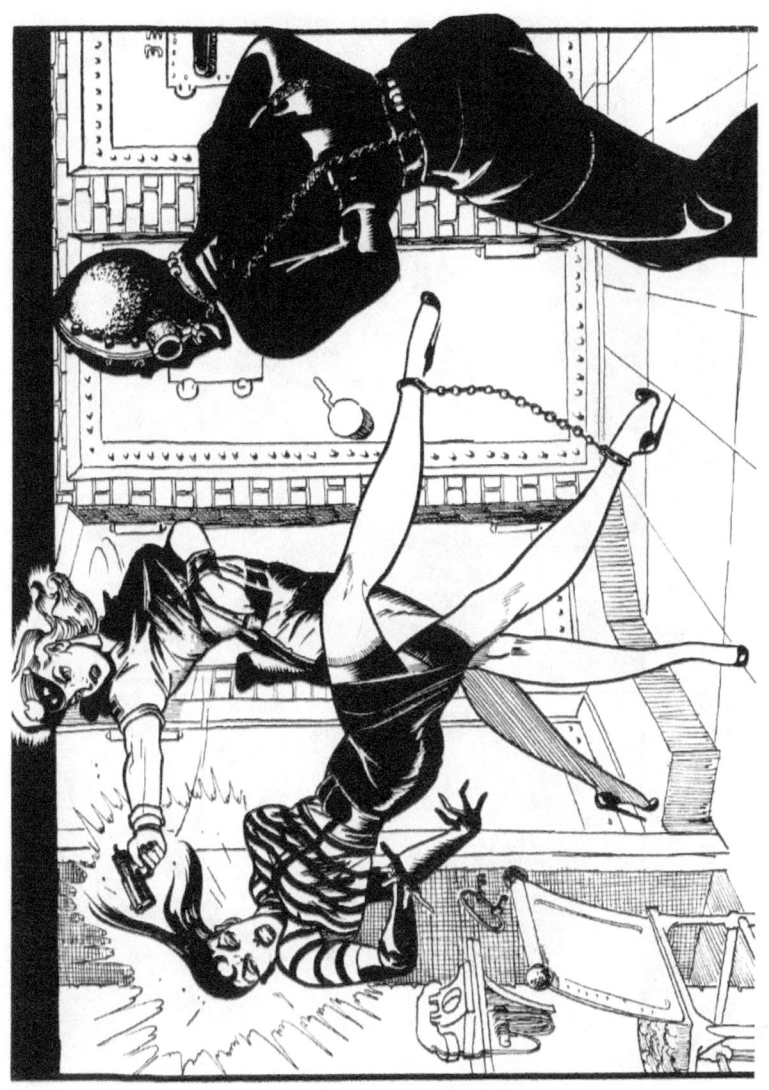

Prison for Women (1952)

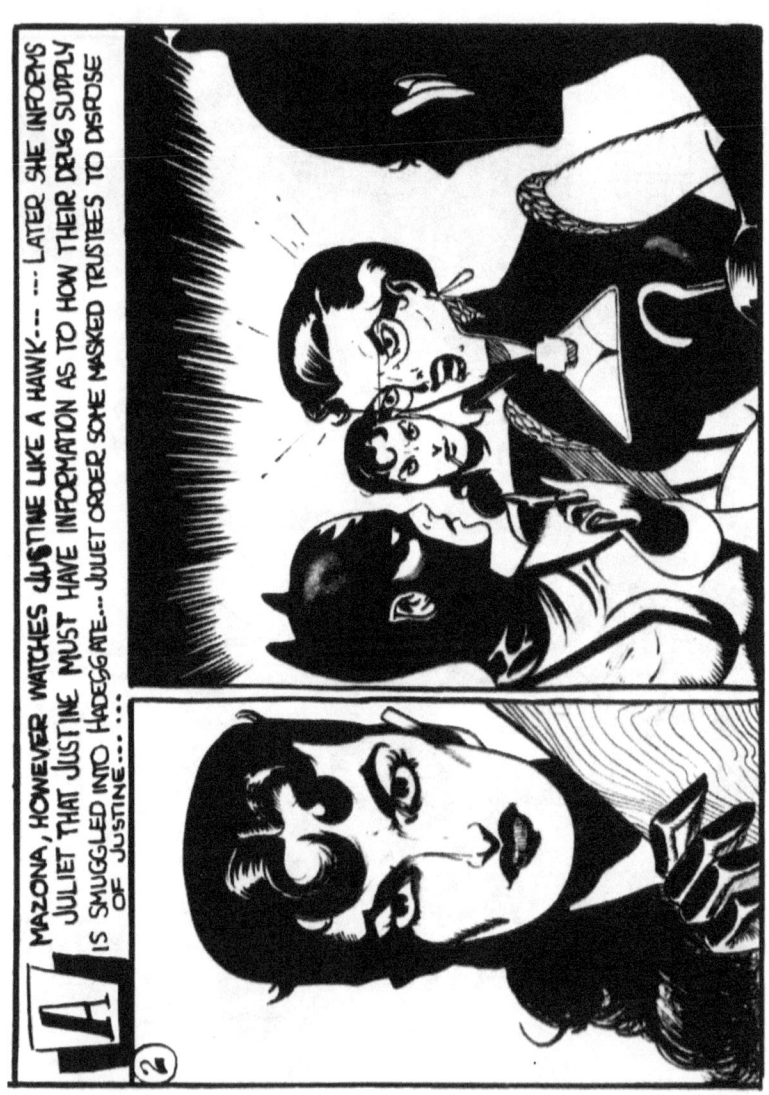

Prison for Women (1952)

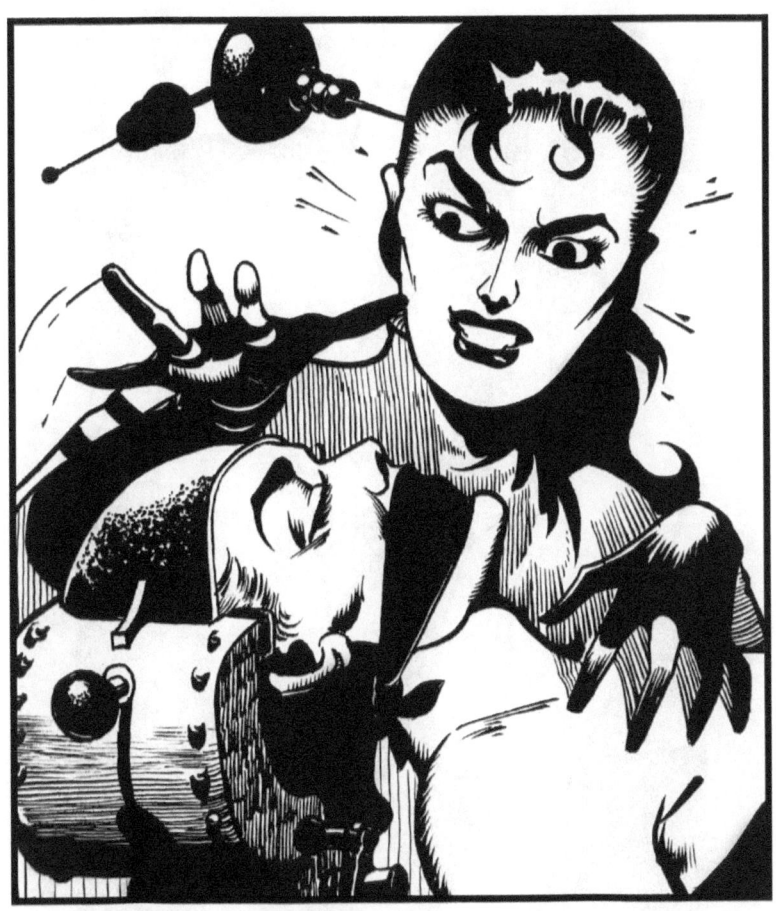

Prison for Women (1952)

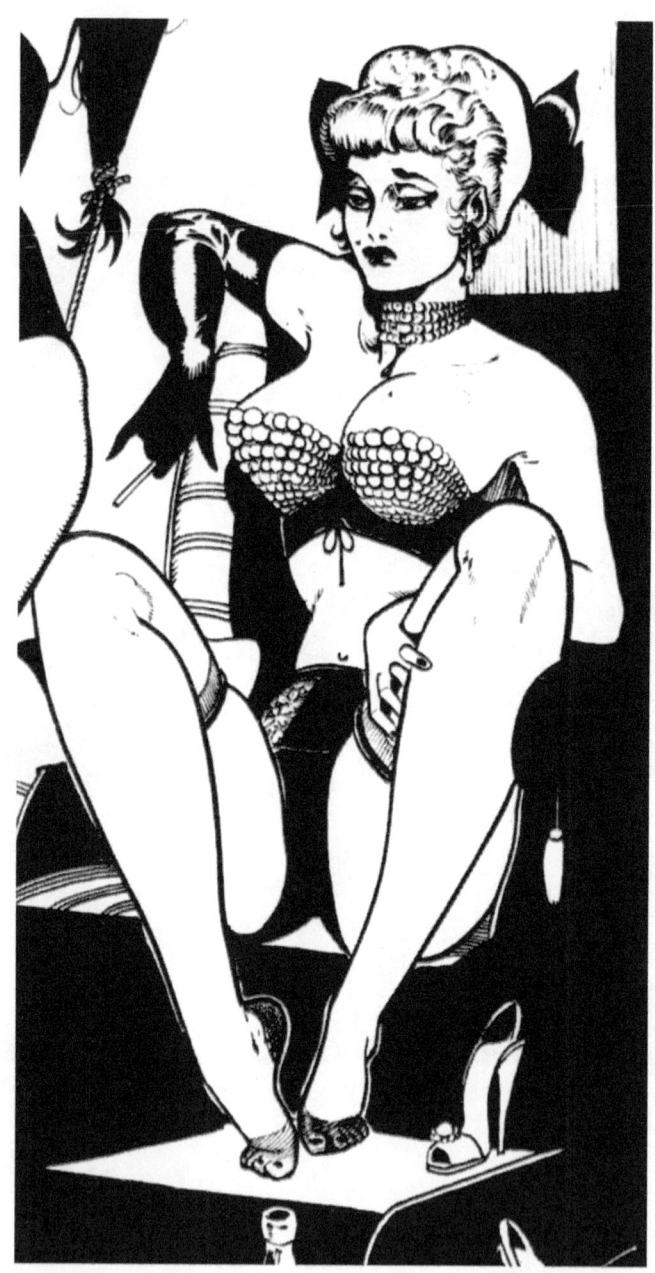

Captives of Madame La Bondage: detail (1953)

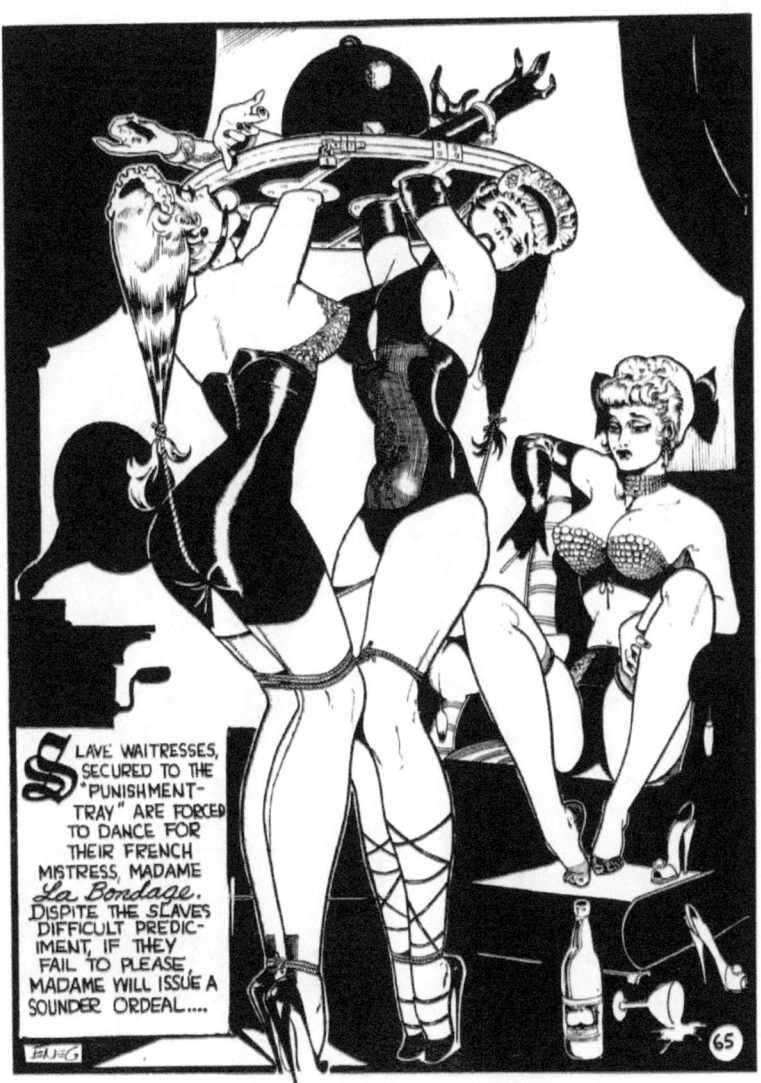

Captives of Madame La Bondage (1953)

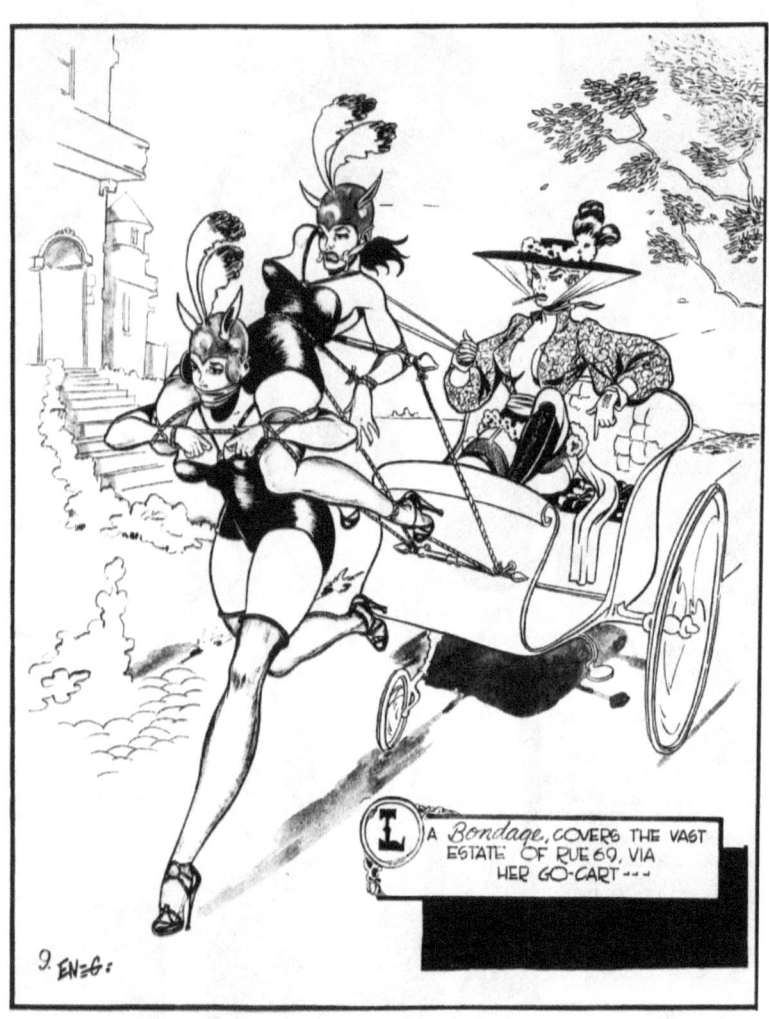

Captives of Madame La Bondage (1953)

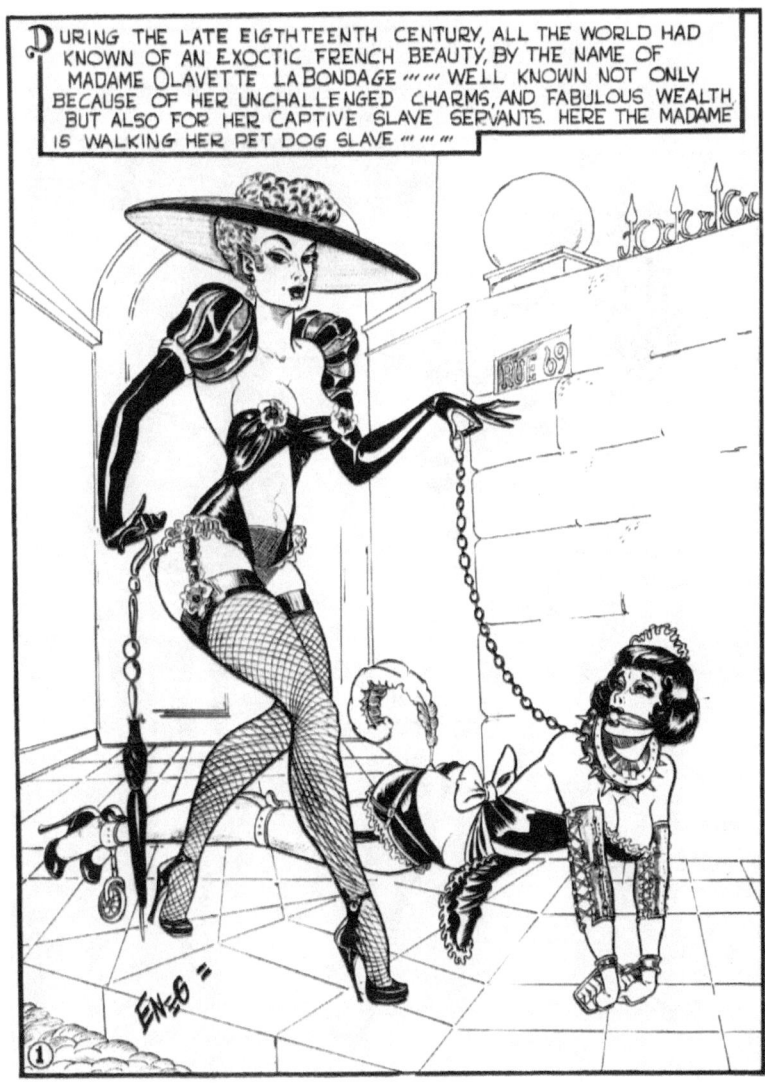

Captives of Madame La Bondage (1953)

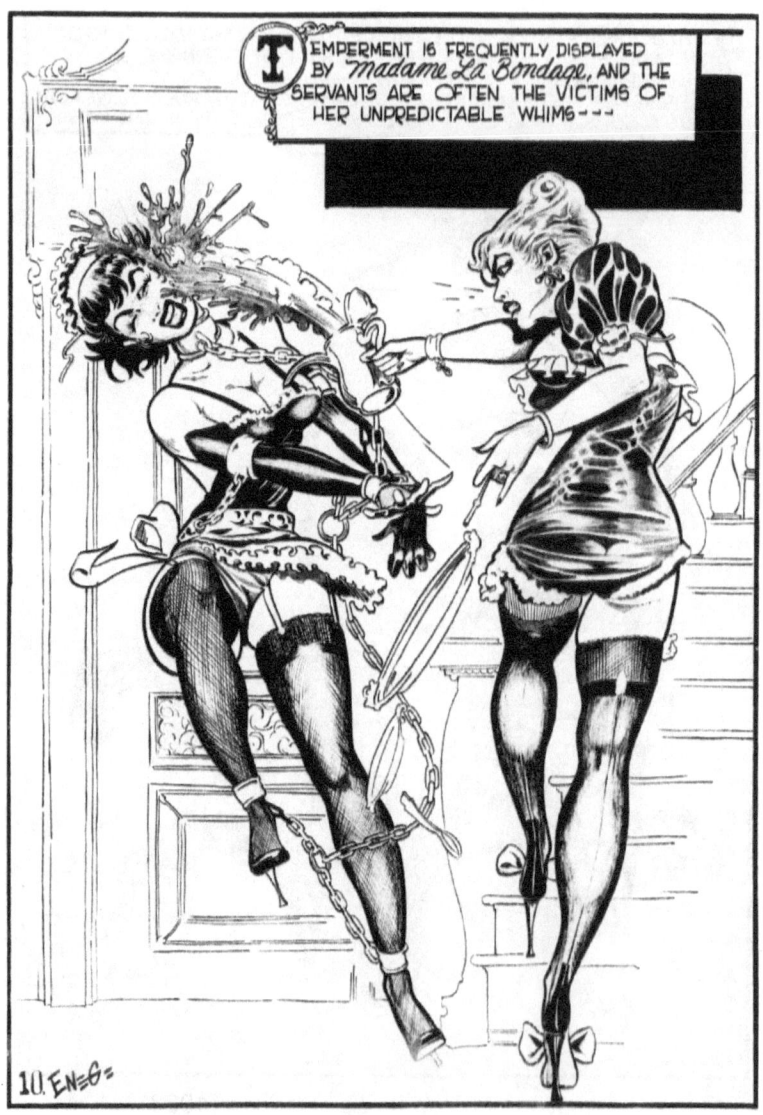

Captives of Madame La Bondage (1953)

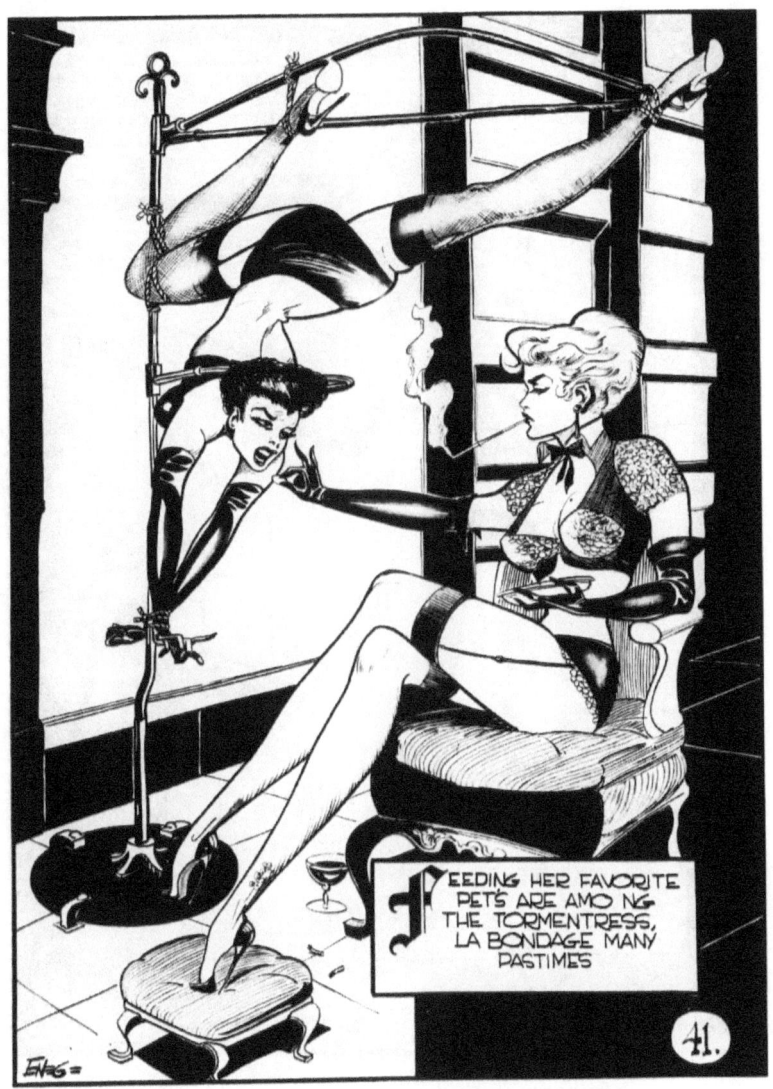

Captives of Madame La Bondage (1953)

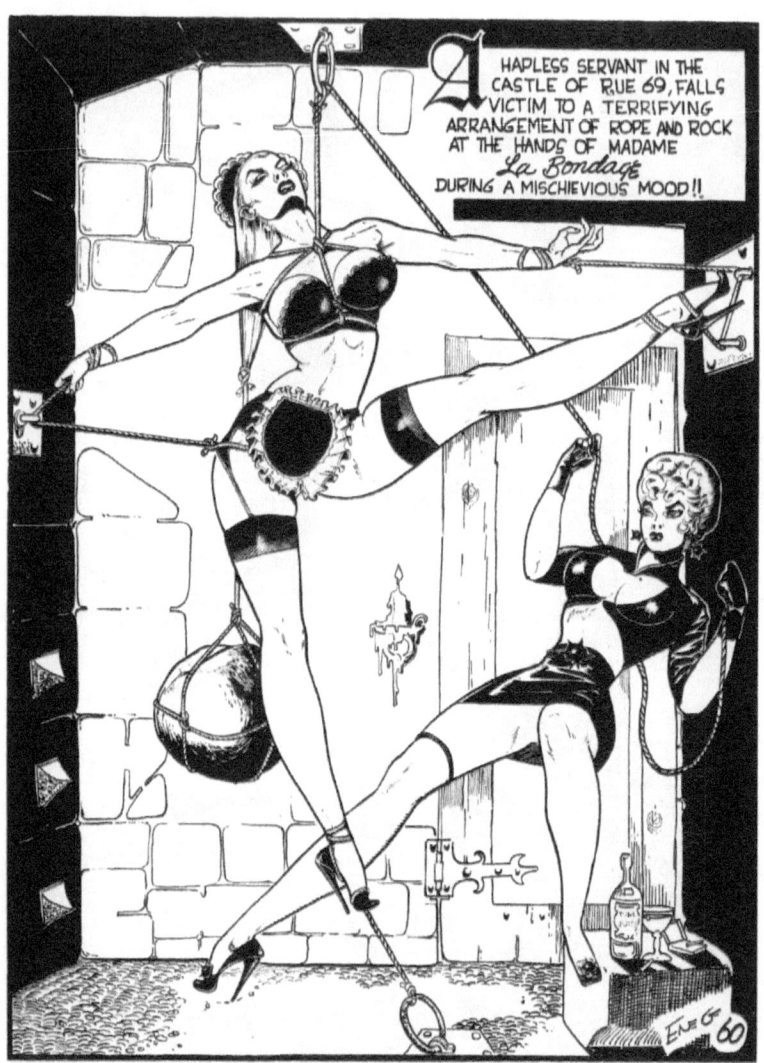

Captives of Madame La Bondage (1953)

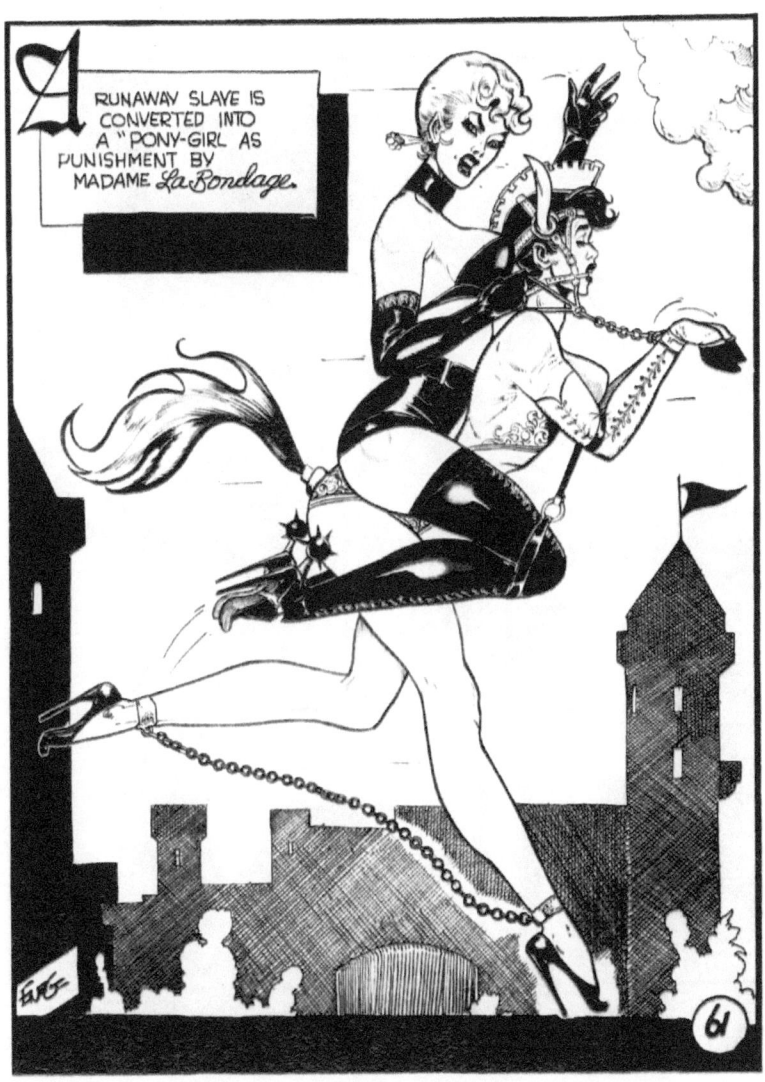

Captives of Madame La Bondage (1953)

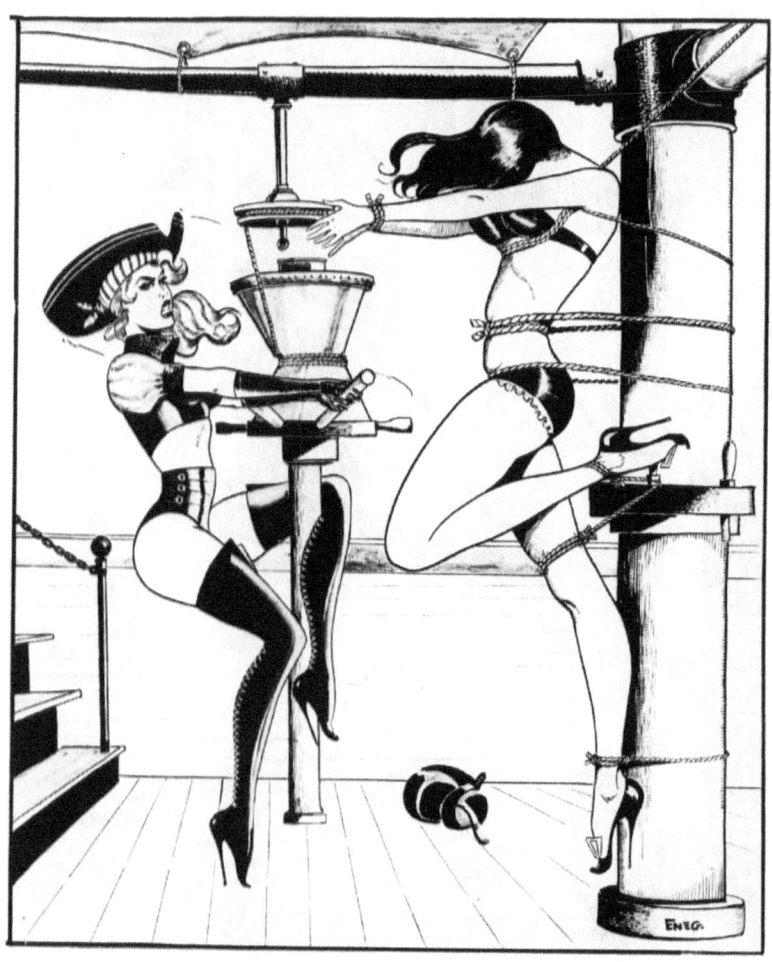

Captain Kidnapp, Lady Pirate (1955)

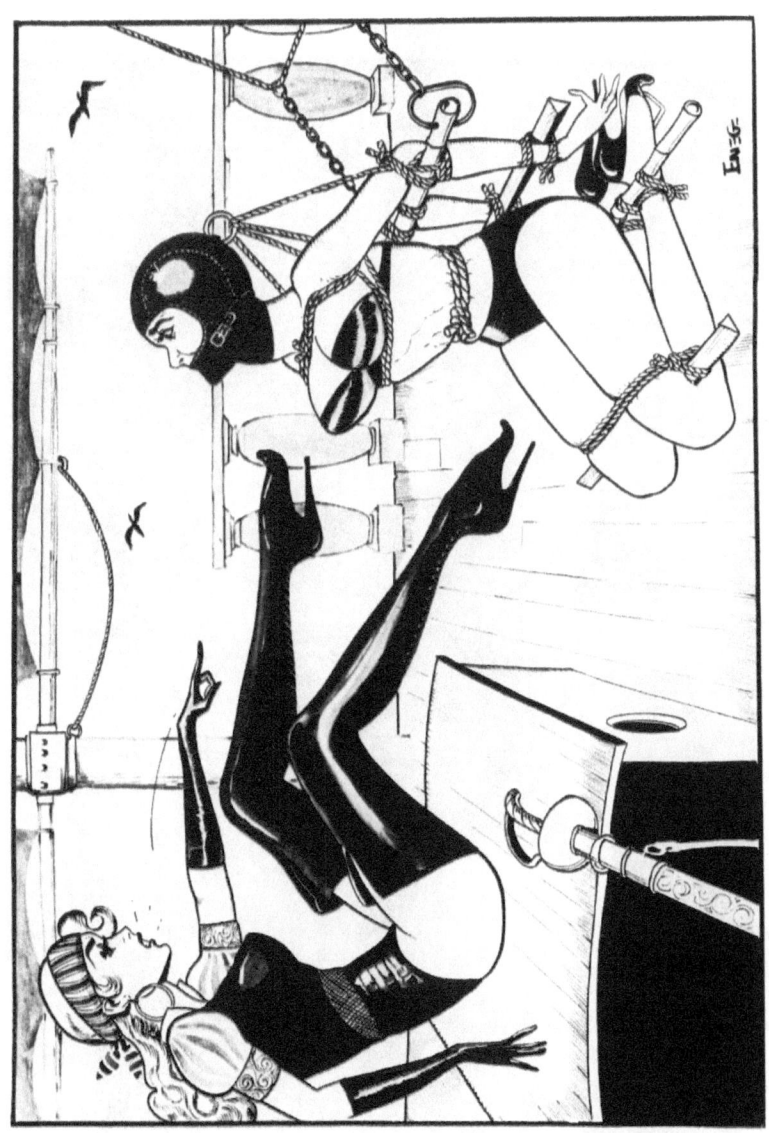

Captain Kidnapp, Lady Pirate (1955)

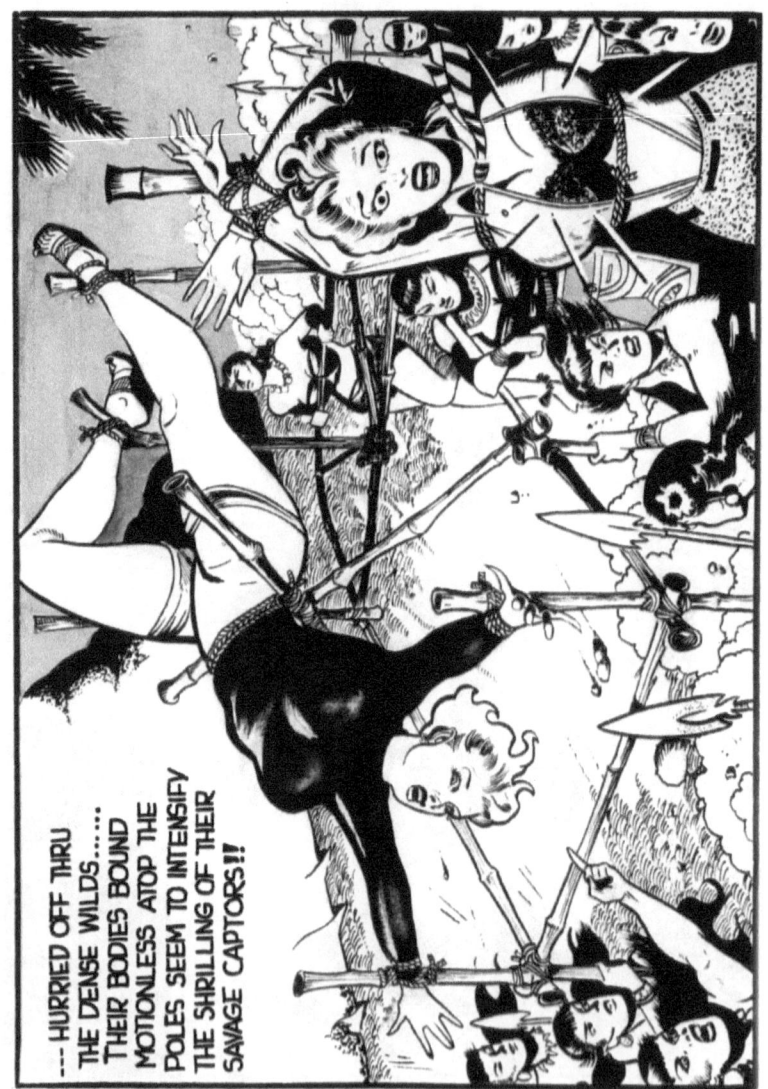

Island of Captive Girls (1953)

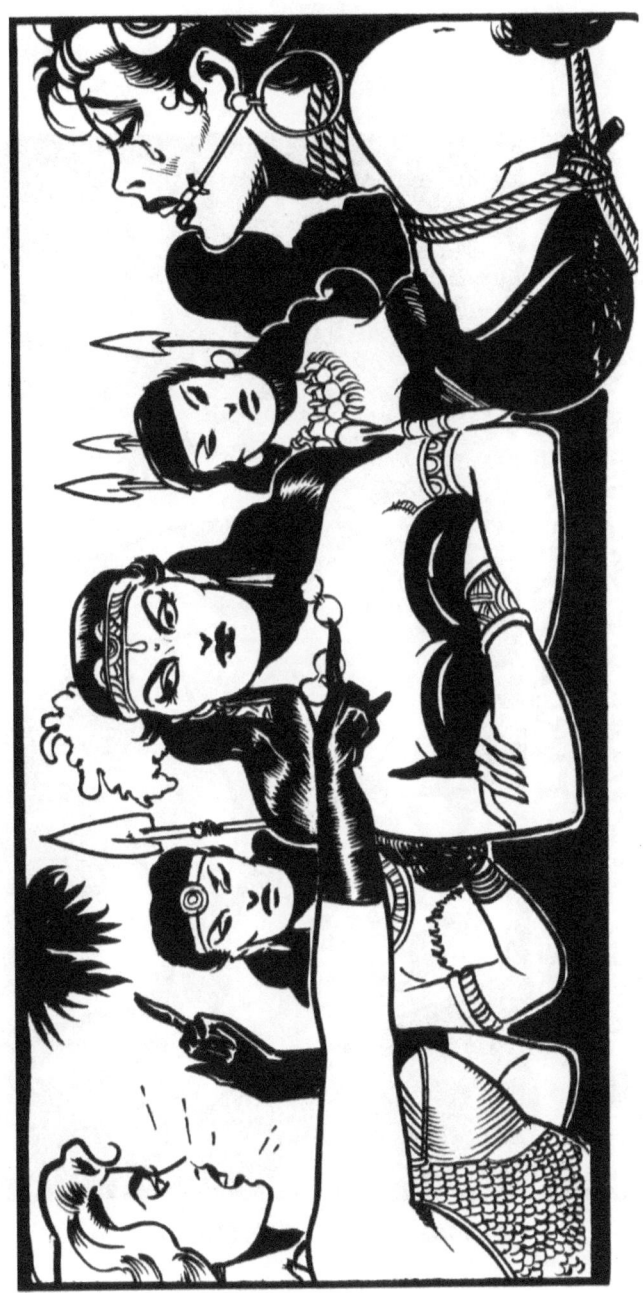

Island of Captive Girls (1953)

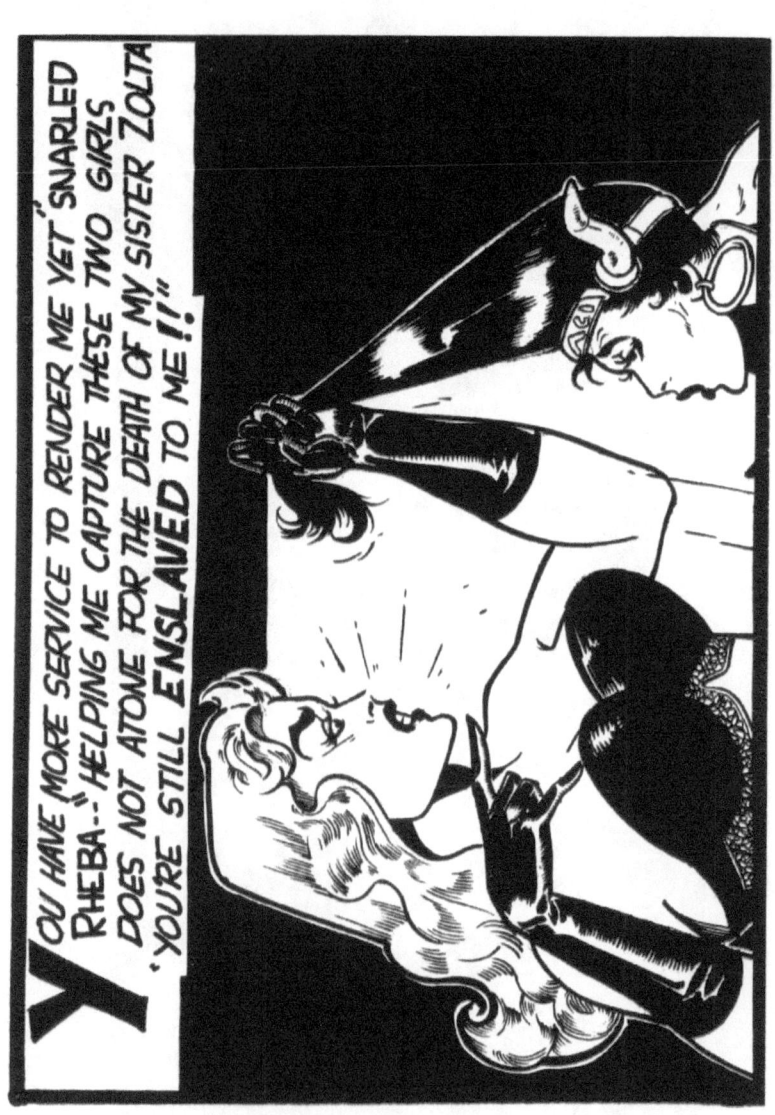

Island of Captive Girls (1953)

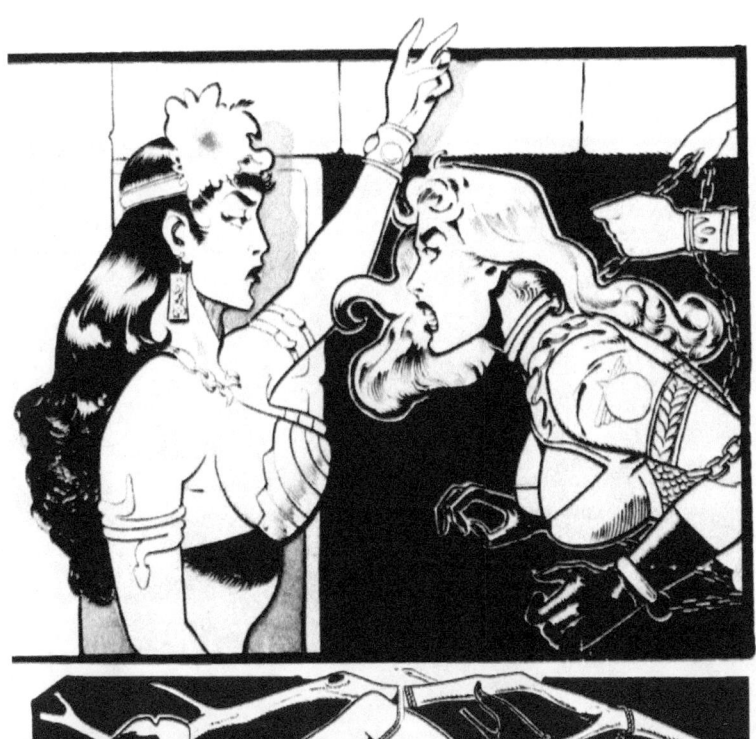

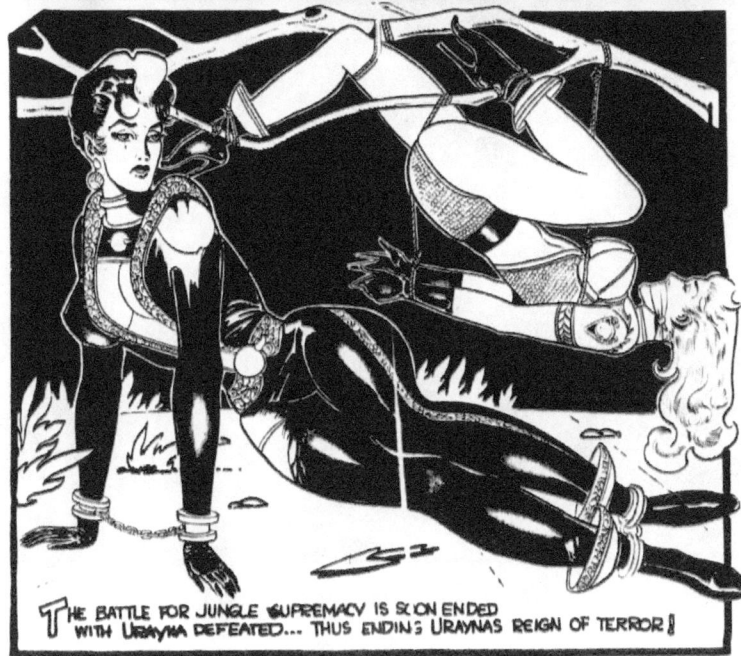

Island of Captive Girls (1953)

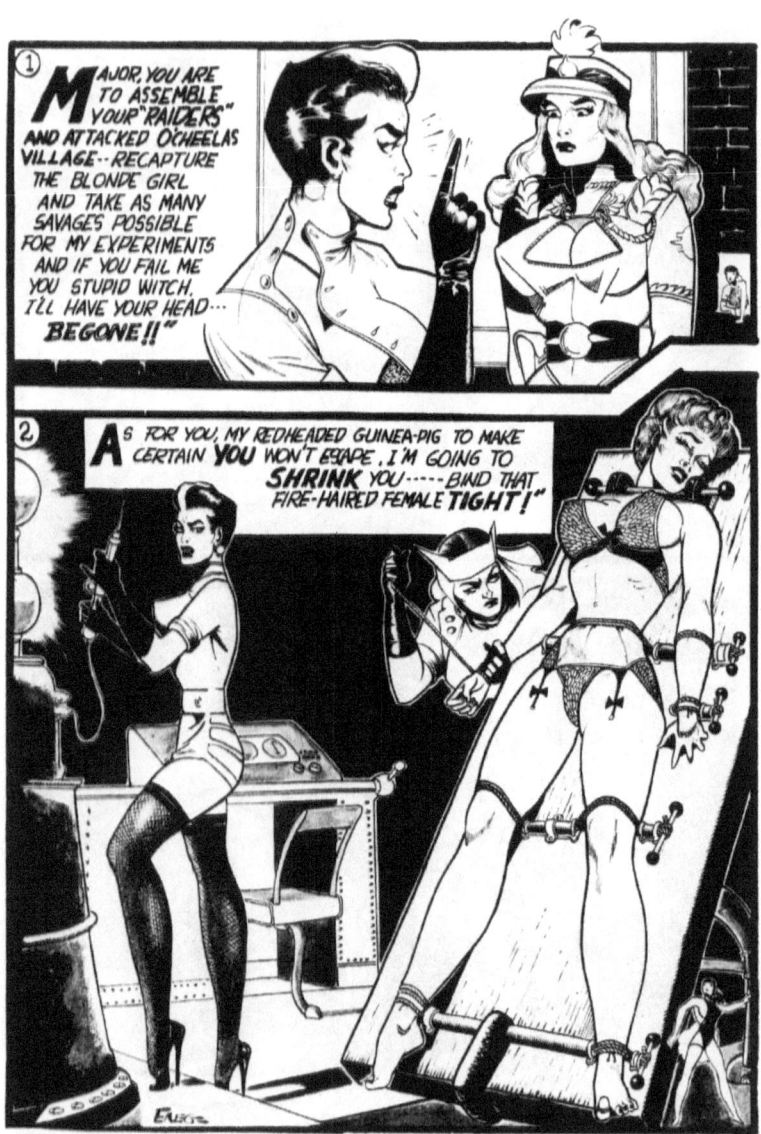

Island of Captive Girls (1953)

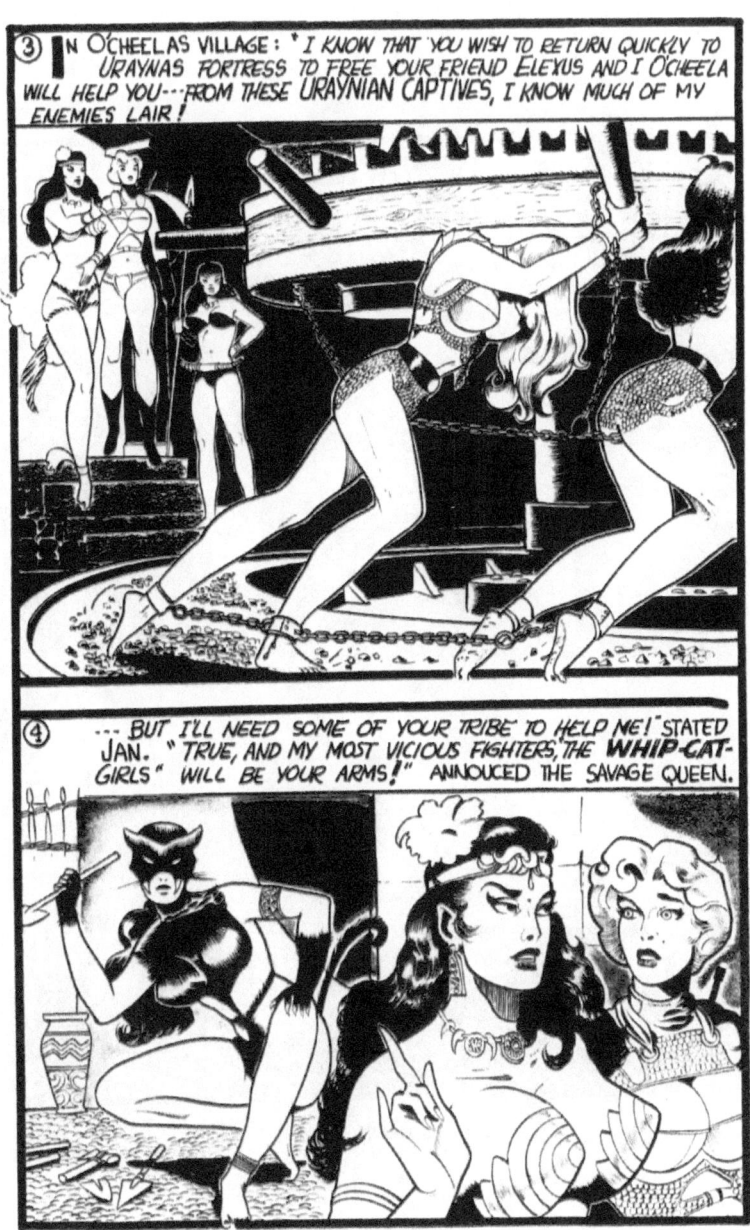

Island of Captive Girls (1953)

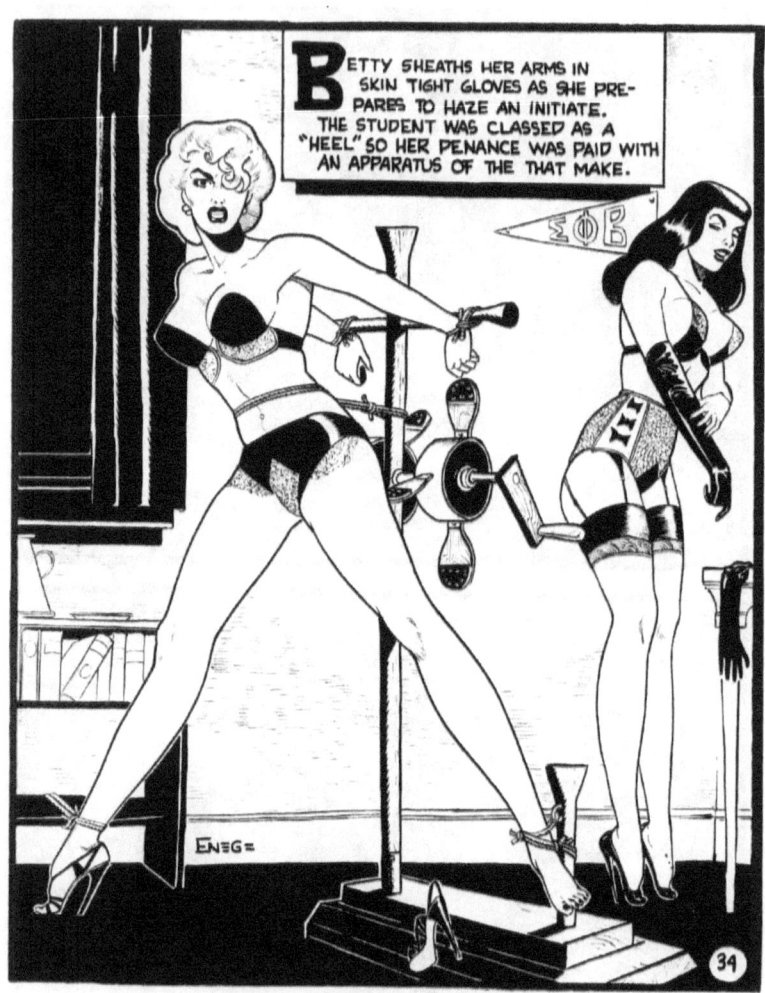

Sorority Girls (1953)

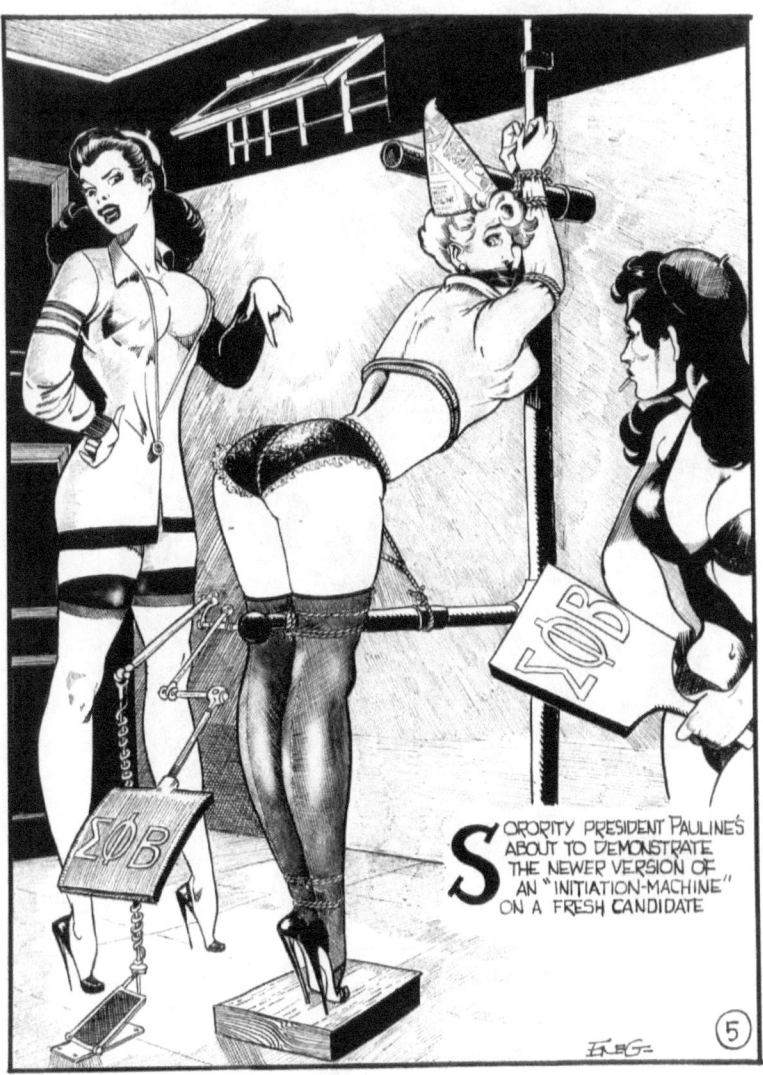

Sorority Girls (1953)

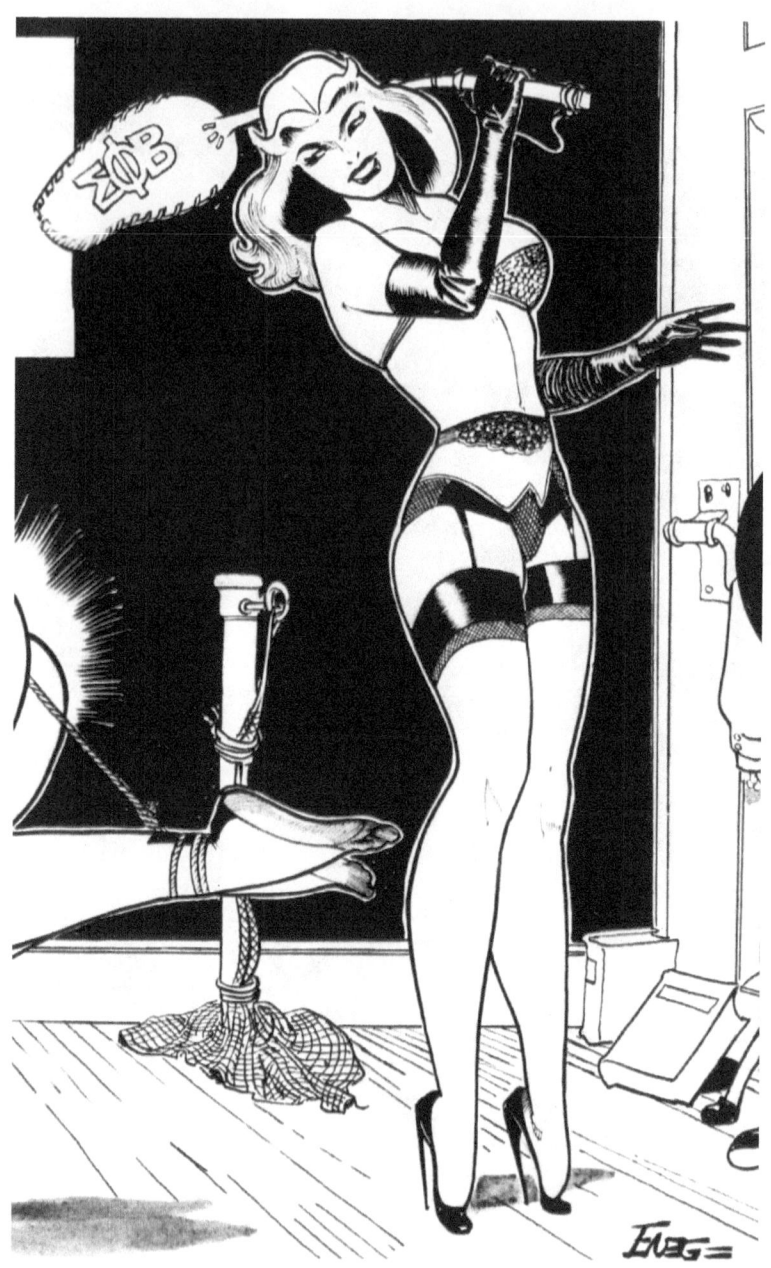

Sorority Girls: detail (1953)

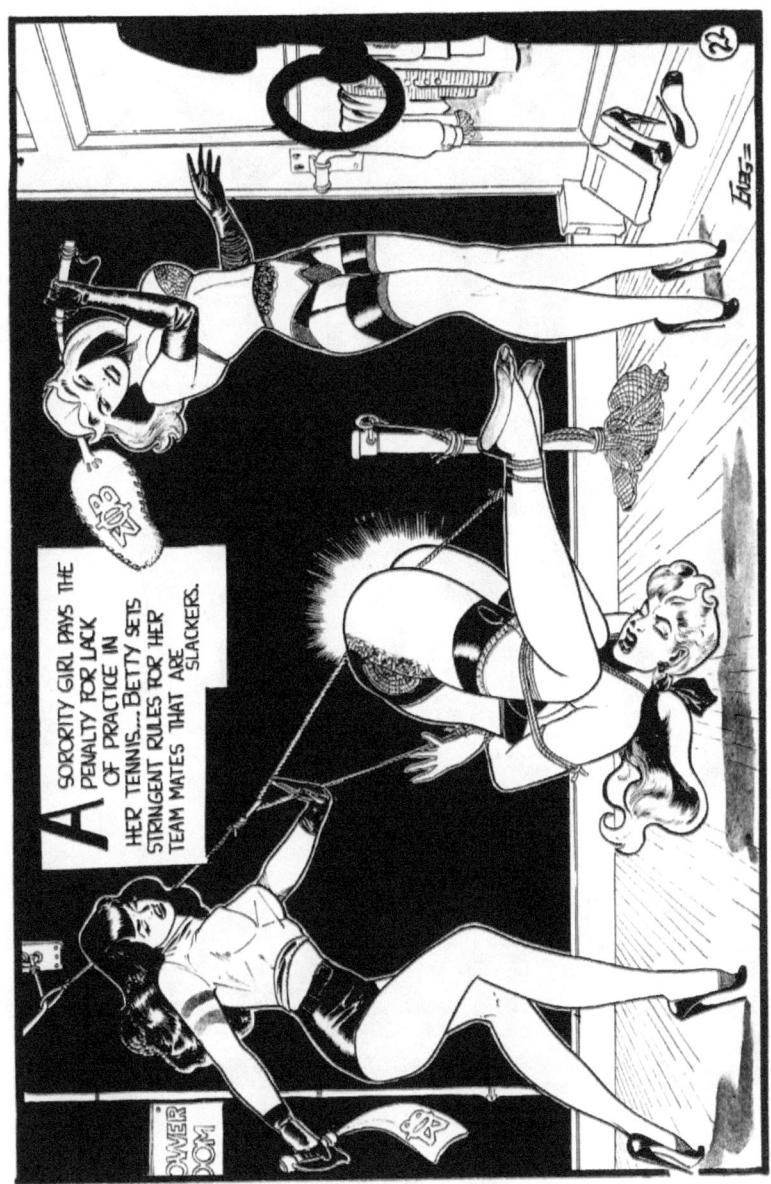

Sorority Girls (1953)

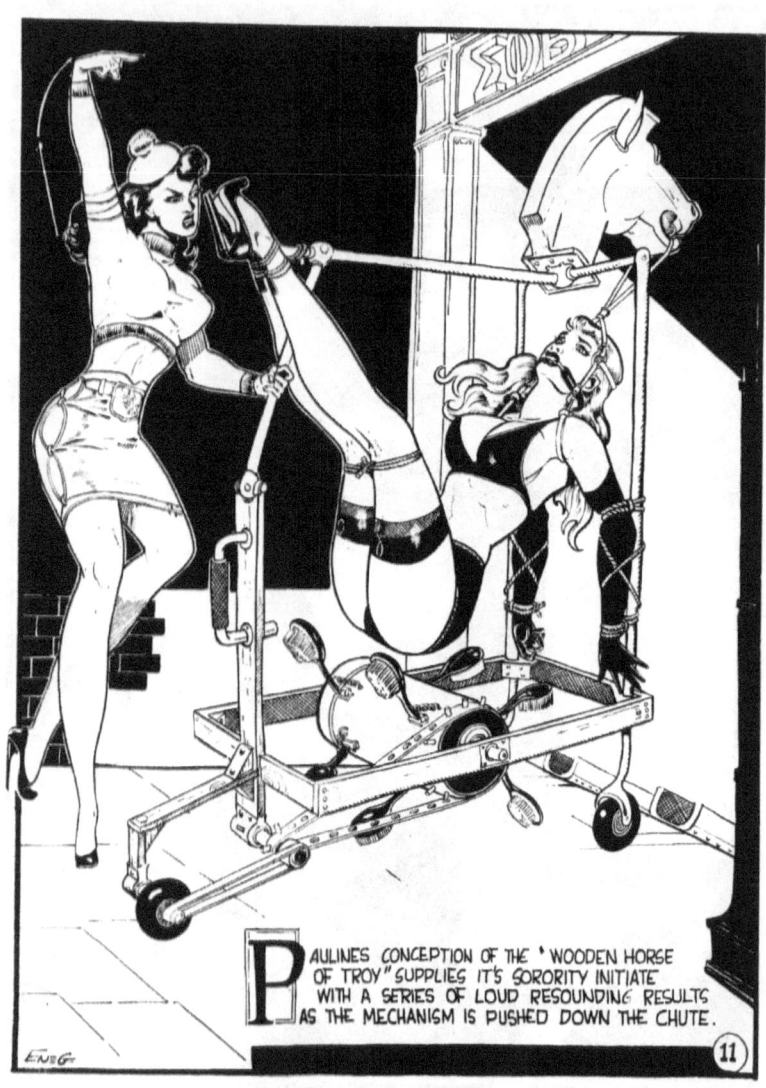

Sorority Girls (1953)

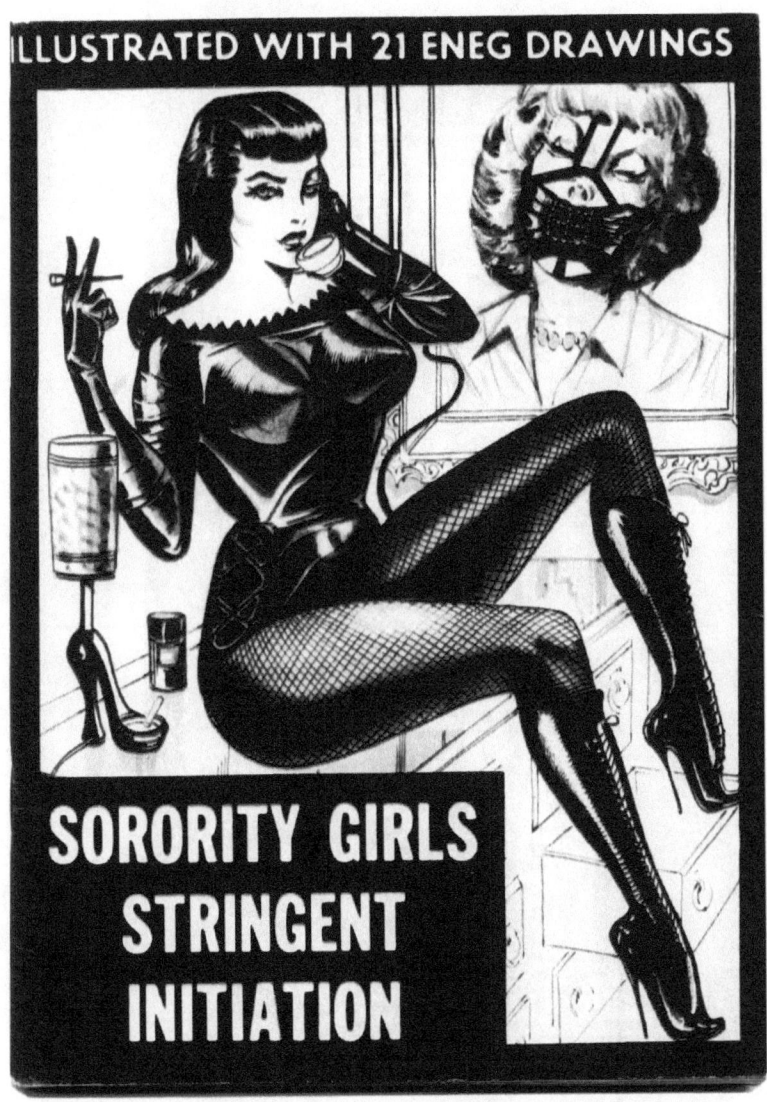

1959 reformatted Nutrix booklet version of *Sorority Girls* lxx

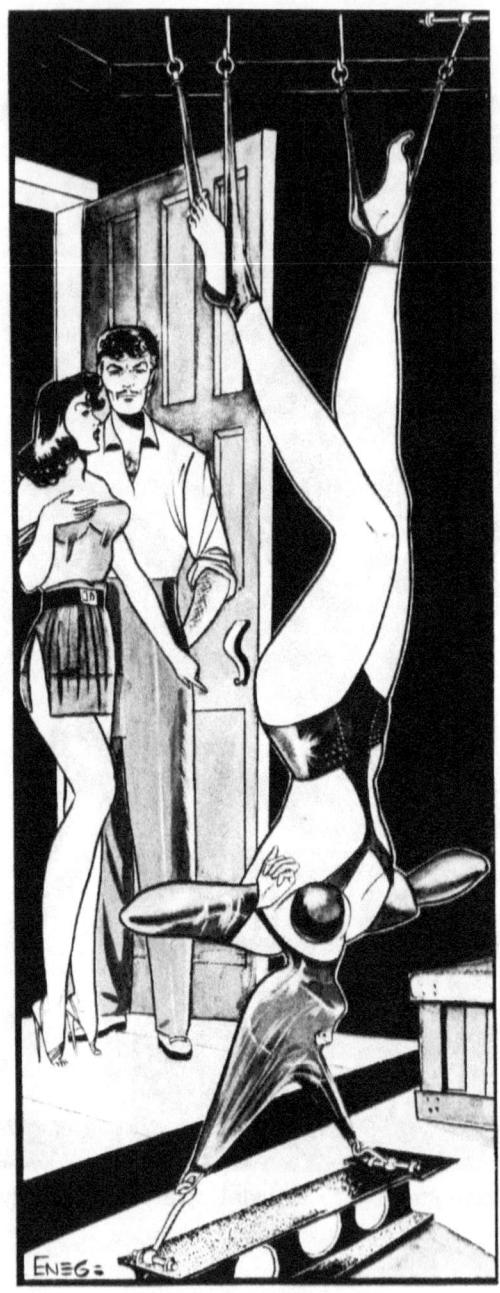

Ladies in Rubber (1954)

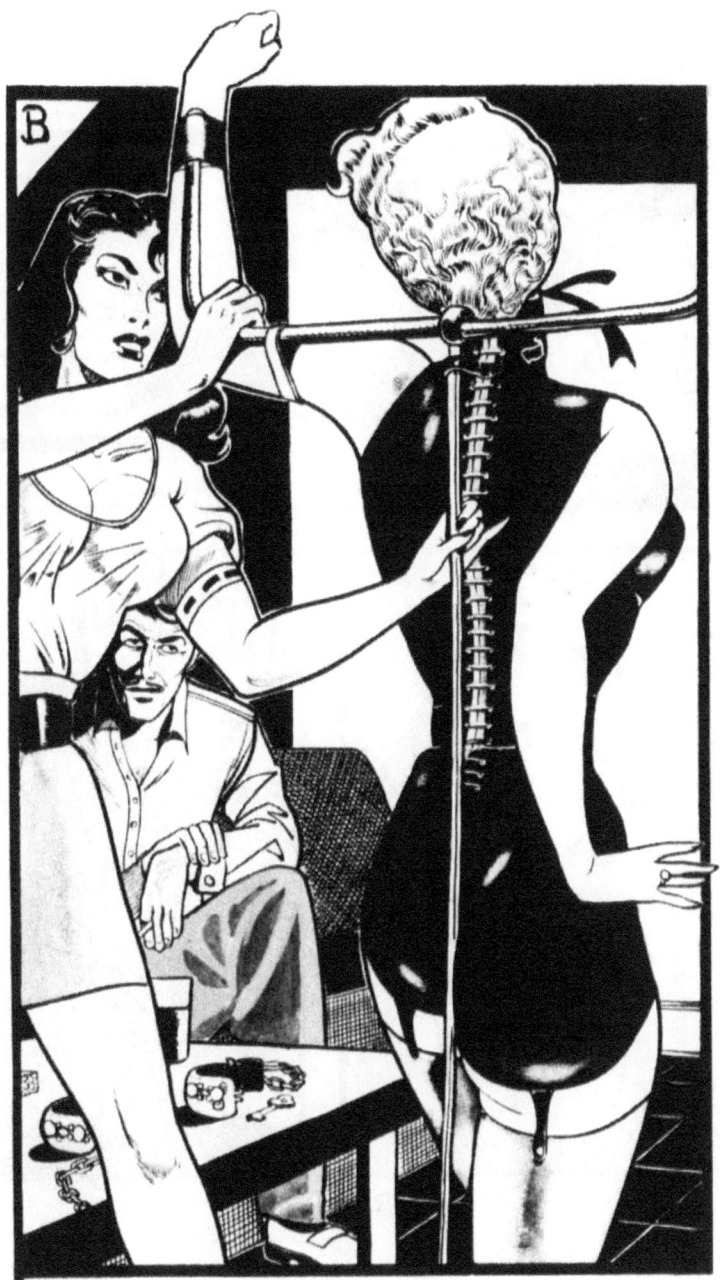

Ladies in Rubber (1954)

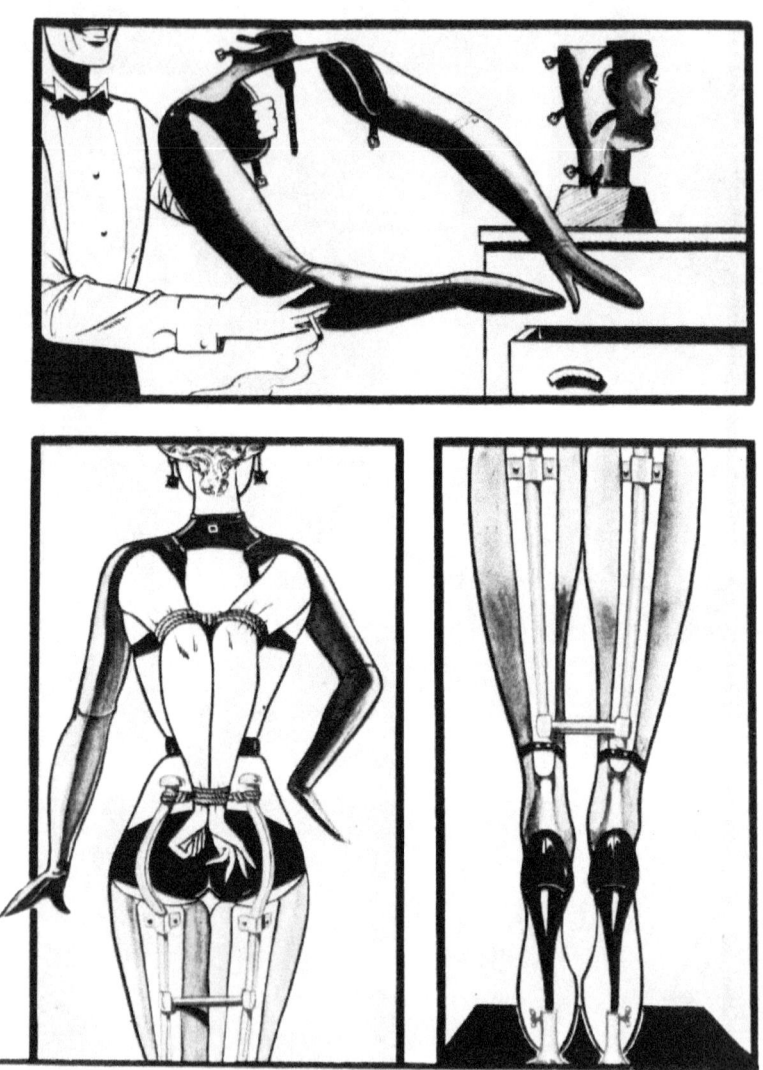

Ladies in Rubber (1954)

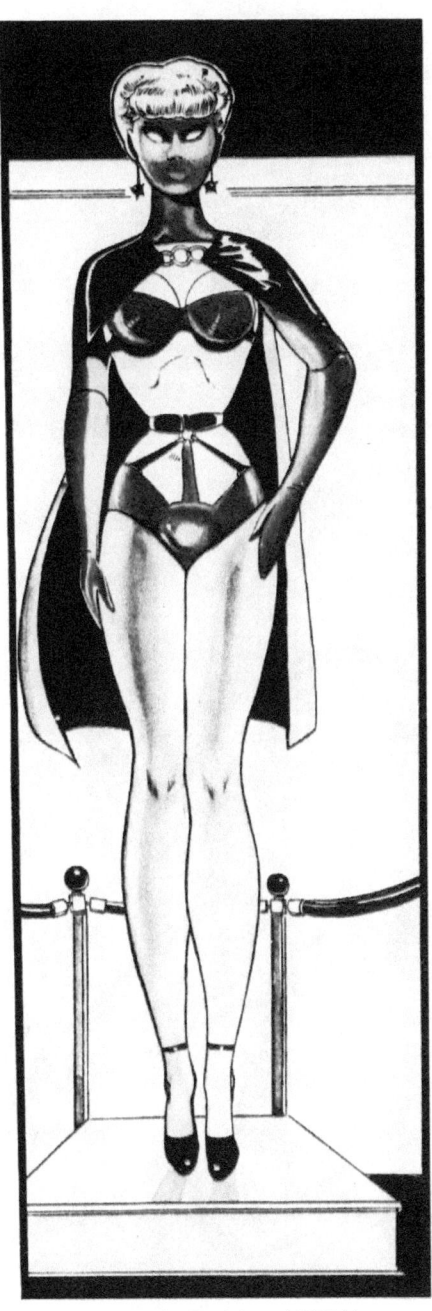

Ladies in Rubber (1954)

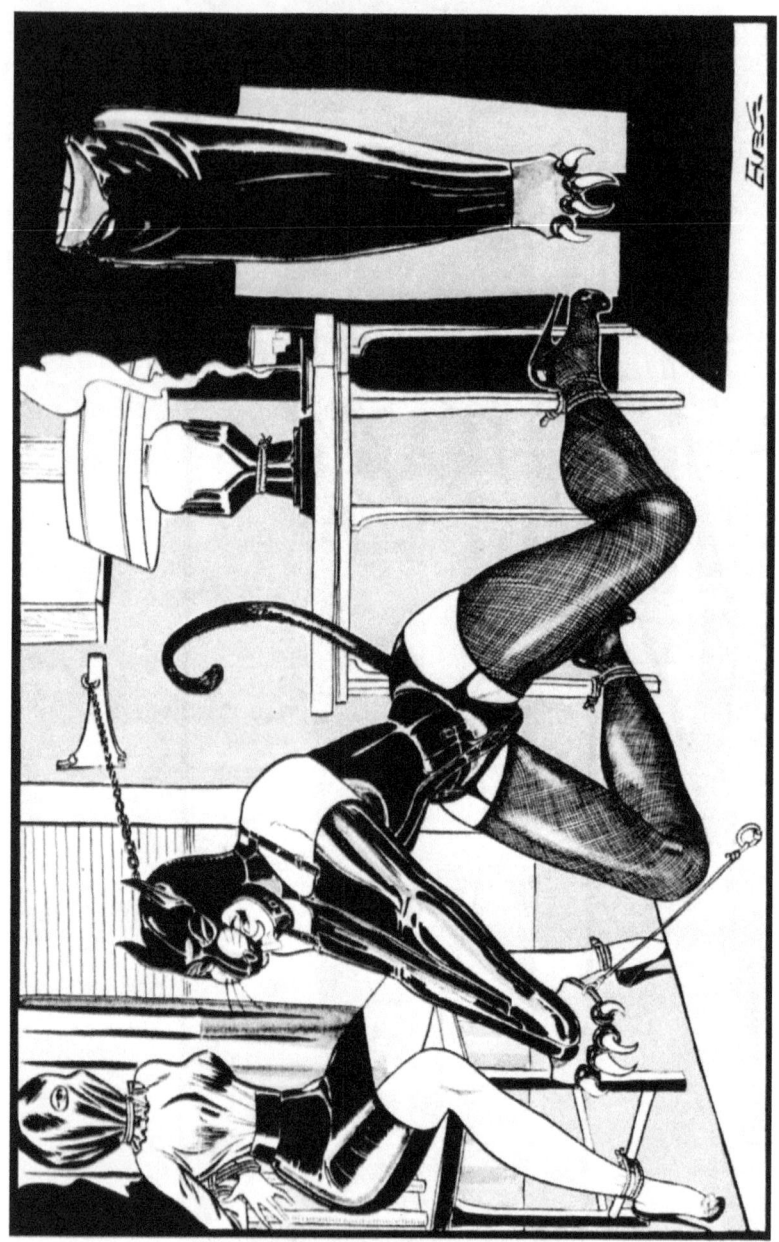

Ladies in Rubber (1954)

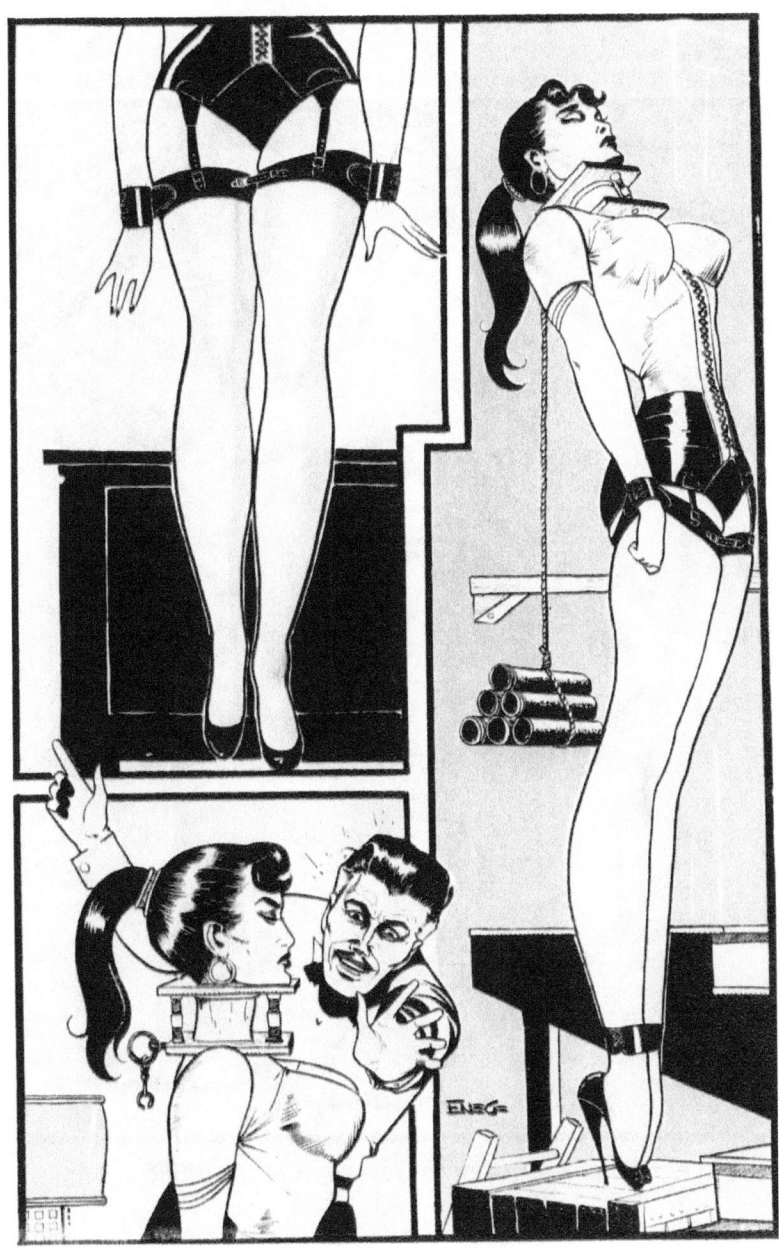

Ladies in Rubber (1954)

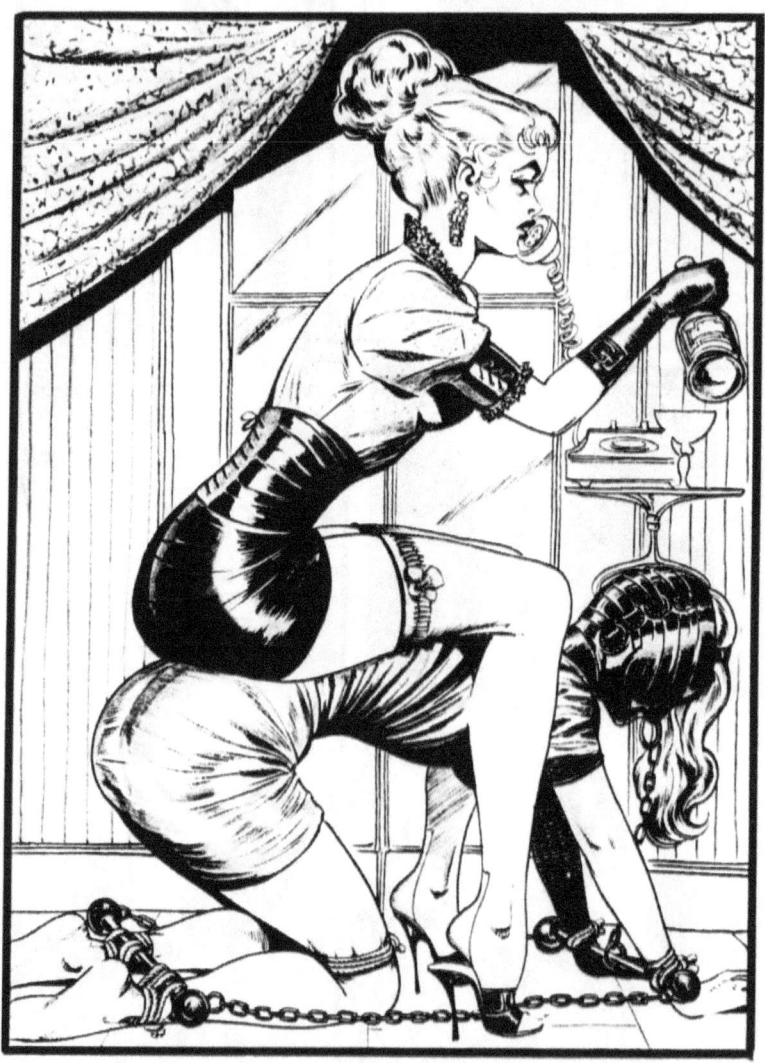

Bondage Society's Gala Slave Ball (1959)

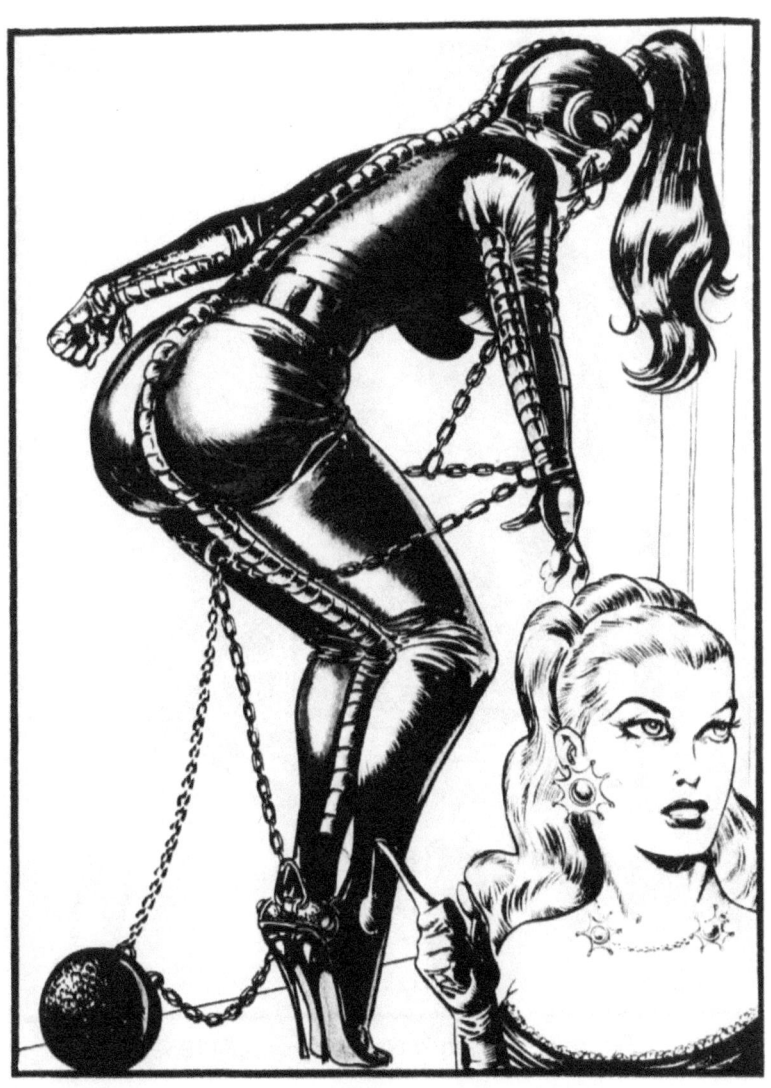

Bondage Society's Gala Slave Ball (1959)

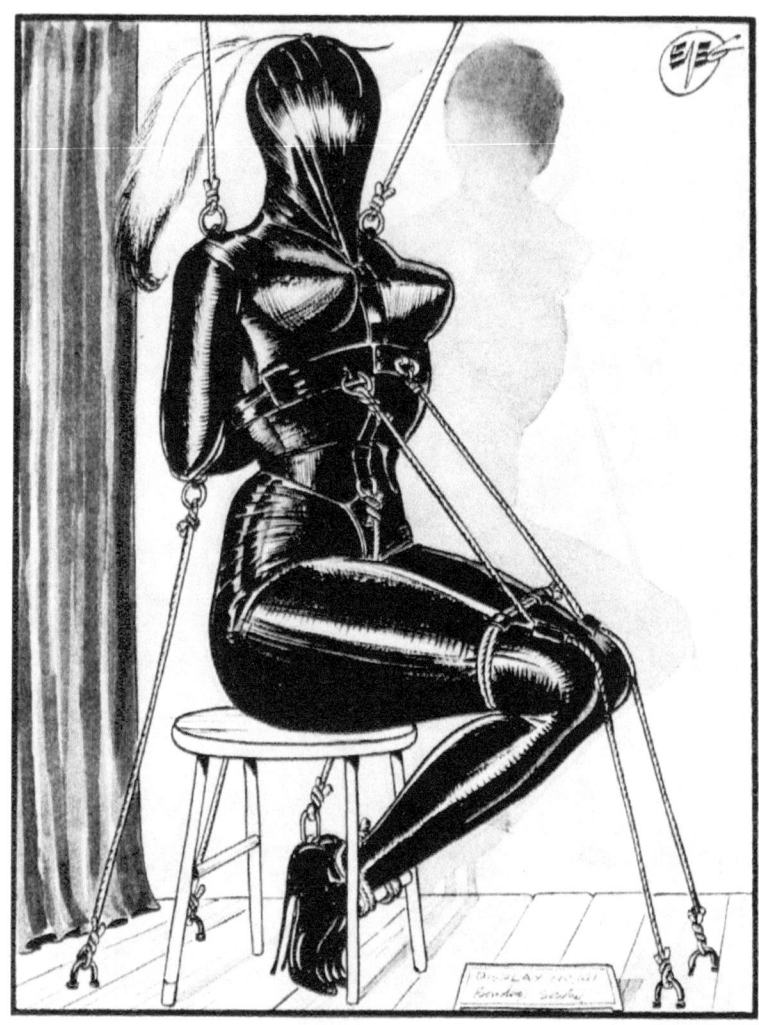

Bondage Society's Gala Slave Ball (1959)

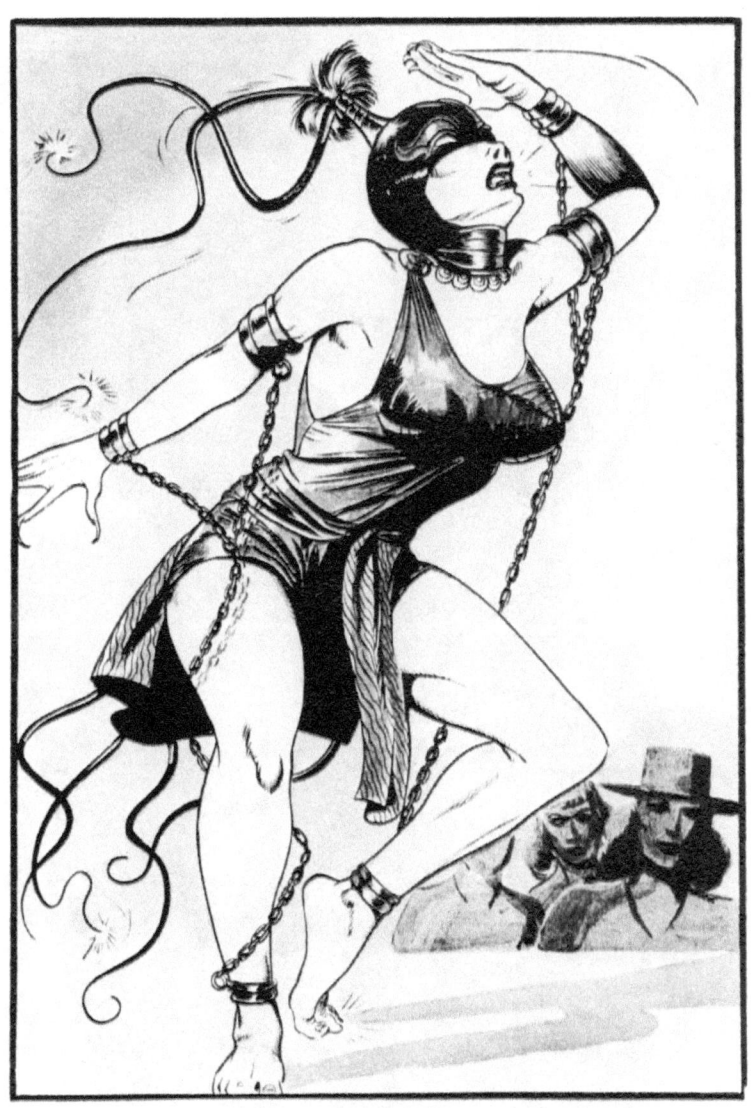

Bondage Society's Gala Slave Ball (1959)

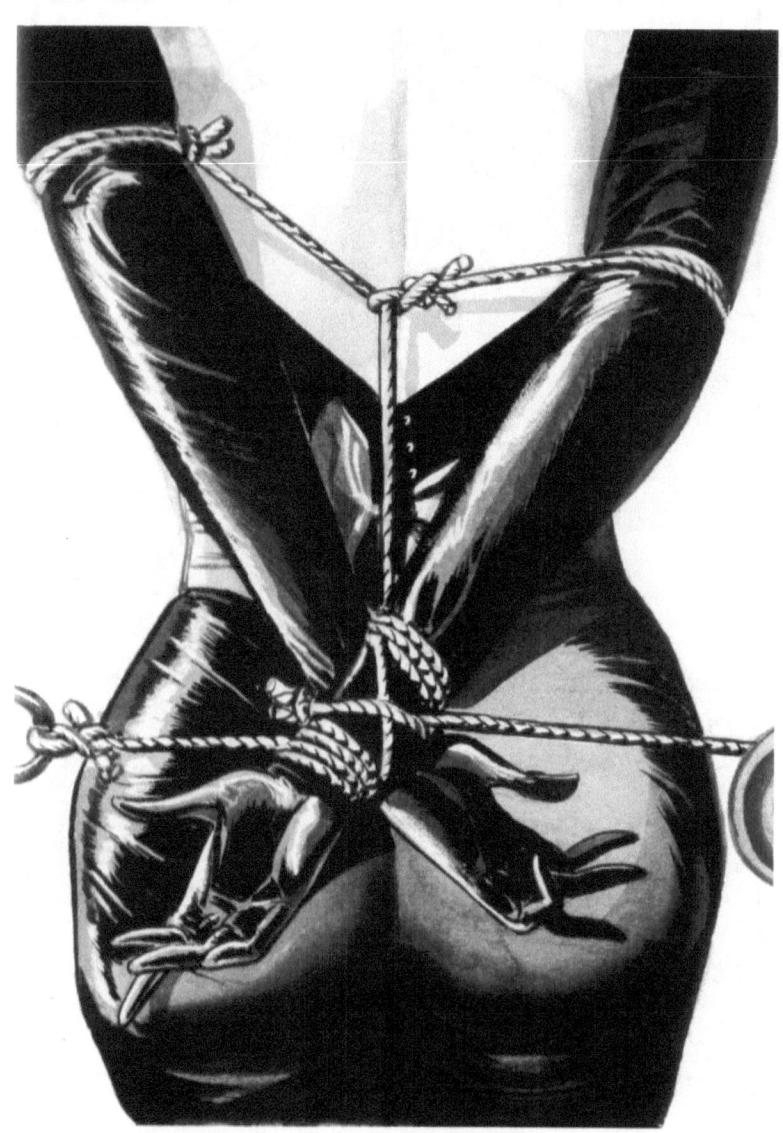

Kidnapped Girl's Sweet Revenge (1959)

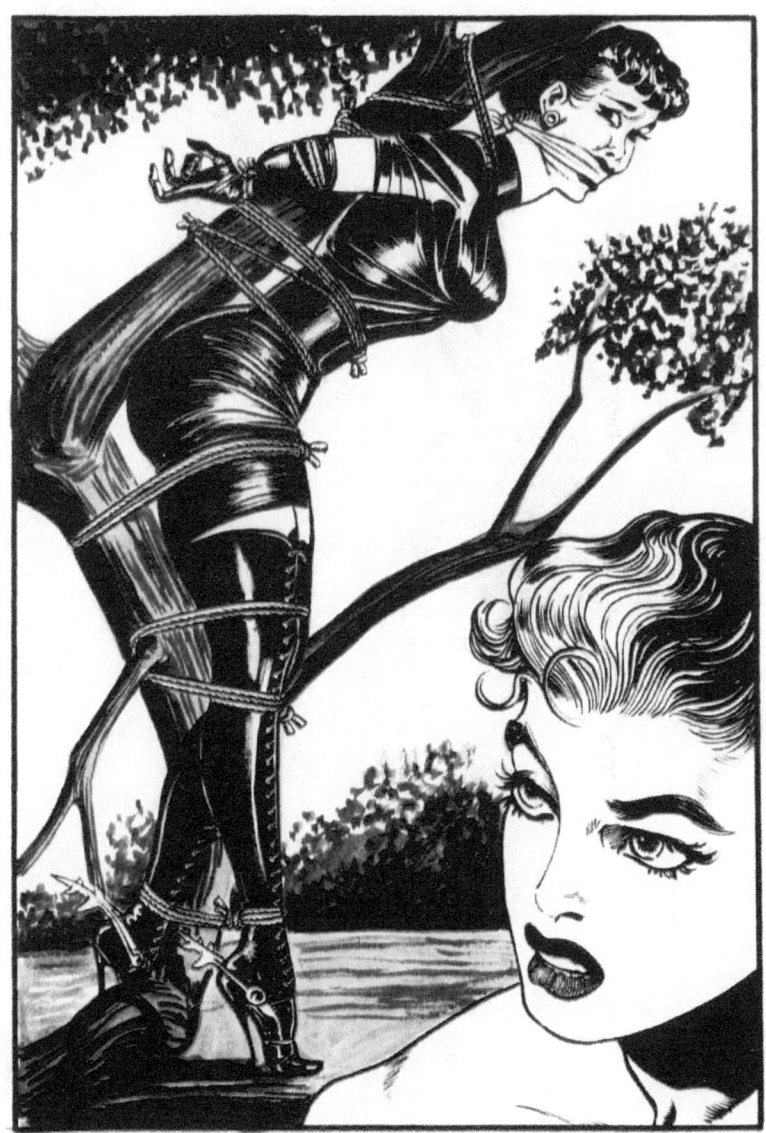

Captive Slaves Dire Distress (1960)

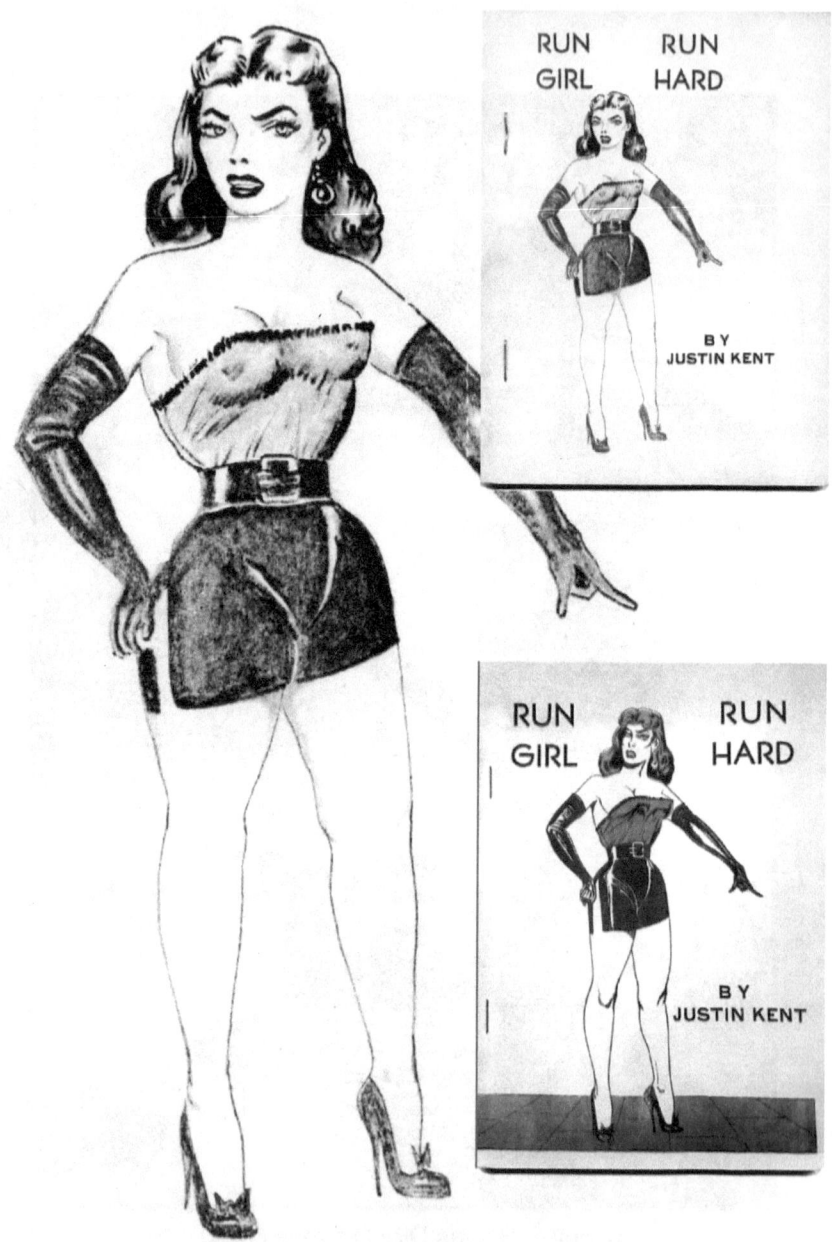

BILBREW/ENEG'S BIZARRE ART CAREER

In a relationship that lasted over a decade, Bilbrew would produce imaginative, often brilliantly executed chapter serials for Klaw, in addition to numbered illustrations and other late '50s booklet art.[lxxi] But, unlike Stanton, Bilbrew never felt any allegiance to Klaw, and quick as he could, he reached out to other patrons. His first after Klaw was evidently Edward "Eddie" Mishkin (right), a man who would snap up anything he produced. (We can see one of Bilbrew's earliest illustrations [former page]—likely one of his first fetish drawings ever—repurposed on the cover of a Mishkin published work, *Run Girl Run Hard,* and later redrawn.)

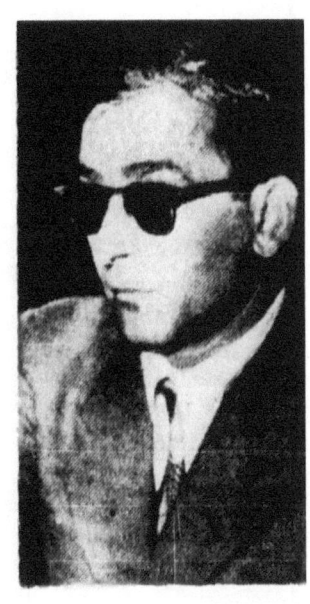

Eddie Mishkin was an old-time bookie who fell into bookstore ownership/operation by 1946.[lxxii] His area of interest was the lively entertainment playground—part misfit magnet, part tourist trap—known as Times Square. Mishkin was also a bold, underground book publisher/distributor, involved in sponsoring original work, as well as—more notoriously—pirating other people's material. (Irving Klaw considered him a major thorn in his side, [lxxiii] although rumors of Mishkin's connection to the underworld may have been enough for Klaw not to take aggressive action.)

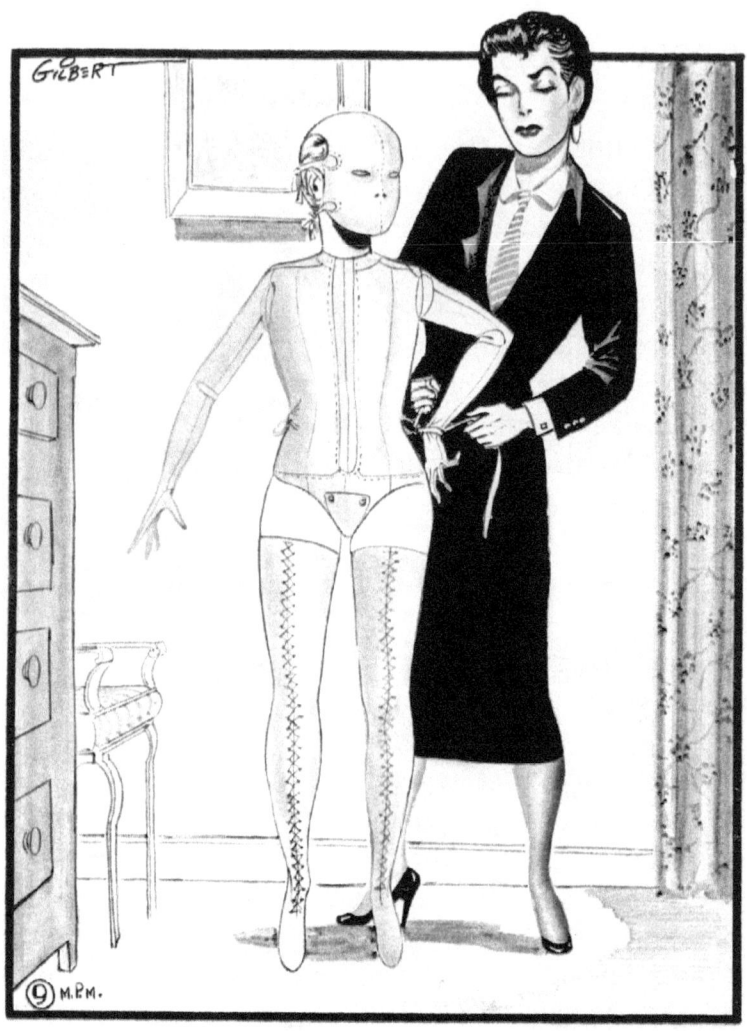

It was for Mishkin (and Mishkin business associate Aaron "Moe" Shapiro[lxxiv]) that Bilbrew/Eneg invented new aliases: "Gilbert" (after Nan Gilbert, author of the crossdressing fantasies he illustrated[lxxv]), "Van Rod" (borrowing the name from the early 20th century French erotica author, Aimé Van Rod[lxxvi]), and "Bondy/ J. Bondy" (obviously a play on "bondage").

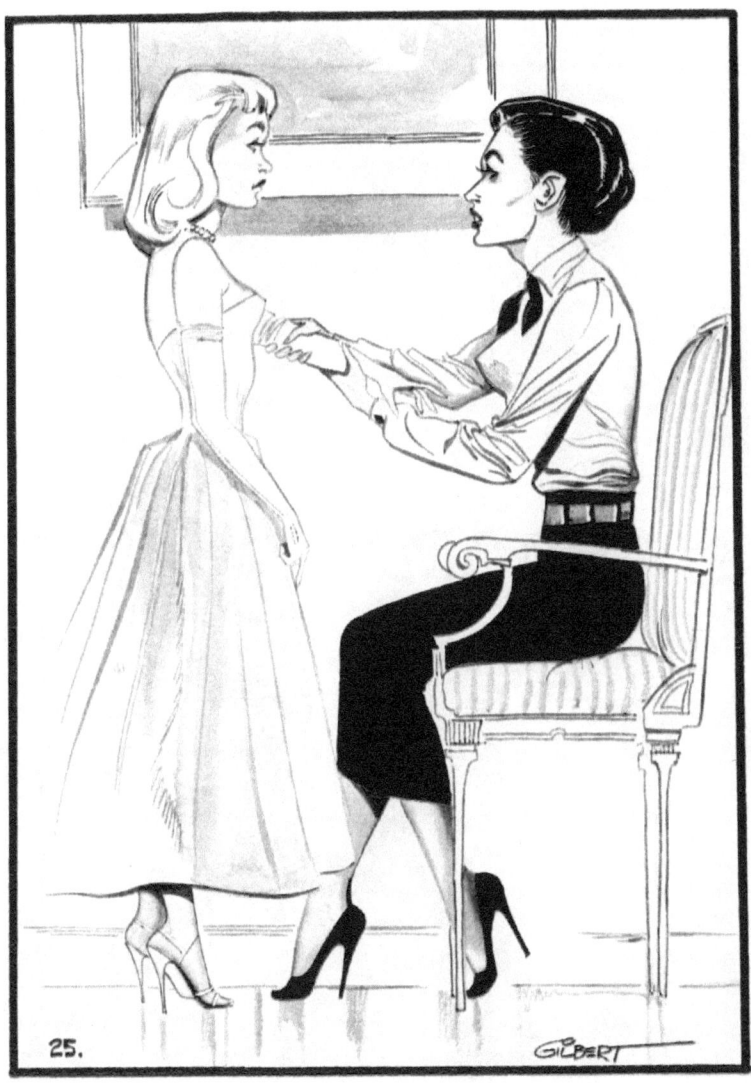

25.   GILBERT

The material produced under the alias "Gilbert" focused on transvestism,[lxxvii] while the "Van Rod" and "Bondy" pseudonyms were used interchangeably for wildly over-the-top sexploitation material full of kinky antics.

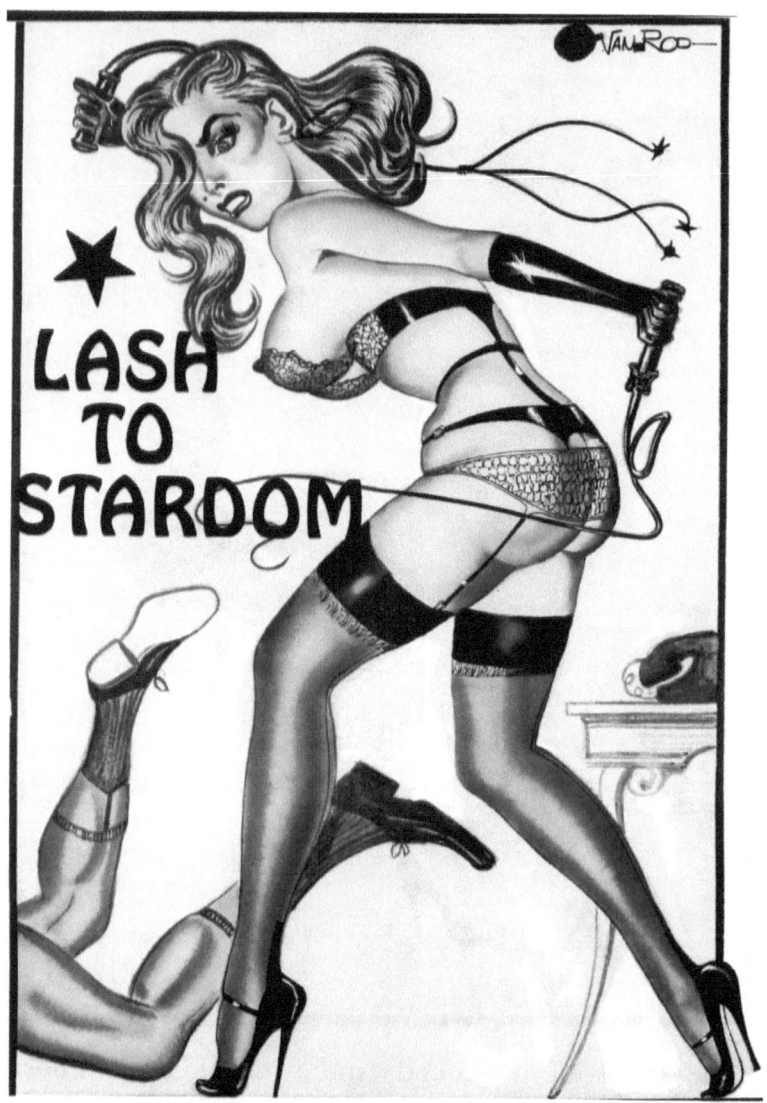

Van Rod, later repurposed by L. Burtman for *Bizarre Life* #10

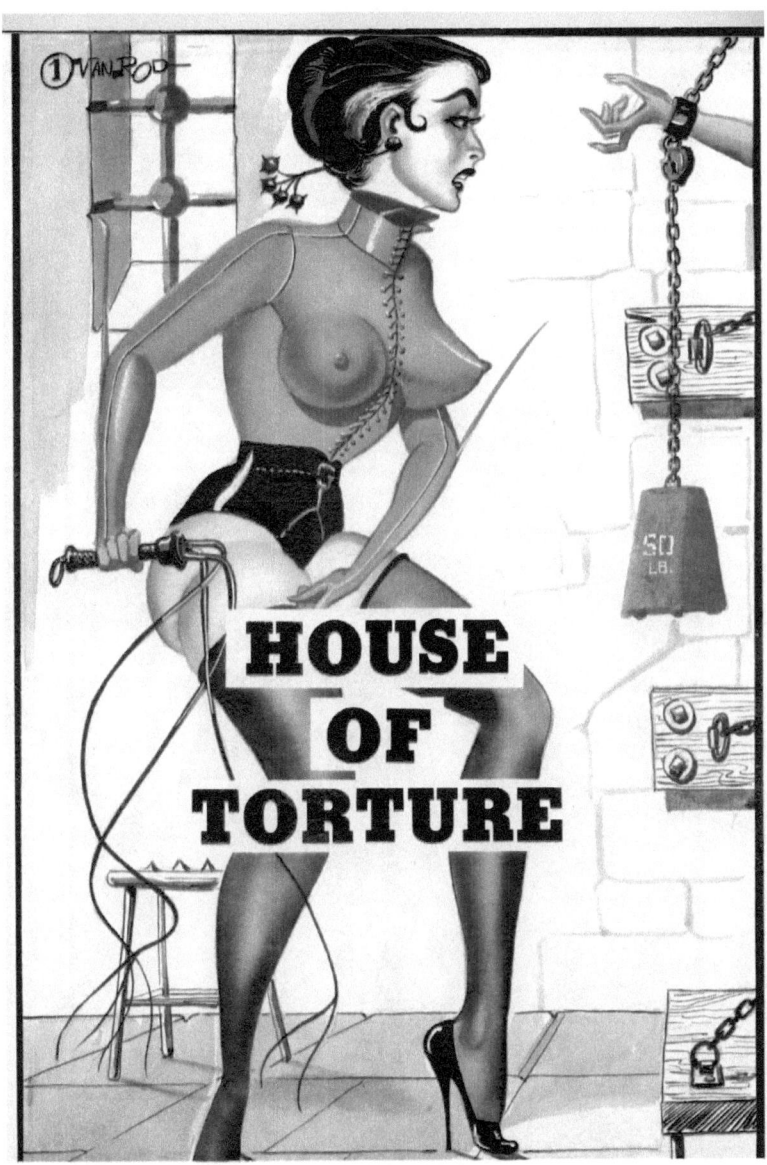

Van Rod, later repurposed by L. Burtman for *Bizarre Life* #11

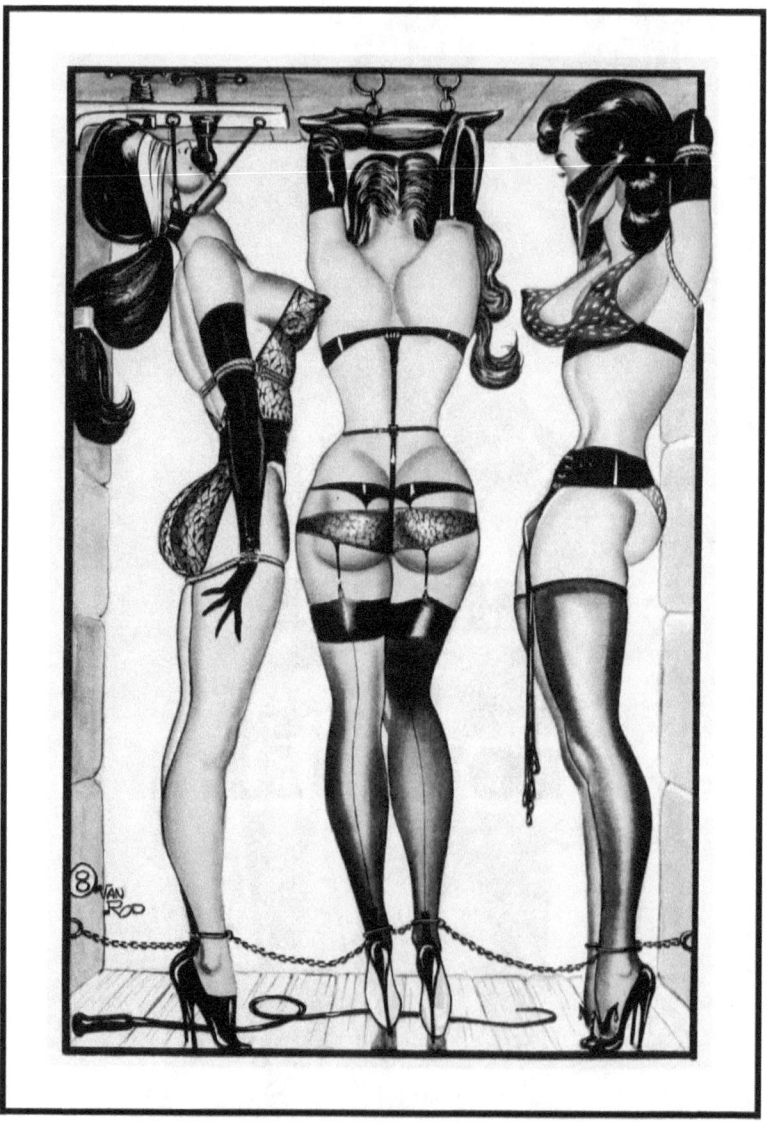

Van Rod, later republished by Burtman (1969) lxxviii

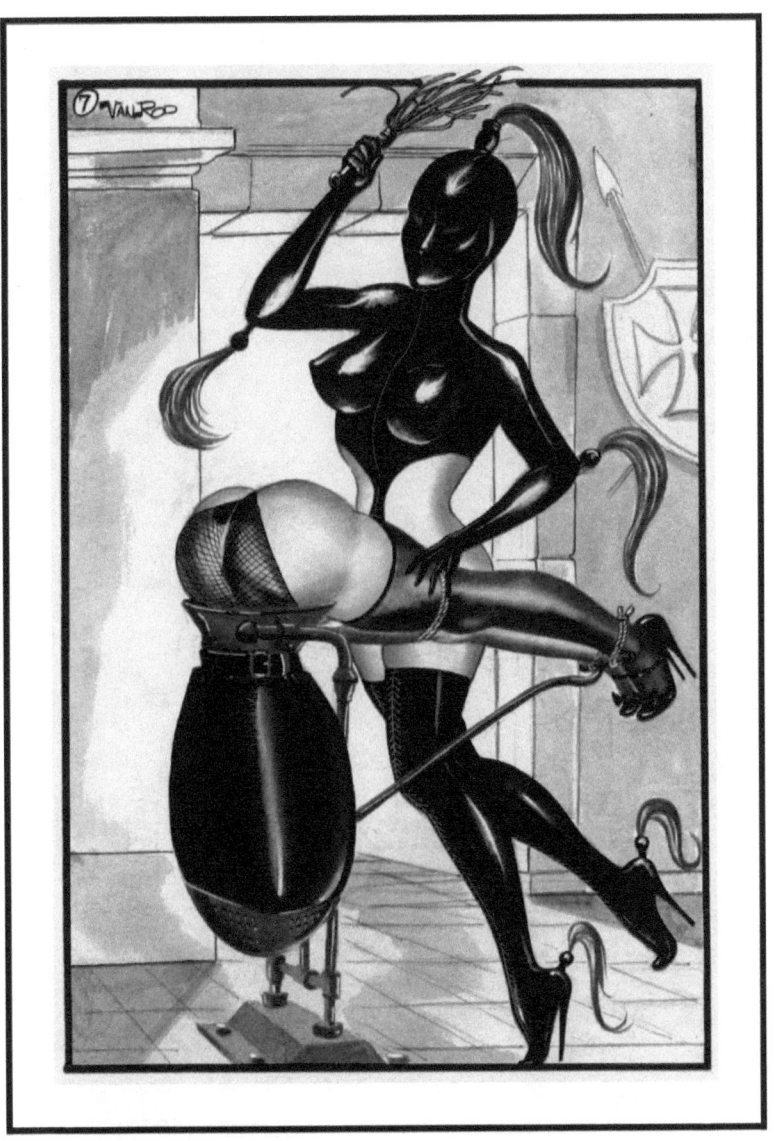

Van Rod, later republished by Burtman (1969)

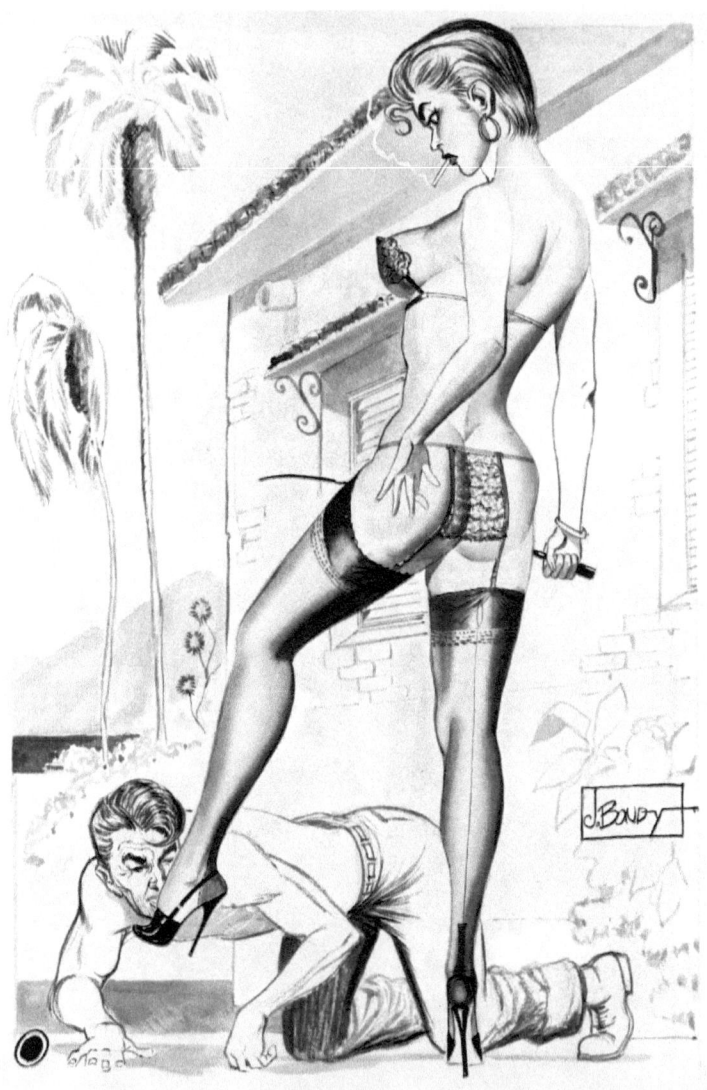

J. Bondy, later republished by Burtman (1970)

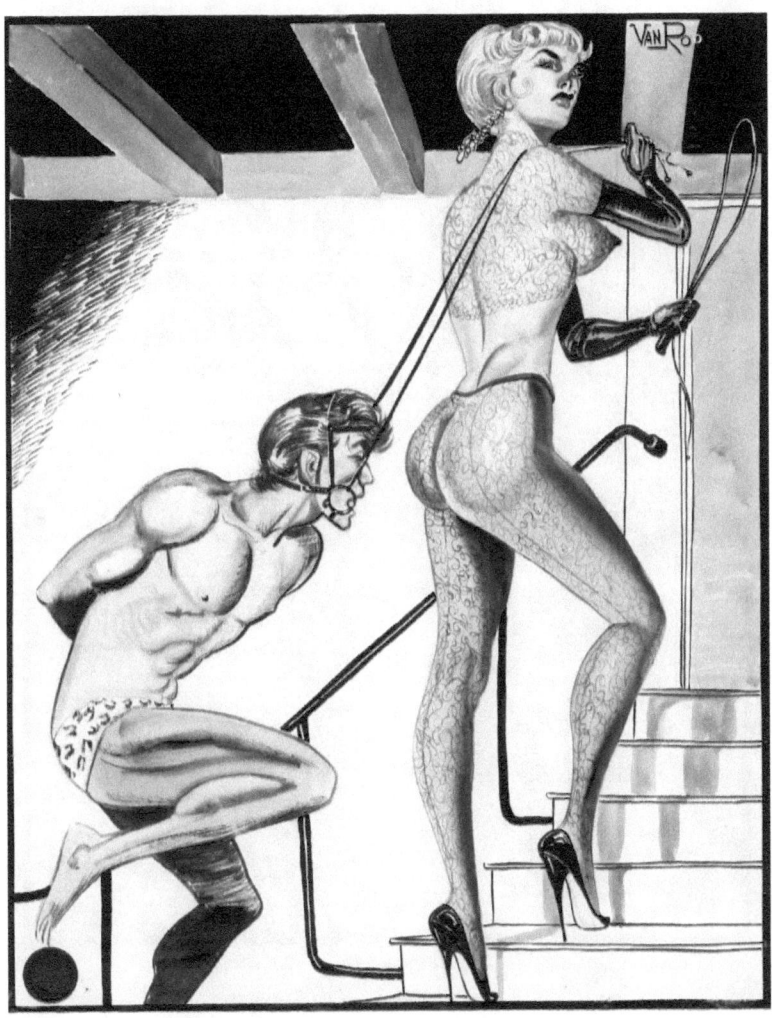

Van Rod, *The Whip Artist* (original art courtesy of Brian Emrich)

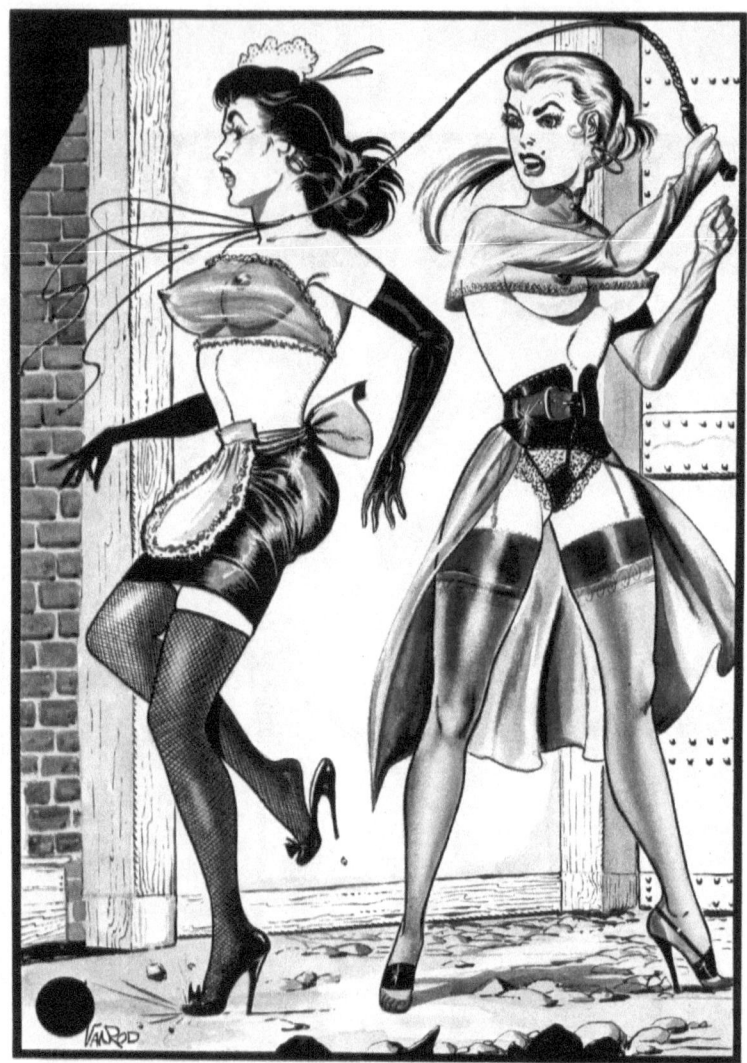

Van Rod, *The Whip Artist*

Bilbrew's most referenced serial as Van Rod is *The Whip Artist*, which featured 48 full-page illustrations, along the lines of others produced for the short-lived 1950s mail order company, Gargoyle Sales Corp.[lxxix]

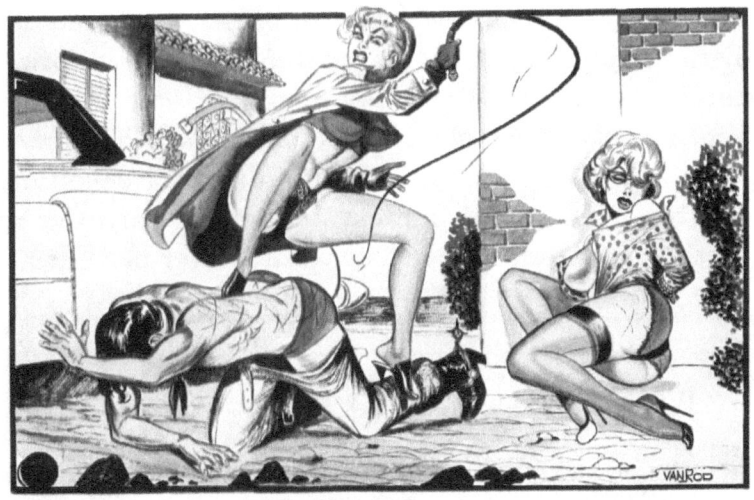

It might be worth noting that Bilbrew (as Gilbert and Van Rod), preceded Stanton in producing trans and "dominant female" themed art.[lxxx]

Both as Van Rod and Bondy, Bilbrew also produced his share of "fighting women" scenarios (usually eight panel narratives), with at least one recurring character: female wrestling champion, "Rita Rio."

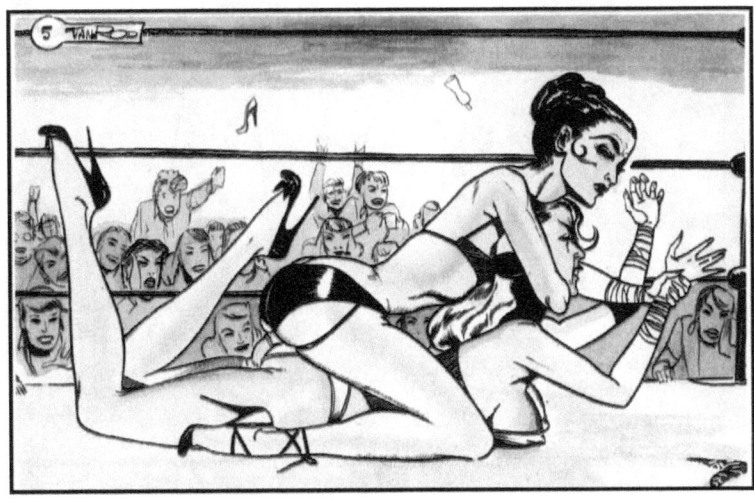

As for other Bilbrew work of merit produced for Mishkin (published in the mid-'50s in book form), standouts include the sci-fi inspired *High Heels in the Heavens,* the noir-inspired *Madame Adista* and *Dangerous Years,* all three containing topless nudity —highly risky in the context of a fetish narrative at the time and something Klaw would never permit.

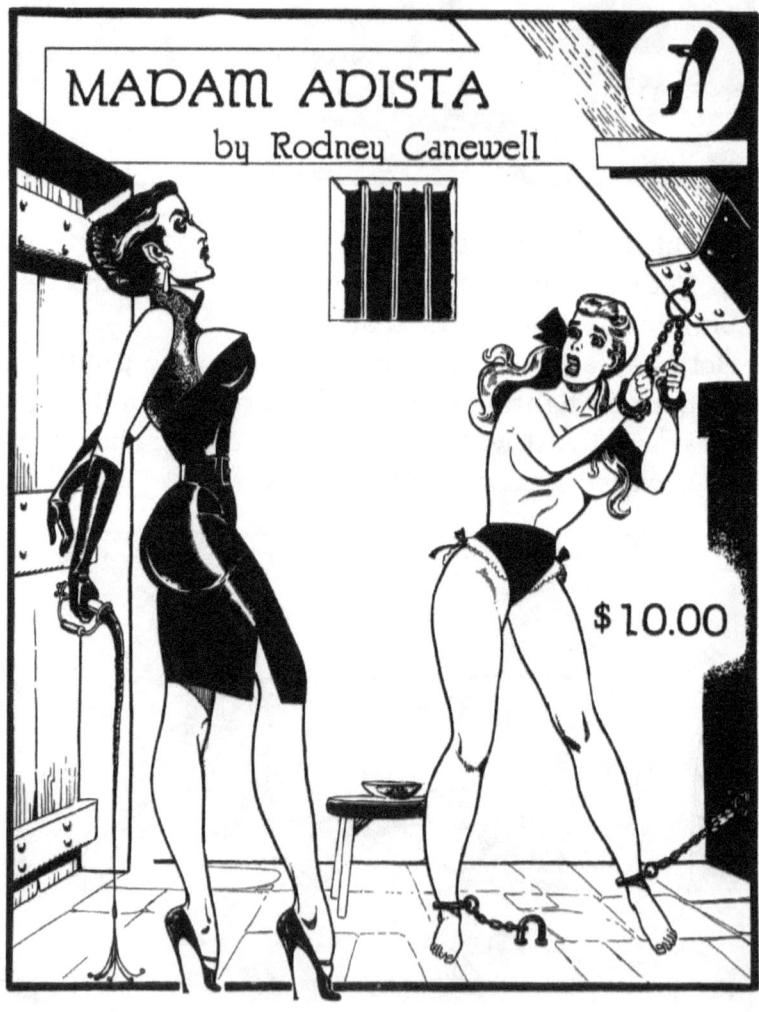

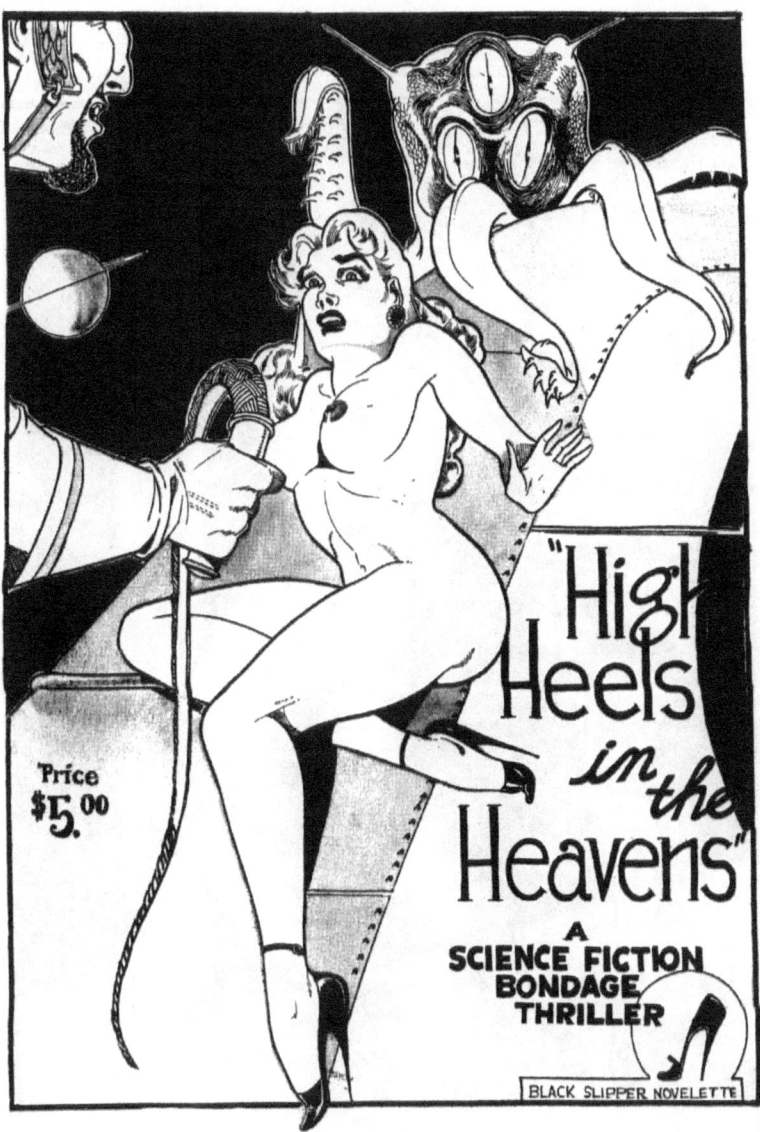

Of the three, the sexploitation content of *High Heels in the Heavens* seems a full decade ahead of its time, anticipating—despite its fetish derivation—the darker films of Russ Meyer and the "roughies" of the 1960s.

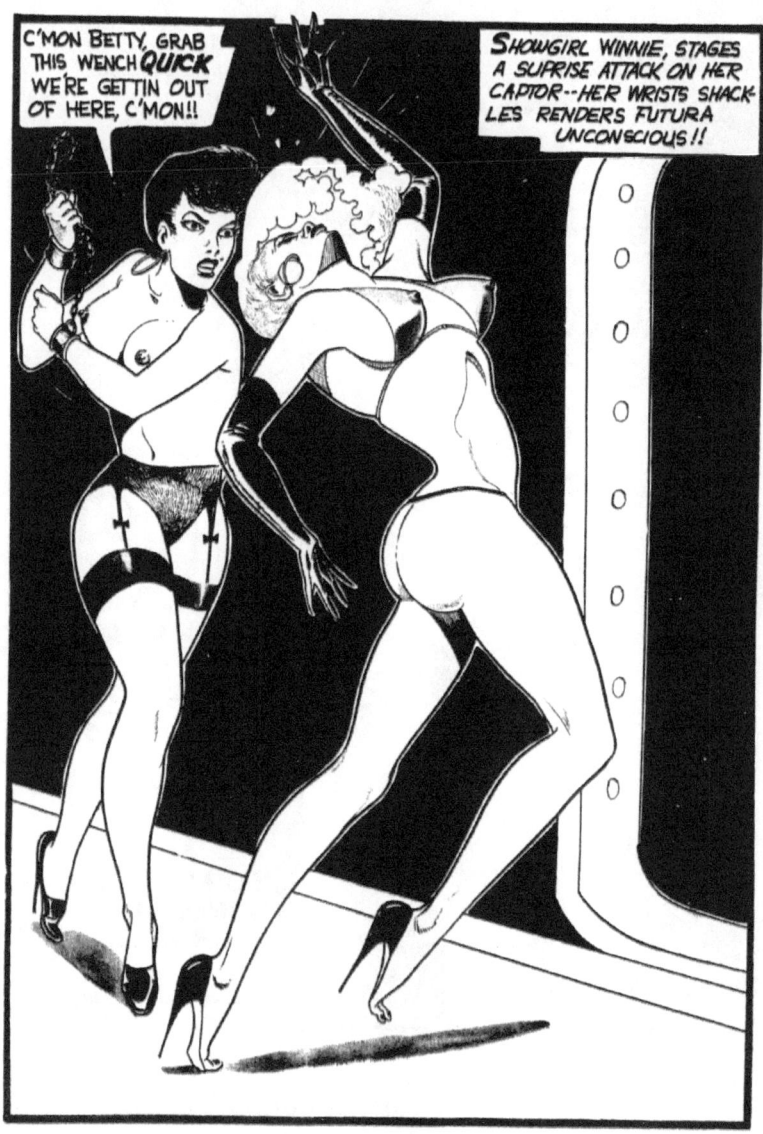

High Heels in the Heavens (1955)

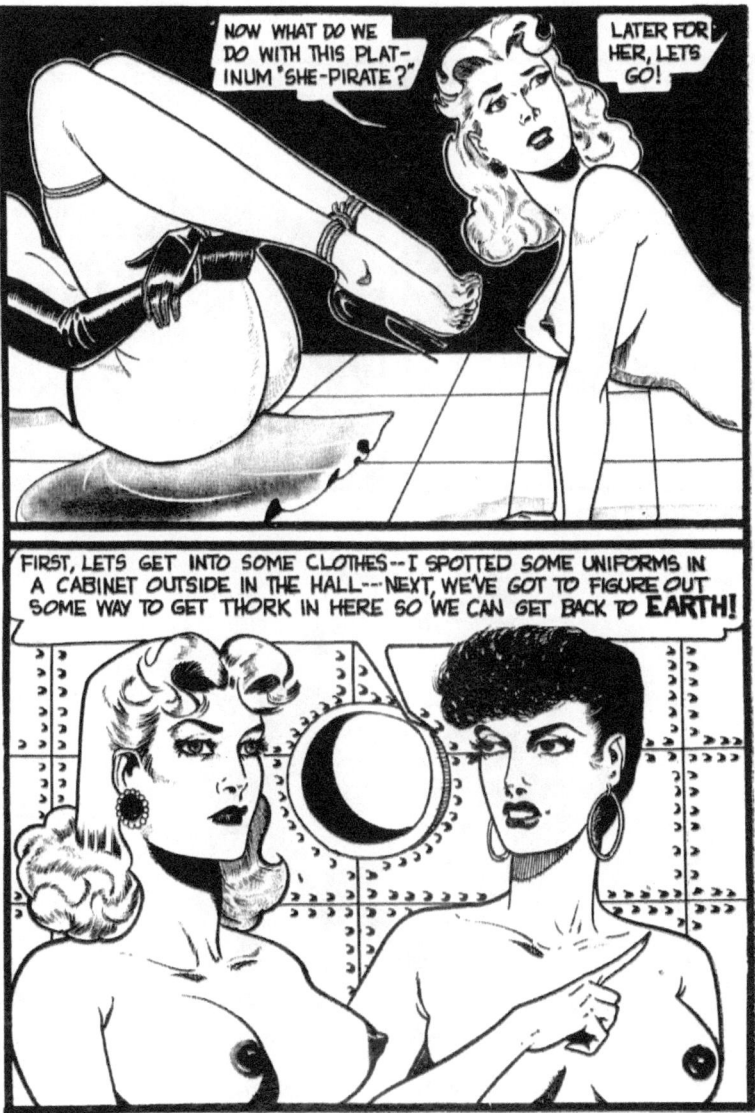

High Heels in the Heavens (1955)

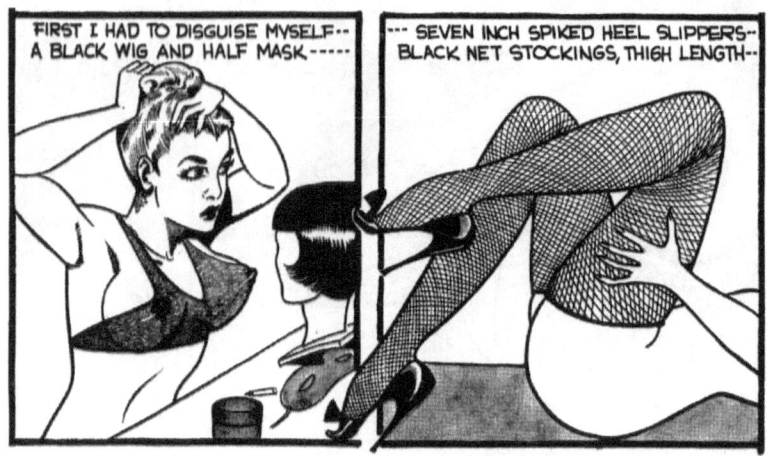

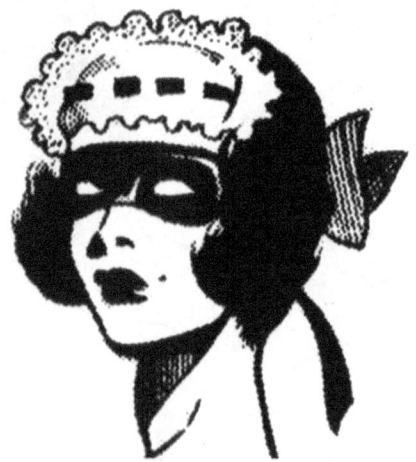

Madame Adista (1955)

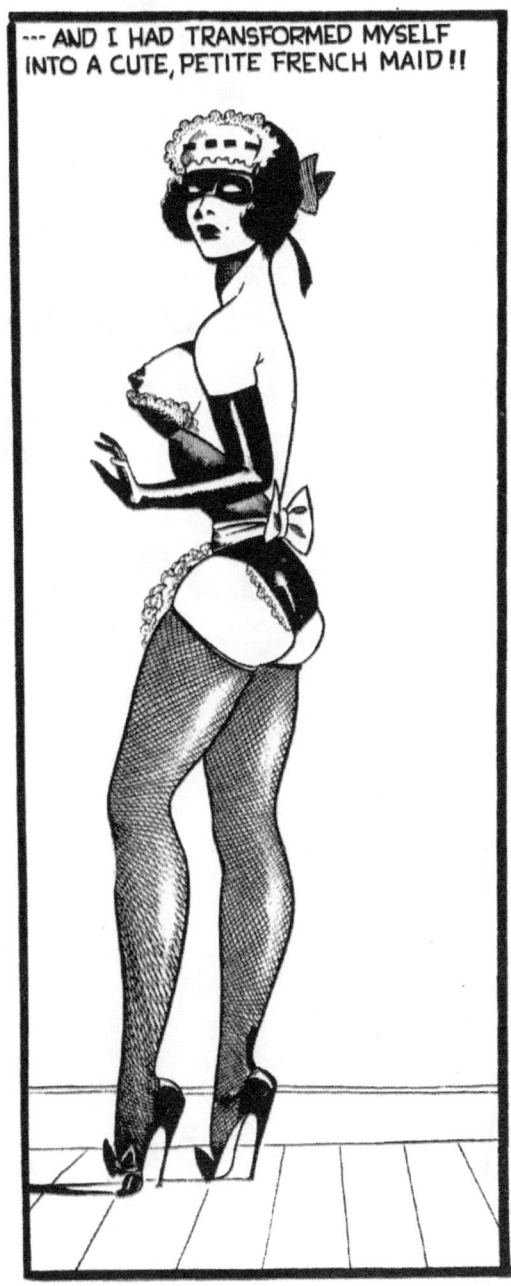

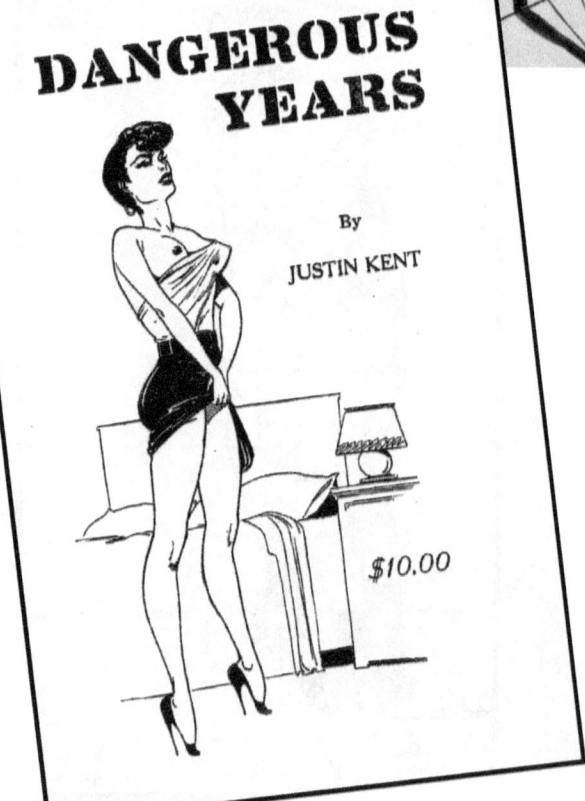

THE DANGEROUS YEARS

I was willing to— to—," He faltered now as if he just couldn't put it into words.

Not that she didn't know the rest of it, but perverse anger made her draw him out. "Willing to what, Jim?" she demanded harshly, suddenly realizing that what he seemed to find it so hard to say was more important than anything he had ever said to her before in all their time together.

"Well," he commenced, a sheepish sort of smile coming on his face, "I haven't been married to my red haired girl for nine years without learning that when she starts getting irritable, it's because Daddy's left off his home work."

That did it.

"Listen," she ...
Jim Ma...
furious, ...

DANGEROUS YEARS

By

JUSTIN KENT

$10.00

(1955)

Bilbrew continued to produce material for Mishkin into the late fifties, after which time Mishkin was famously arrested, brought to trial, and convicted— in the language of the court—"of violating § 1141 of the New York Penal Law for publishing, hiring others to prepare, and possessing with intent to sell obscene books."[lxxxi]

Through a series of legal appeals, Mishkin was able to stave off his three-year prison sentence until 1966, during which time his case rose all the way to the US Supreme Court, where the decision was conclusively upheld.

Seventy-two titles were used as evidence against Mishkin, most with art by Bilbrew and Stanton.

No. Title of Book (with artist):

1 *Chances Go Around* (Stanton)

2 *Impact* (Stanton)

3 *Female Sultan* (Stanton)

4 *Satin Satellite* (Bilbrew)

5 *Her Highness* (Stanton)

9 *The Whipping Chorus* Girls (Bilbrew)

15 & 47 *Bound In Rubber* (Bilbrew/Stanton/Klaw piracy)

19 & 50 *Women In Distress* (Bilbrew/Stanton/Klaw piracy)

20 & 54 *Pleasure Parade* No.1 (Bilbrew/Stanton/Klaw piracy)

21 & 57 *Screaming Flesh* (Stanton)

22 & 58 *Fury* (Bilbrew)

23 *So Firm So Fully Packed* (Stanton)

24 *I'll Try Anything Twice* (Bilbrew)

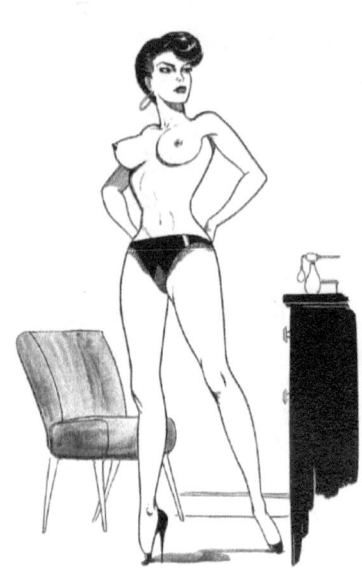

25 & 59 *Masque* (Stanton)

26 *Catanis* (Bilbrew)

27 *The Violated Wrestler* (Stanton)

28 *Betrayal* (Bilbrew)

29 *Swish! Bottom!* (Bilbrew)

30 *Raw Dames* (Stanton)

32 *Dangerous Years* (Bilbrew)

51 *Pleasure Parade* No. 4 (Bilbrew/Stanton/Klaw piracy)

52 *Pleasure Parade* No. 3 (Bilbrew/Stanton/Klaw piracy)

53 *Pleasure Parade* No. 2 (Bilbrew/Stanton/Klaw piracy)

55 *Sorority Girls Stringent Initiation* (Bilbrew/Klaw piracy)

56 *Terror At The Bizarre Museum* (Stanton/Klaw piracy)

60 *Temptation* (Bilbrew)

63 *Mrs. Tyrant's Finishing School* (Stanton/Klaw piracy)

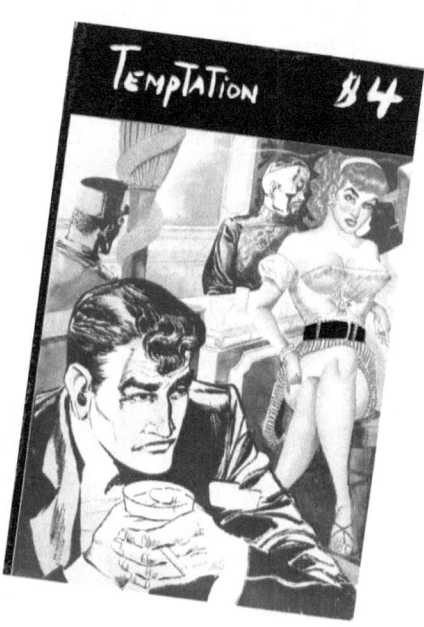

68 *Bondage Correspondence* (Stanton/Klaw piracy)

69 *Woman Impelled* (Stanton)

70 *Eye Witness* (Bilbrew)

71 *Stud Broad* (Stanton)

72 *Queen Bee* (Bilbrew)

Interestingly, both Bilbrew and Stanton were called to testify against Mishkin in 1960, though they wisely offered little information that assisted the prosecution. During the tedious proceedings, they were asked about their dealings with the publisher and to identify their own artwork obtained in police raids. (One such raid involved Stanton and Steve Ditko's art studio.)

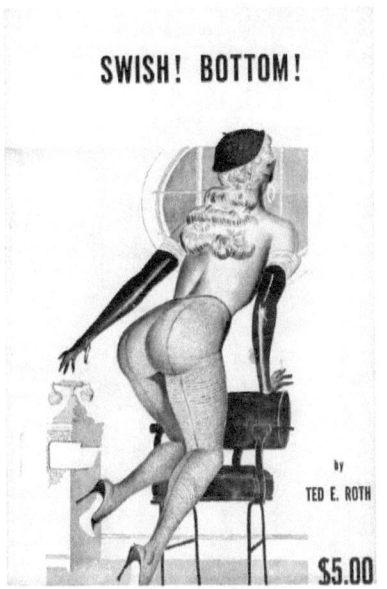

SWISH! BOTTOM!

by

TED E. ROTH

$5.00

In his court appearance, Bilbrew identified artwork from ten of his books: [lxxxii]

- *Satin Satellite*
- *Catanis*
- *Betrayal*
- *Swish! Bottom!*
- *Temptation*
- *Eye Witness*
- *Queen Bee*
- *Fury*
- *The French Girl On The Stairs, Parts 1 and 2*

Asked on the stand *where* he was paid for his artwork, Bilbrew alluded to Publishers Outlet (Mishkin's main base of operation at the time) or Kingsley Books (another Mishkin controlled 42nd Street shop). [lxxxiii]

Asked *how much* he was paid per illustration, Bilbrew generally responded: "About twenty-five to thirty dollars." Grilled if he read the books he provided illustrations for, Bilbrew replied no. The judge cited one book in particular (exhibit 22, *Fury*): [lxxxiv]

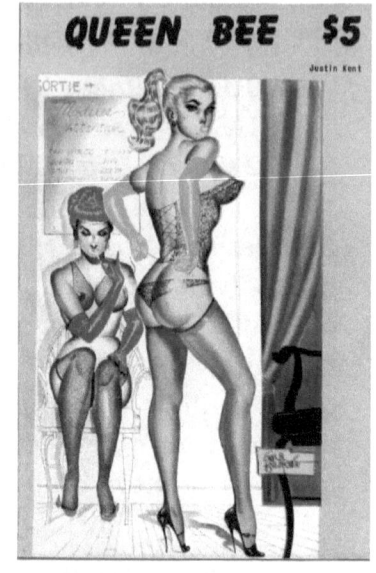

Justice Gassman: *Well, tell me: How did you know what sort of a cover to put on this without reading the book?*

Bilbrew: *Well, let's say I would—I, more or less, learn the psychology of the type of work, what's appealing—*

Justice Gassman: *But you didn't read the book. How did you know that the cover was going to fit the book?*

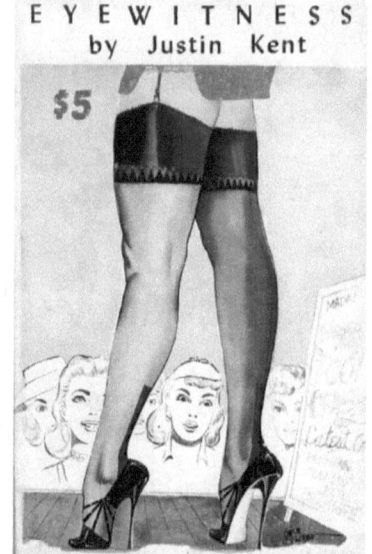

Bilbrew: *Actually speaking, I didn't.*

Justice Gassman: *You just made a cover without knowing whether it fitted the book or it didn't fit the book?*

Bilbrew: *That's the way I have been working.*

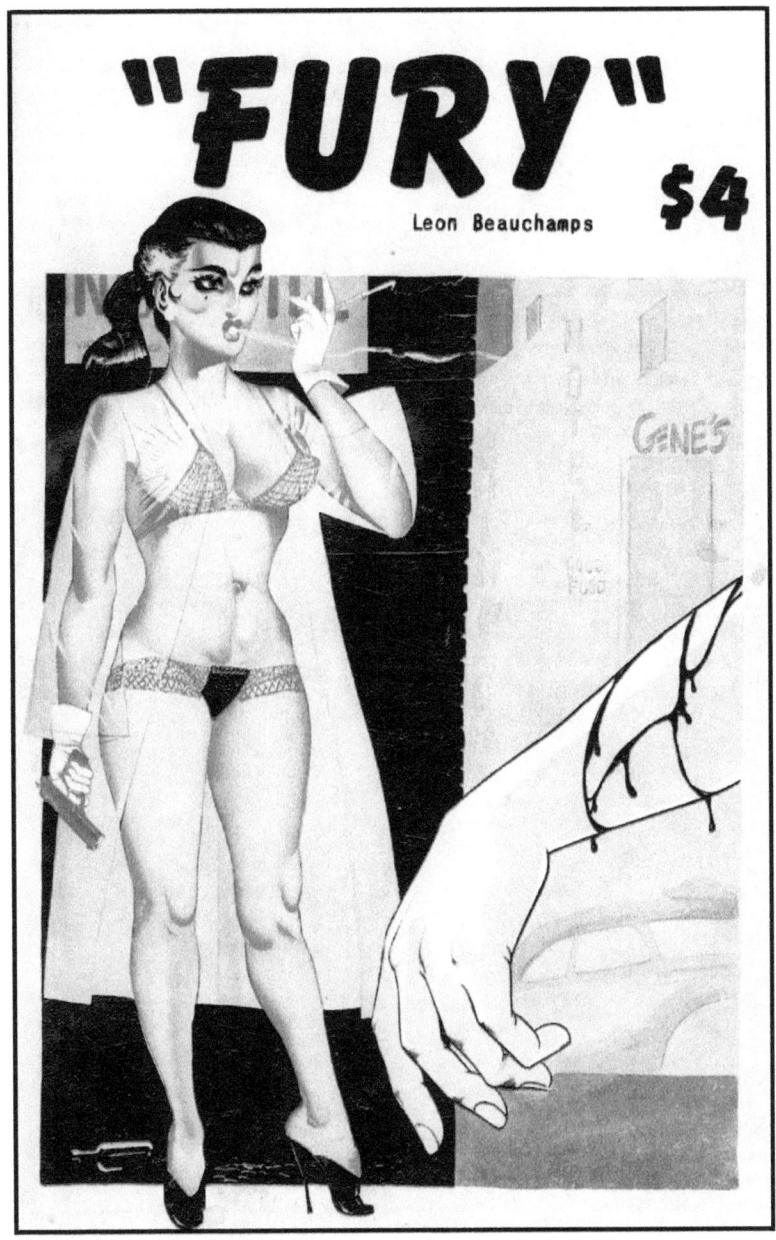

Exhibit 22 at Mishkin's trial. (Note "Gene's" bar)

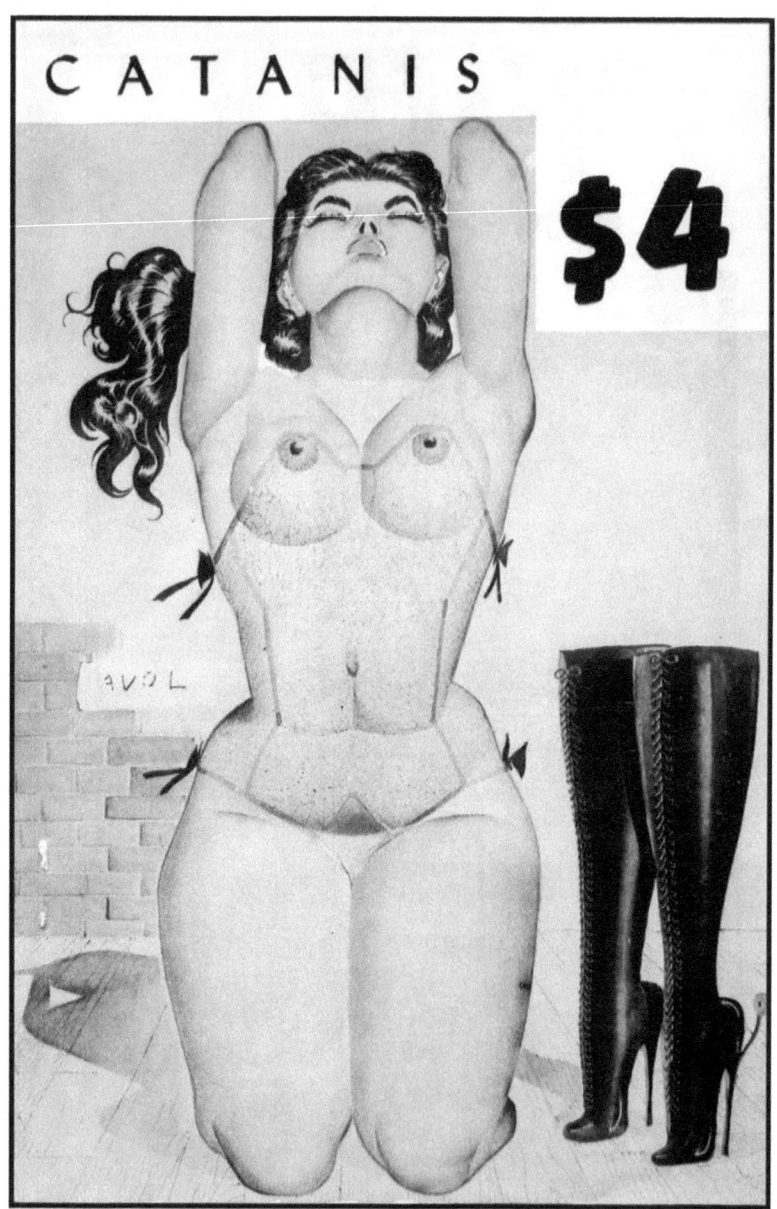

Exhibit 26A at Mishkin's trial

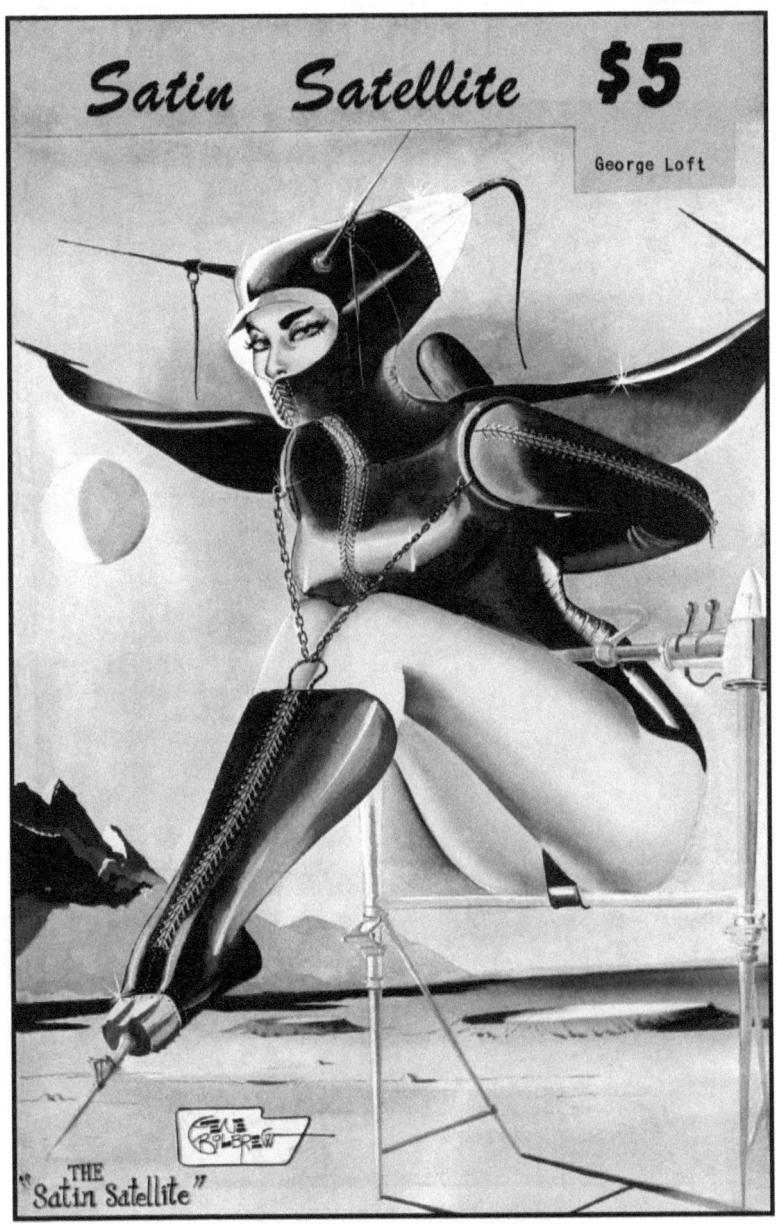

Exhibit 4A at Mishkin's trial

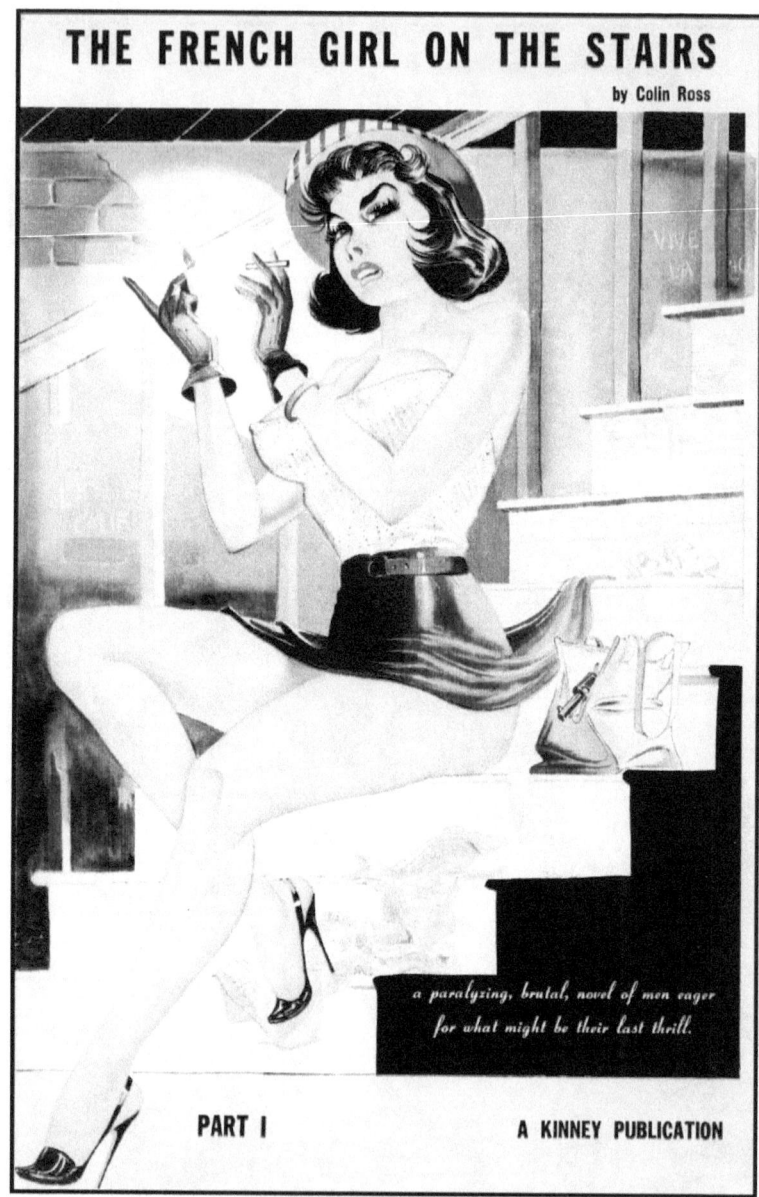

Exhibit 35 at Mishkin's trial

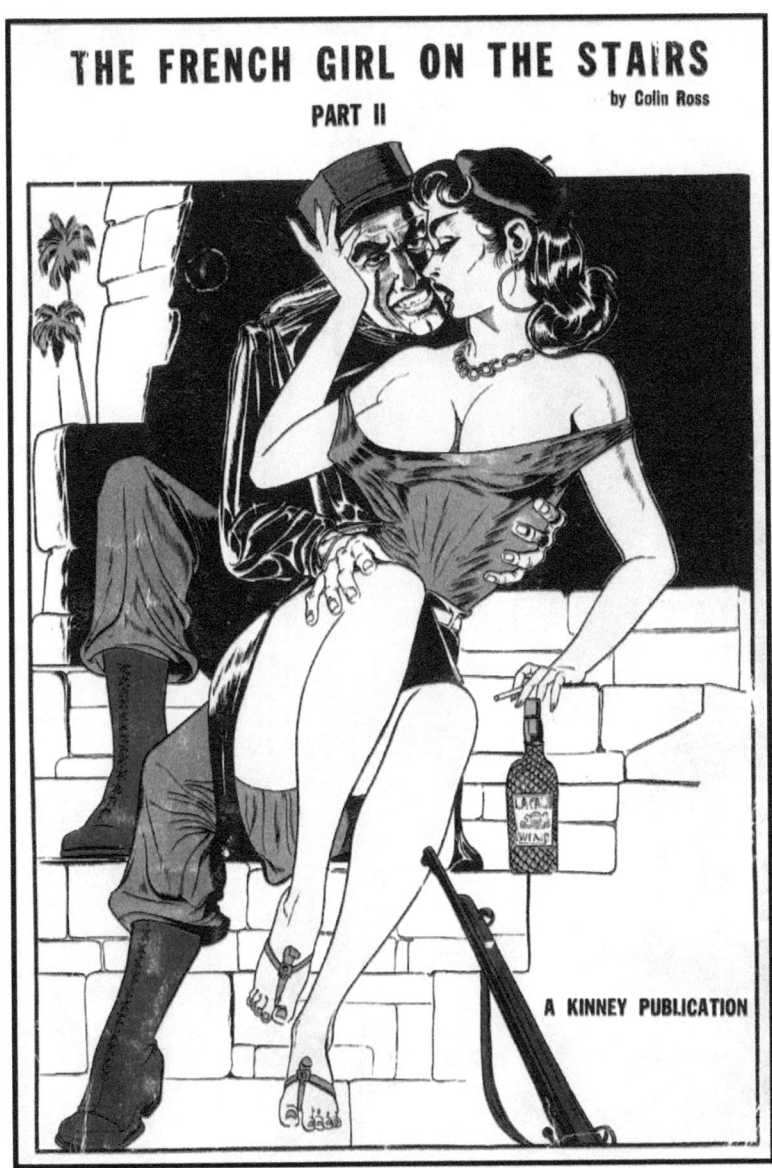

Exhibit 36 at Mishkin's trial

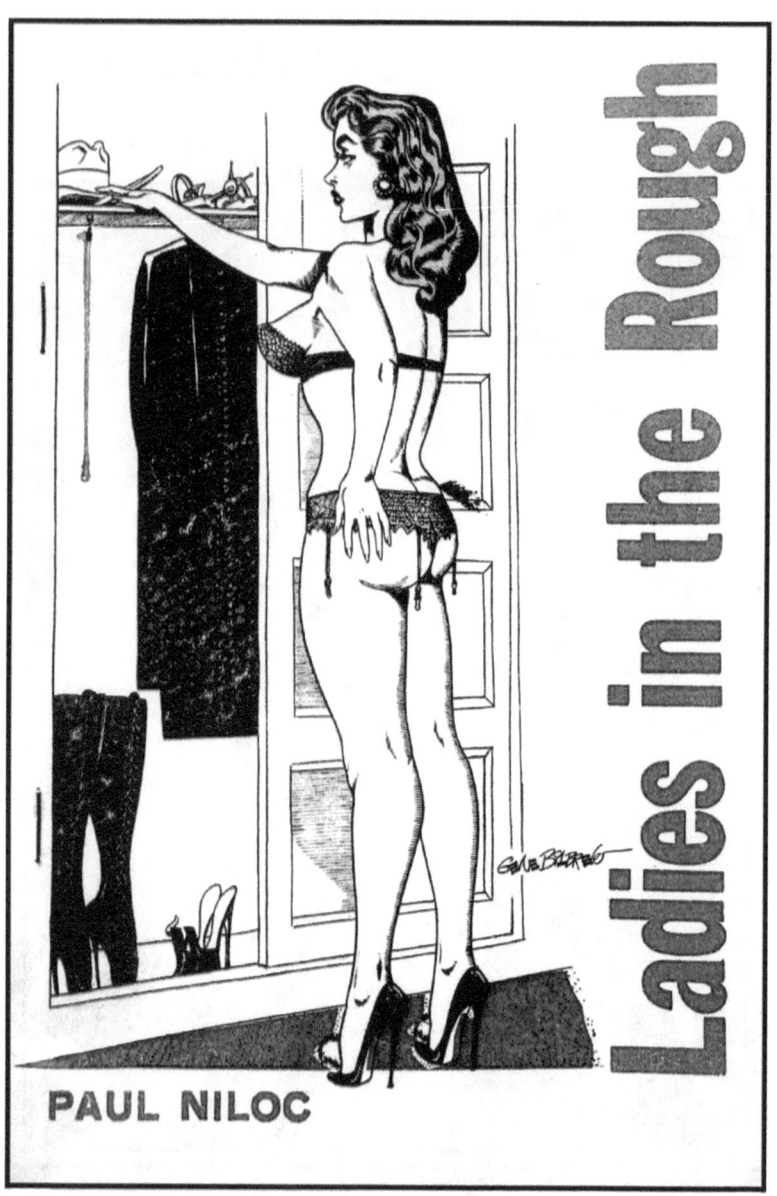

For Mishkin c.1958 lxxxv

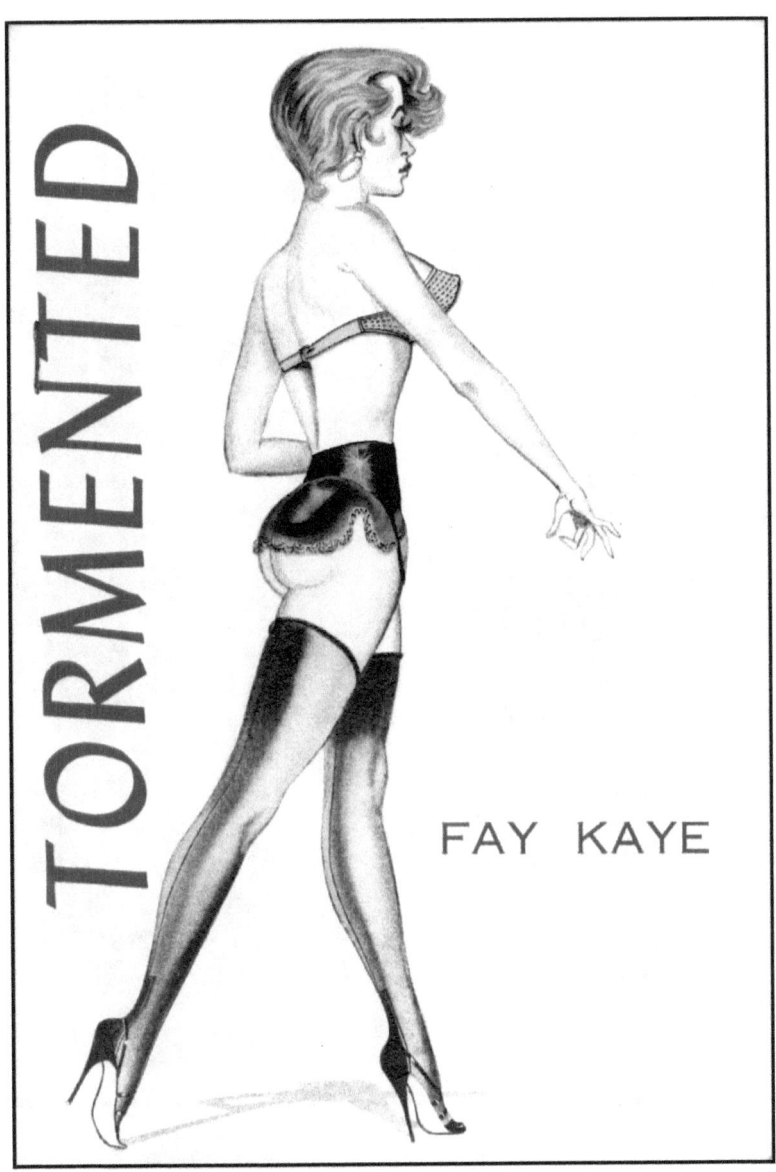

TORMENTED

FAY KAYE

For Mishkin c.1958

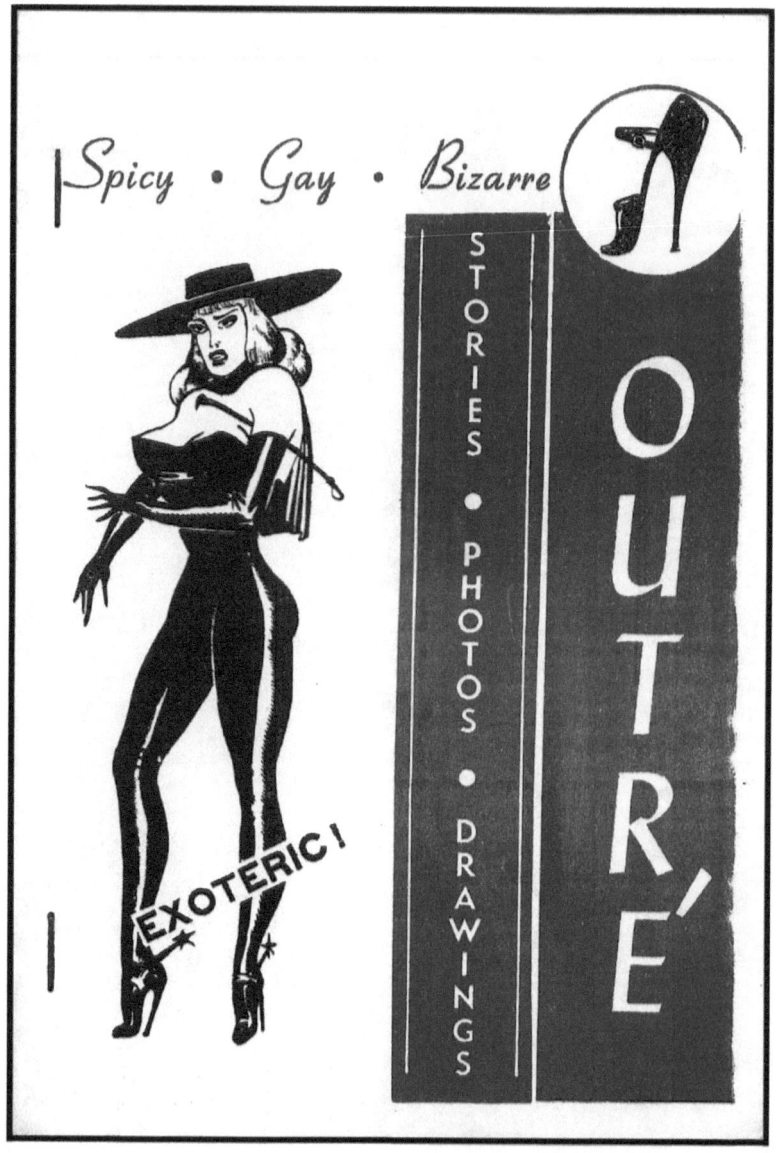

Not mentioned at the trial, Bilbrew also contributed art for Mishkin-published "novelettes" like *Handsome Abductor,* [lxxxvi] *Pink Chemise*; plus, other magazines and books, some of which were primitively produced.

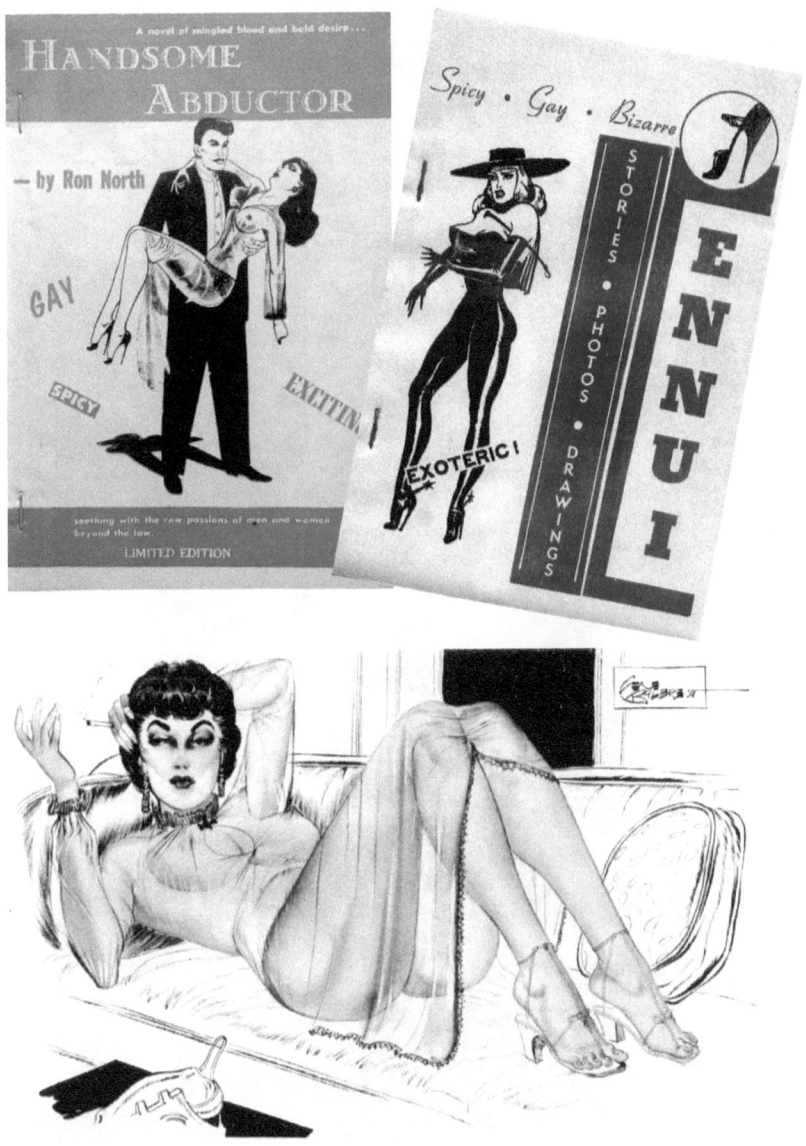

As Mishkin thought nothing of publishing the same magazine with different titles, *Ennui* was identical to *Outré*. (The exclamation "Exoteric" would also appear as the name of a sham publishing imprint.)[lxxxvii]

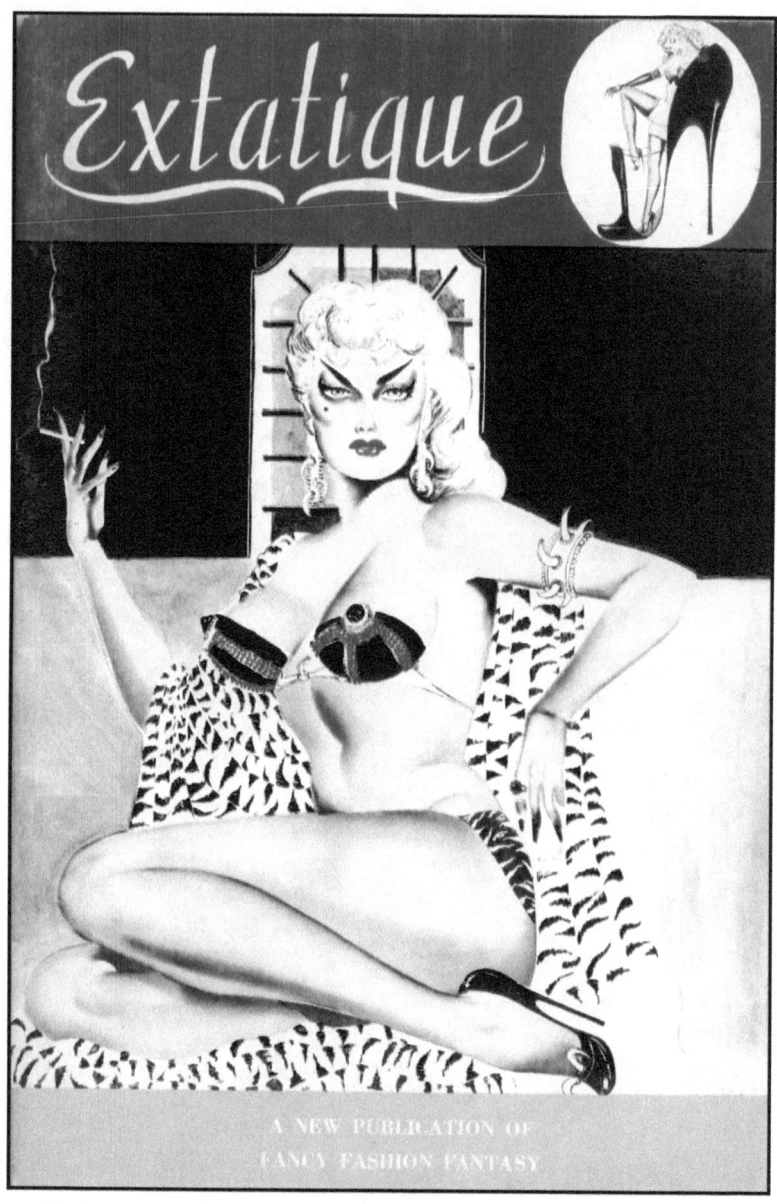

Tele-Foto Publishing Corp./ Mishkin, late 1950s (undated)

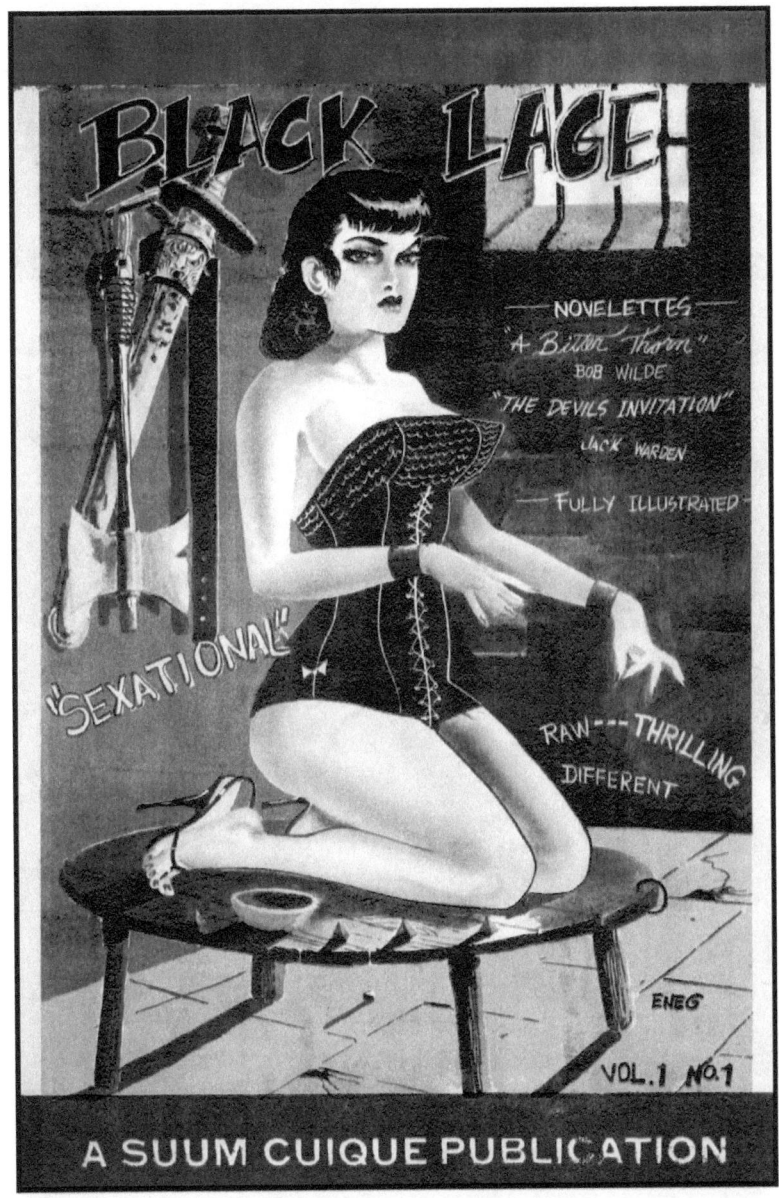

Sold by Tele-Foto Publishing Corp./ Mishkin, late '50s (undated)

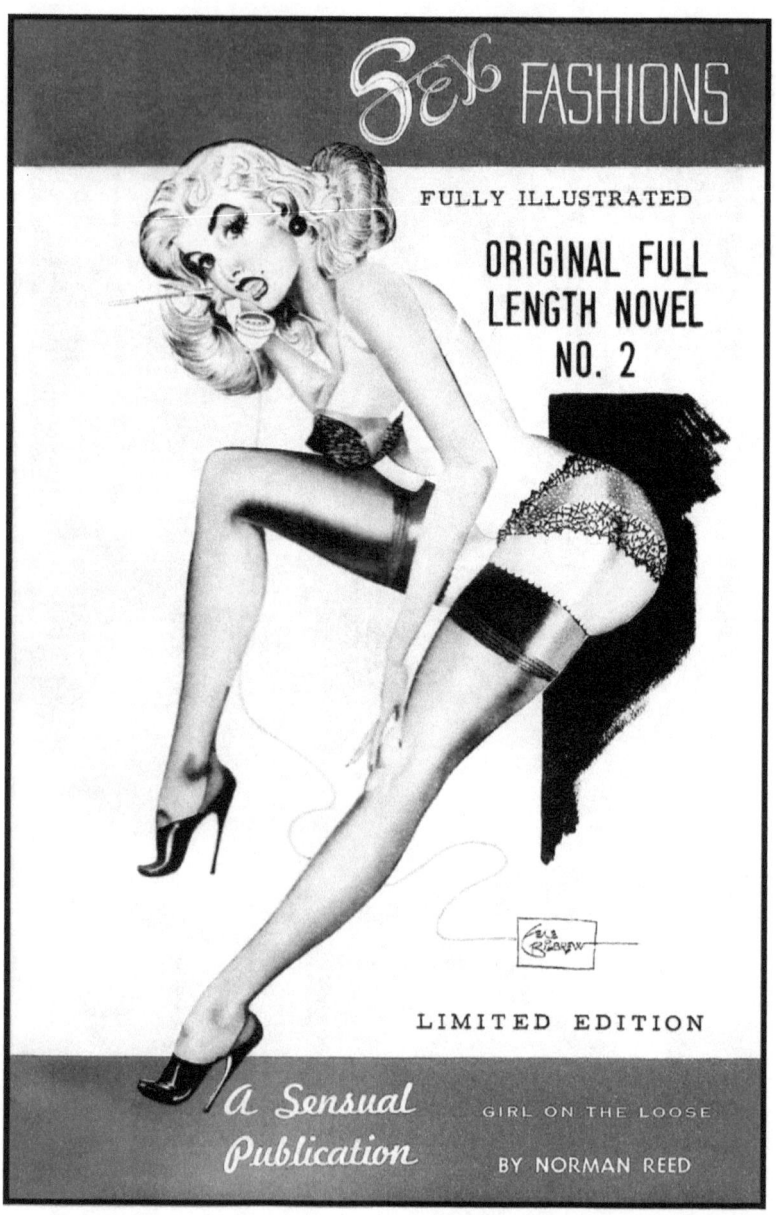

Tele-Foto Publishing Corp./ Mishkin, late '50s (undated)

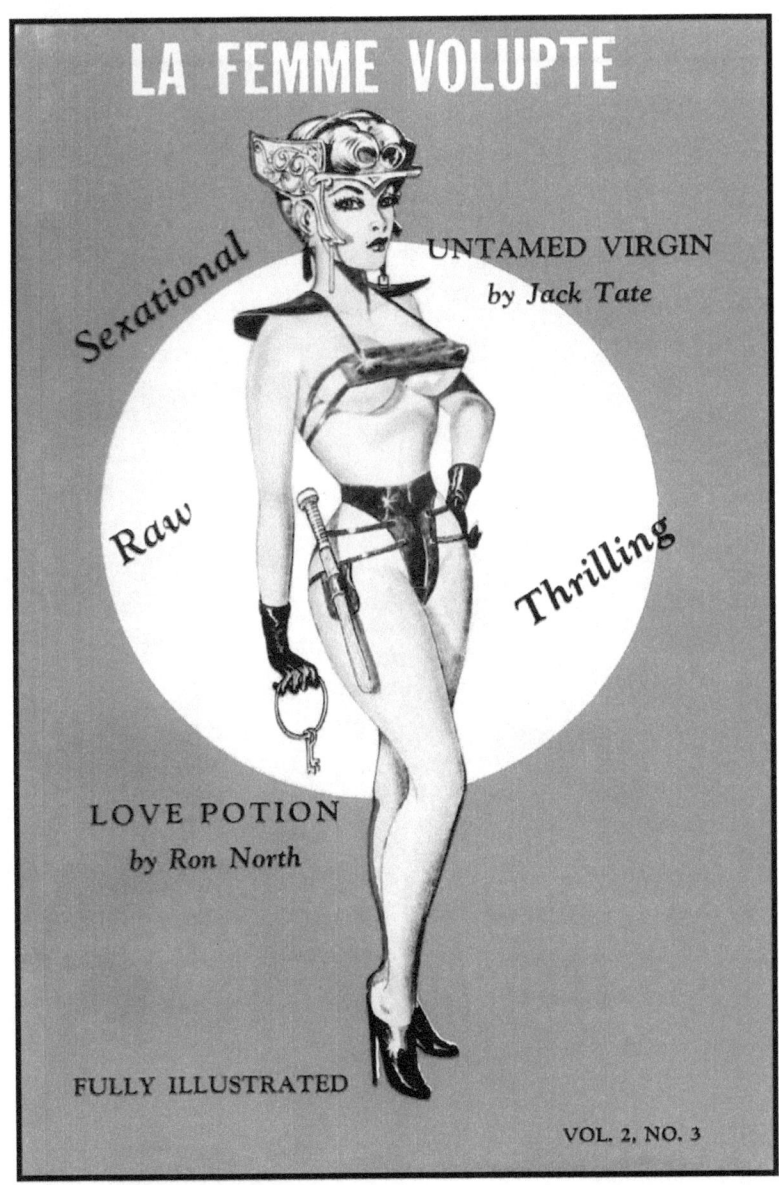

"Exoteric Publication"/ Mishkin, late '50s (undated)

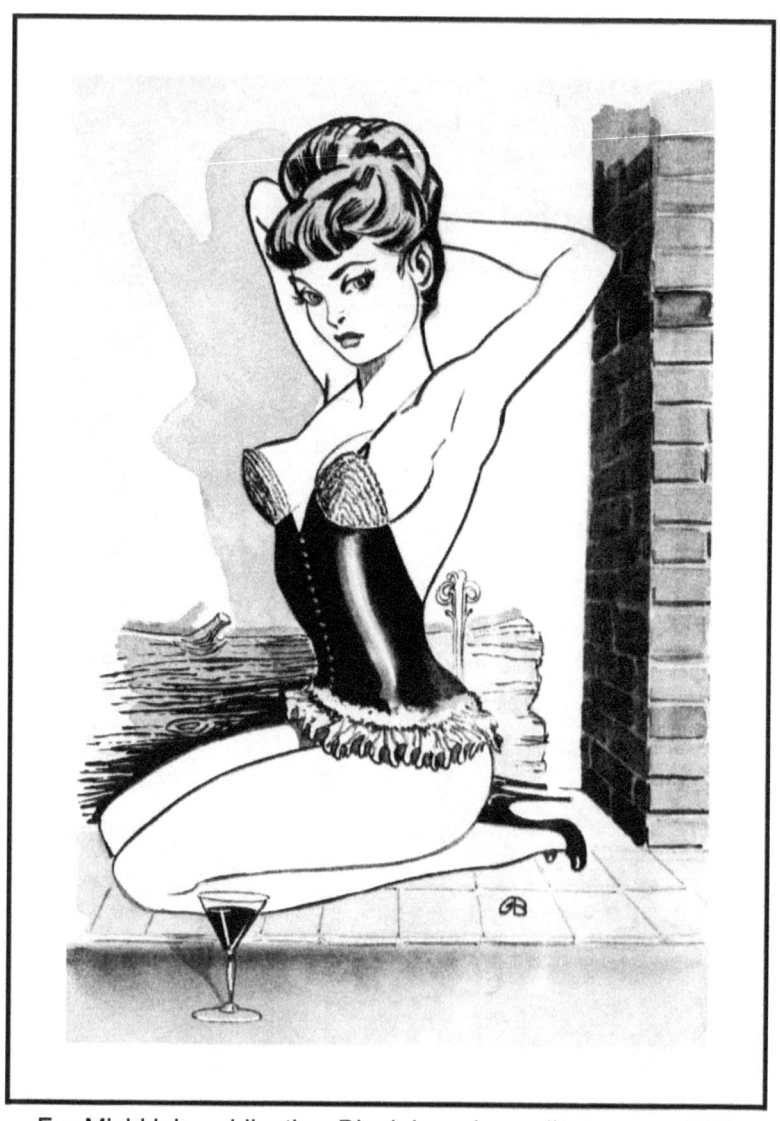

For Mishkin's publication *Black Lace* issue #1 (see pg. 111)

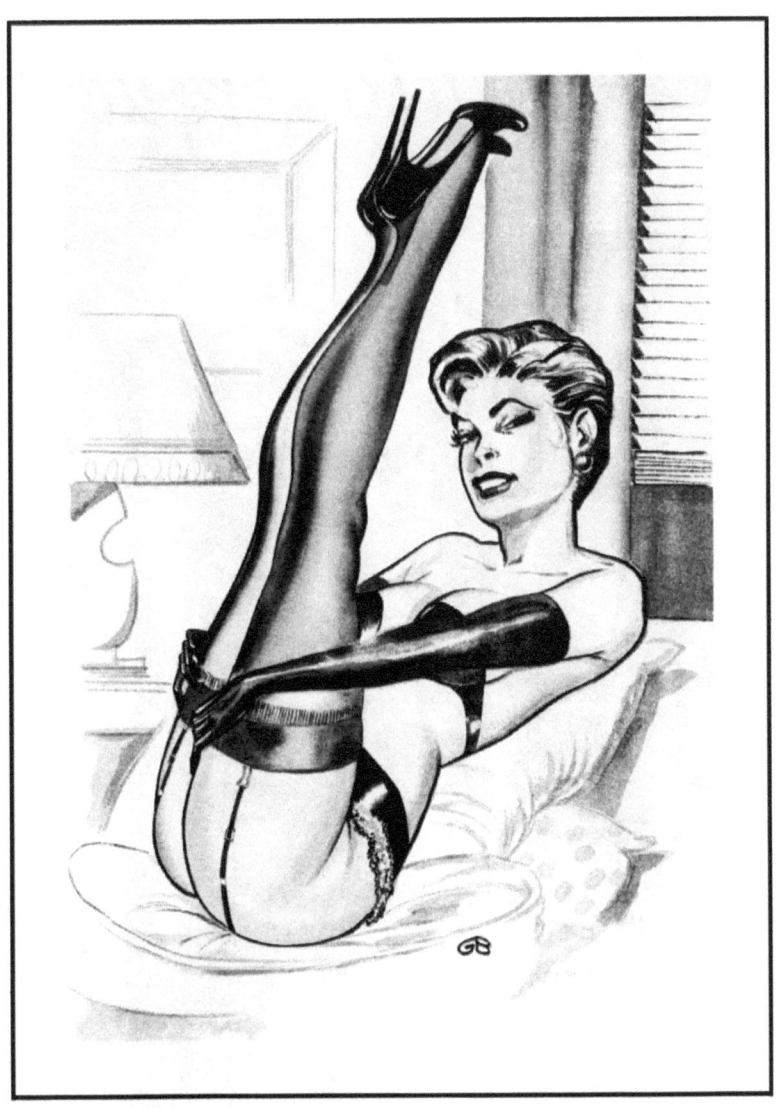

For Mishkin's publication *Black Lace* issue #1

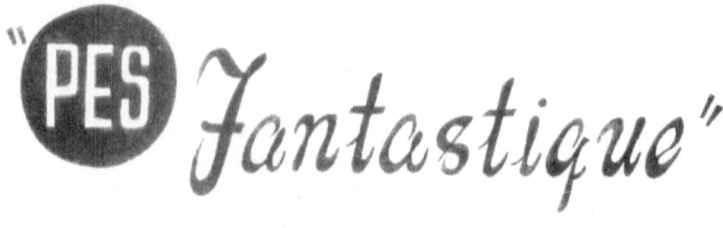

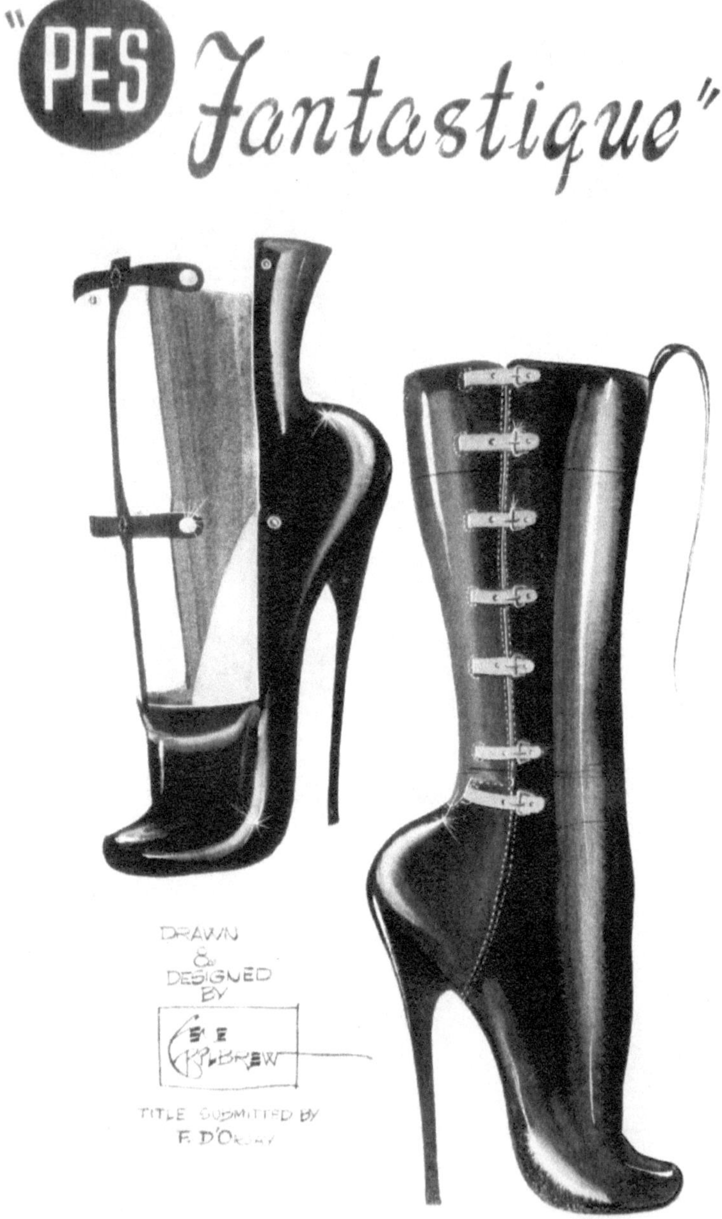

"**PES** *Fantastique*"

DRAWN
&
DESIGNED
BY

TITLE SUBMITTED BY
F. D'OR...

For Mishkin's publication *Extatique* issue #3 (pg. 110)

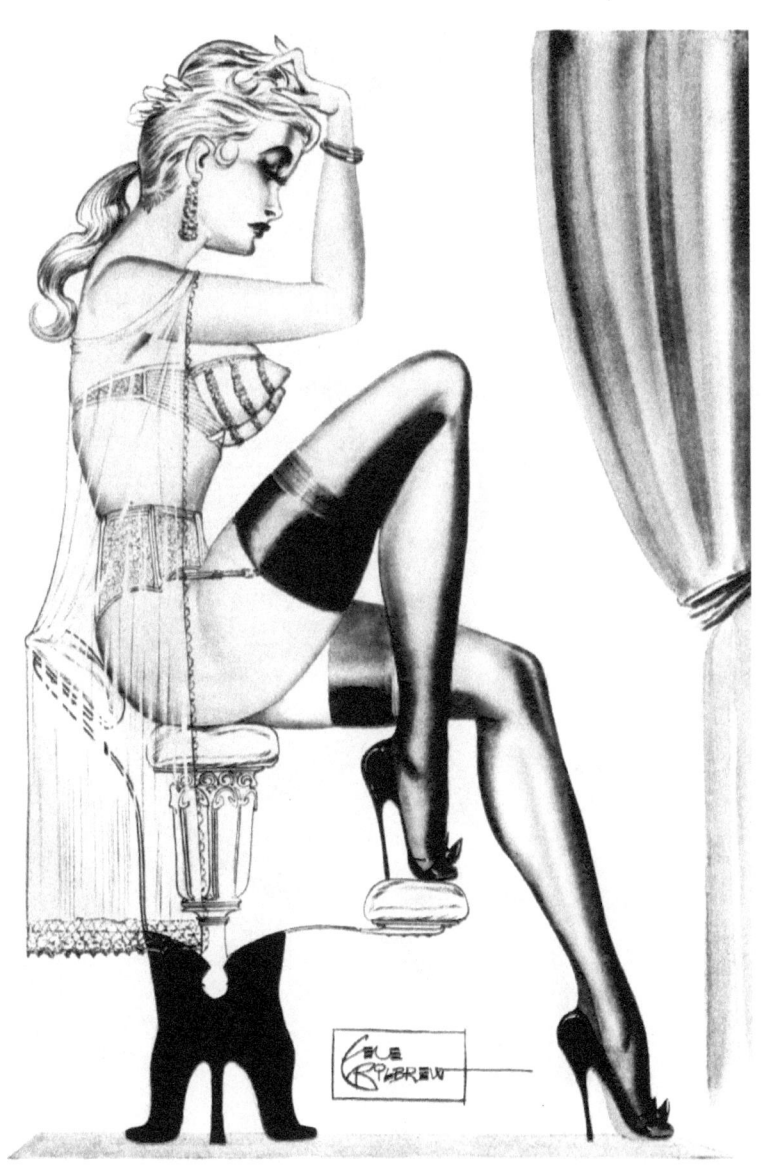

For Mishkin's publication *Extatique* issue #3

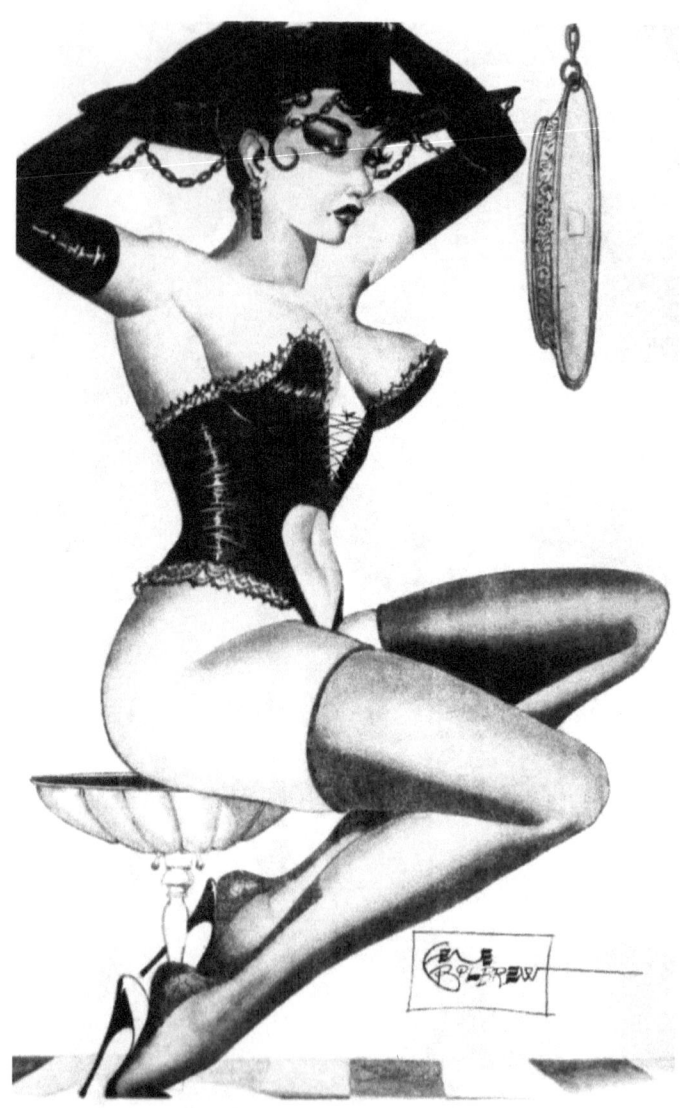

For Mishkin's novelette, *Bus Ride*

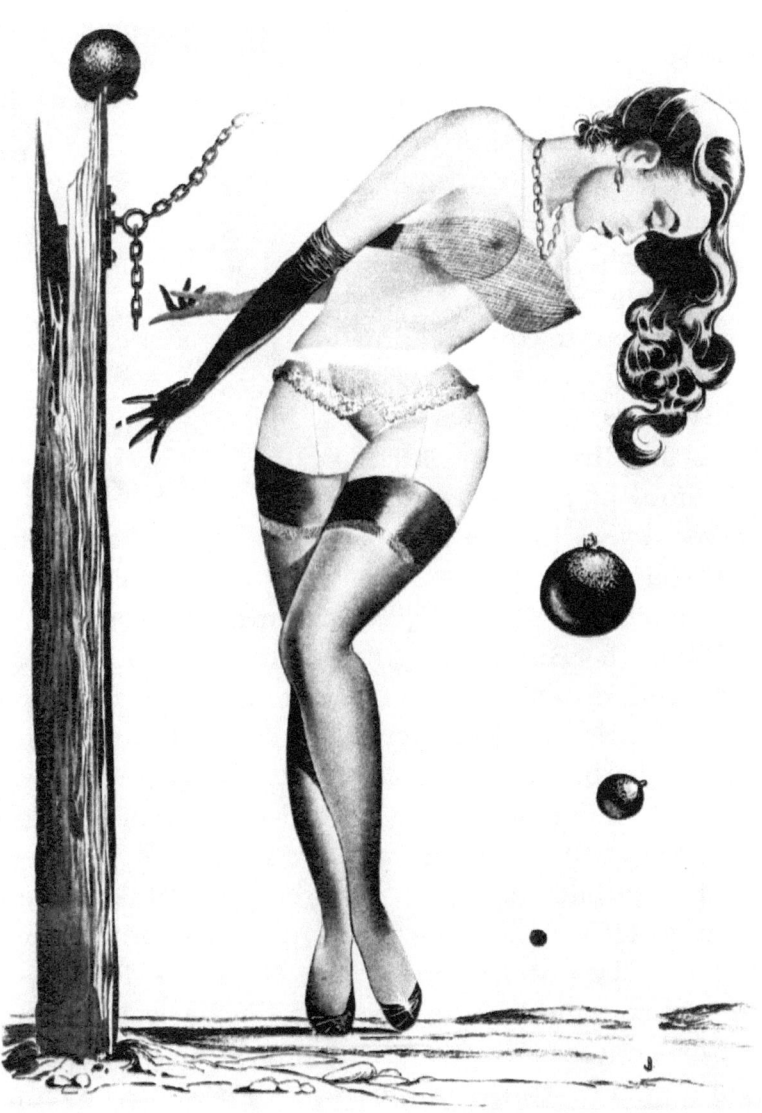

Cover art for *The Burning End* (a.k.a. *Painful Memoirs of Mollie*)

LEONARD BURTMAN

It was likely through Mishkin that Bilbrew met, arguably, his most important '50s patron: Leonard "Lennie" Burtman.

In the 1940s, Burtman was an electronics engineer whose career highlight included being part of the research staff that contributed to the making of the atom bomb.[lxxxviii]

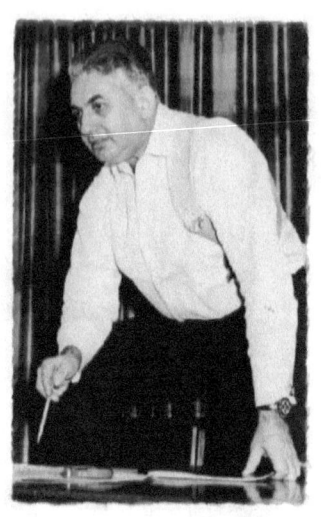

By 1949, in connection with theft and fraud,[lxxxix] Burtman fell afoul of the law and even served a year in federal prison. He then drifted to the east coast, where circa 1951 he reinvented himself as a sexploitation photographer and magazine editor.

While a Burtman publication named *Exotica* appeared in late 1954, it wasn't until the following year that Burtman launched his breakthrough print venture: a "bizarre" fashion-oriented magazine underscored by high vamp style named *Exotique*, for which he tapped Bilbrew as primary artist.

This publication was inspired by John Willie's seminal fetish magazine, *Bizarre,* and another more obscure UK publication named *Fads and Fancies*—while also adopting the aesthetic of Charles Guyette, the originator of bizarre (i.e., fetish) style in America, still then a costumer of theatrical/burlesque fashion. Predating Irving Klaw, Guyette had gained notoriety as a mail-order pioneer, dealing primarily in fetish-themed photographs, some of which graced *Exotique.*

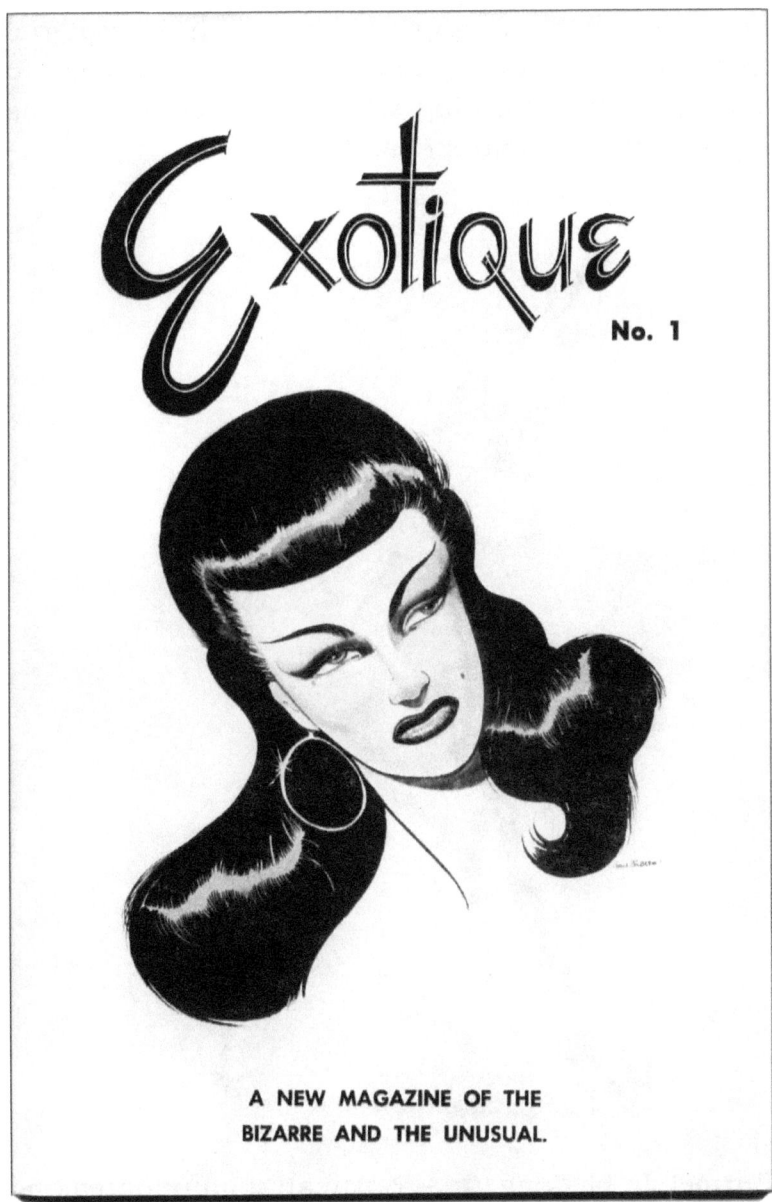

As per the publication's intended audience, *Exotique* needed an elegant, somewhat feminine touch, and Bilbrew's then delicate, stylized ladies seemed a perfect fit. In fact, Bilbrew was so at home with the material that from issue #1 he was signing his real name to cover art, underscoring what he believed was the legitimacy of the enterprise.

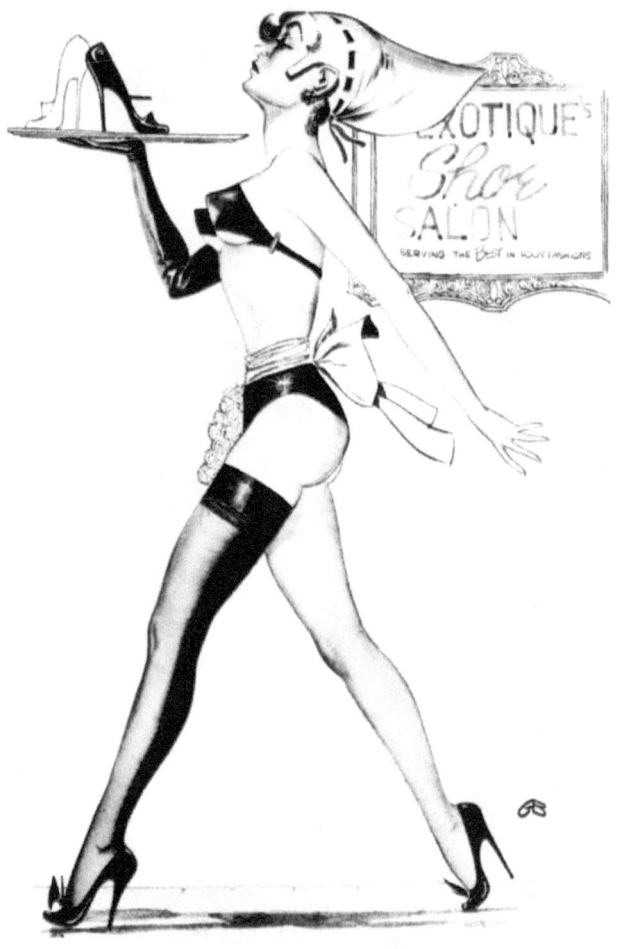

Burmel Publishing Co.—Burtman's groundbreaking publishing imprint—would also branch out to issue illustrated novelettes (much like Mishkin's), photo-fiction (narrative, fetish-themed booklets made up only of photographs, no words) and other bizarre-related one-shot specialty publications; while Burtman and business partner Benedict Himmel also fabricated sham (or hit-and-run) imprints through which they published what was then more risky or "borderline" material featuring Bilbrew work.

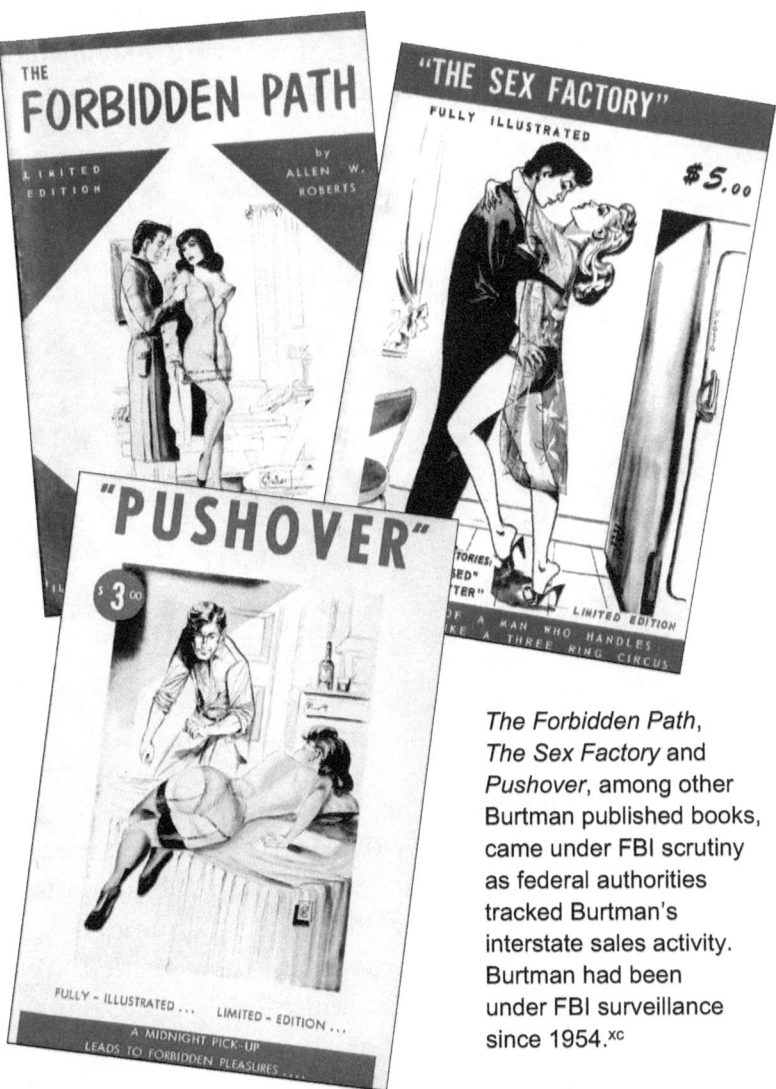

The Forbidden Path, *The Sex Factory* and *Pushover*, among other Burtman published books, came under FBI scrutiny as federal authorities tracked Burtman's interstate sales activity. Burtman had been under FBI surveillance since 1954.[xc]

Bilbrew produced thirty-one of the thirty-six *Exotique* magazine covers, many of them iconic—in addition to the bulk of the magazine's interior art—before Burmel Publishing Co. was brought down by federal authorities on charges of obscenity.[xci]

Used as evidence against Burtman, were three novelettes: two (below) featuring cover and interior art by Bilbrew (the other by Stanton, who also briefly became an artist for Burtman in late 1956).

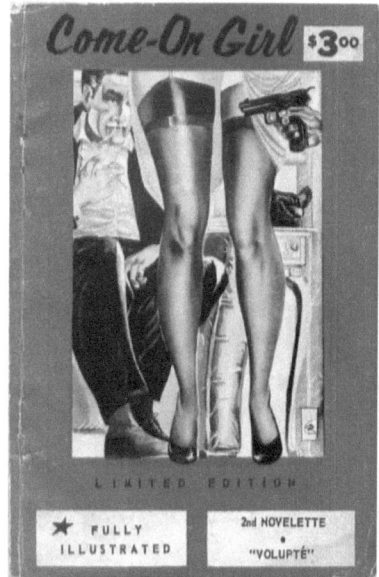 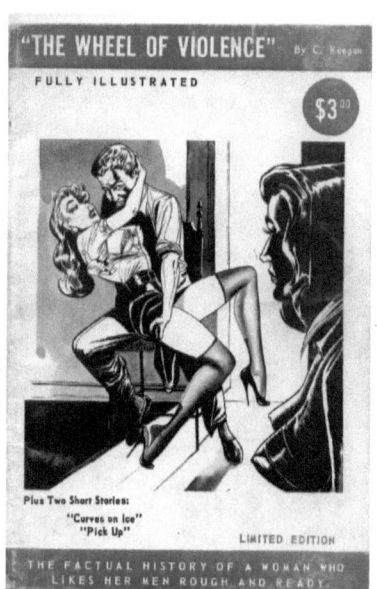

Two of the three titles that effectively ended Burmel.

Burtman's final attempt to reinvent Burmel under a new name—Kaysey Sales Co. Inc.[xcii]—proved short-lived, and within a year it too followed the same fate as Burmel.[xciii] For Burtman, the 1950s concluded with two final issues of *Exotique* magazine (now retitled "*New Exotique*"), in addition to several other publications—all with Bilbrew artwork.

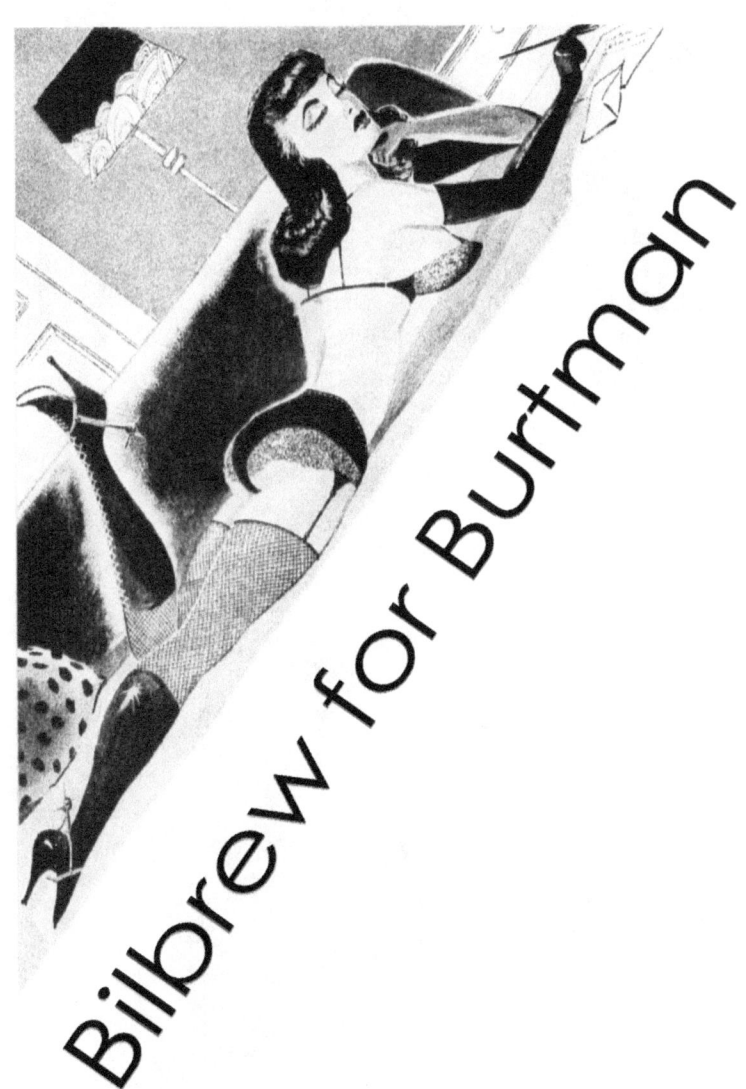

Bilbrew for Burtman

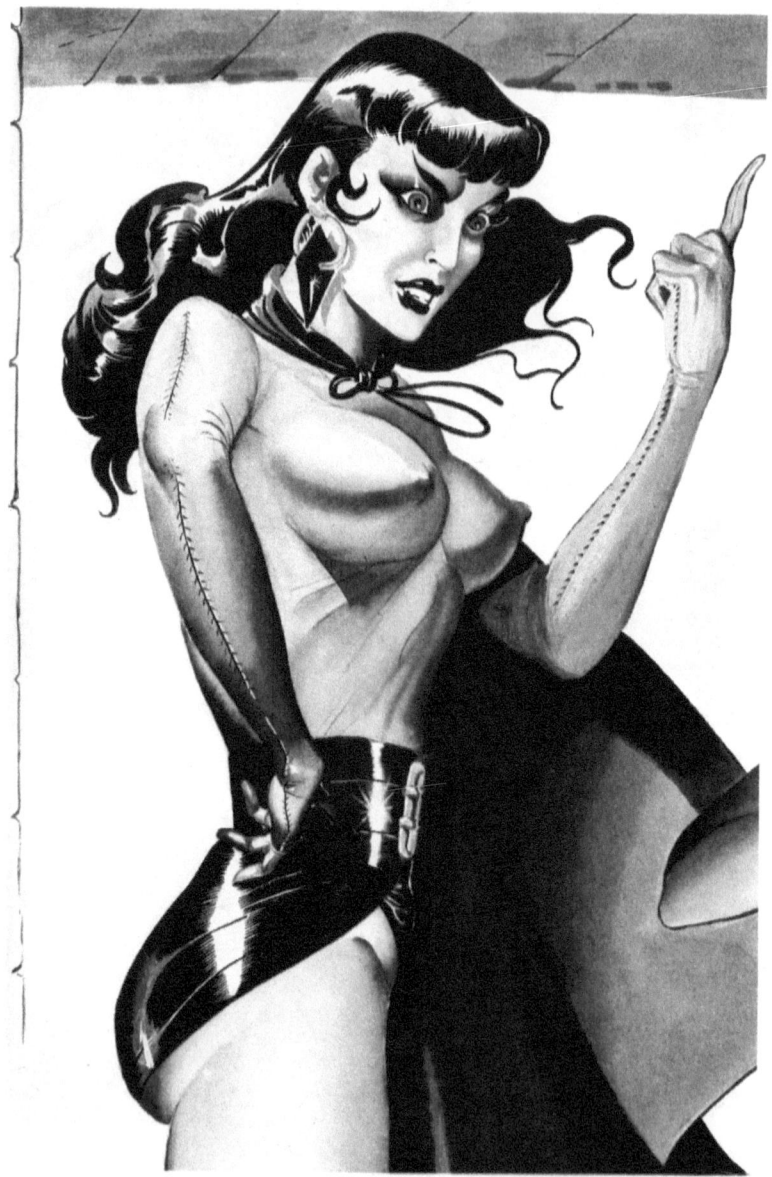

For Burtman, fragment (c. 1957)

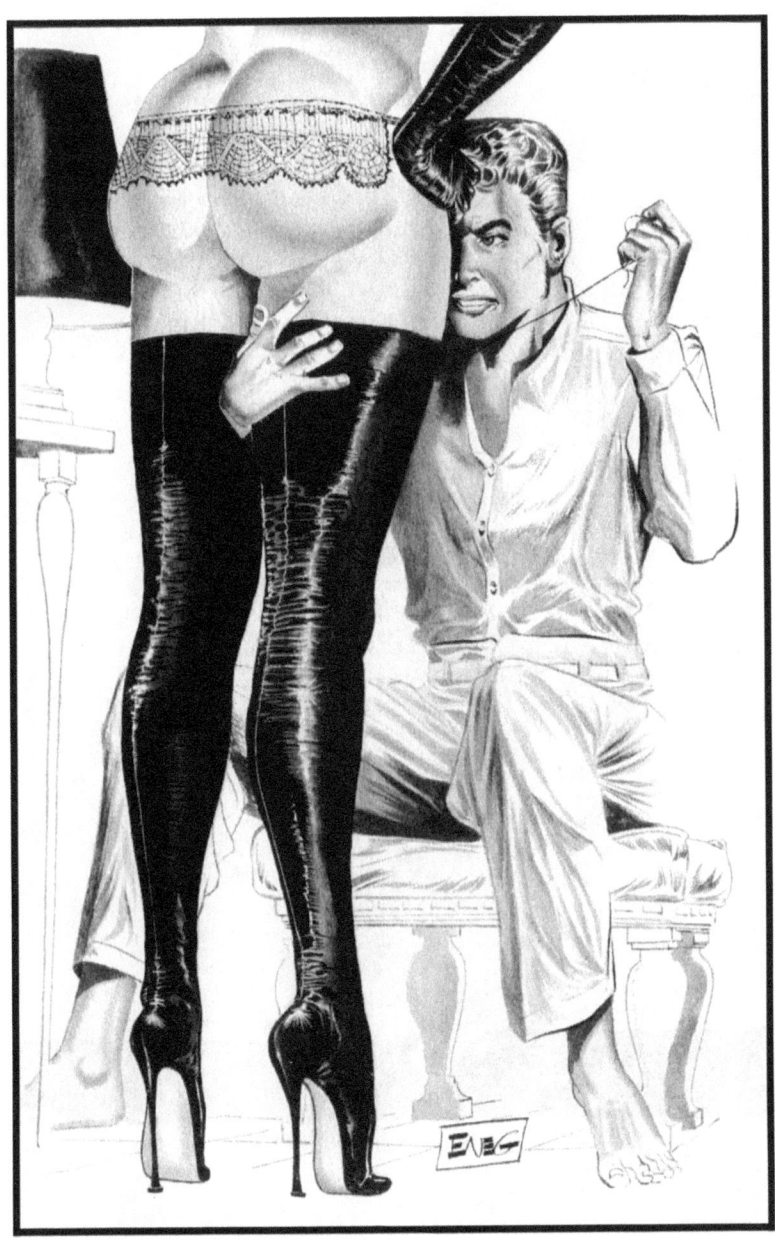

For Burtman's novelette, *Bizarre Desires* (1958)

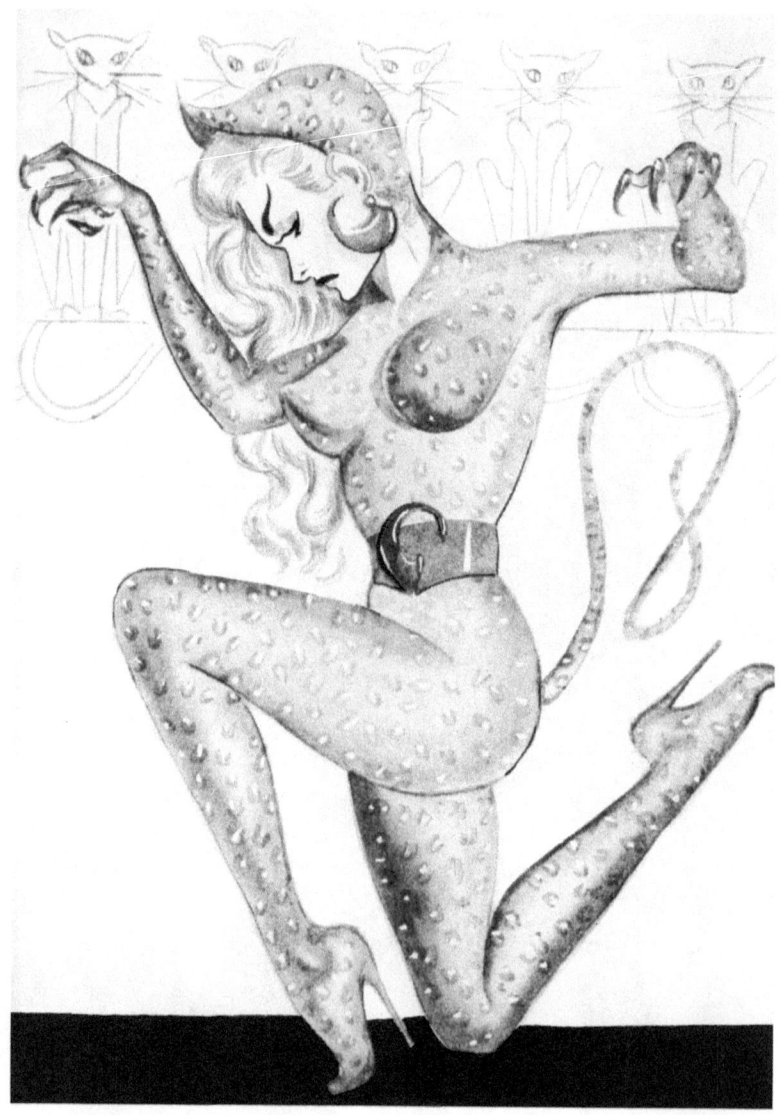

For *Exotique* issue #10 (1956)

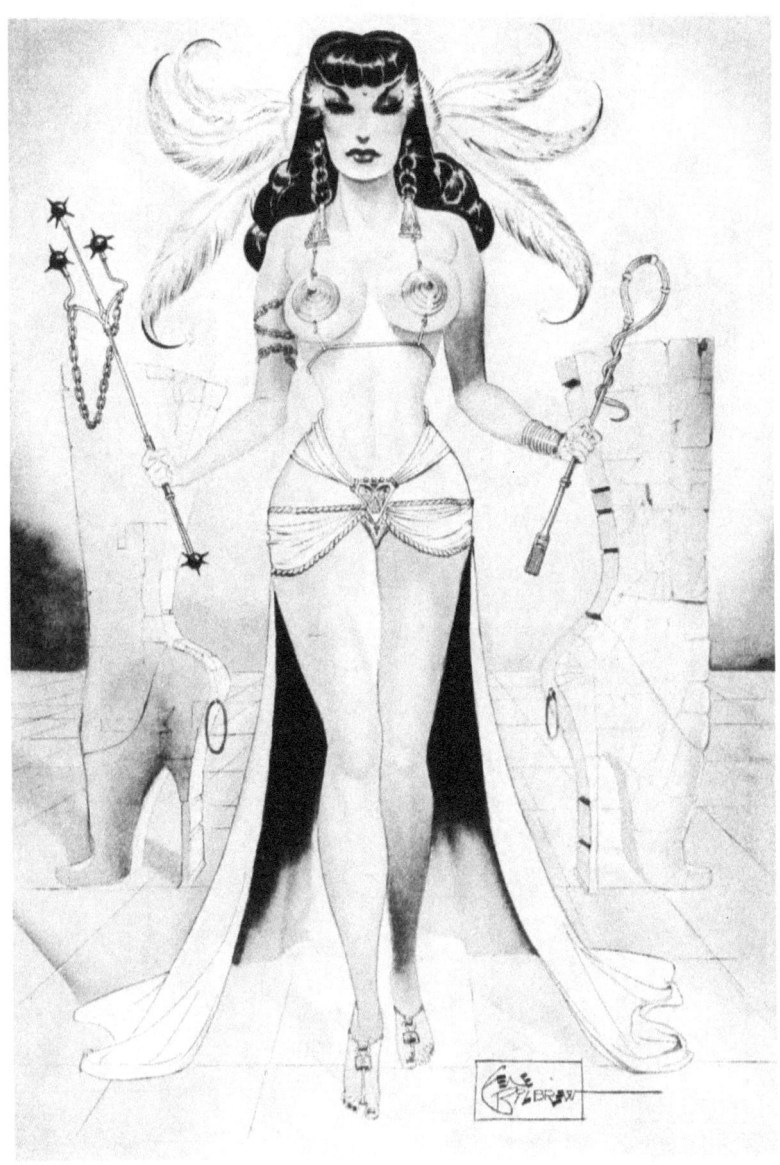

For *Exotique* issue #17 (1957)

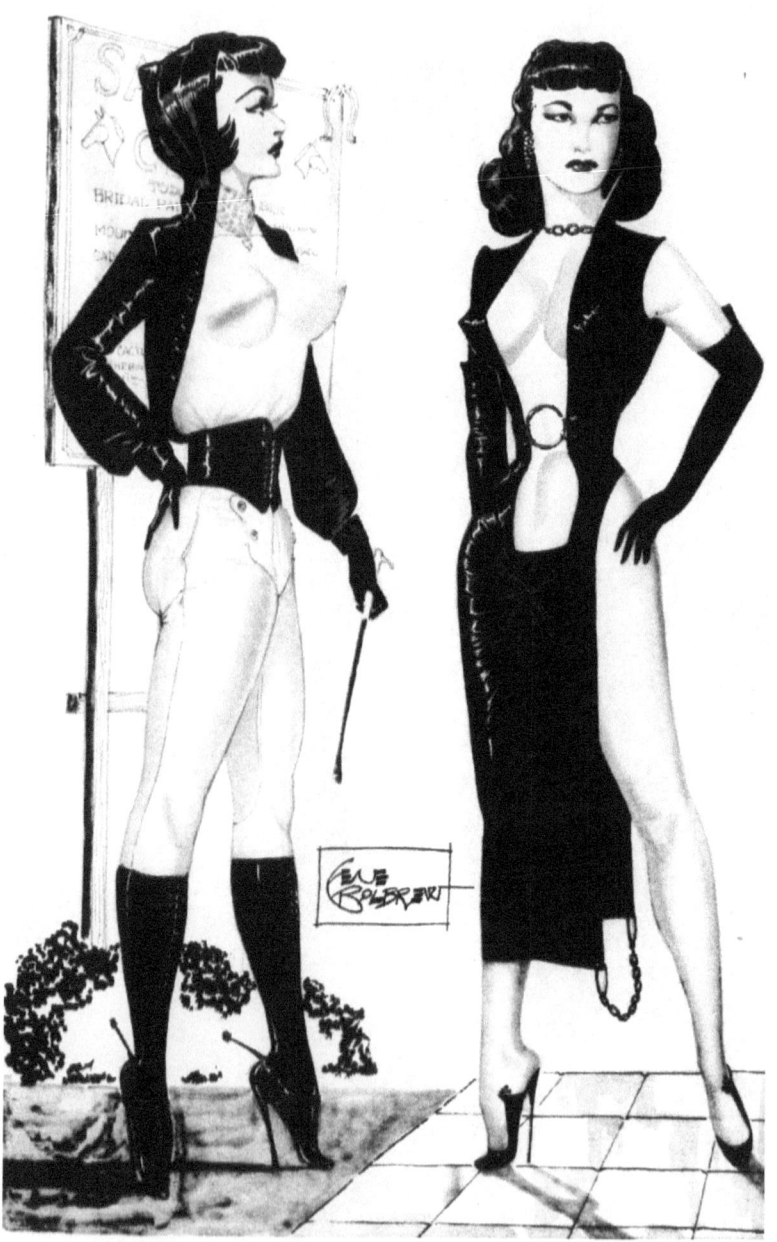

For *Exotique* issue #15 (1957)

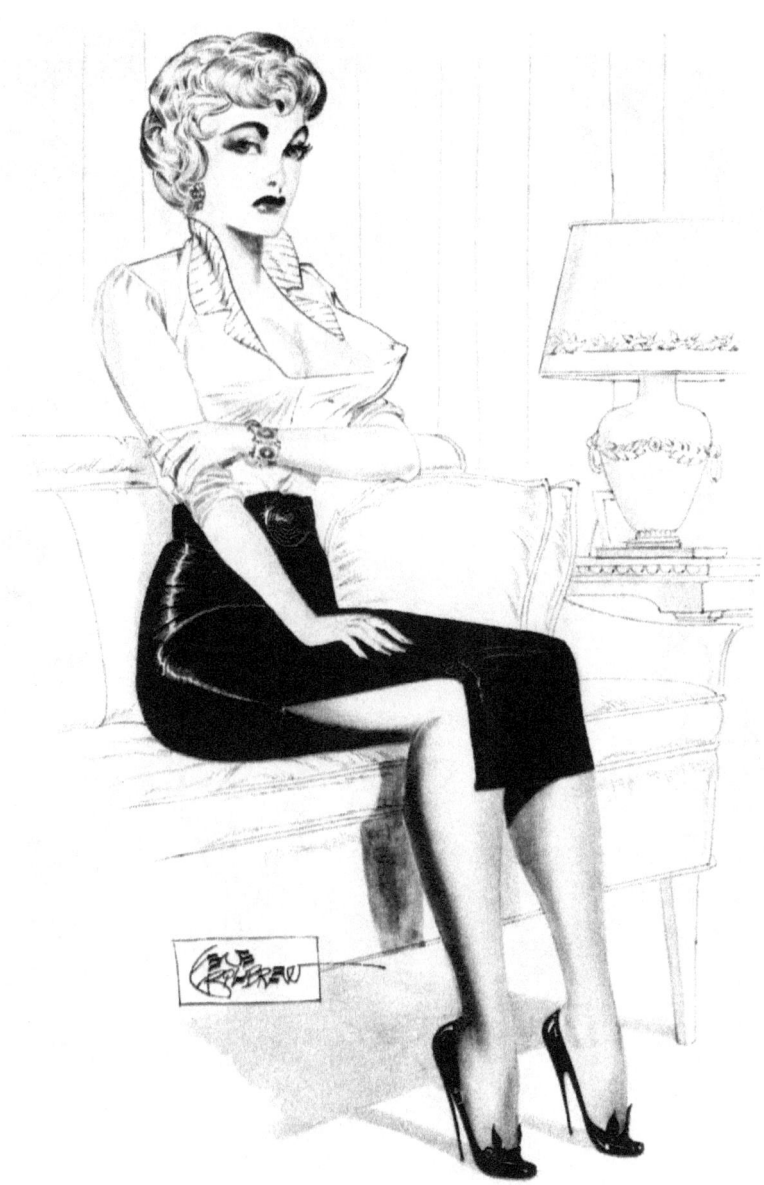

For *Exotique* issue #15 (1957)

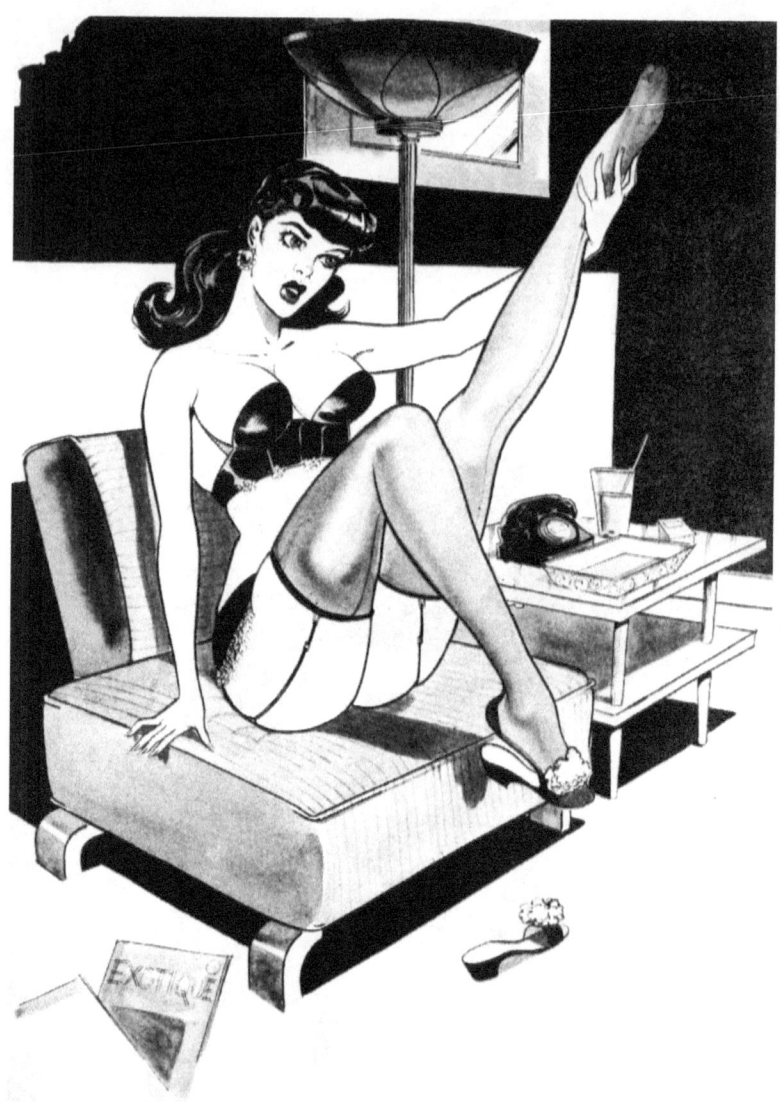

For *Exotique* issue #2 (1955)

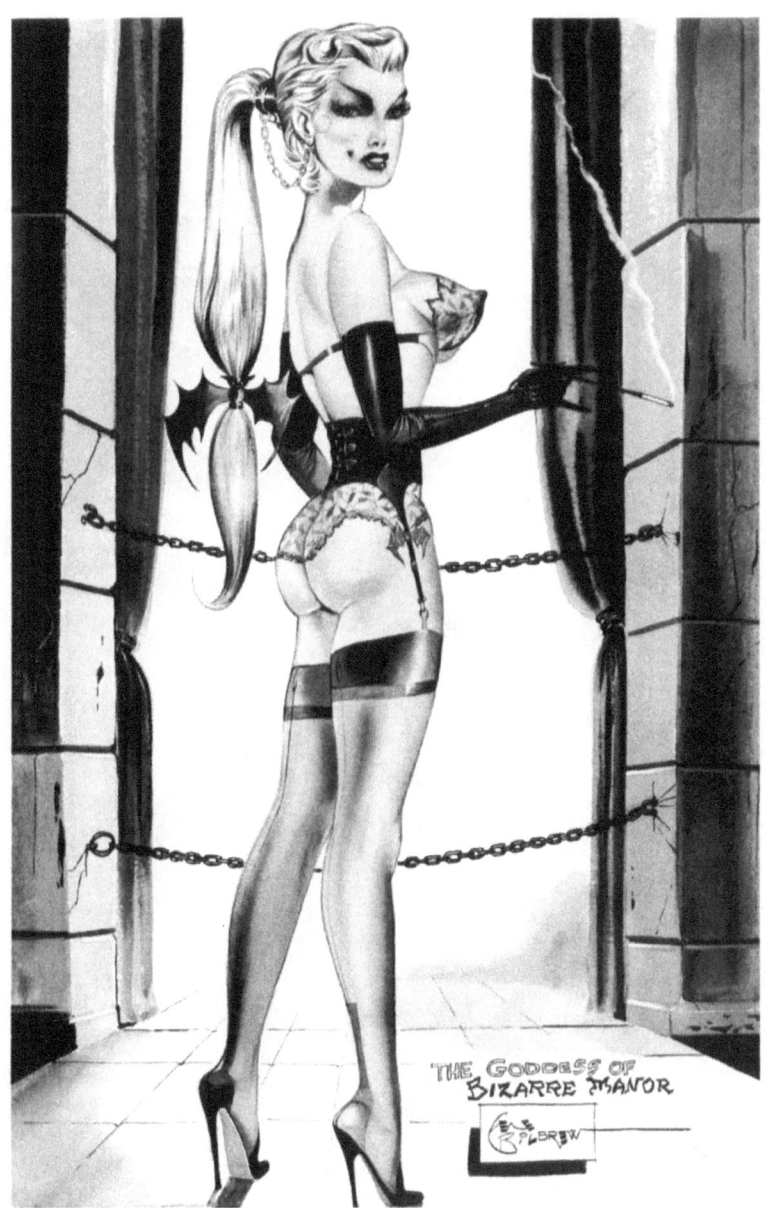

For *Exotique* issue #20 (1957)

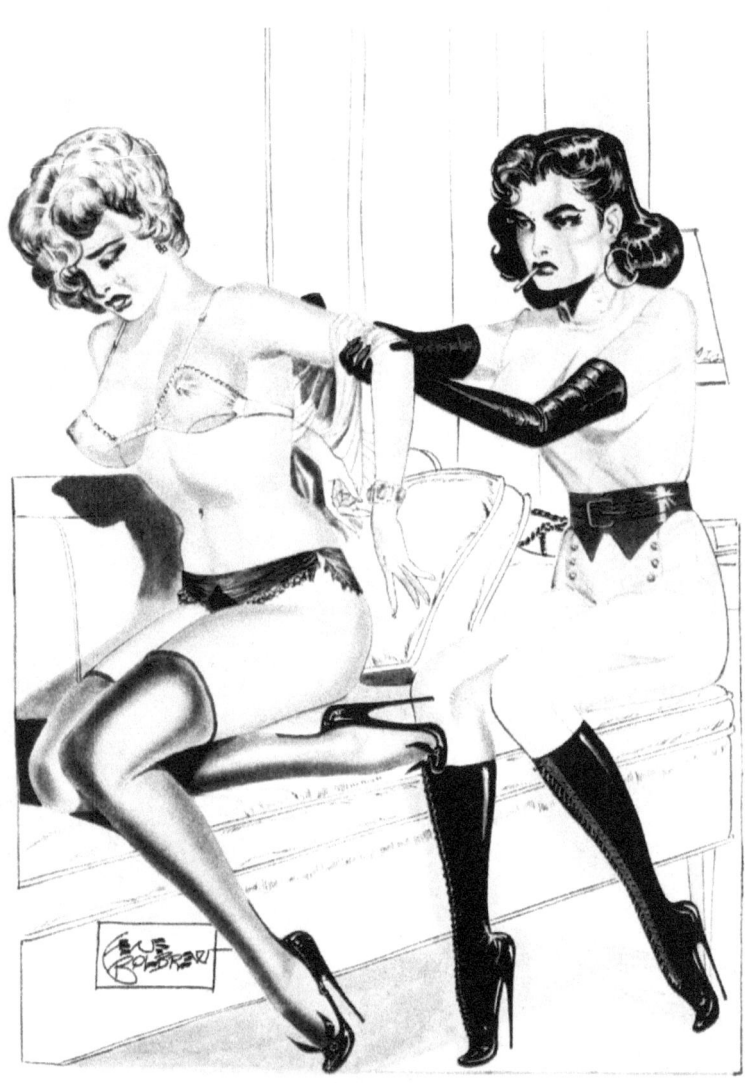

For *Exotique* issue #15 (1957)

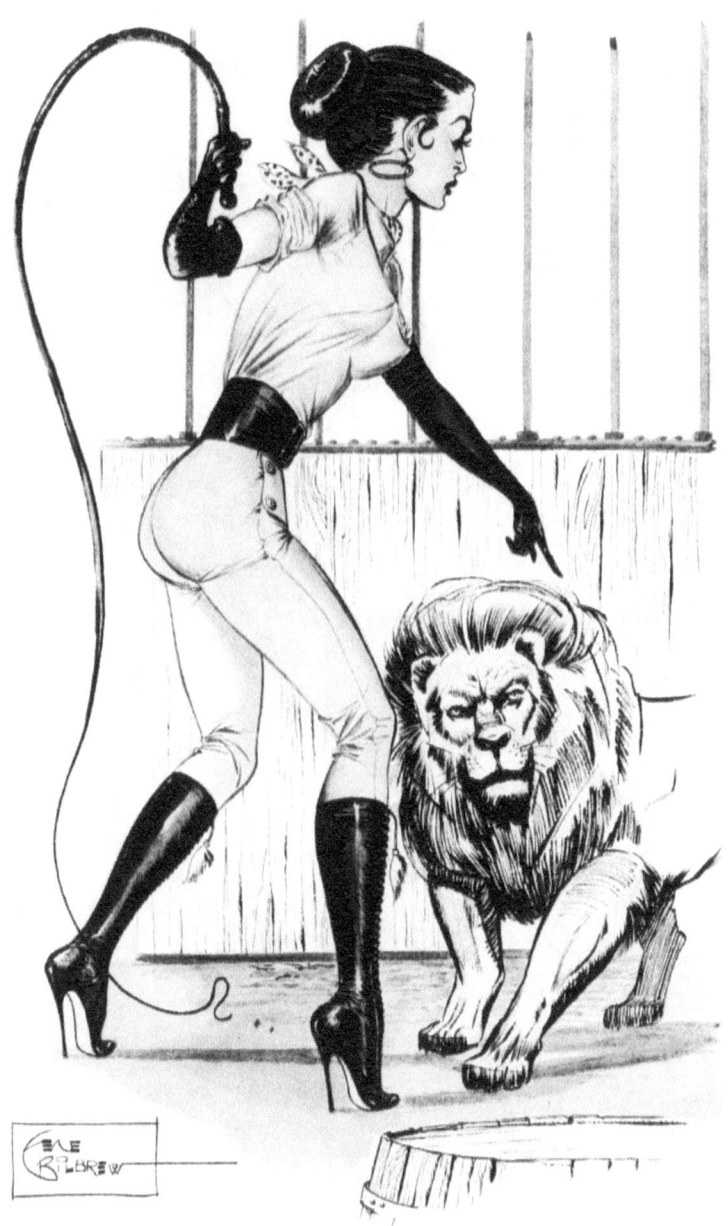

For *Exotique* issue #16 (1957)

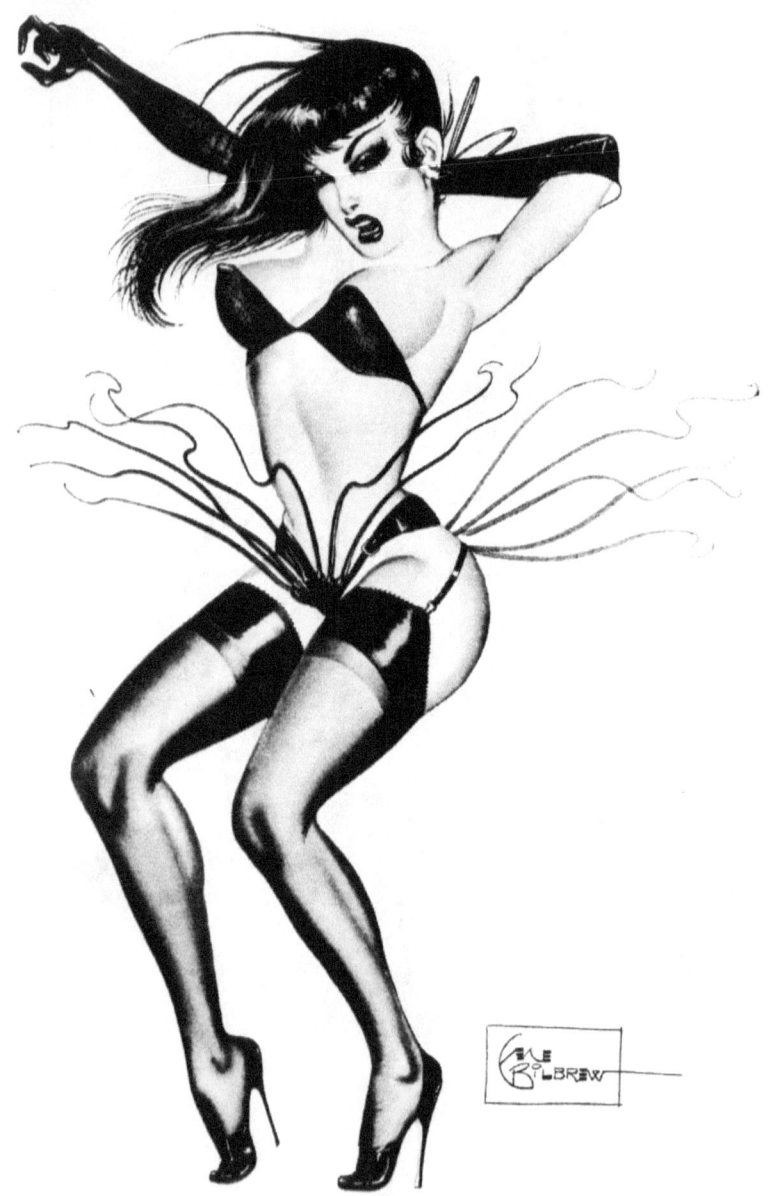

For *Exotique* issue #18 (1957)

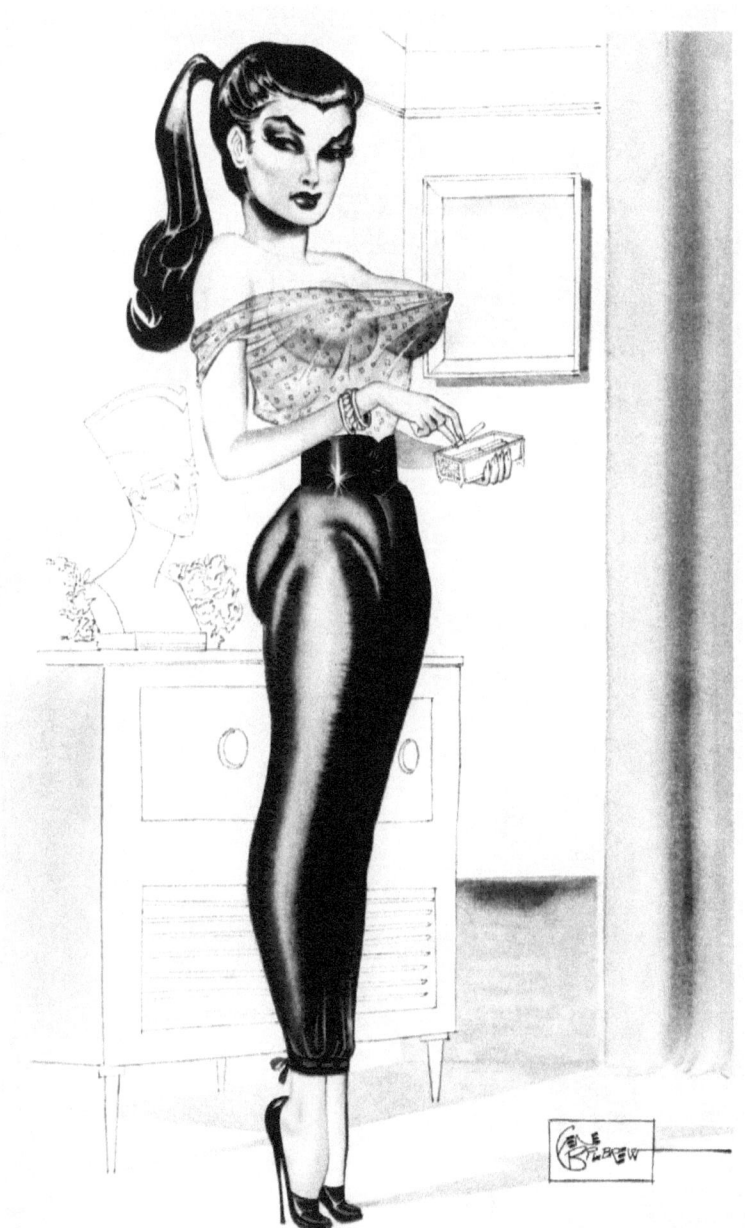

For *Exotique* issue #19 (1957)

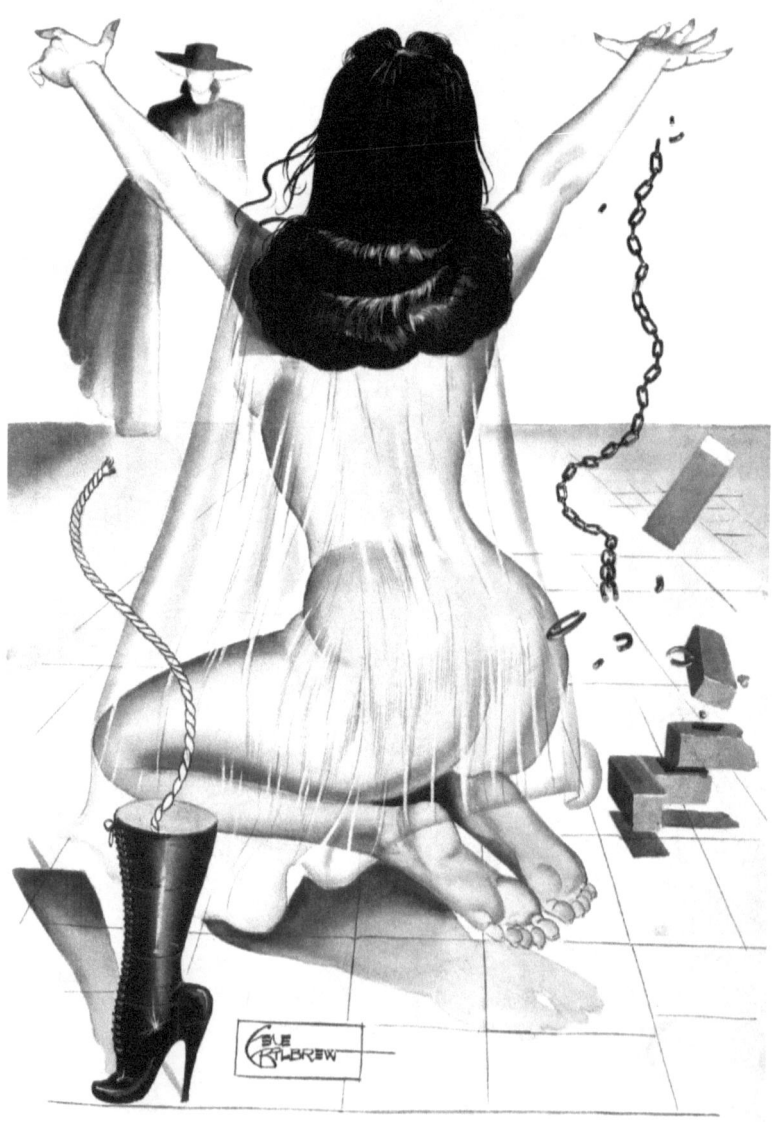

For *Exotique* issue #23 (1957)

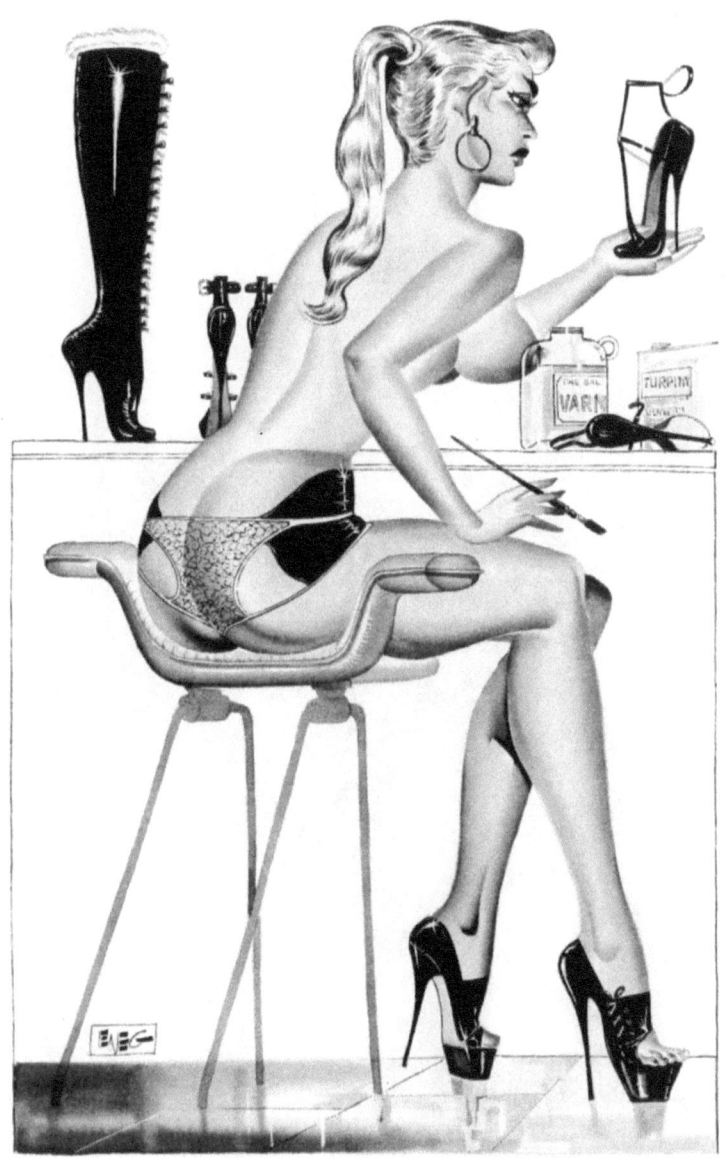

For *Exotique* issue #28 (1957)

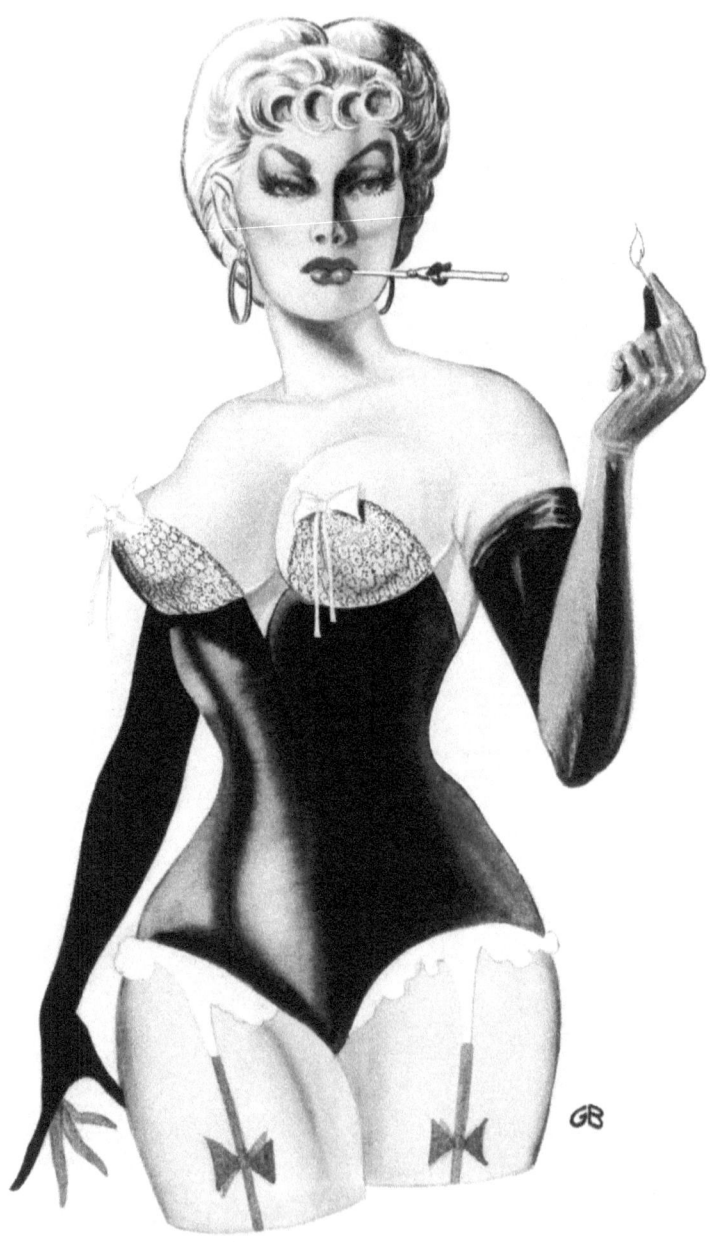

For *Exotique* issue #7 (1956)

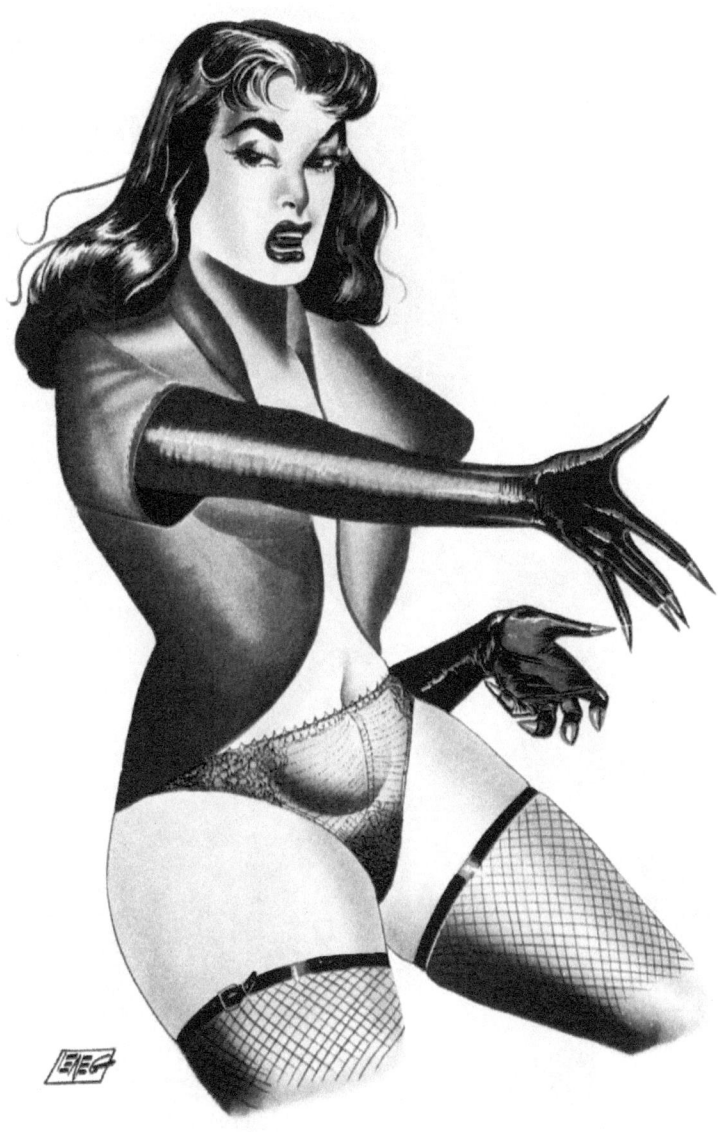

For Burtman's novelette, *Myrna Learns the Ropes* (1958)

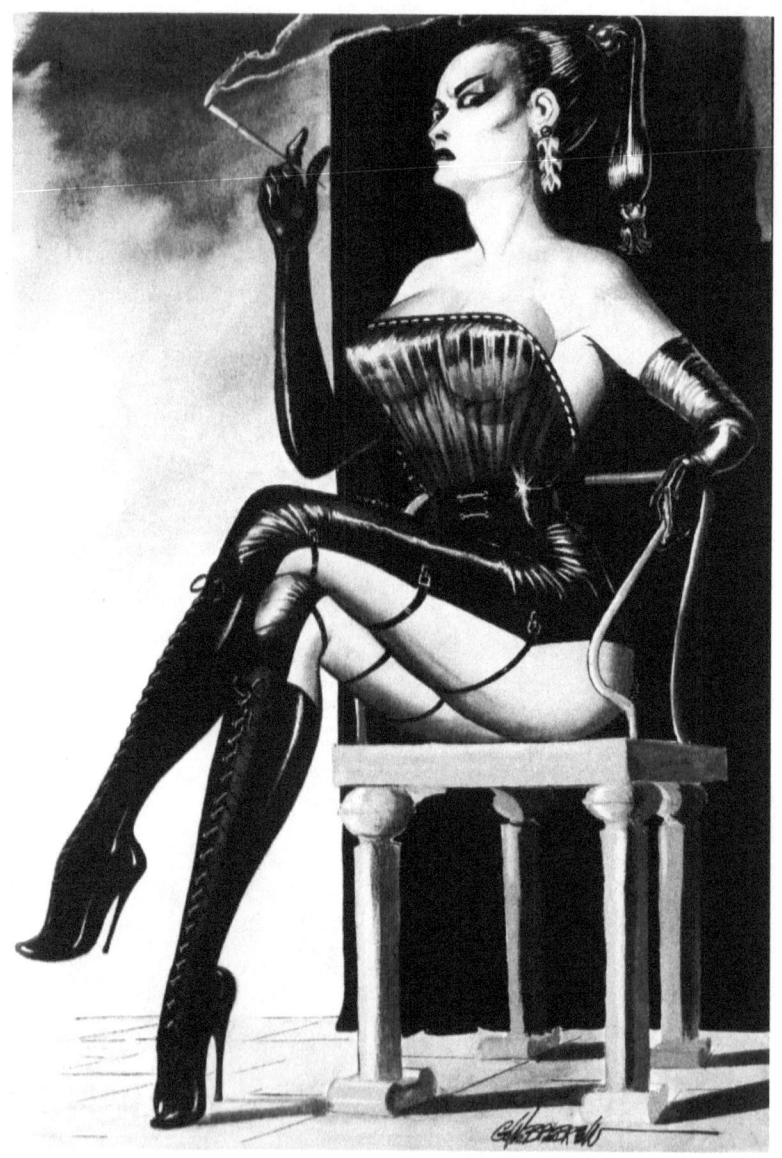

For Burtman (c. 1956)

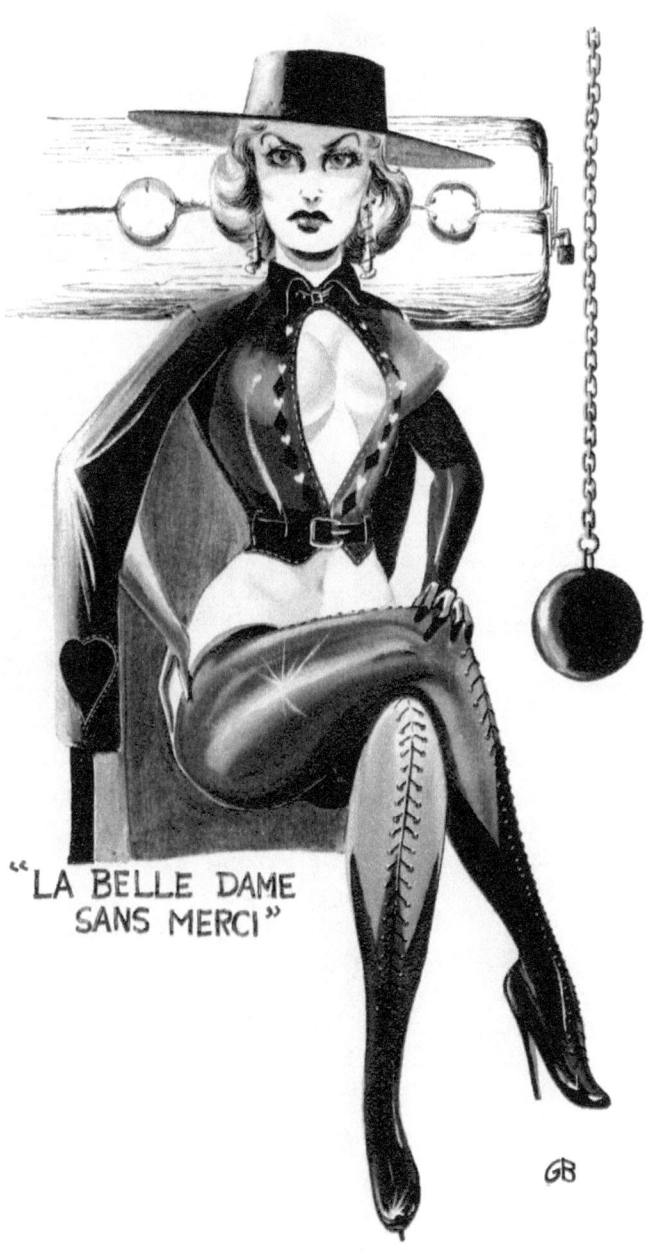

"LA BELLE DAME
SANS MERCI"

For *Exotique* issue #9 (1956)

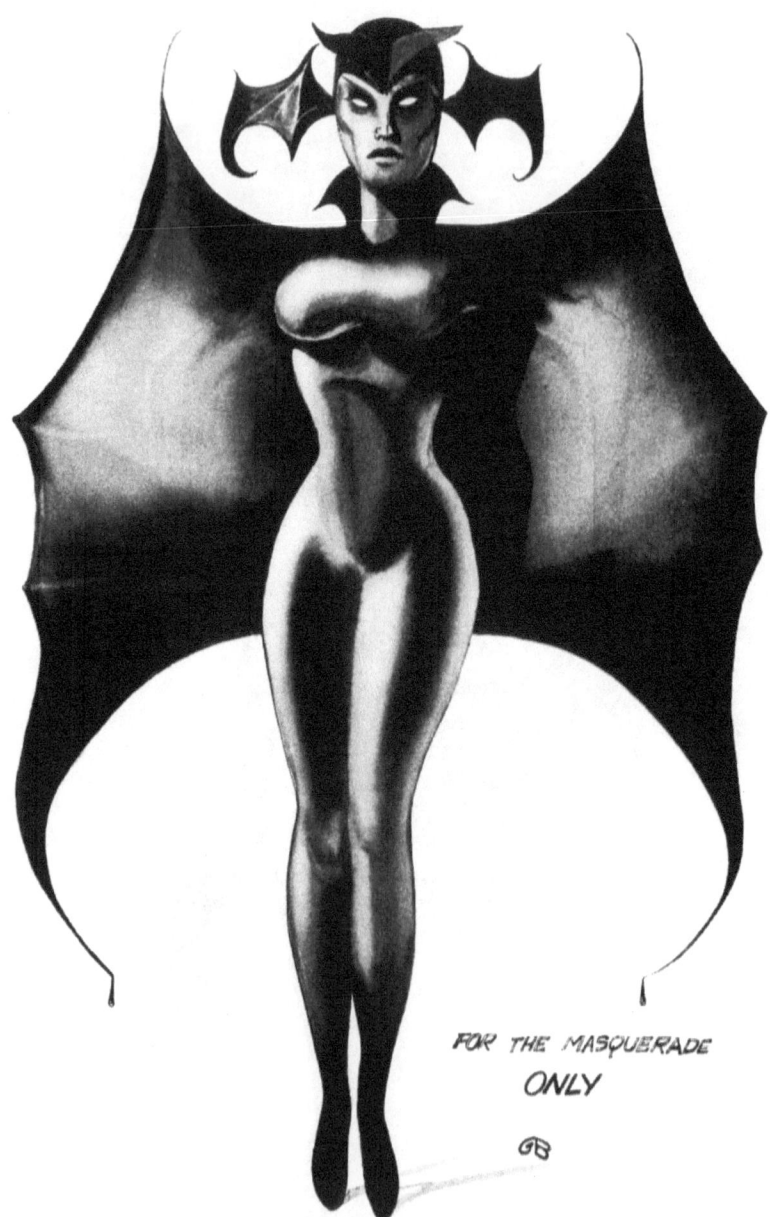

For *Exotique* issue #9 (1956)

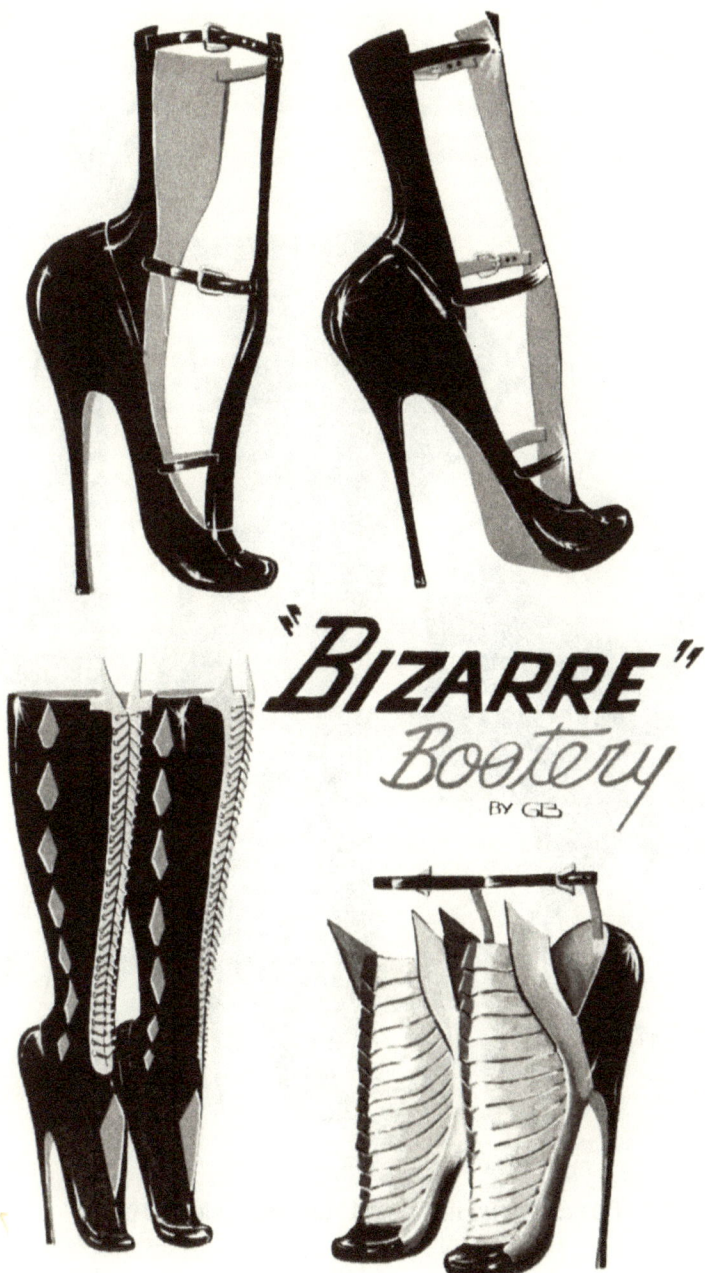

For *Exotique* issue #10 (1956)

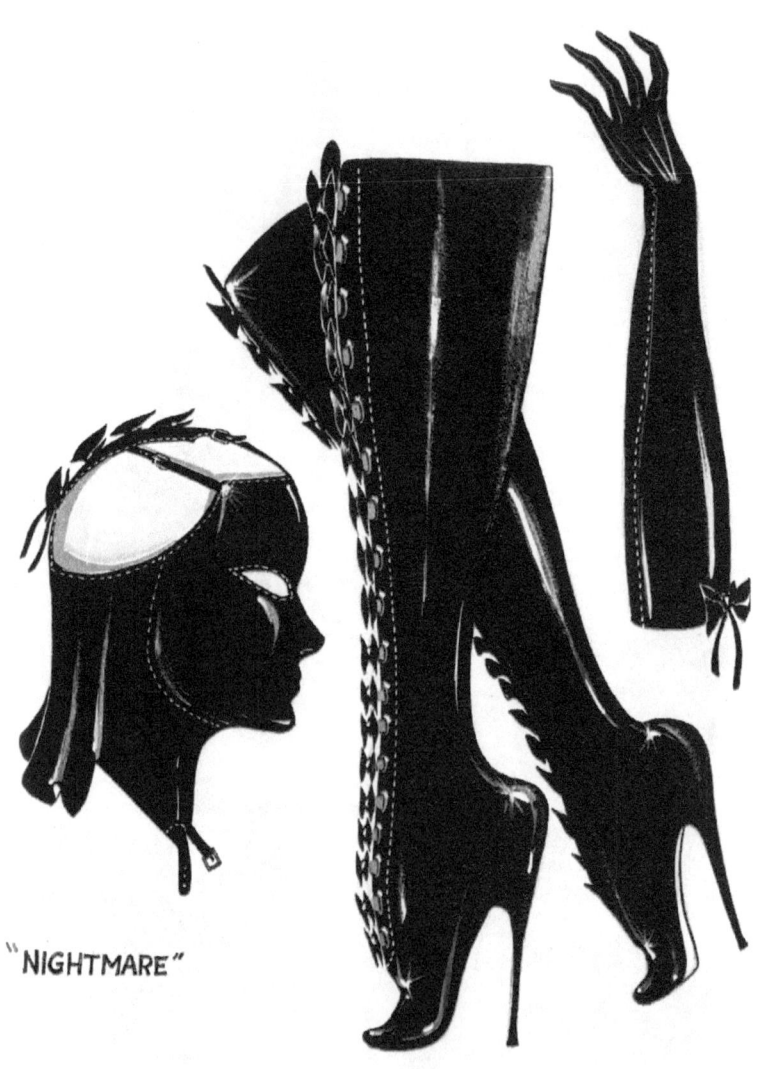

"NIGHTMARE"

For *Exotique* issue #11 (undated, likely 1957)

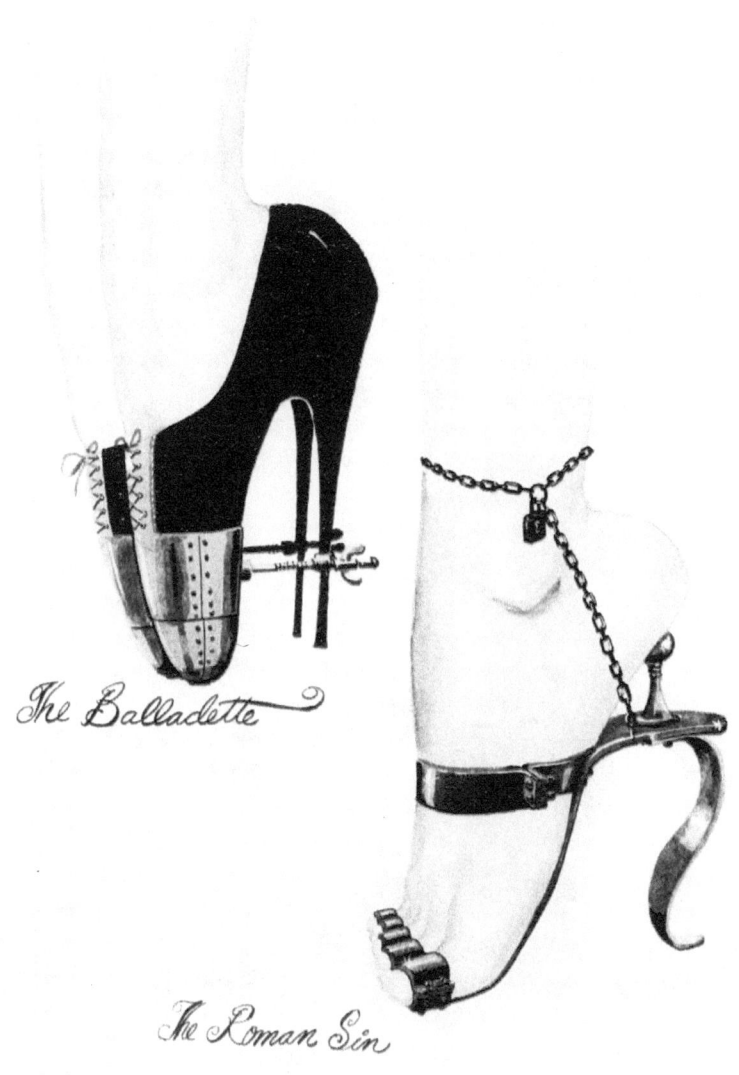

The Balladette

The Roman Sin

For *Exotique* issue #6 (1956)

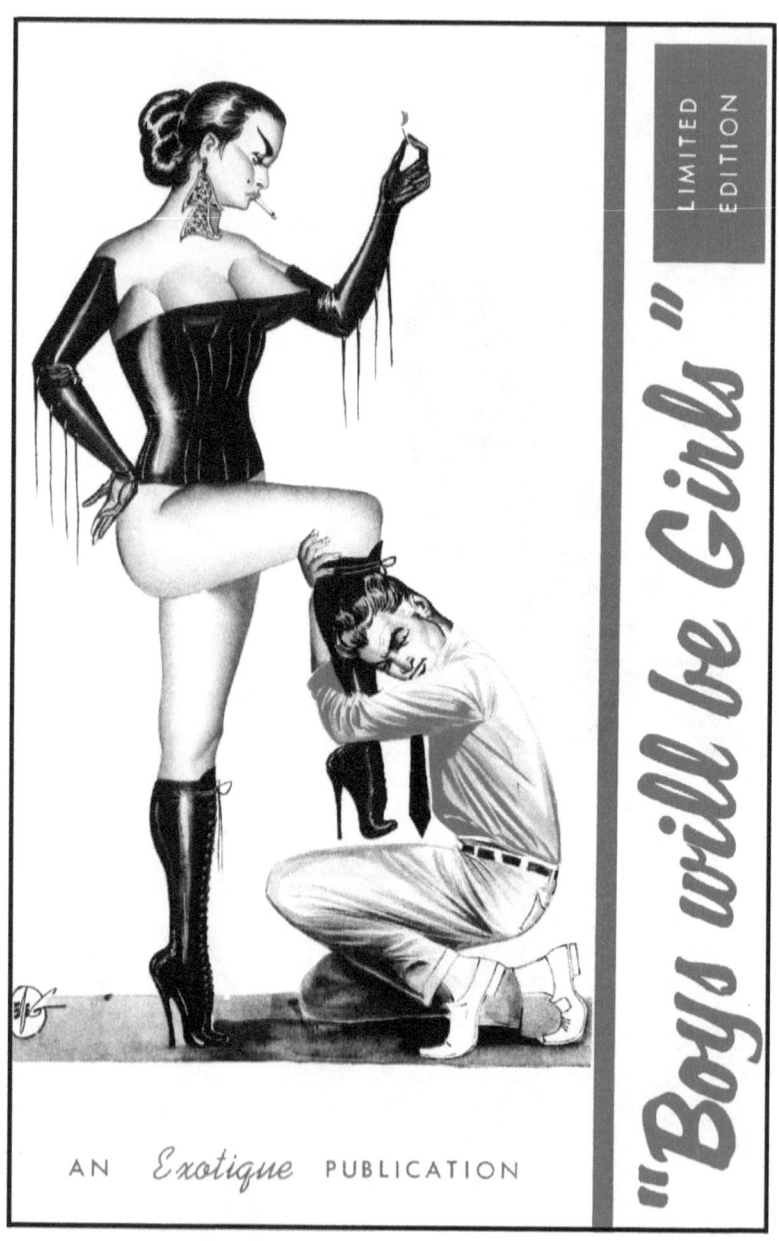

For Burtman, undated (c. 1958)

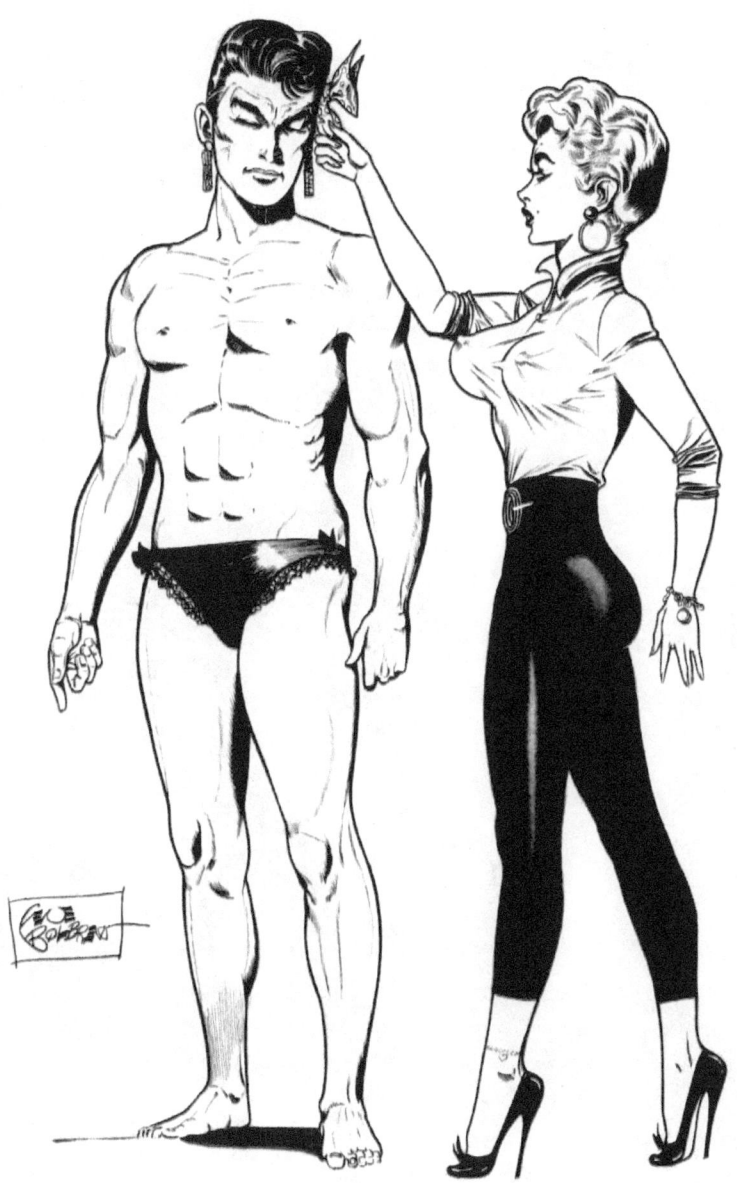

For *Exotique* issue #19 (1957)

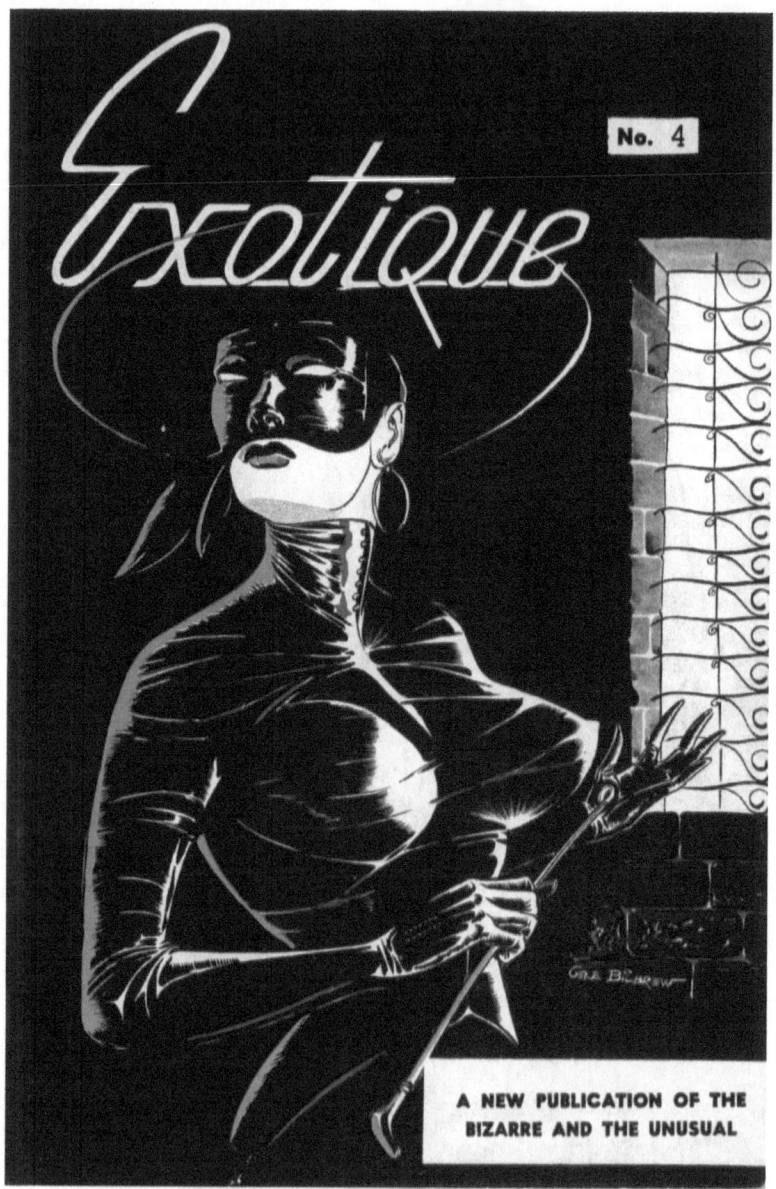

For Burtman (undated, likely 1956)

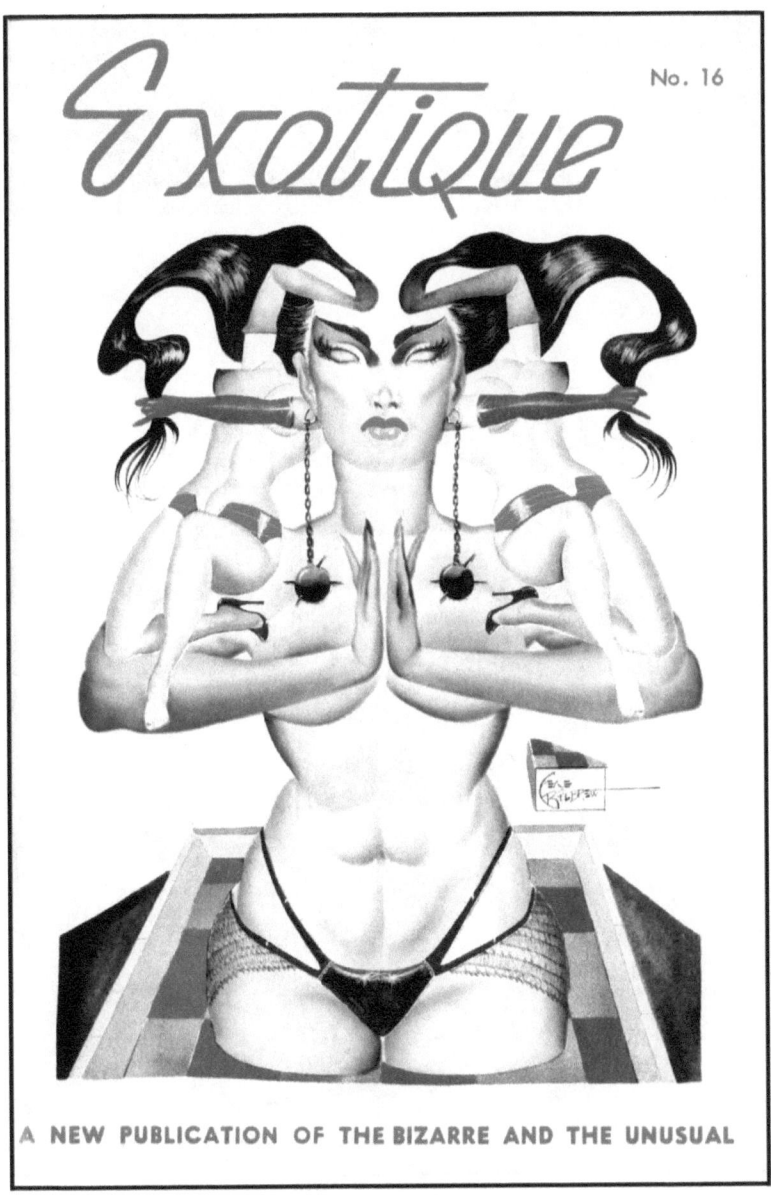

For Burtman (1957)

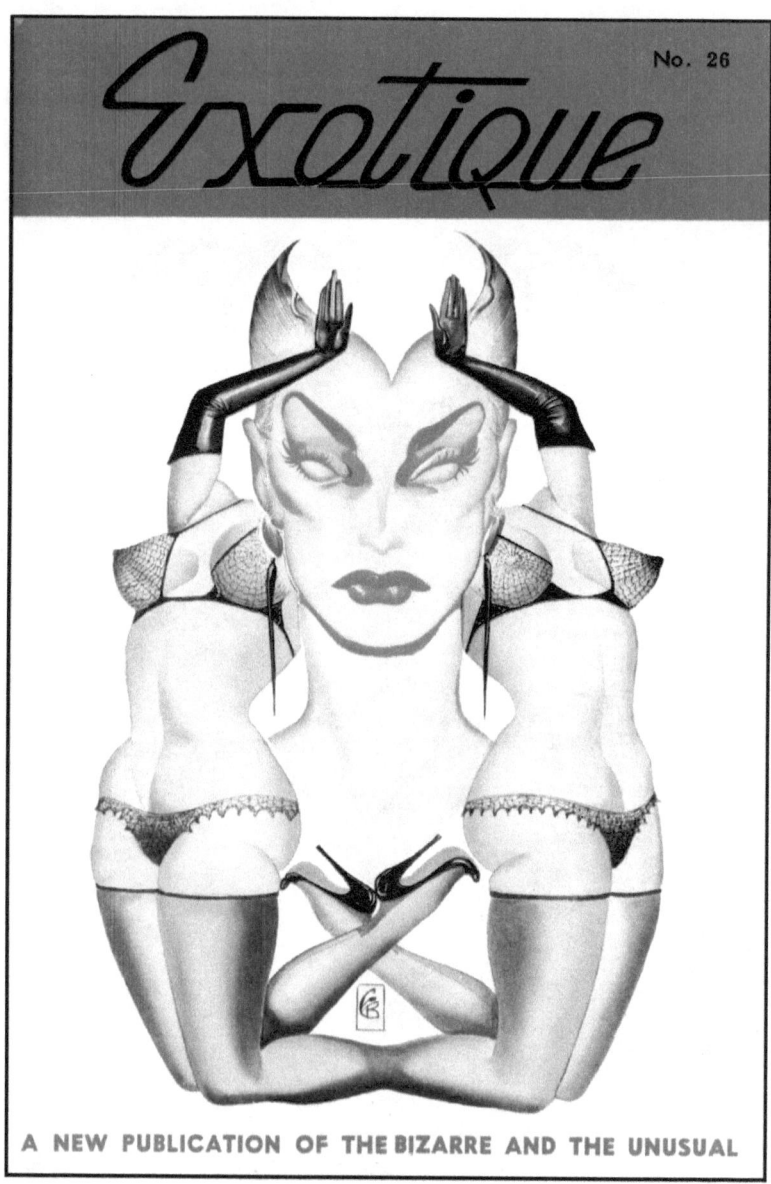

For Burtman (1958)

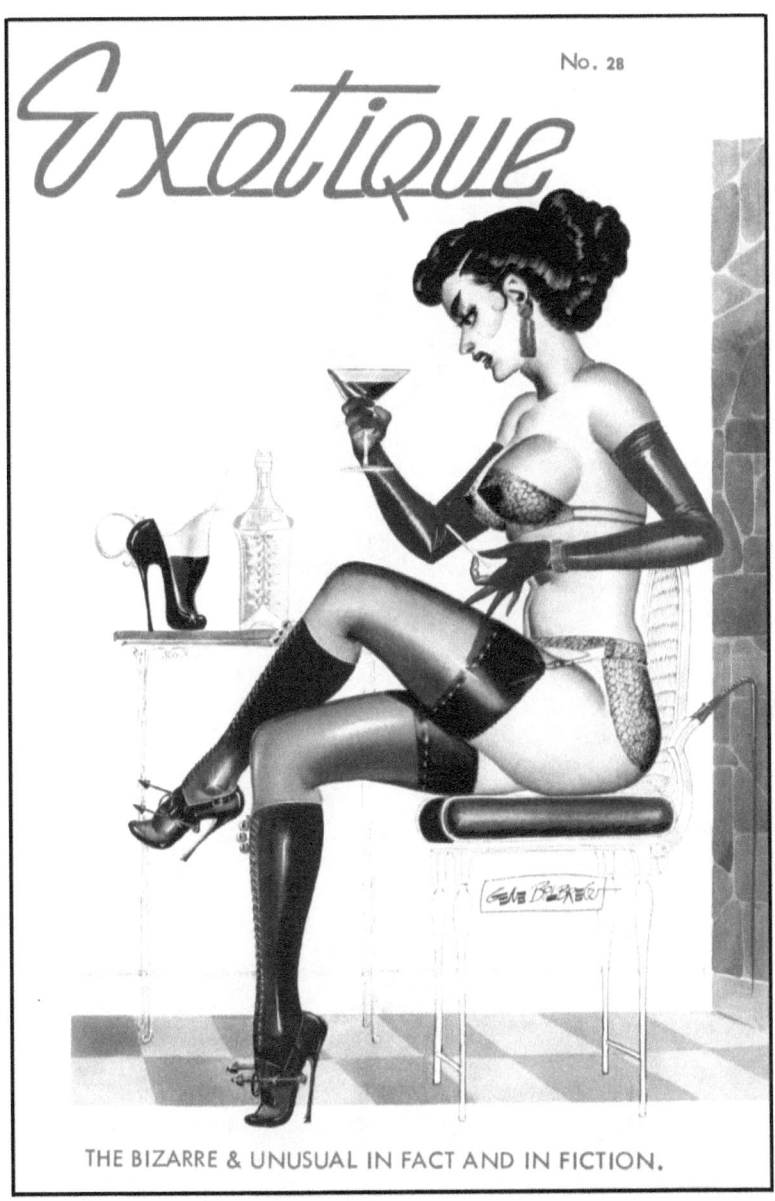

For Burtman (1958)

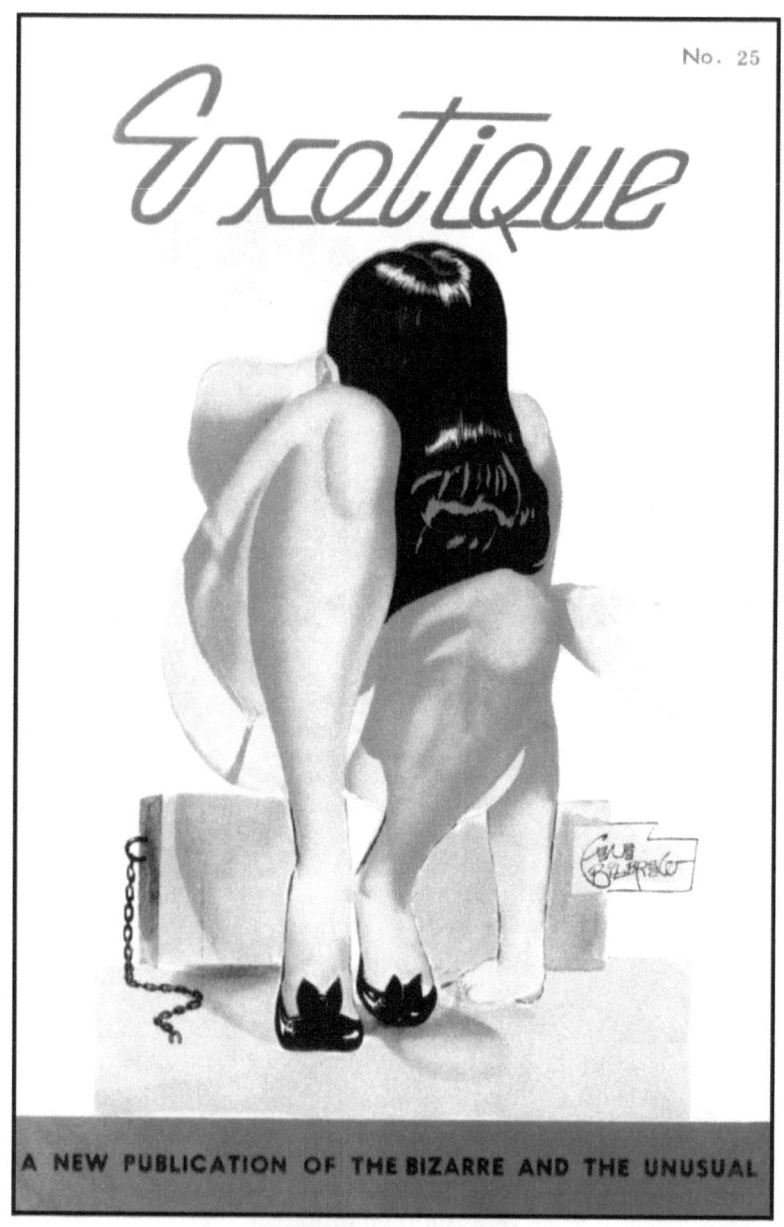

For Burtman (1958)

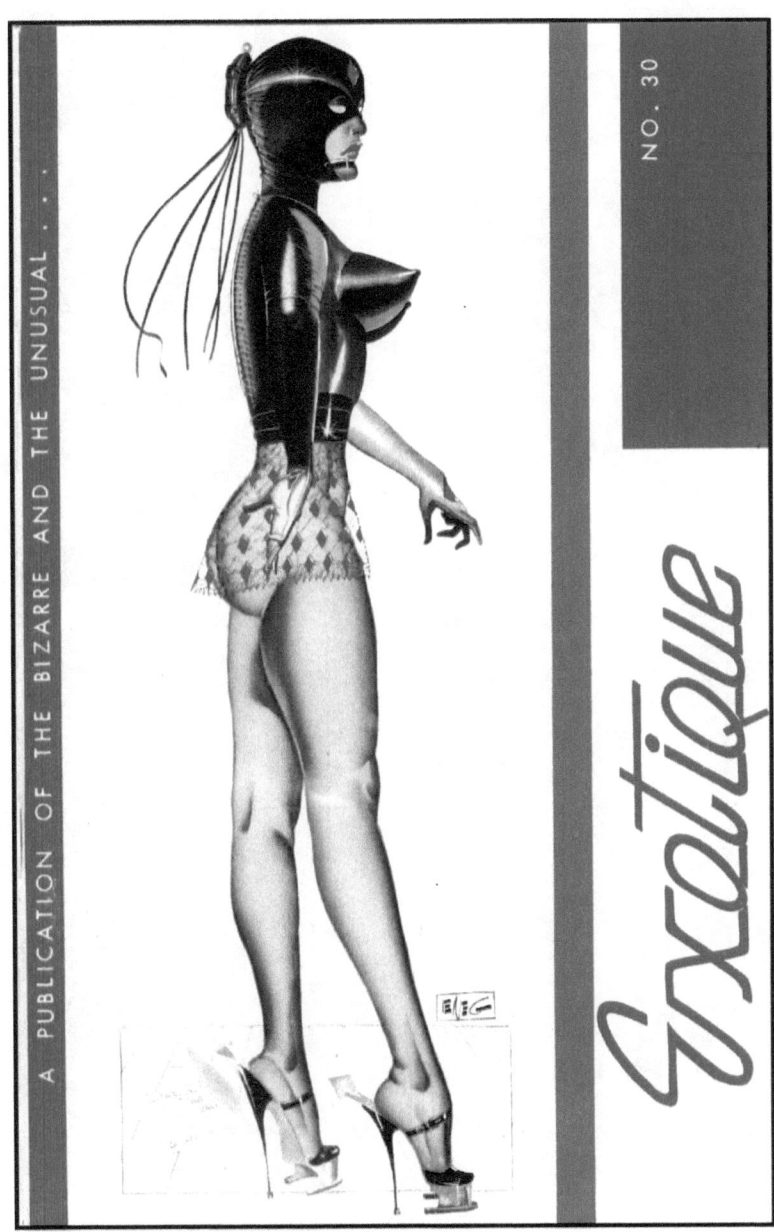

For Burtman (1958)

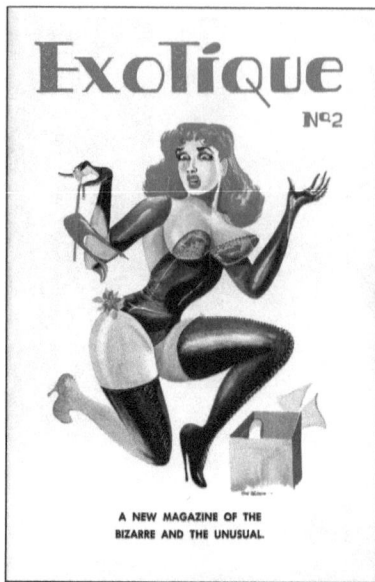
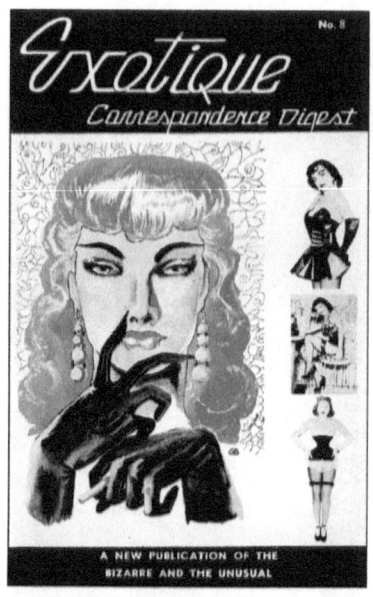
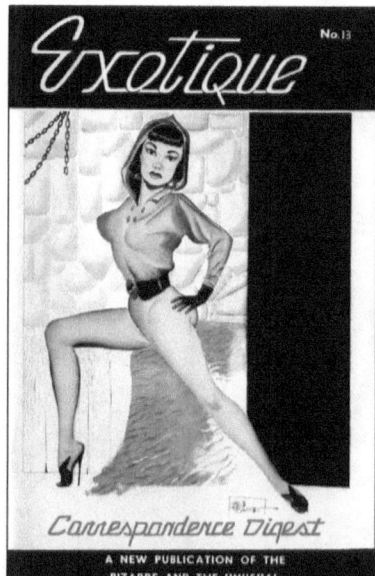
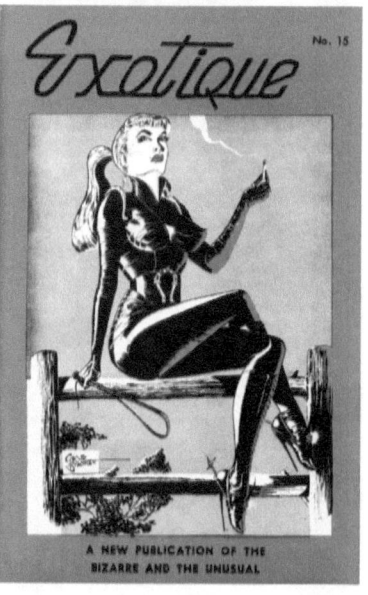

For Burtman, *Exotique* #2 (1955) #8 (1956); #13, #15 (1957)

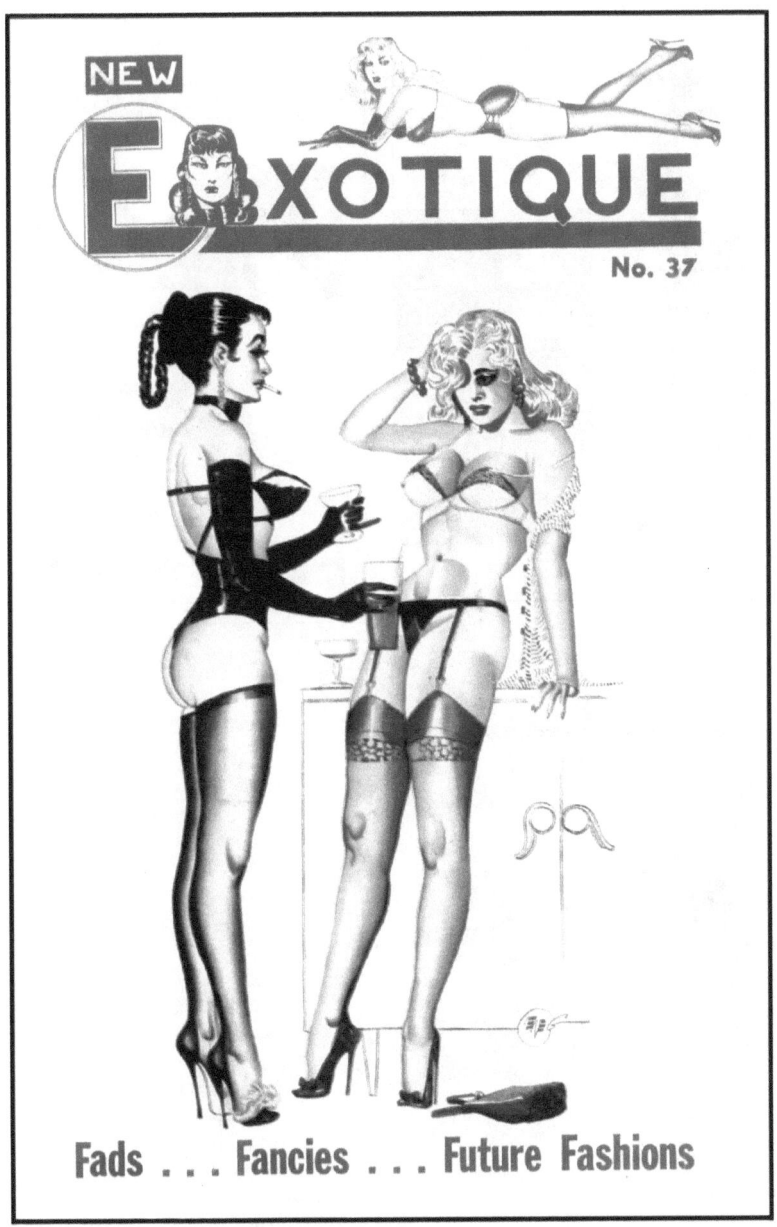

For Burtman, *New Exotique* #37 (1959)

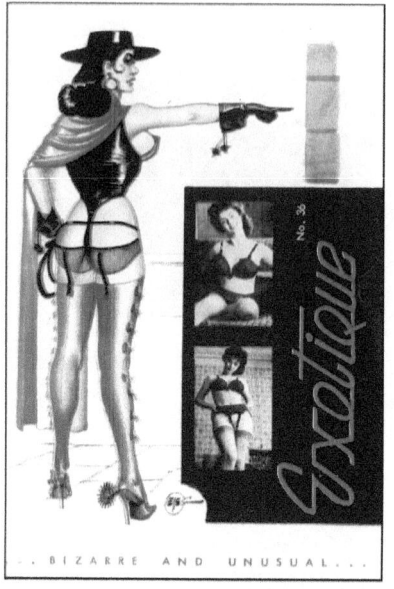
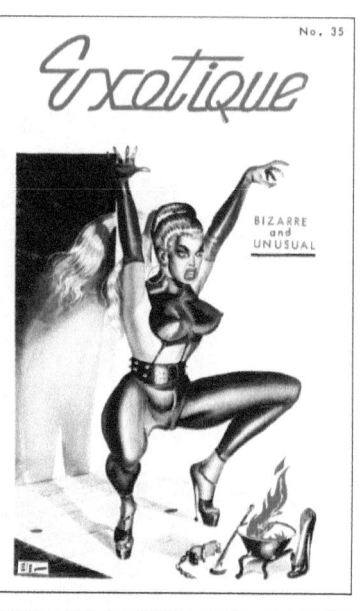
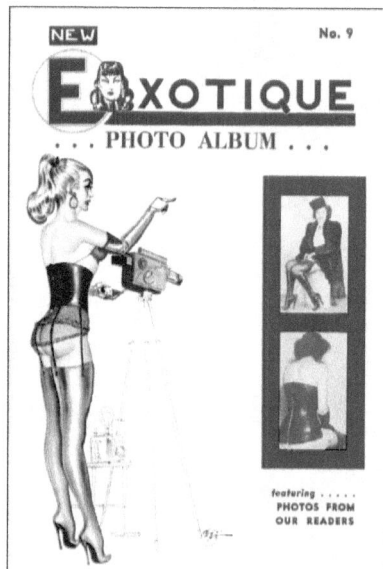
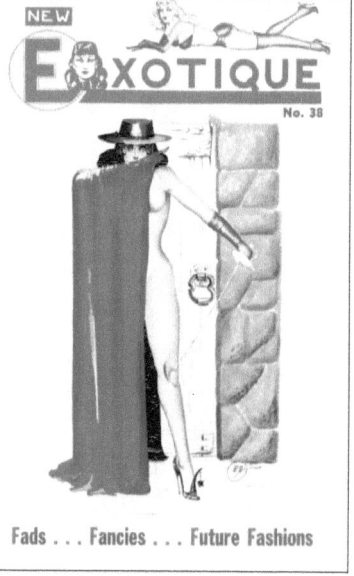

Exotique #36, #35, *New Exotique* publications (1959)

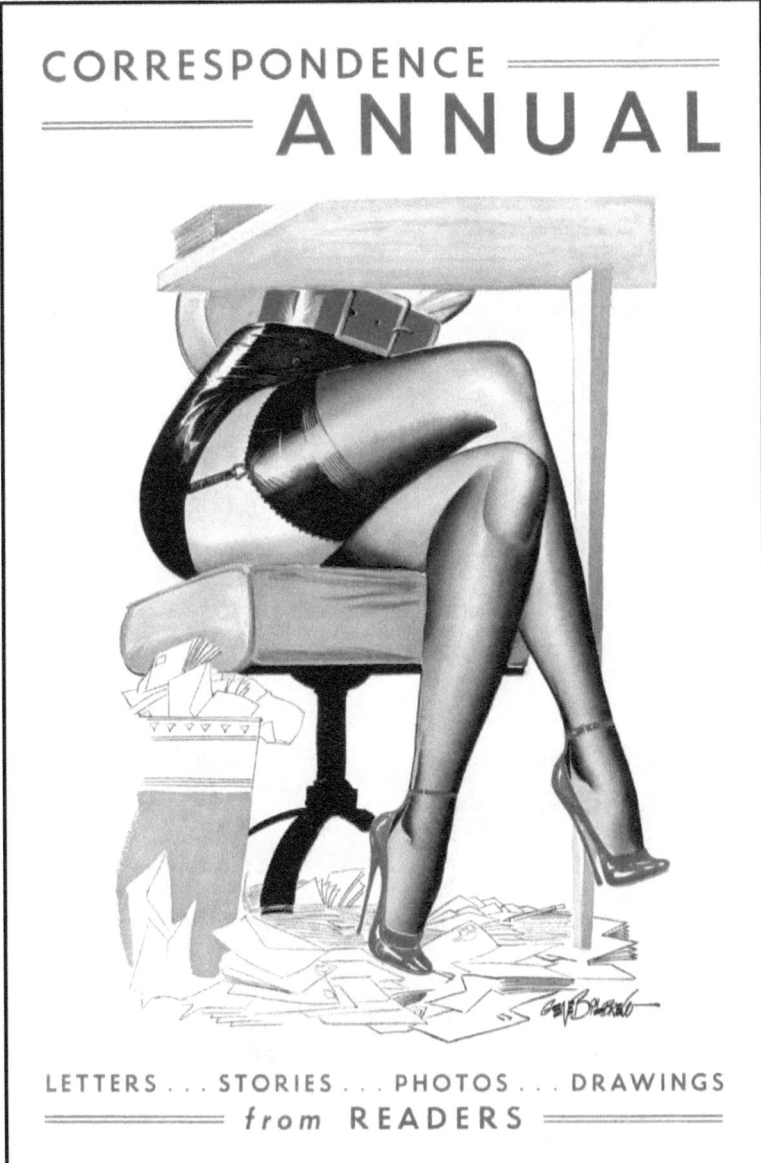

For Burtman, Kaysey Sales Co. Inc. (1959)

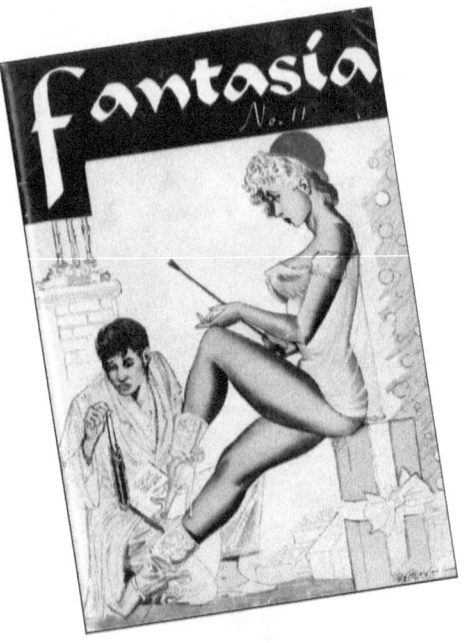

Not one to tie himself to a single employer, Bilbrew's artwork also adorned the covers of competing, if lesser magazines: Mishkin's short-lived *Extatique* (pg. 110), *Hum*, *Ultra*, and *Fantasia*. Bilbrew even contributed several covers to the UK publication *Fads and Fancies*, which at one point was distributed in the US by Burtman, though it's likely that these issues were reprints or repurposed editions of the original magazine.[xciv]

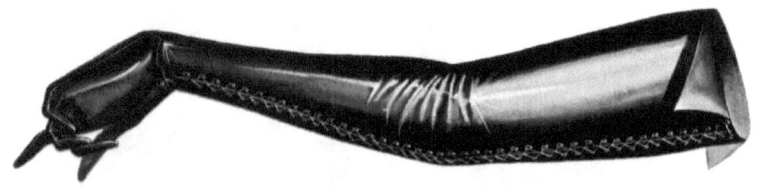

And speaking of repurposed material, evidence also suggests that Utopian Press, the UK publisher of *Fads and Fancies*, changed ownership by the late 1950s—by then sporting a Los Angeles publishing address and offering repackaged Bilbrew/Van Rod/Bondy fetish art originally commissioned by Mishkin (opposite page).

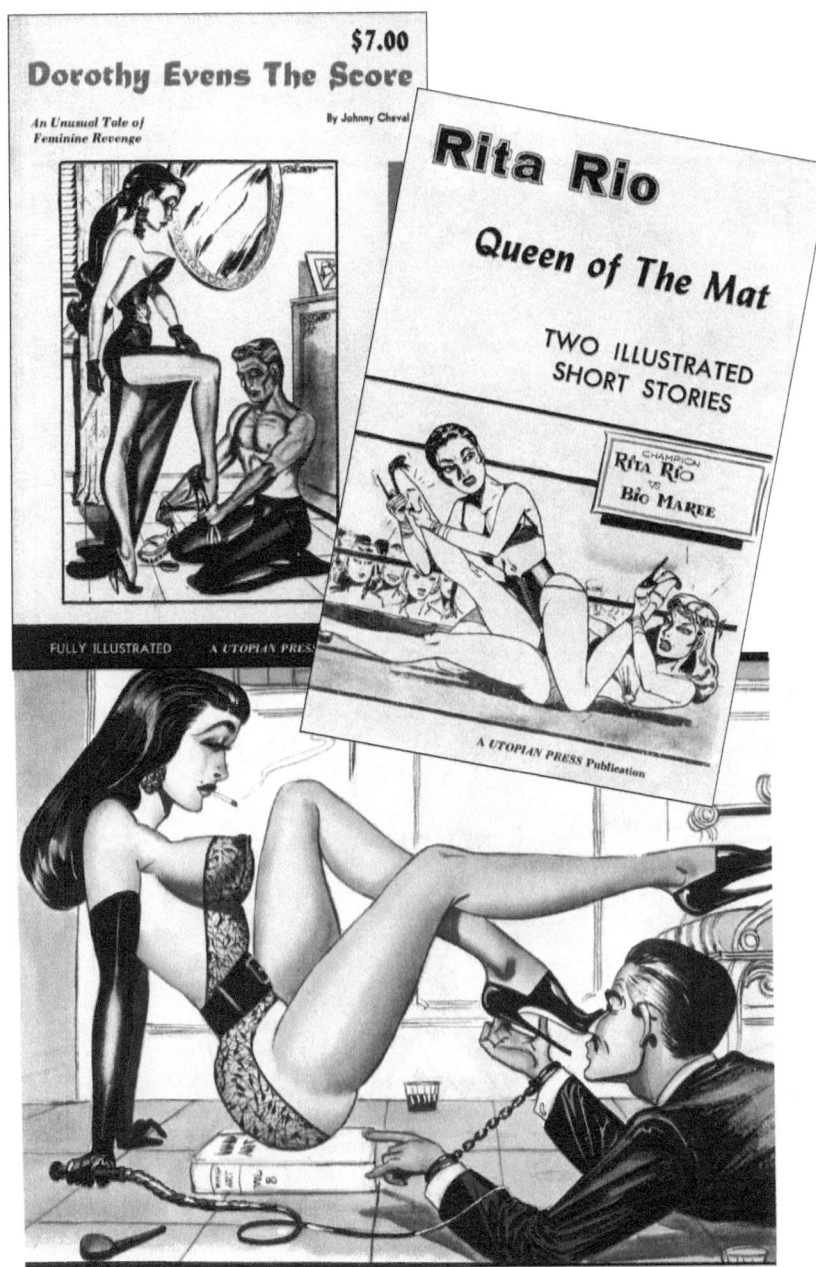

Utopian Press (1958)

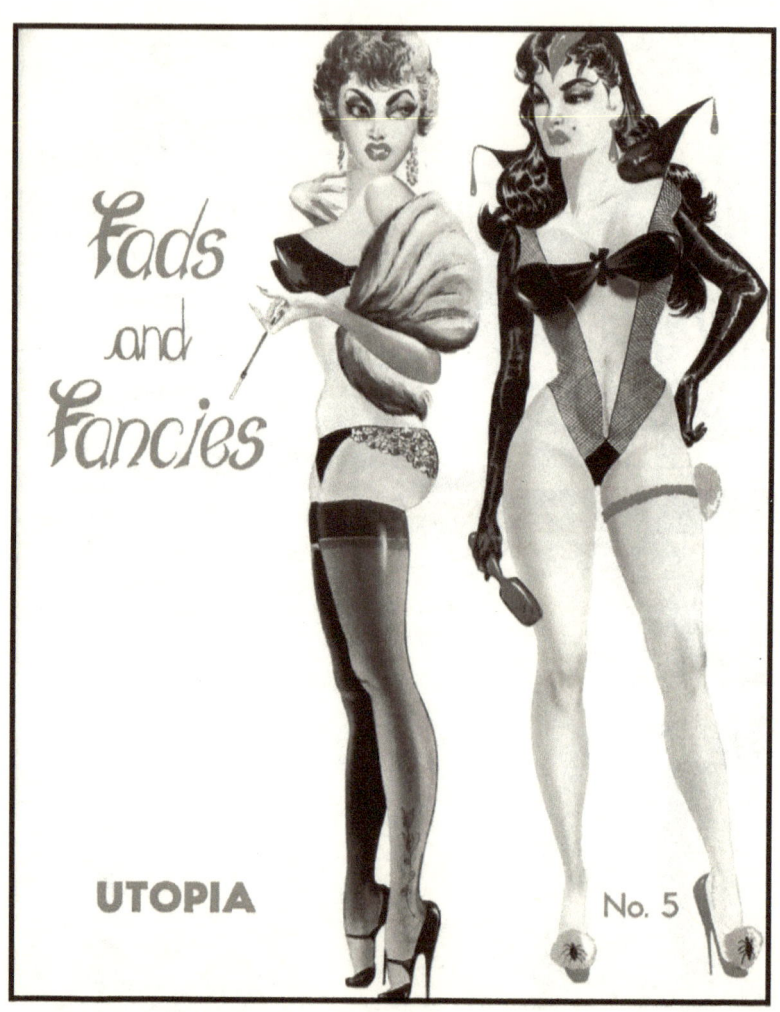

For Utopian Press/Burtman (1957)

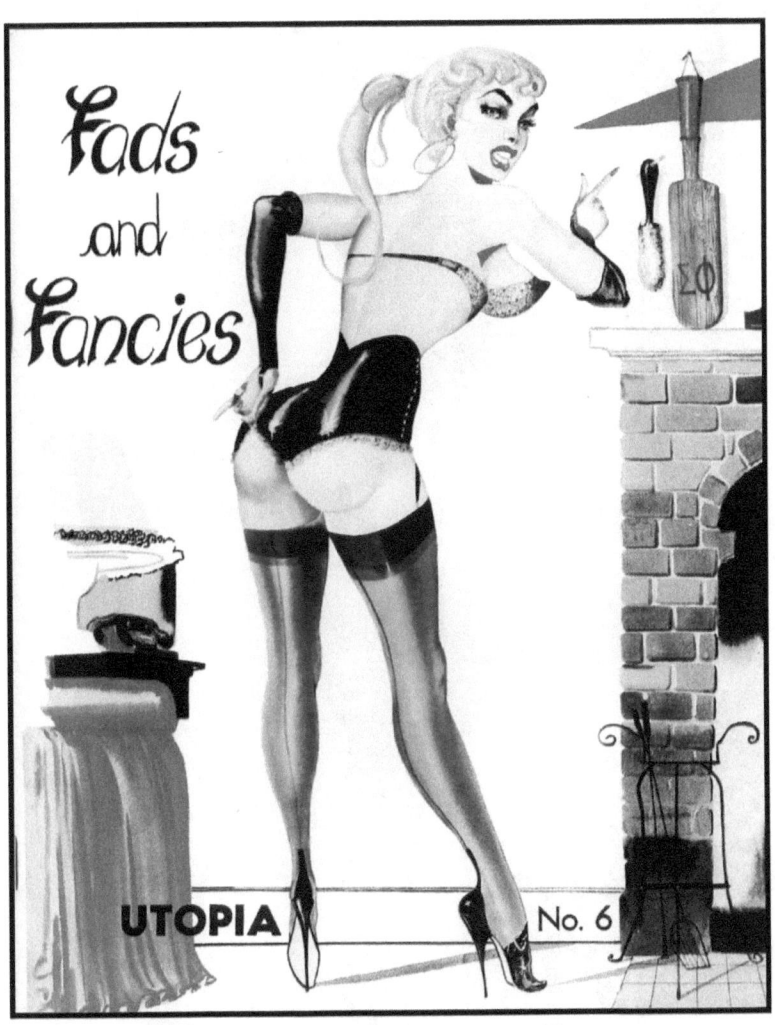

For Utopian Press/Burtman (1957)

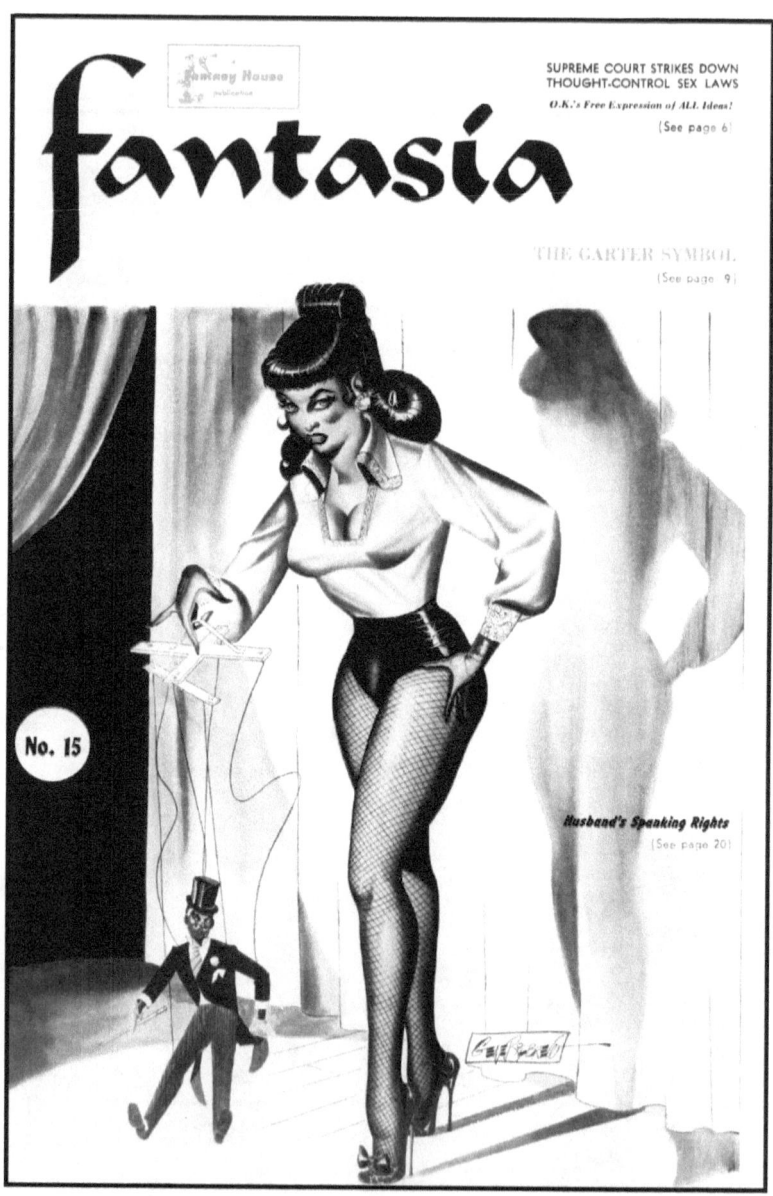

For Fantasy House, a.k.a. Lucian Press (1959)

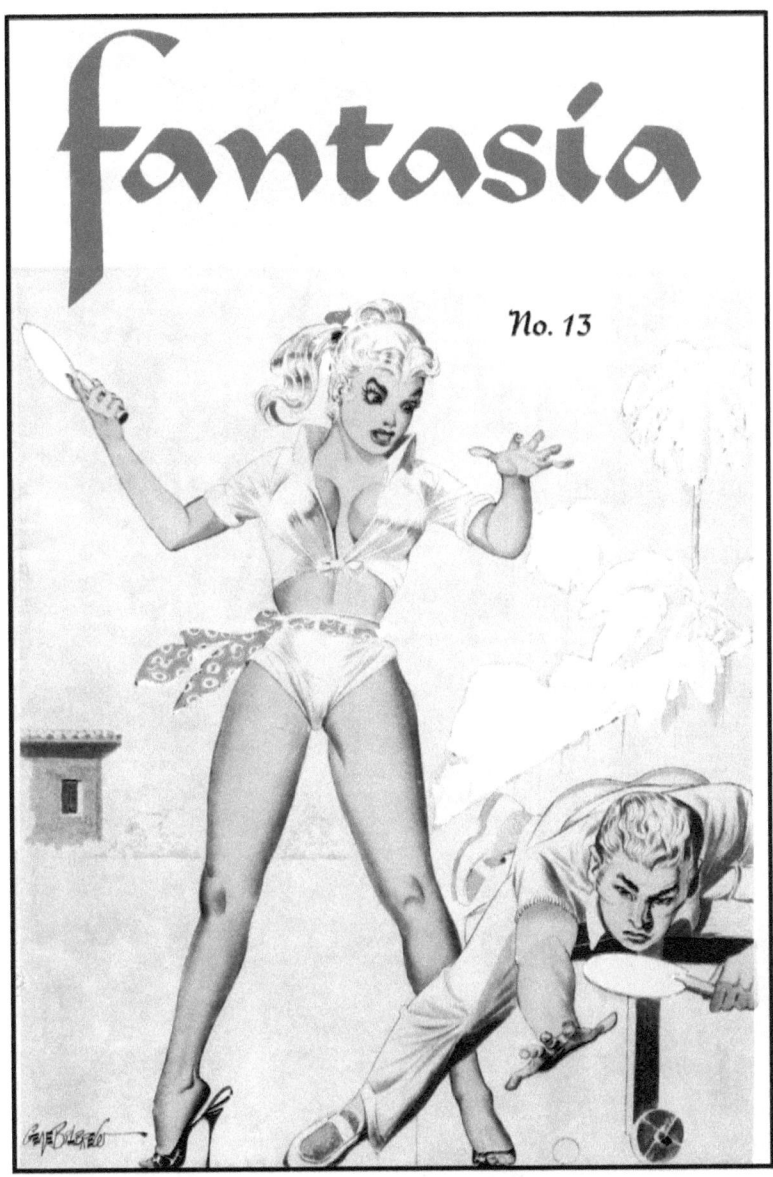

For Lucian Press (c. 1958). Bilbrew contributed to 8 issues.[xcv]

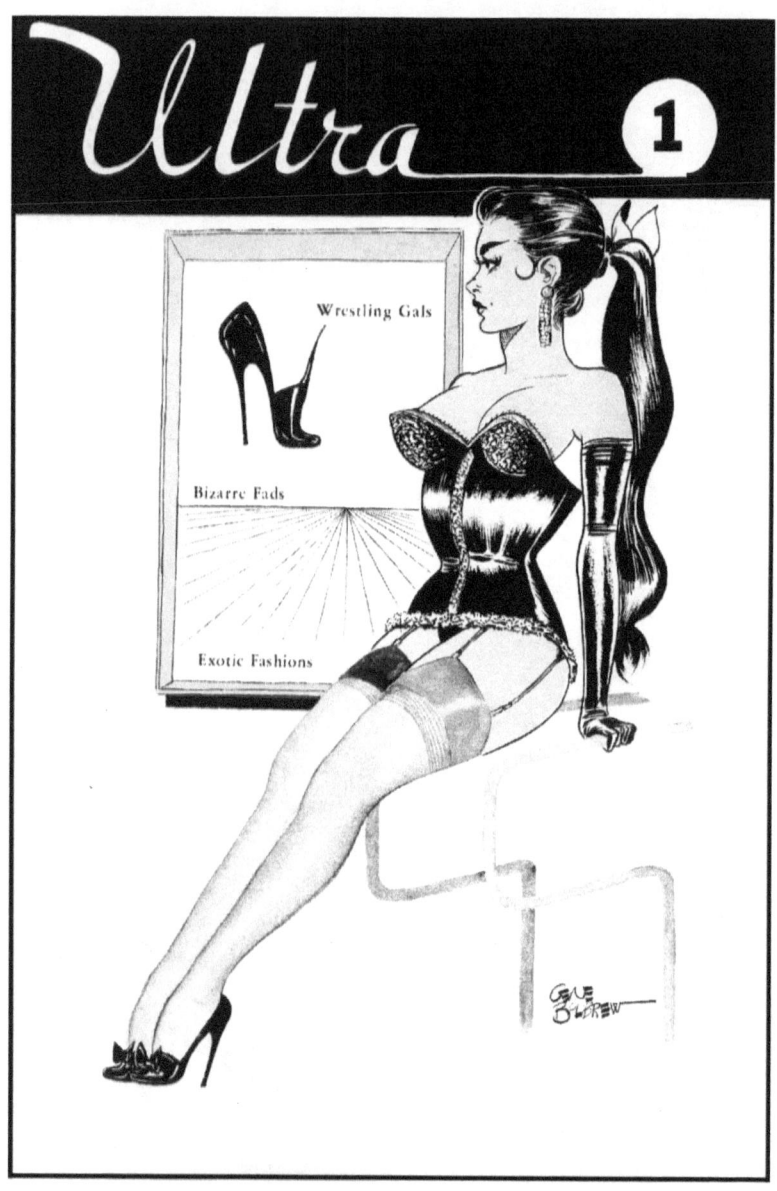

For Ultra Sports Co./Hal Zucker as "Zucca" xcvi (1957)

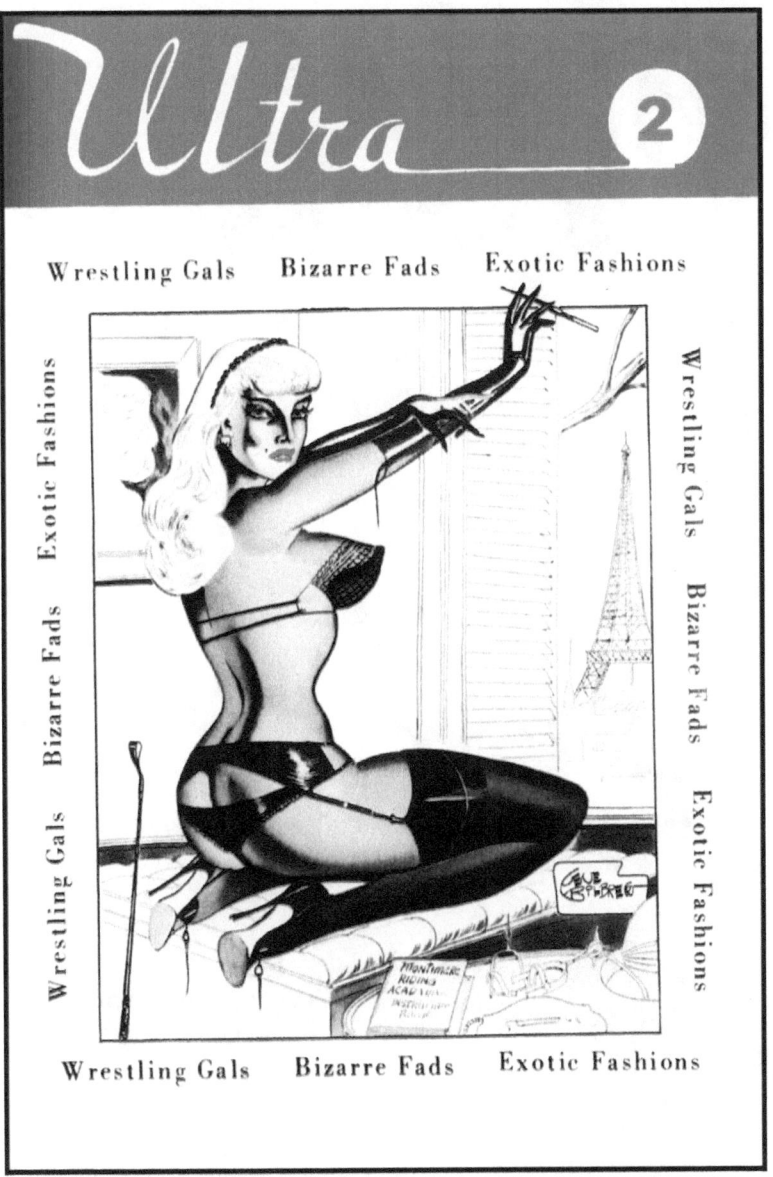

For Hal Zucker (1957). Bilbrew art graced all 4 issues.

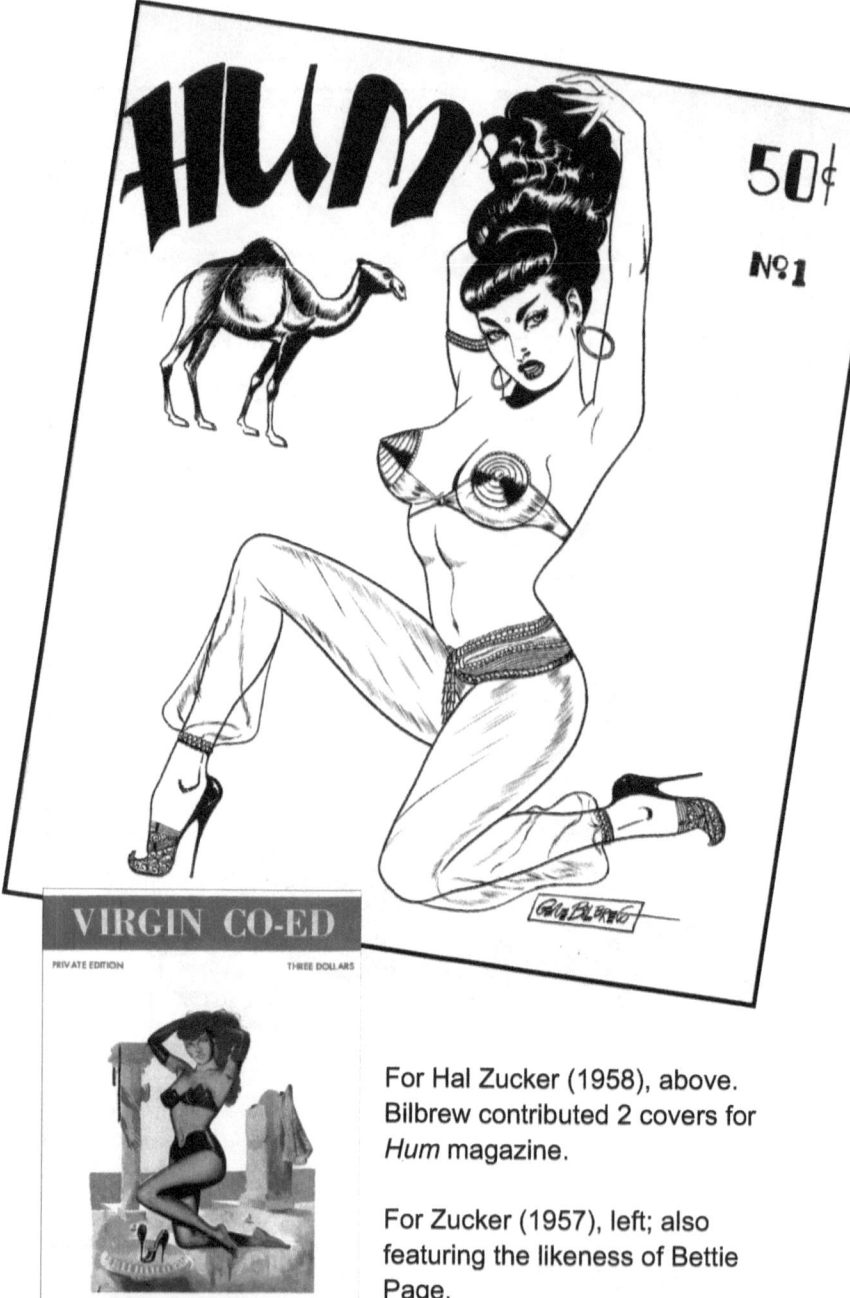

For Hal Zucker (1958), above. Bilbrew contributed 2 covers for *Hum* magazine.

For Zucker (1957), left; also featuring the likeness of Bettie Page.

170

Although Bilbrew was not obsessed with Bettie Page to the extent that Eric Stanton was, her image still appeared in a fair share of the artist's work, most notably *Sorority Girls* (1953) for Klaw, *Exotique* #23 for Burtman (following page), *Hum* #1 and *Virgin Co-Ed* (opposite), and perhaps most beautifully, *Celeste* (pg. 171), a 1957 novelette for Burtman.

Was Bilbrew the first to draw Bettie Page? His alternate dust jacket art (below) for the 1951 book, *Drawing, Painting, and Sculpture from Live Models* suggests it—even predating her arrival at Klaw's—if we can trust that the jacket art was produced at the same time as the book and not simply added later for special resale value in Times Square shops.[xcvii]

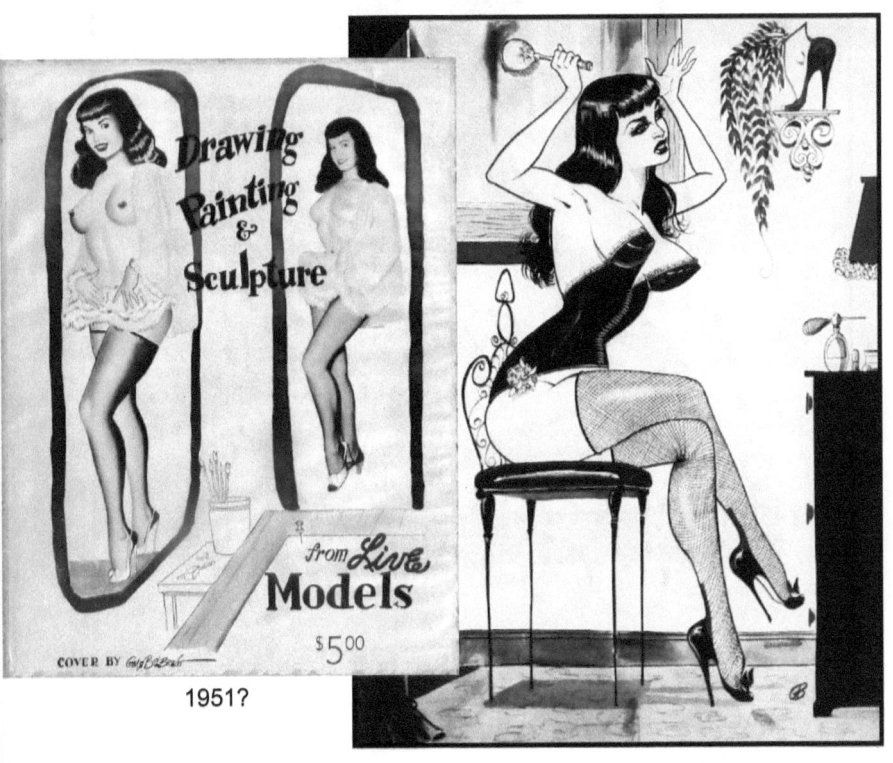

1951?

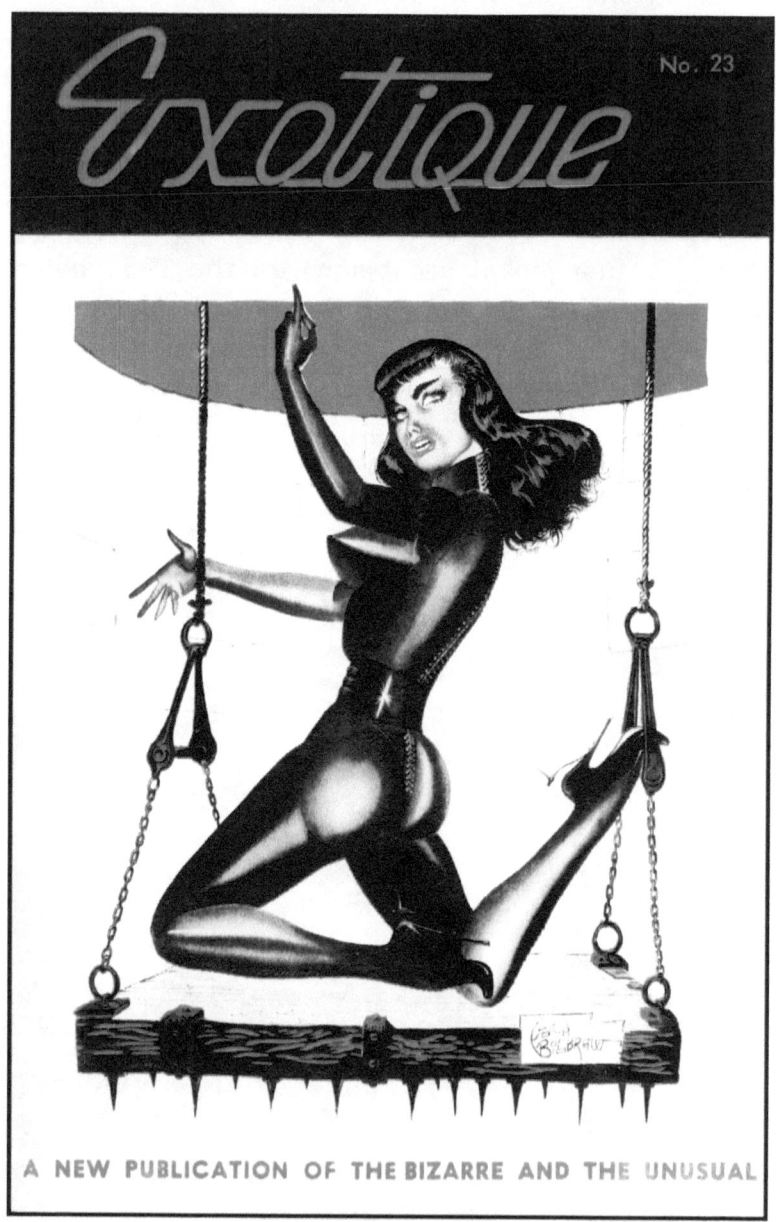

For Burtman (1957)

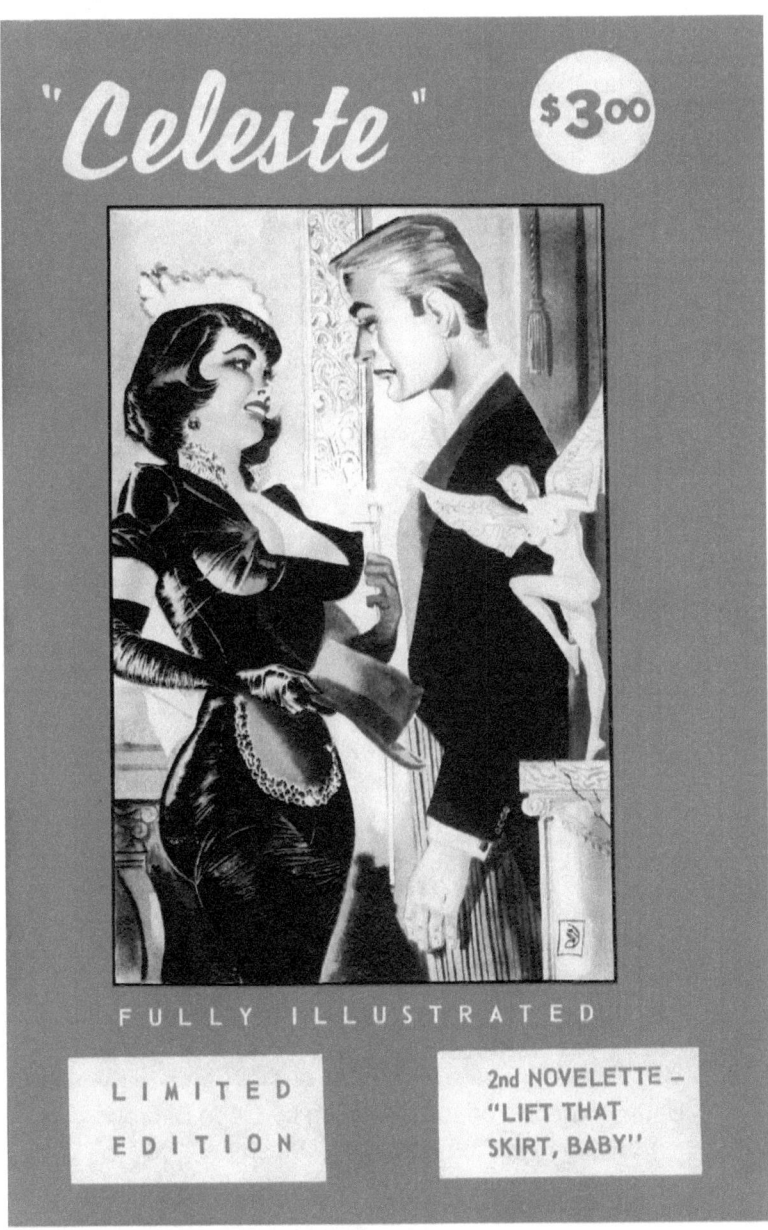

For Burtman (1957). Another book on the FBI list.[xcviii]

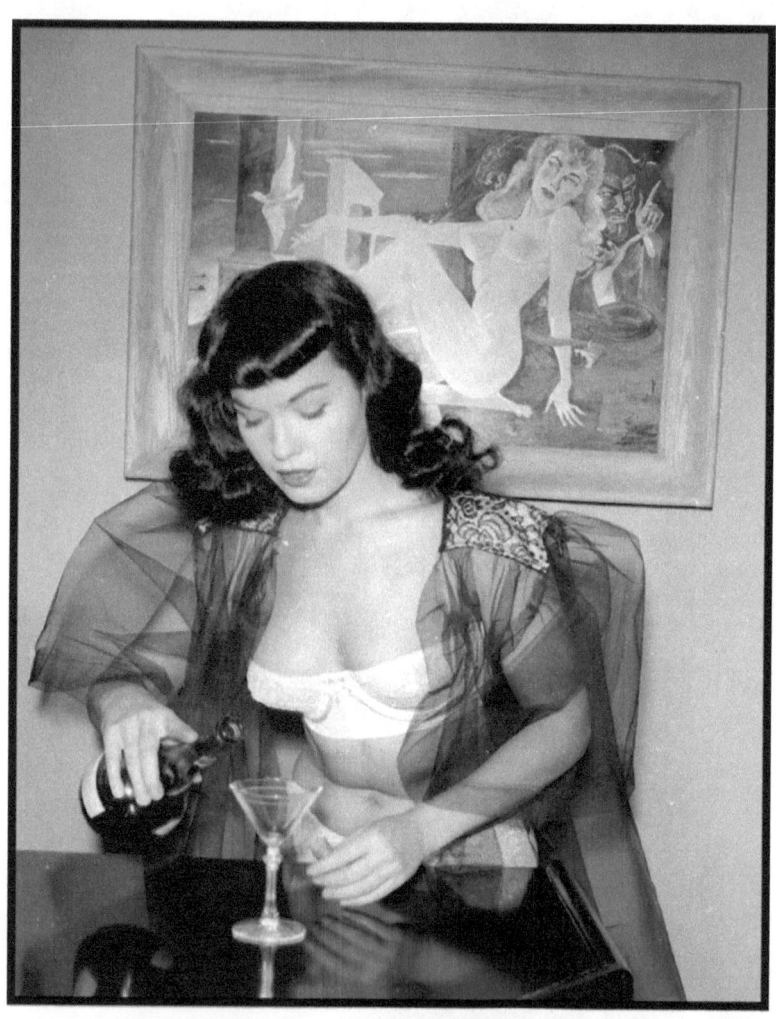

Bettie Page in front of a painting by Gene Bilbrew.
She retired from modeling in December 1957.

BILBREW

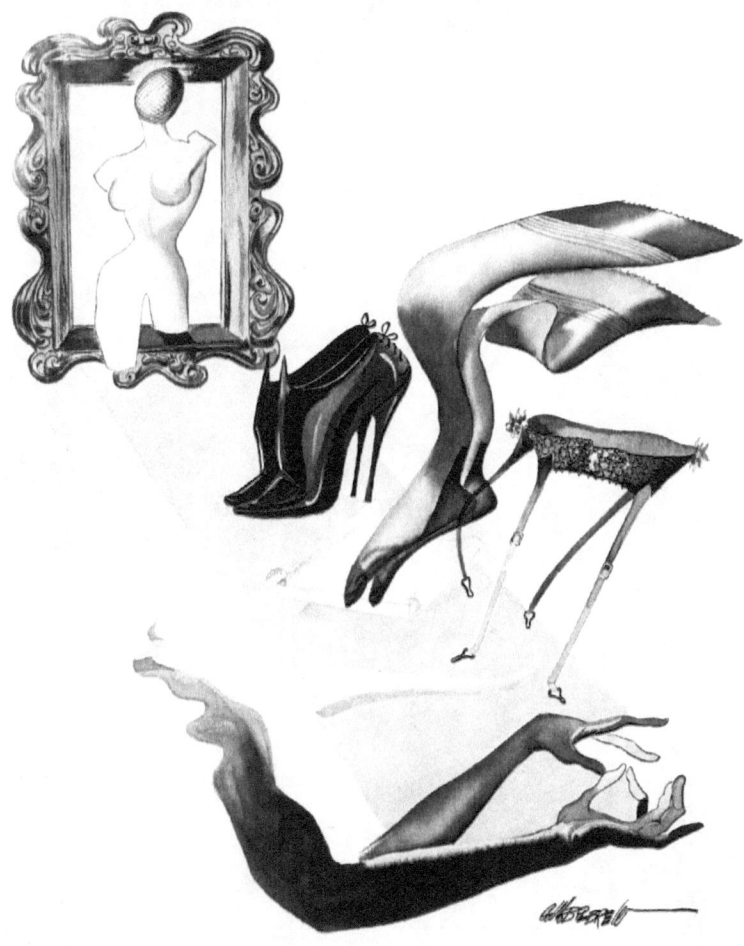

IN THE 1960s

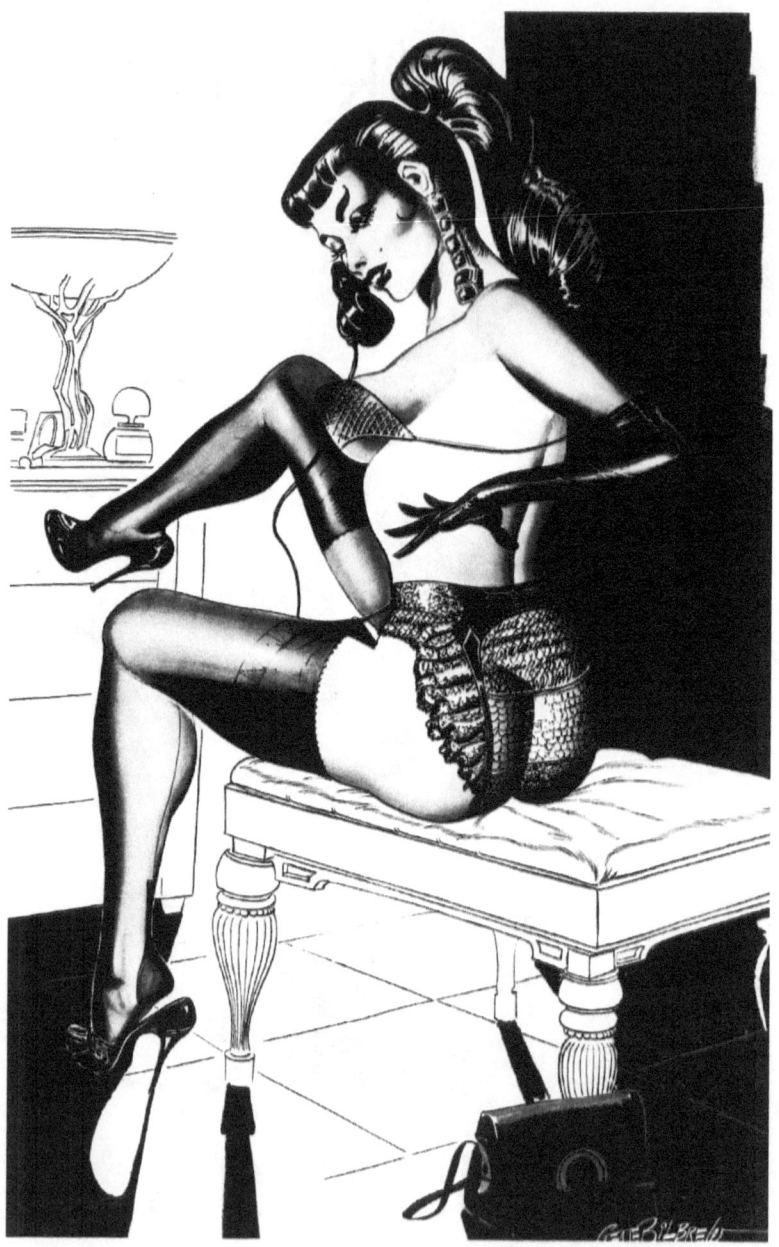

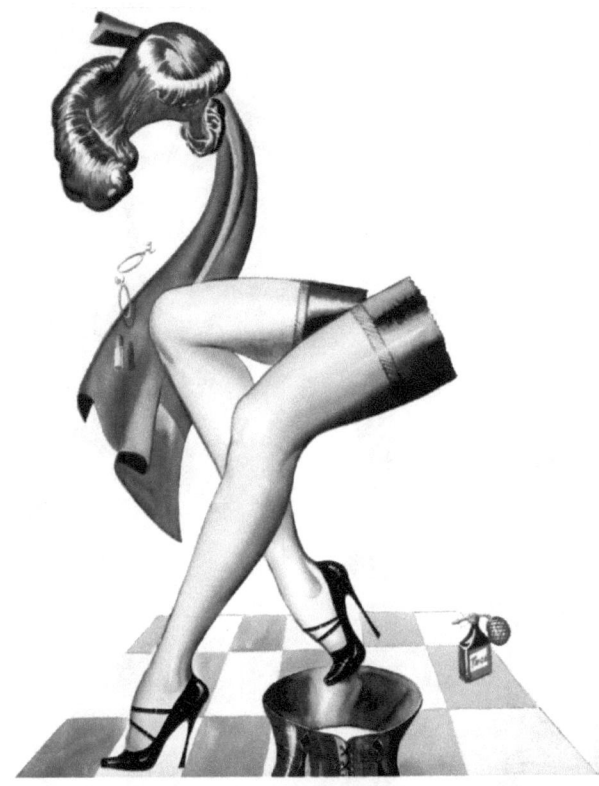

Following the government crackdown that resulted in the demise of Burmel Publishing Co. and the imprint of Kaysey Sales Co. Inc., Burtman and partner Benedict Himmel reinvented themselves most notably under a new company: Selbee Associates, Inc. Their signature magazine, similar in format and style to *Exotique,* was named *Masque.* The year was 1960. On board as head artist was Bilbrew.

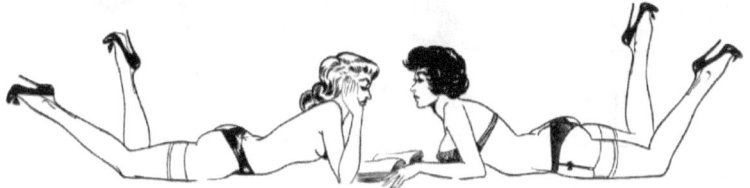

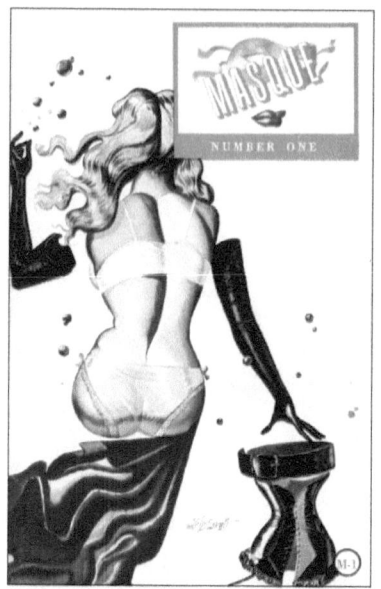
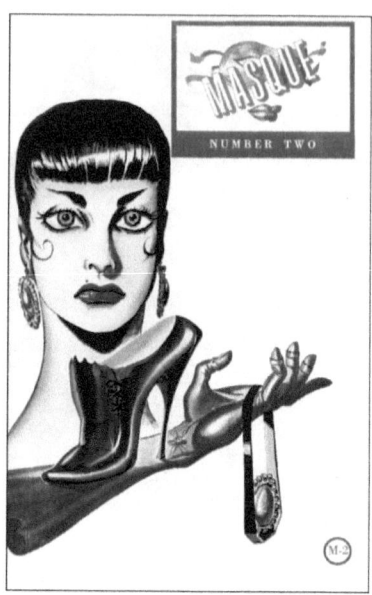
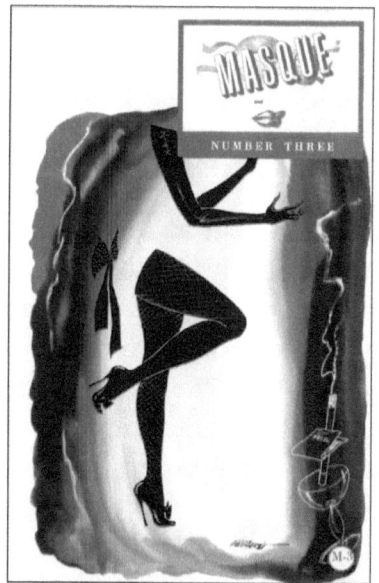
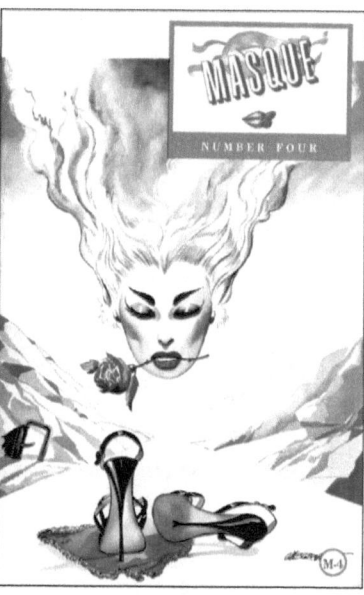

After the first four issues of *Masque*, the magazine was renamed *Connoisseur*—with the interior pages of issue #1 (opposite) still titled *Masque*.

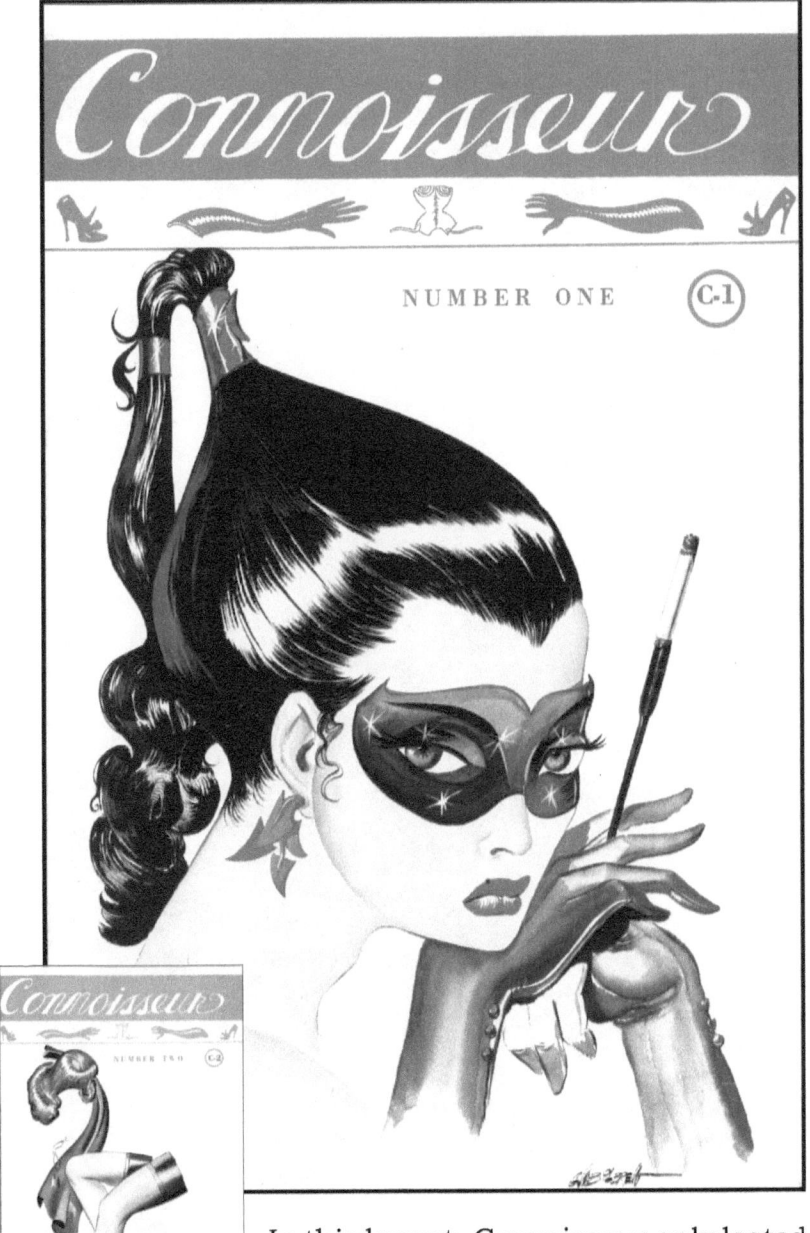

In this layout, *Connoisseur* only lasted two issues, though Bilbrew's artwork throughout was excellent.

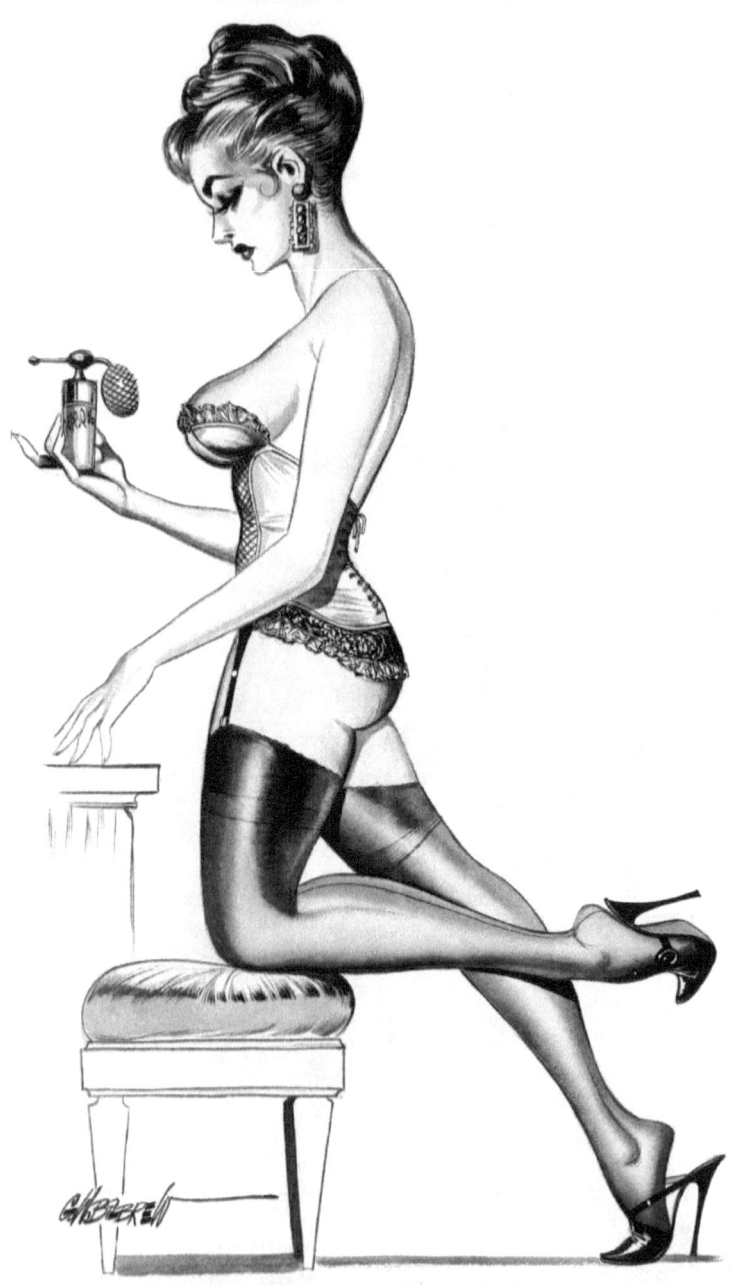

For *Connoisseur* issue #1 (1961)

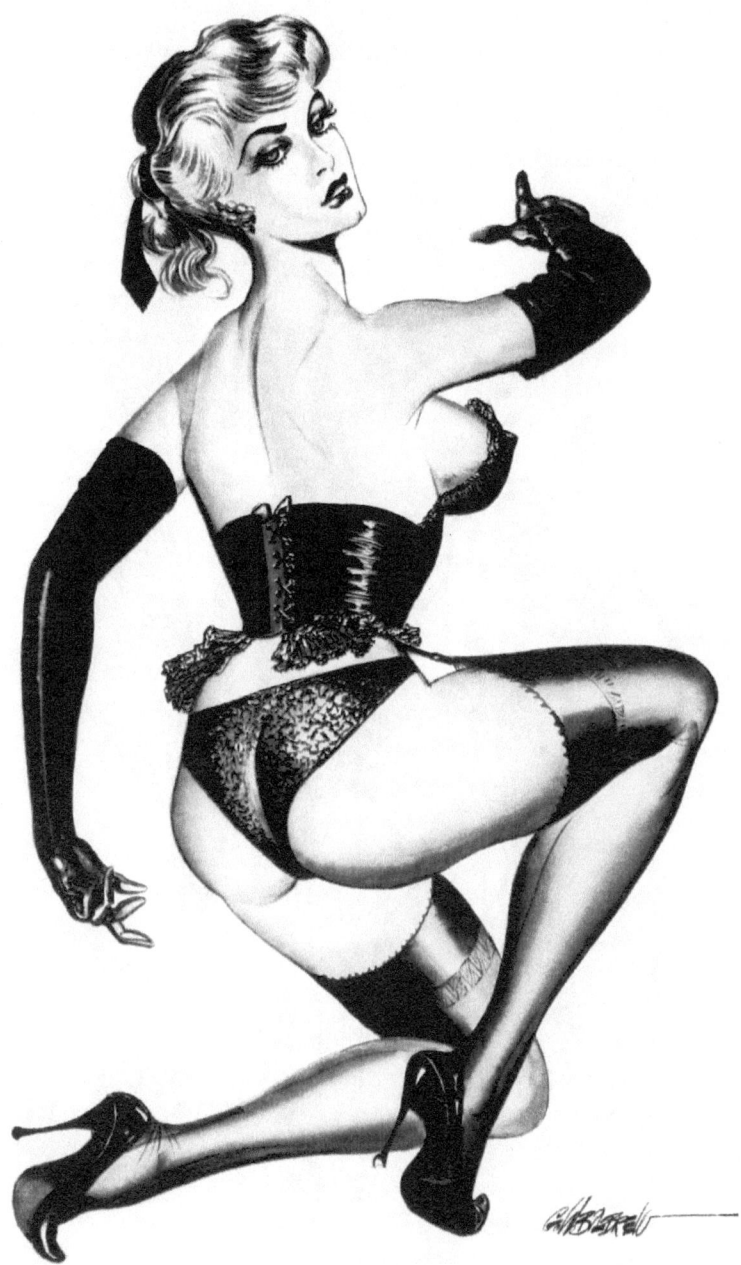

For *Connoisseur* issue #2 (1961)

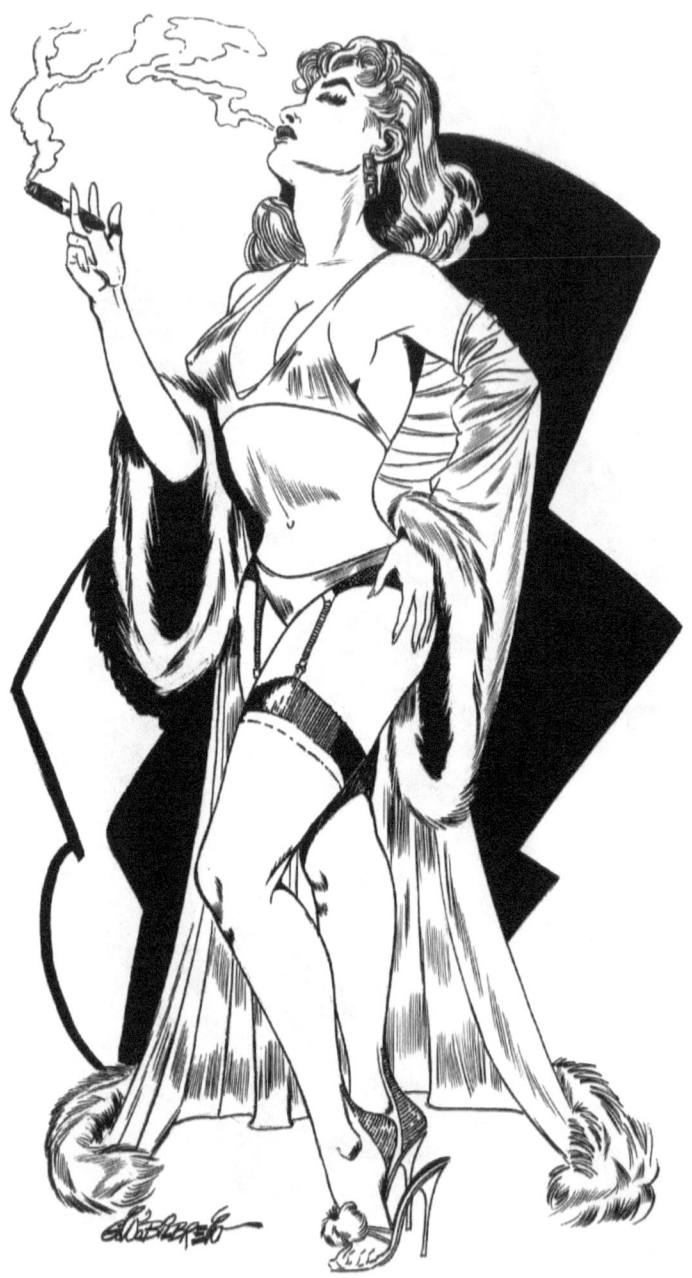

For *Masque* issue #4 (1960)

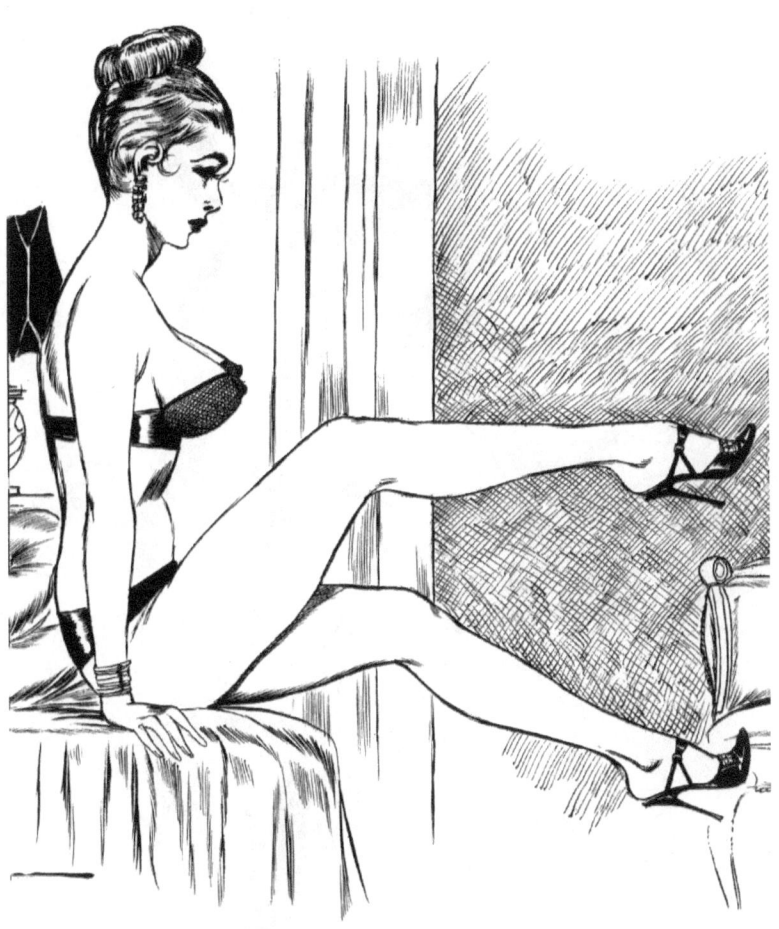

Connoisseur period, early Selbee (1961)[xcix]

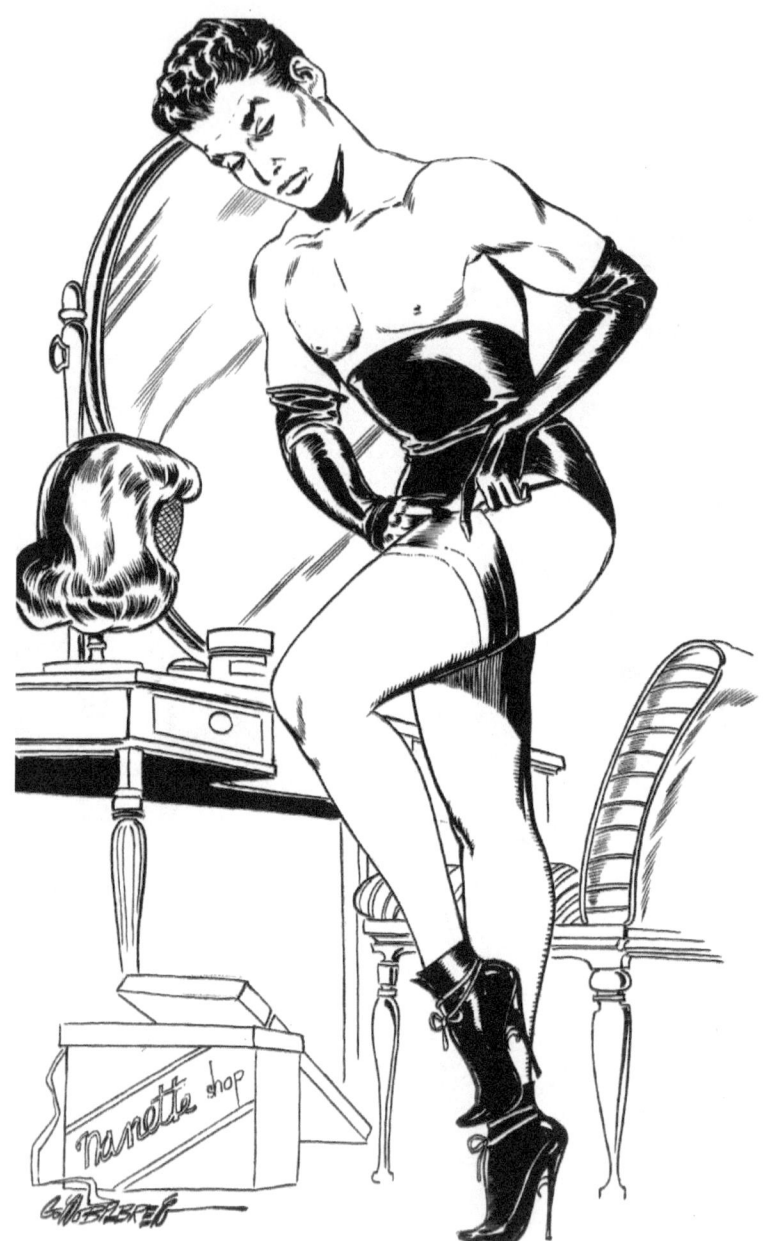

For *Masque* issue #4 (1960)

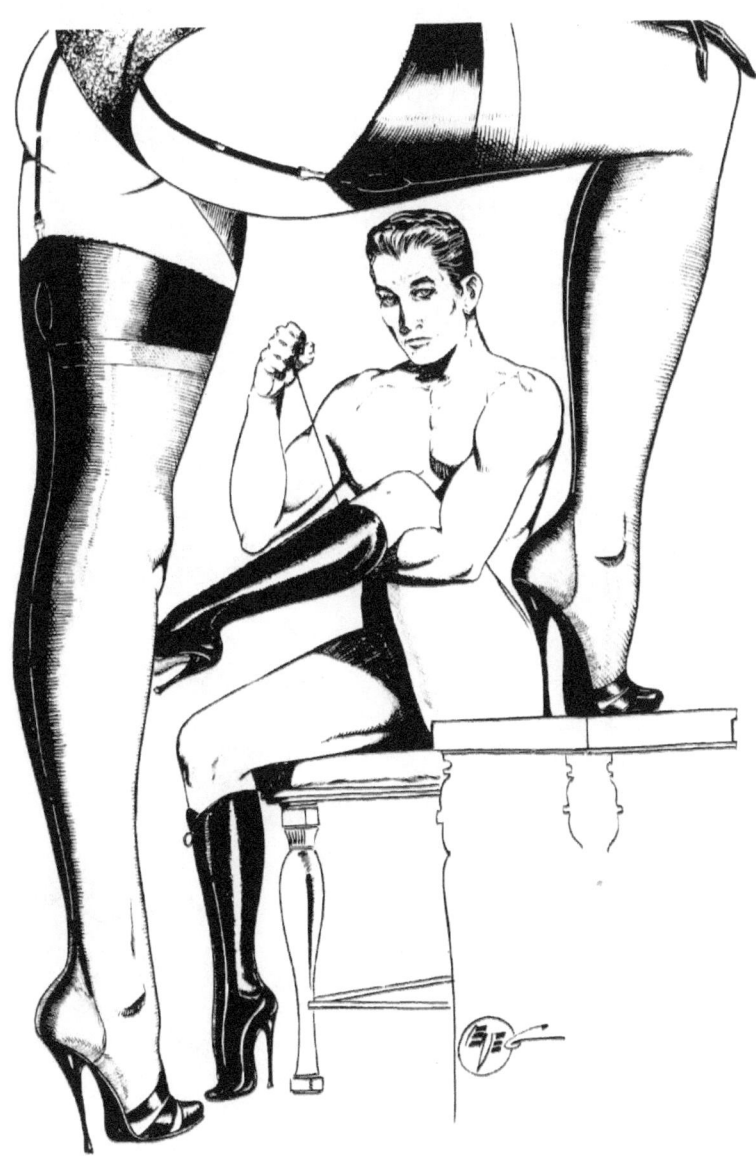

For *Connoisseur* issue #2 (1961)

In 1961, Burtman shifted his focus from digest-sized publications like *Masque* and *Connoisseur* to full-size magazines that were closer to "heel n' hose" slicks, which were then popular. Although these magazines were mostly filled with spreads of busty ladies in high heels and stockings, Bilbrew provided risqué cartoon art typical of men's magazines at the time, in addition to several, short-lived cartoon strips.

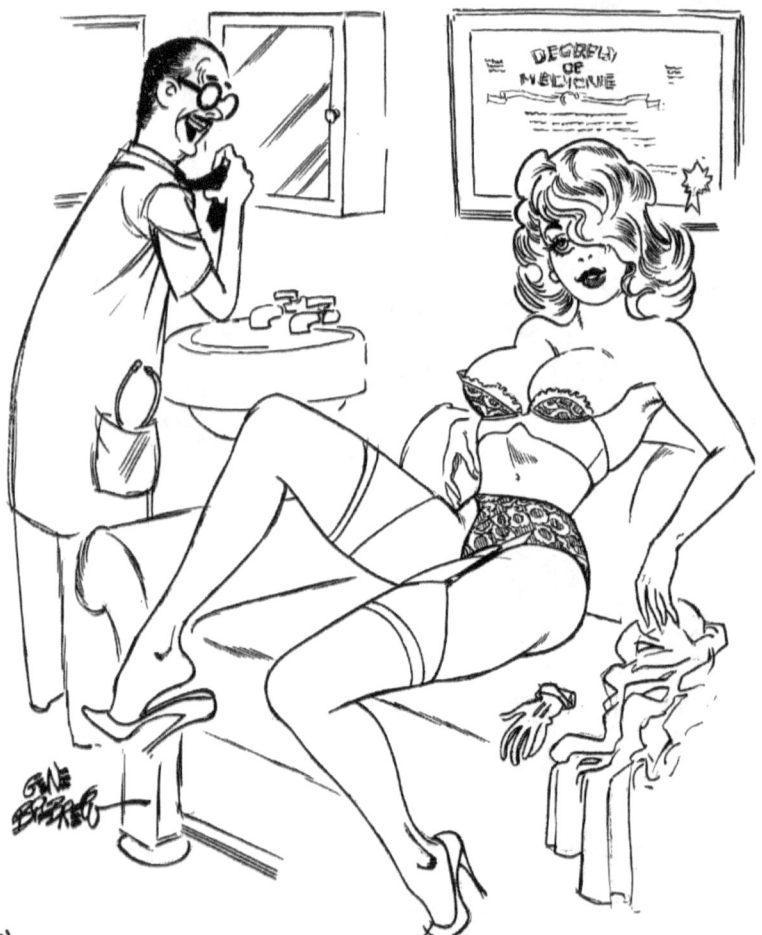

"*NOW, THEN, MRS. CANNONBERRY, WHAT SEEMS TO BE YOUR TROUBLE?*"

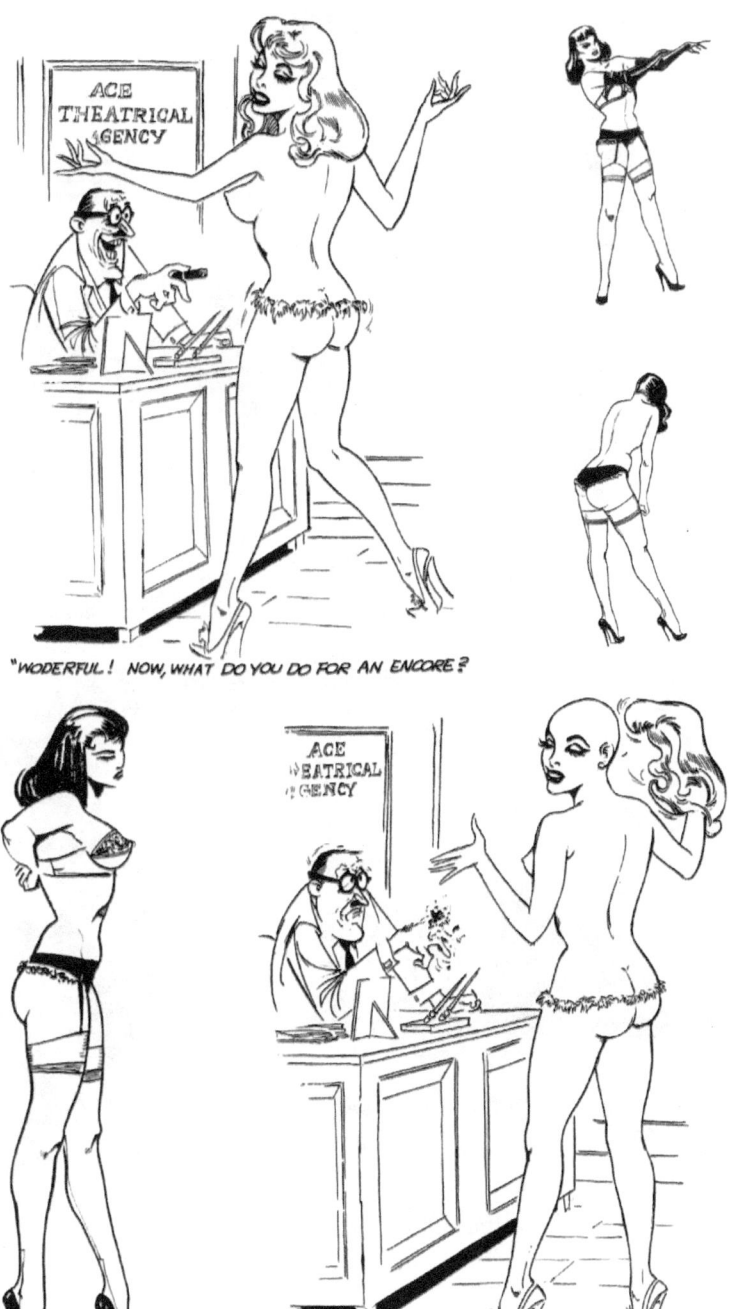

"WODERFUL! NOW, WHAT DO YOU DO FOR AN ENCORE?"

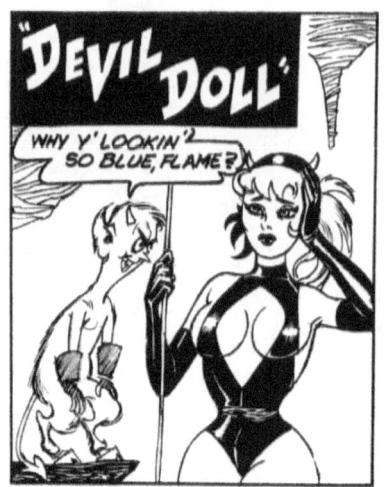
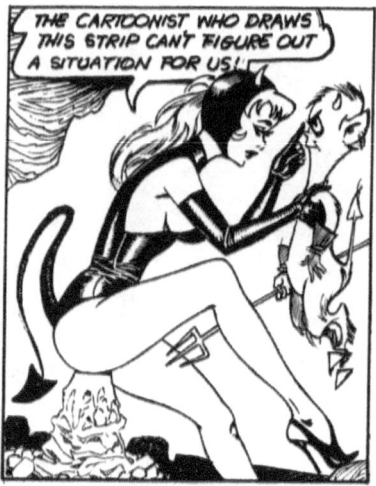
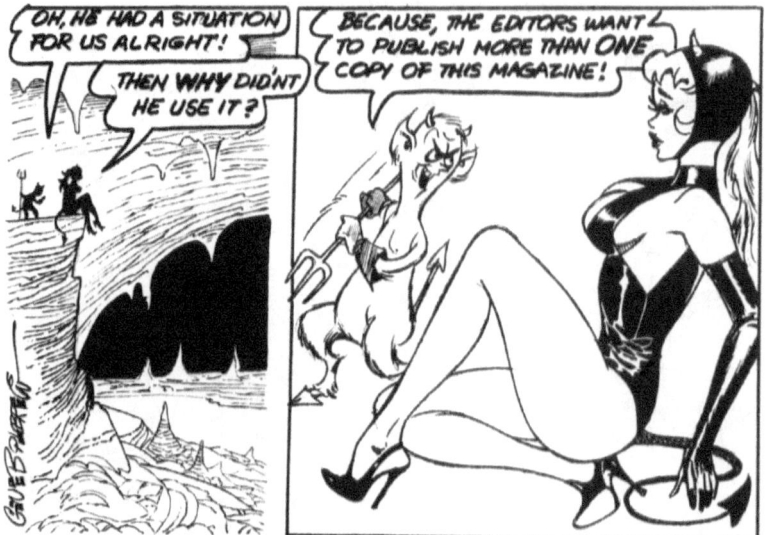

For the magazine, *Diabolique*^c

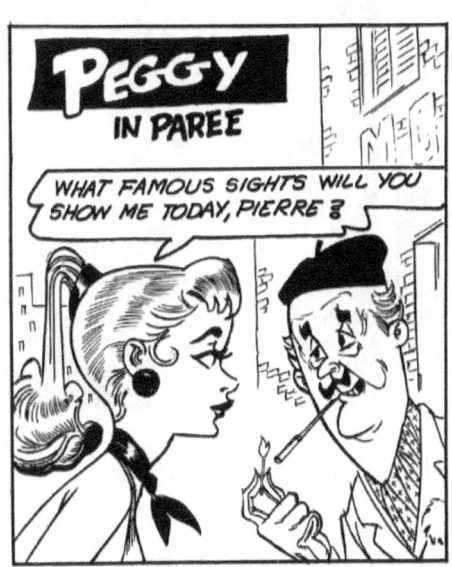
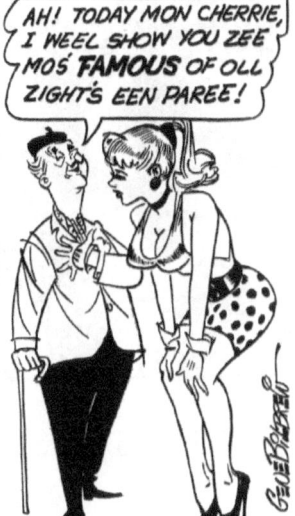
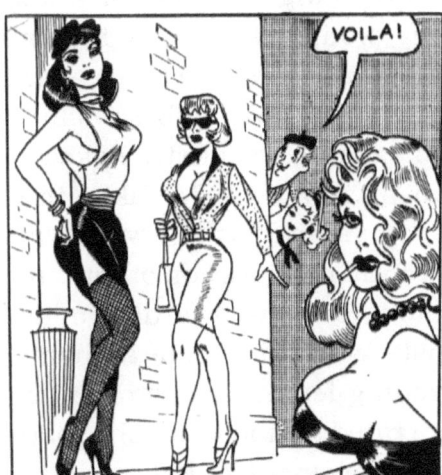
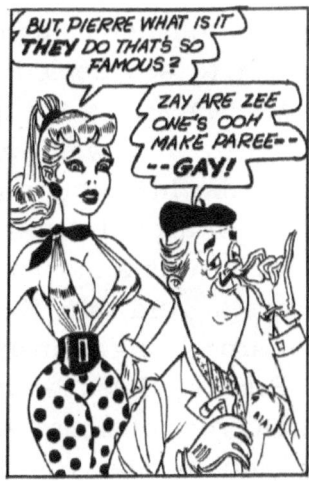

For the magazine, *Paris Taboo*

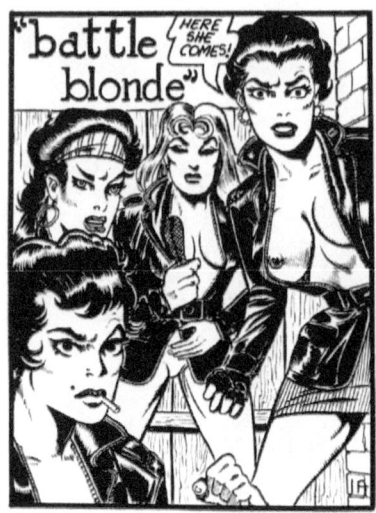
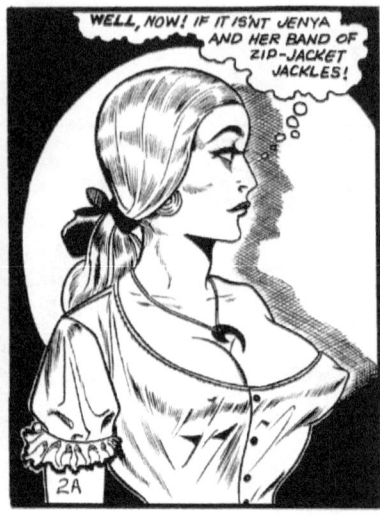

PEERLESS SALES & FIGHTING WOMEN

Did Bilbrew deal with issues of race in his comics? Rarely.[ci] It was only in producing material for a low-end publisher of fighting women fetish art that we begin to see depictions of African Americans—and not always in a flattering light. Was Bilbrew simply catering to a white audience? Very likely. Asked to describe his occupation at the 1960 Mishkin trial, Bilbrew used the term "commercial artist," well aware that he was an artist producing work for others, not himself. And, like Stanton, Bilbrew was determined to earn a living as an artist—albeit for a niche audience.

Peerless Sales, a wrestling-fetish and "strong girl" mail order business—operated by niche-fetish, sports aficionado Max Stone—supplemented its catalog of photos and female wrestling/jiu-jitsu/judo movies by selling 4-page cartoon narratives of fighting women. At first, these were primitively laid-out comics drawn

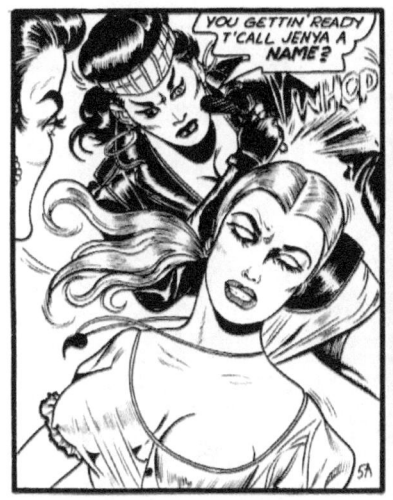
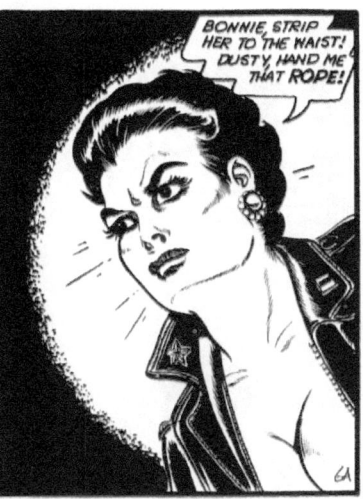

by amateur artists until Stanton came along in 1958 and essentially reinvented the subgenre.

By 1960, while Stanton and Stone wrangled over artist's wages, Stone braced himself for Stanton's potential departure by having a replacement artist waiting in the wings: Bilbrew.

Was this a source of resentment for Stanton? It was. Especially considering that Stanton believed he single-handedly elevated Stone's business.[cii] But Bilbrew's attitude was to serve up some payback to Stanton, who after all had responded to Bilbrew's complaints of censorship with Klaw by saying: "Hey, I'm just doing a job..."[ciii]

Bilbrew's first 4-pager for Stone was installment #77 (next page). Oddly, the story hinges on a white woman being attacked by a black man, who she ultimately trounces. So why the negative racial stereotype? Was it an expression of internalized racism, or hostility toward Caucasian women—or was Bilbrew just goofing around?

191

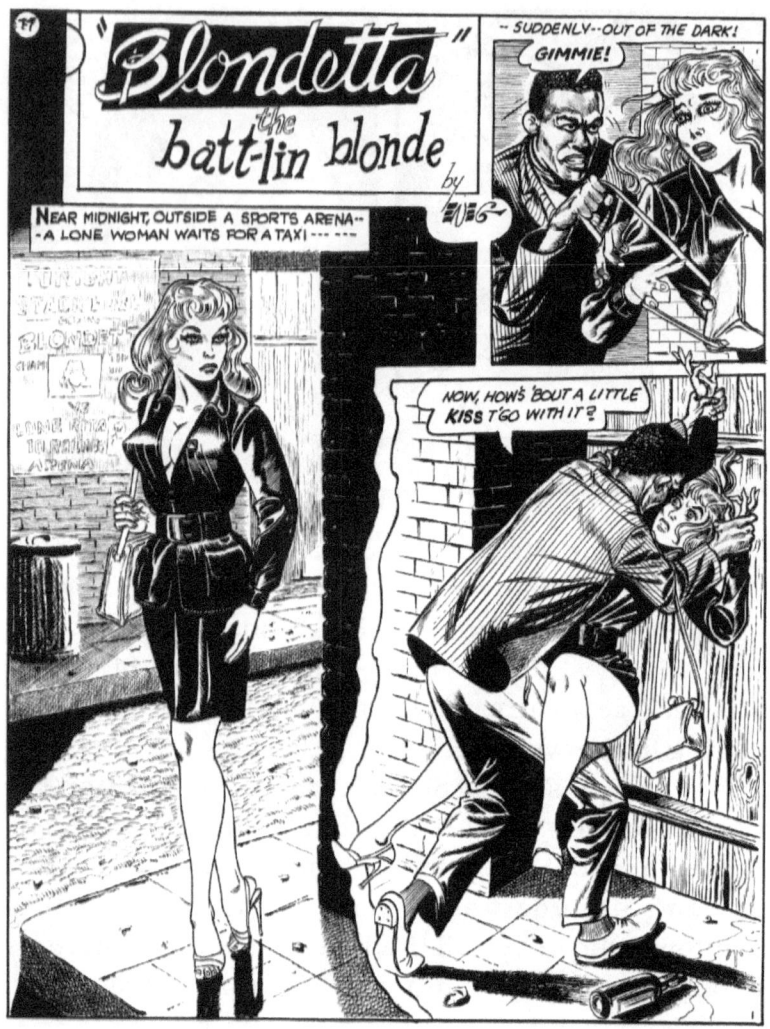

Stanton suggested racial self-loathing on the part of Bilbrew when he stated, "Eneg was a white man in black. He wished he was white..."[civ] But here again, was Stanton expressing his own hostility toward his strongest competitor and sometimes rival? According to publisher J.B. Rund, who knew Stanton intimately for over twenty years: "Bilbrew went so far as to call

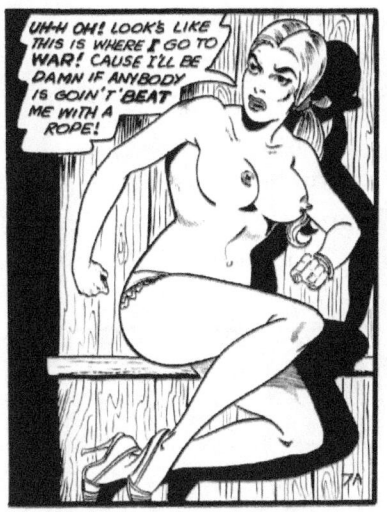
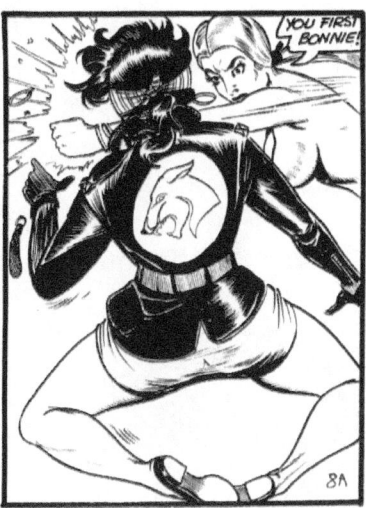

Eric racist, which he wasn't." Was it more a matter of two sensitive, contending artists swept up in petty jealousy? There's no question that Bilbrew and Stanton also kept a close eye on each other's artistic progress and played off each other creatively.

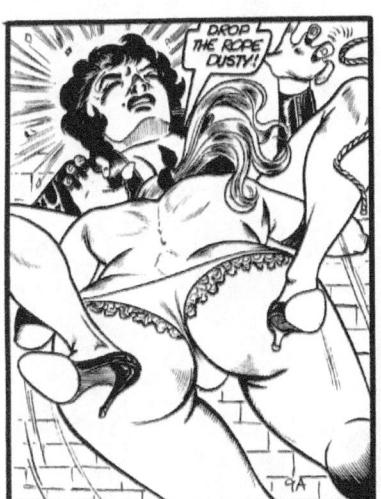
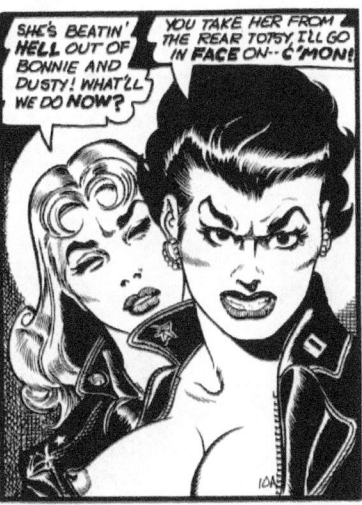

"Battle Blonde," one of 66 cartoon narratives for Peerless Sales

As far as the fighting women comics produced for Max Stone, is it a mistake to read too deeply into them? Essentially, most are sexploitation forays into slapstick comedy, where everyone takes a beating.

Among Eneg's greatest hits for Peerless Sales were: "Maid From Mars," "Battle Blonde," "Foul Fowl Feud," "Lydia," "The Fighters," and "The Husband Beater."

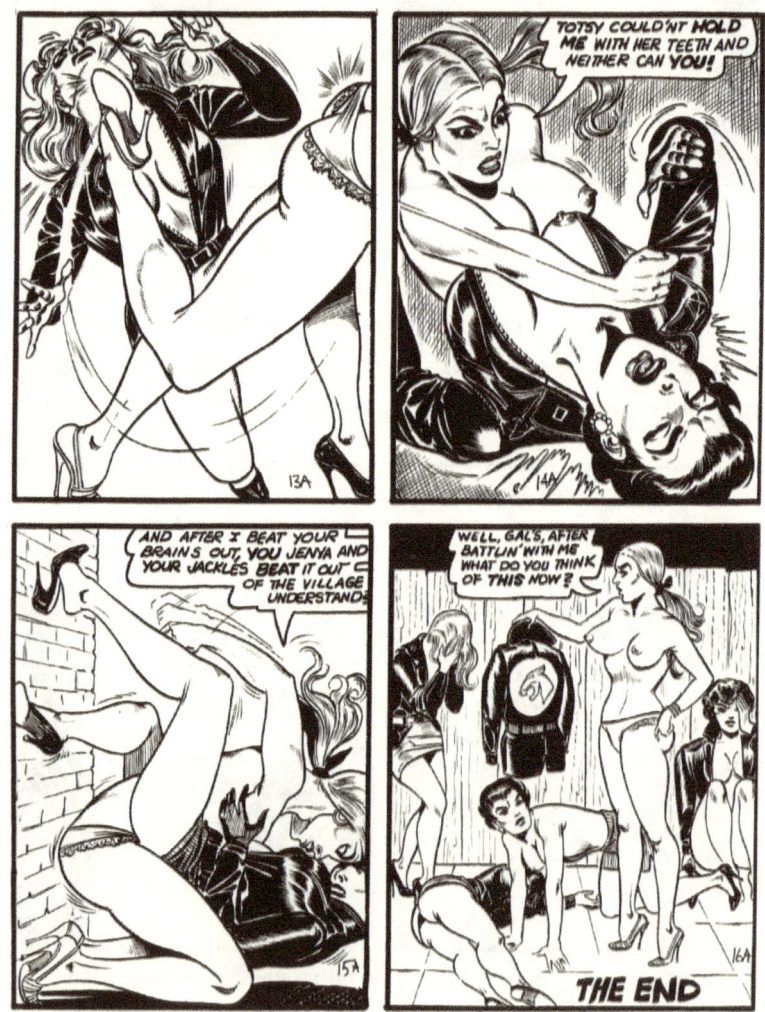

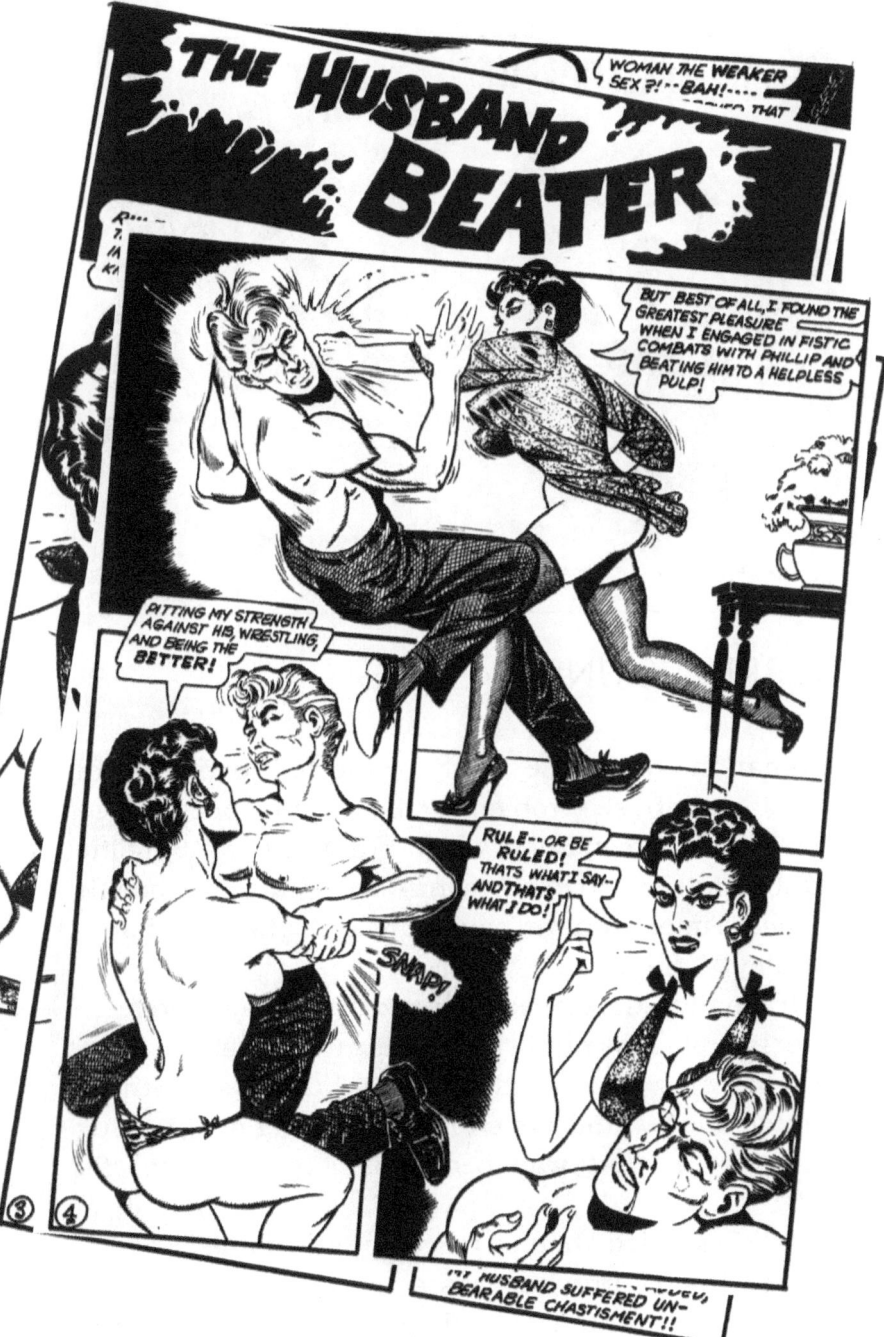

For Max Stone, Peerless Sales cartoon #129

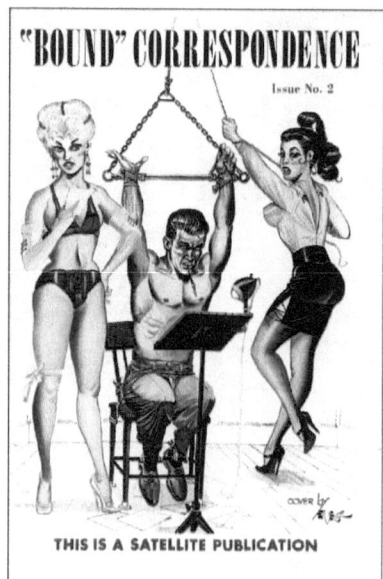

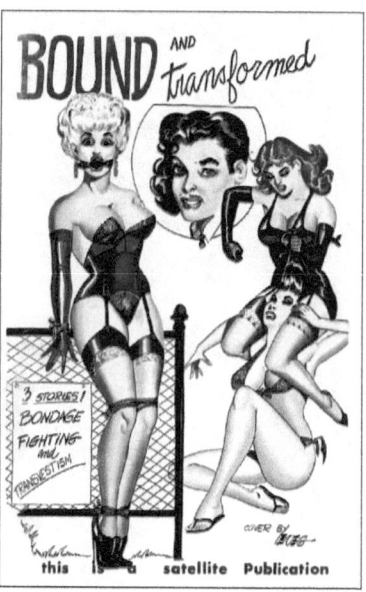

BILBREW'S UNRAVELING

Intimations of decline, likely connected to persistent substance abuse problems,[cv] began to appear circa 1962 in Bilbrew/Eneg work produced for Satellite Publishing Co., an entity controlled by another bookie turned Times Square bookstore operator/publisher, Stanley Malkin.

Originally, Malkin had tapped Stanton as creative director of his publishing venture (Stanton later insisted that he signed on as a business partner), though they would have an early falling out, leaving Bilbrew—in what was becoming a pattern—to "fill in."[cvi]

Malkin's fetish-themed magazine was named *Bound*, and early on—in what was a unique occurrence—Bilbrew and Stanton teamed up on several covers, both signing the artwork. The most telling collaboration, illustrating their prickly, competitive relationship, appeared on issue #1 (1961).

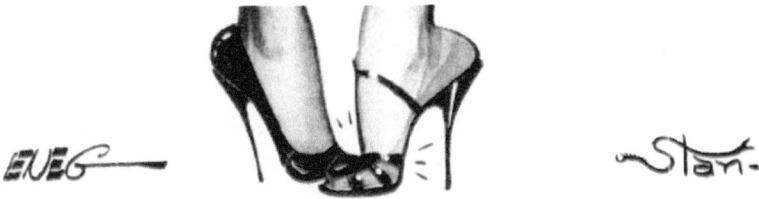

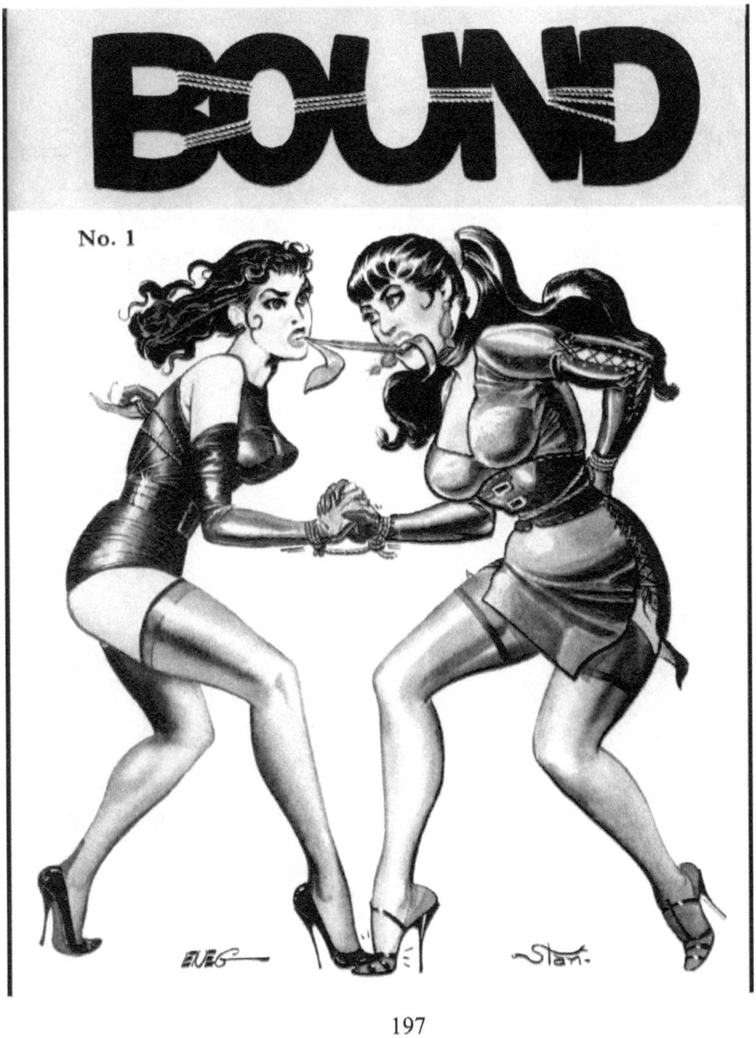

Not all the art Bilbrew produced for Satellite was poor or careless, and—to be objective—there was always some inconsistency in work Bilbrew produced for others. Even at his height—with Leonard Burtman, Edward Mishkin, and Irving Klaw—his artwork could run from brilliant to inept. Take, for example, the serial *Captain Kidnapp, Lady Pirate*, produced for Klaw in 1955. Compare a panel from episode/page 6 (below) with one from episode/page 3:

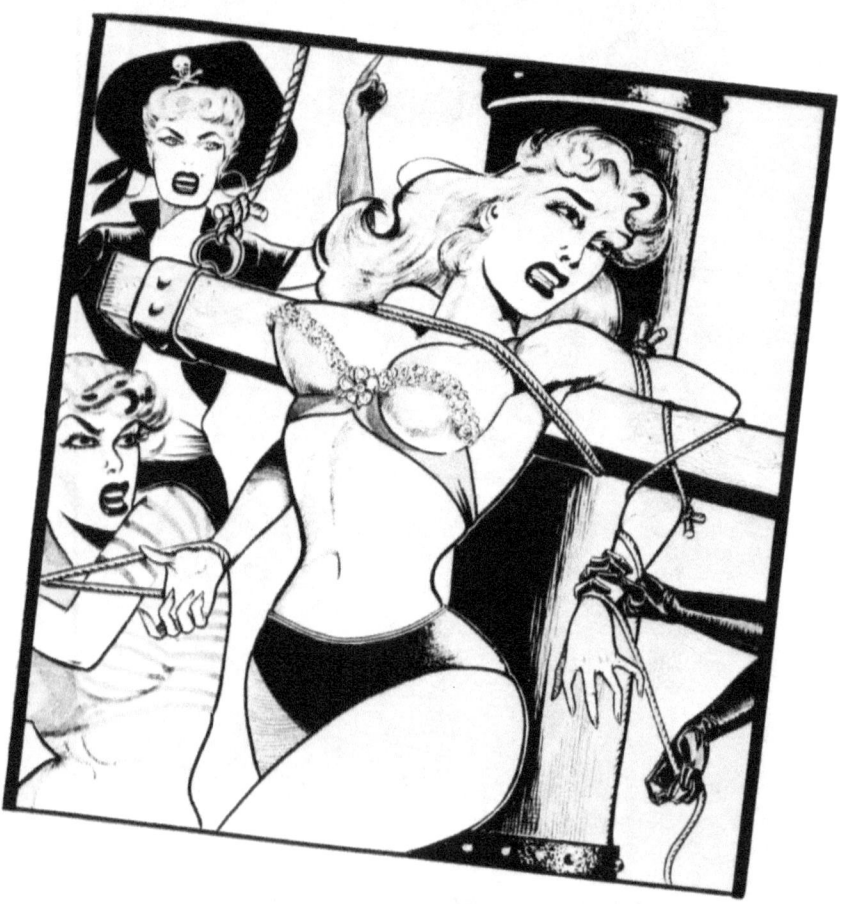

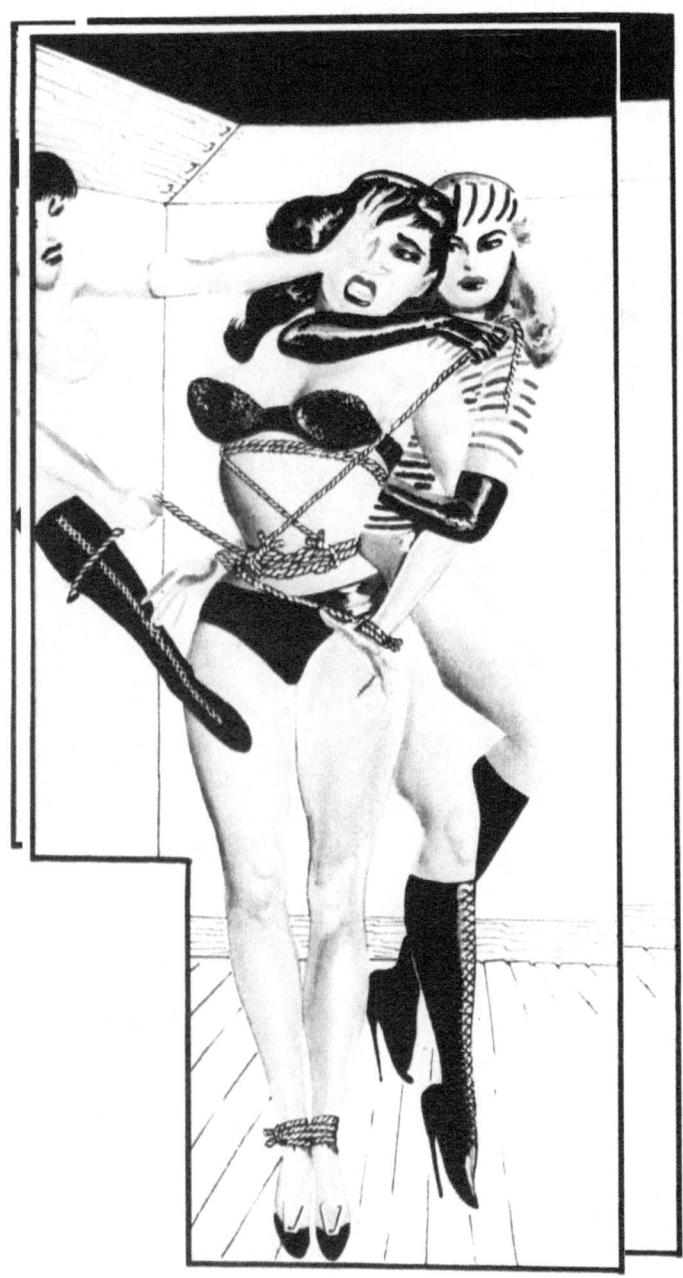

Kidnapp, Lady Pirate panel, page 3

Did Bilbrew pick up his partying habits in his days with the Basin Street Boys—or was it something he indulged in later? We don't know. But alcohol and later drugs played a big part in his life. As the 1960s progressed, this was more and more the case.

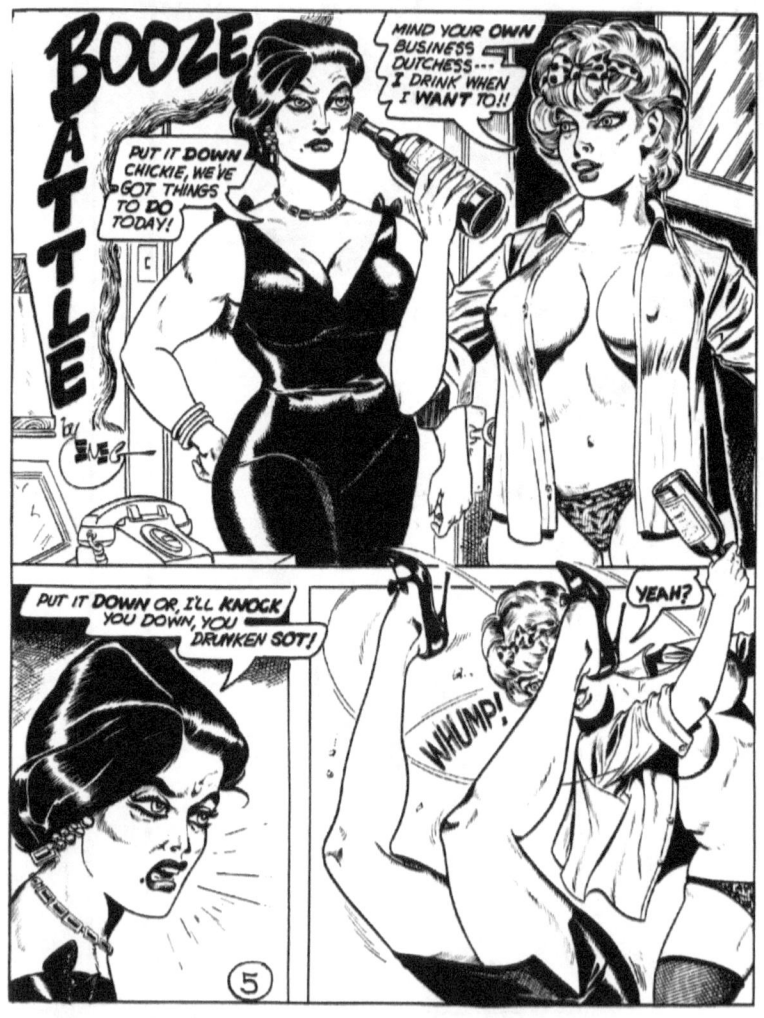

Bilbrew's final comic for Peerless Sales (cartoon #251)

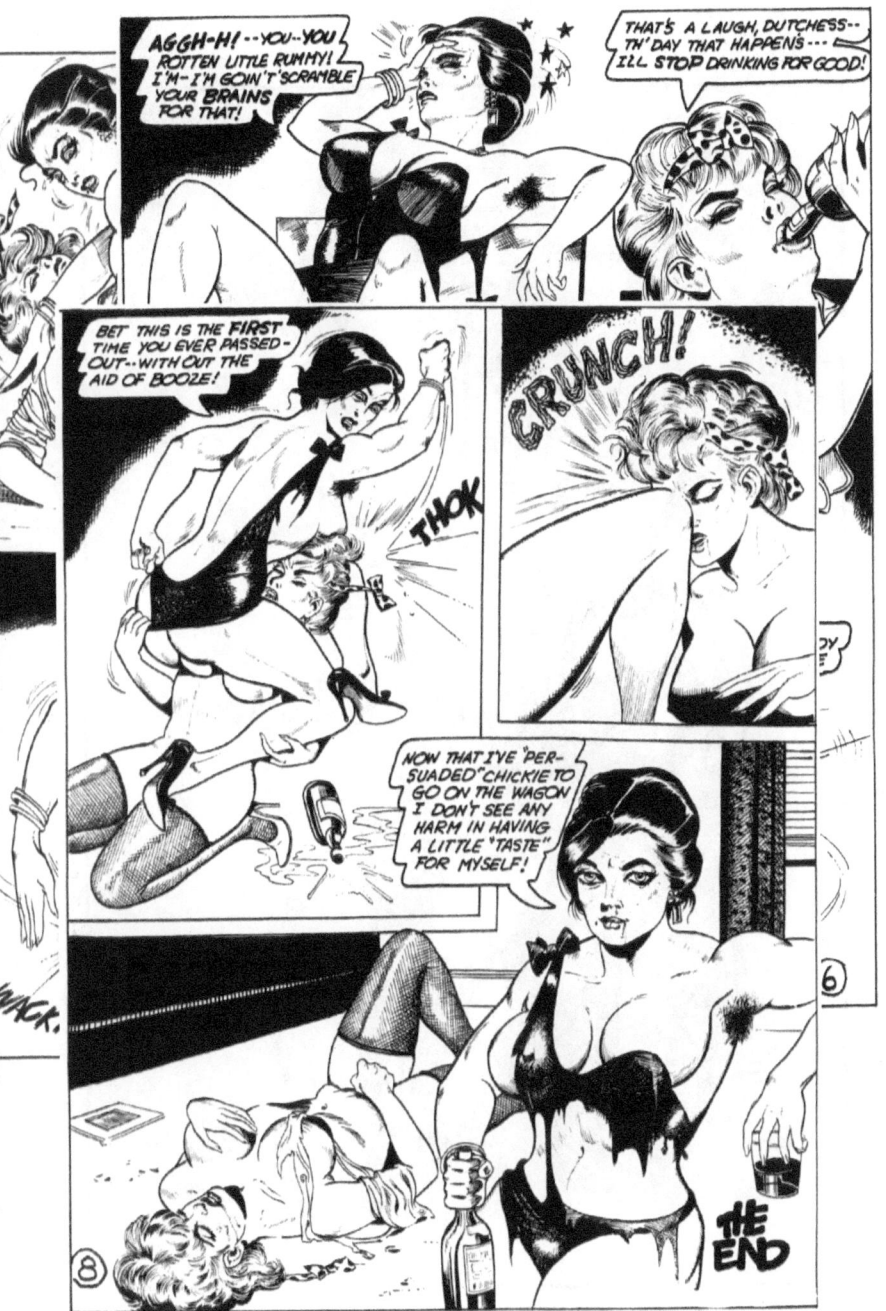

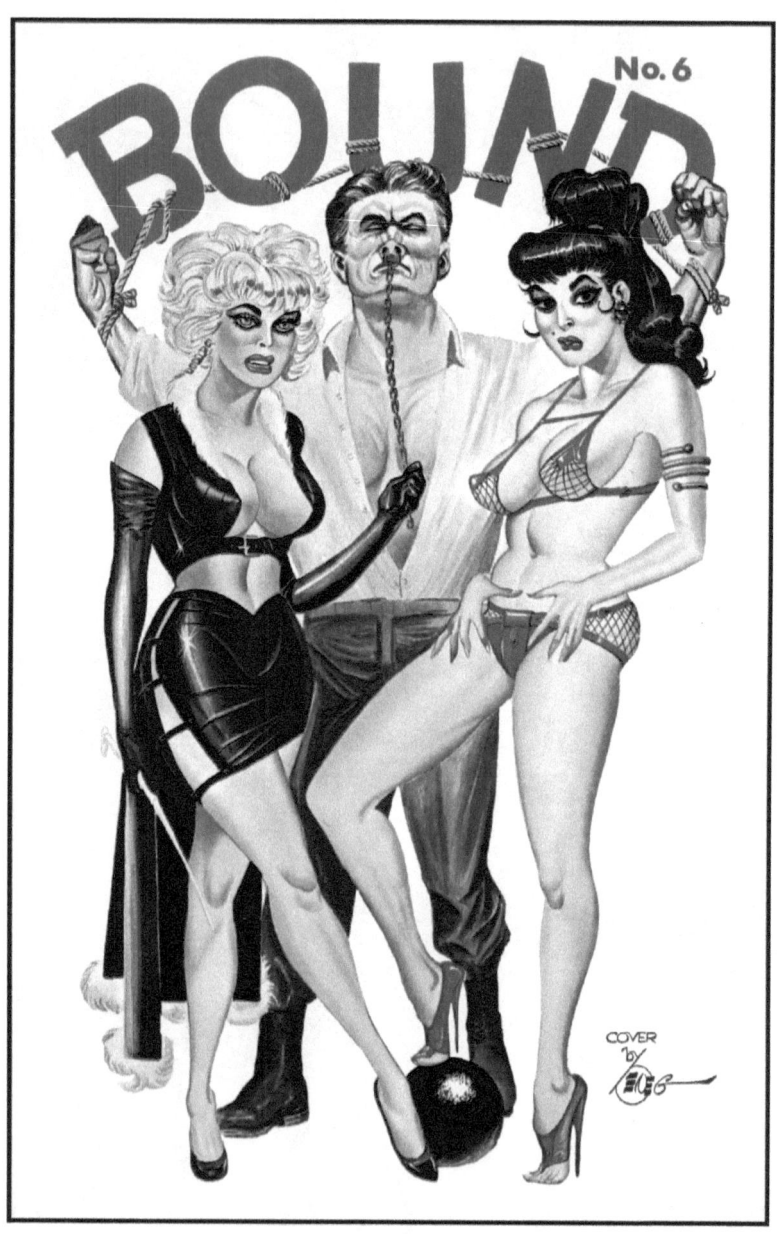

For Malkin's Satellite Publishing Co. (1962), one of his best

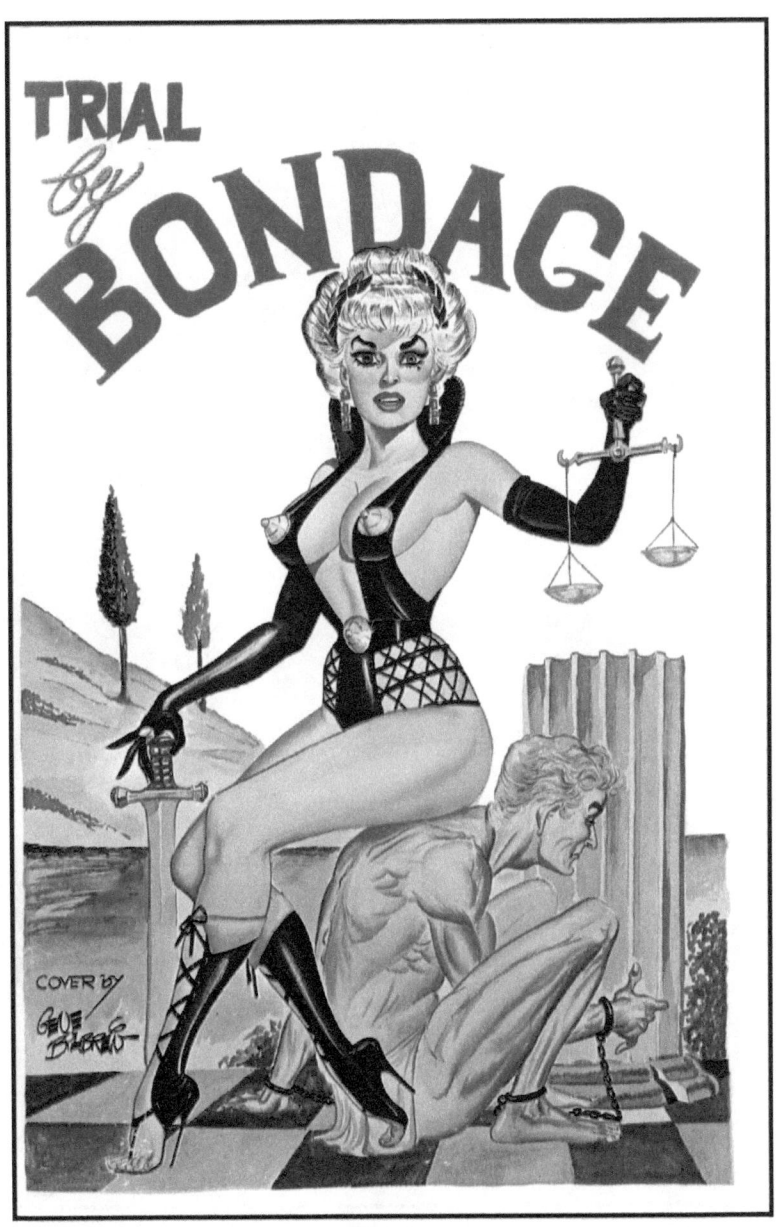

For Malkin (1962), one of his best

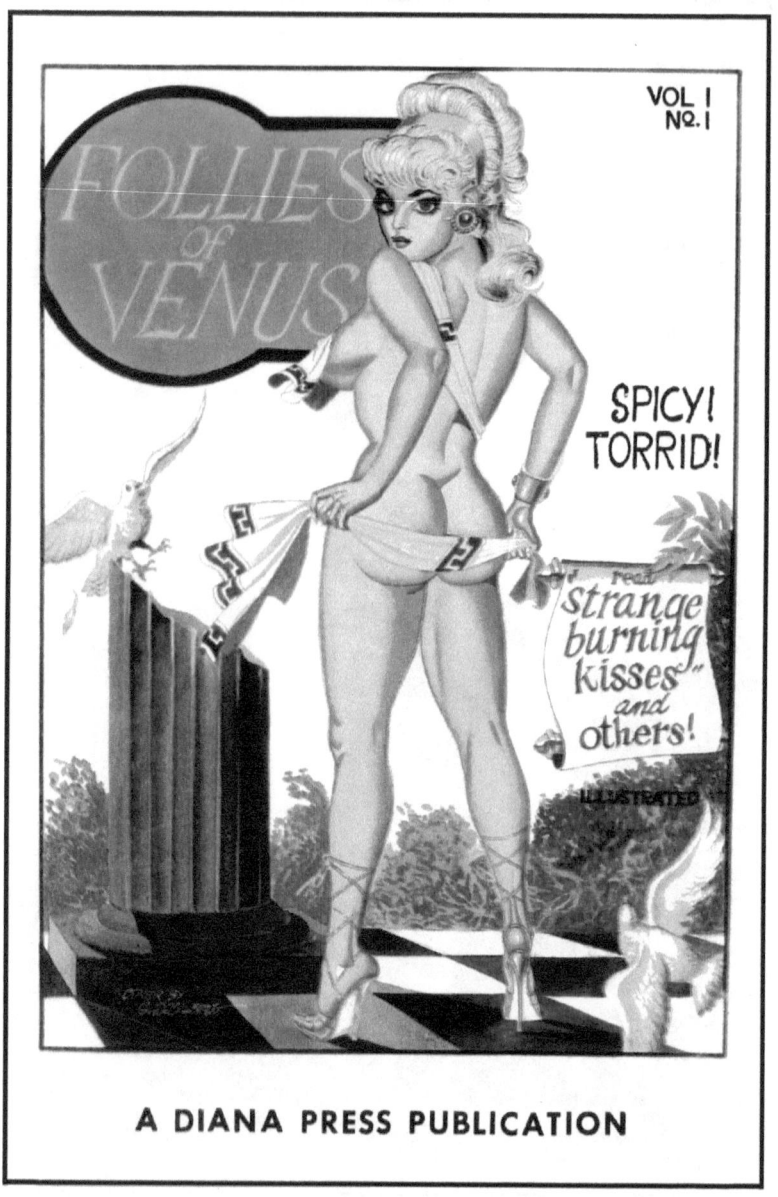

For Malkin (1962). "Diana Press" was an alternate imprint.

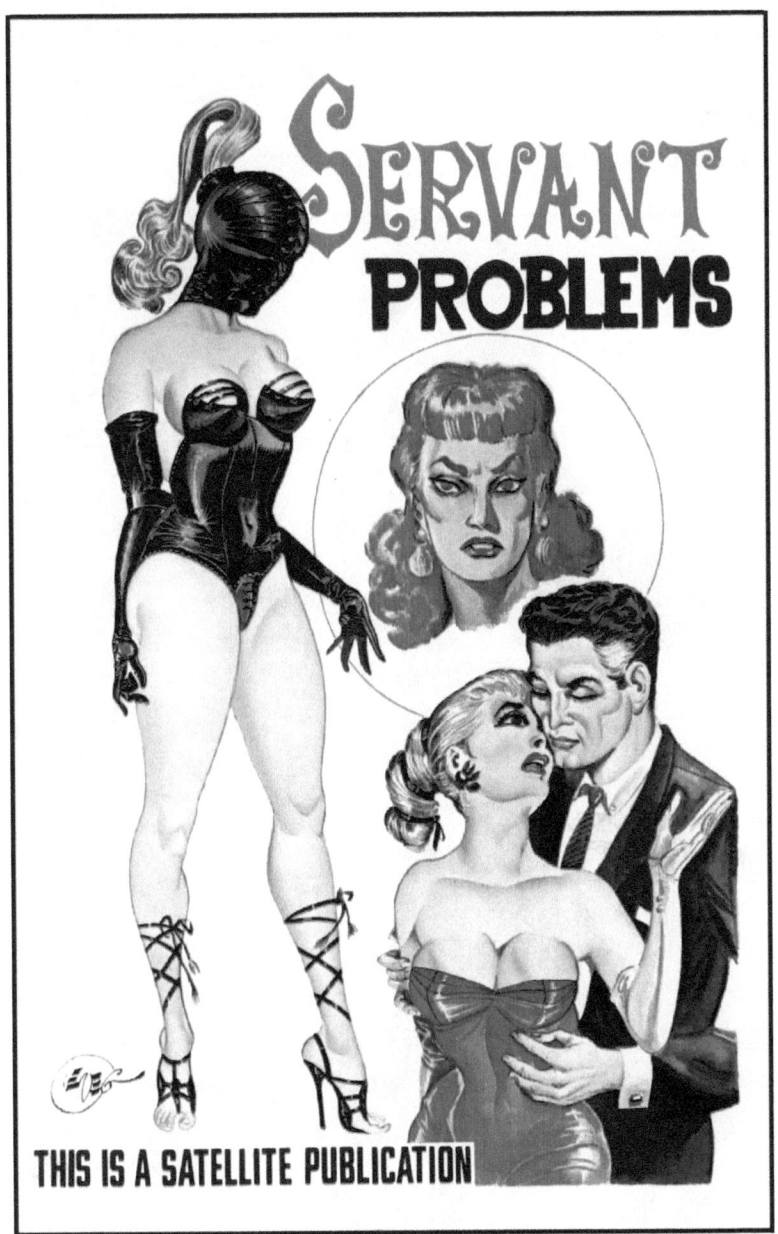

For Malkin (1962), one of his better efforts

As illustrated, even with Satellite Publishing Co., there are attention-grabbing examples of Bilbrew art. At his best with Malkin, his work has a subversive sideshow appeal; at his worst, we have the excessive rigidity or unnaturalness of his posed figures, which to some extent always characterized Bilbrew's style.

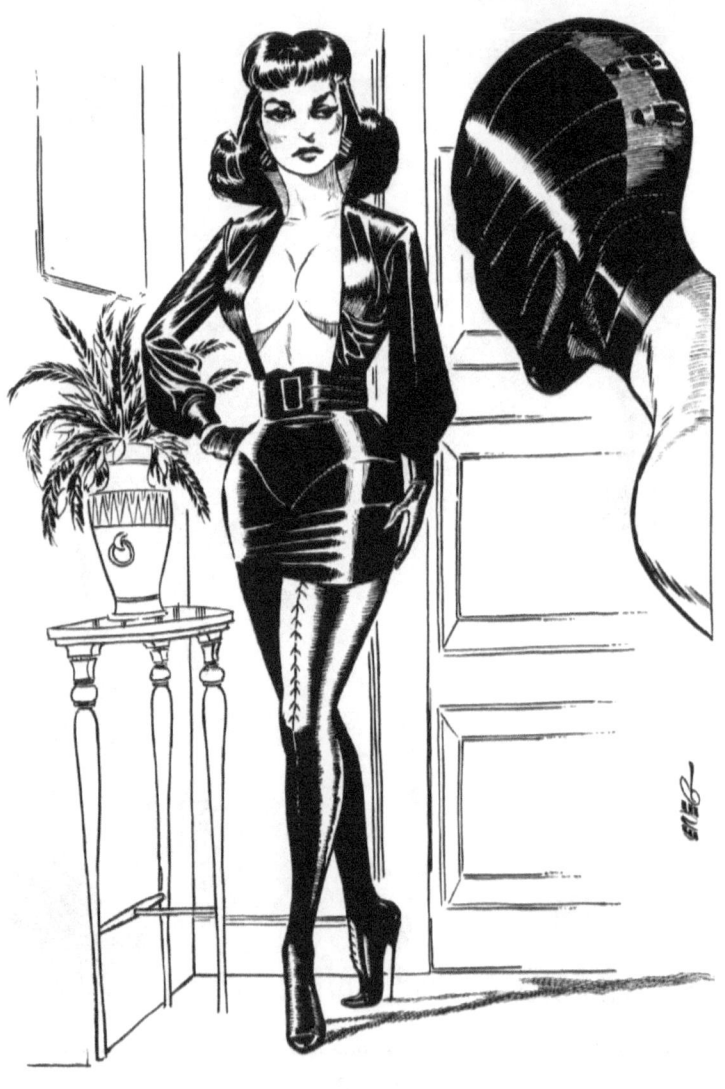

To understand how naturally gifted Bilbrew was, he produced what's generally regarded as his greatest work, *Island of Captive Girls* (see pages 54-59) only three years after switching careers.[cvii] (*Prison for Women,* produced in 1952, is also exceptional.)

In 1953, it may be of no surprise that Stanton stepped up his game, producing his first great work, *Duchess of the Bastille* and finally his masterpiece for Klaw, *Bound In Leather.*

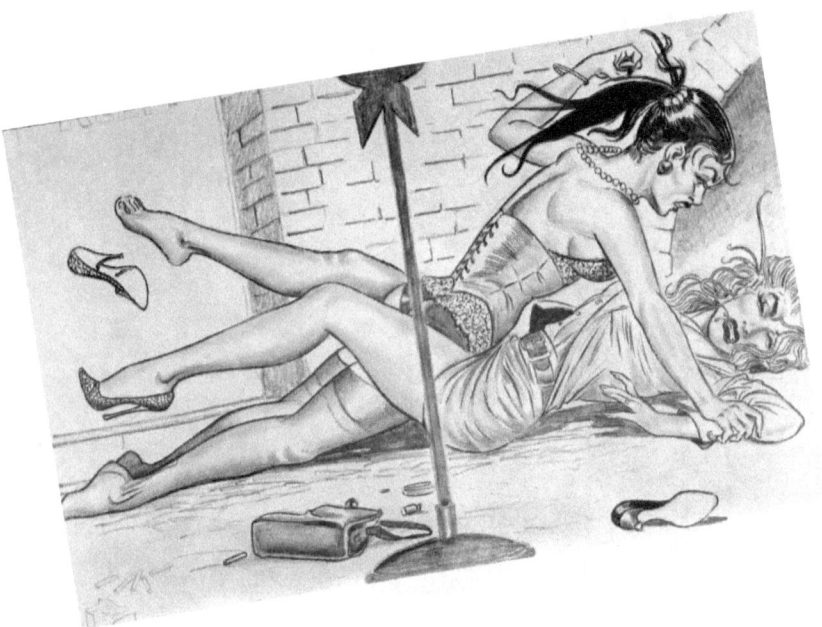

Circa 1961, Bilbrew began to produce graphite illustrations for Satellite Publishing Co. Is it a coincidence that Stanton also switched to pencil/charcoal that year when he had previously relied on the technique of wash to achieve depth and tone in his illustrations?

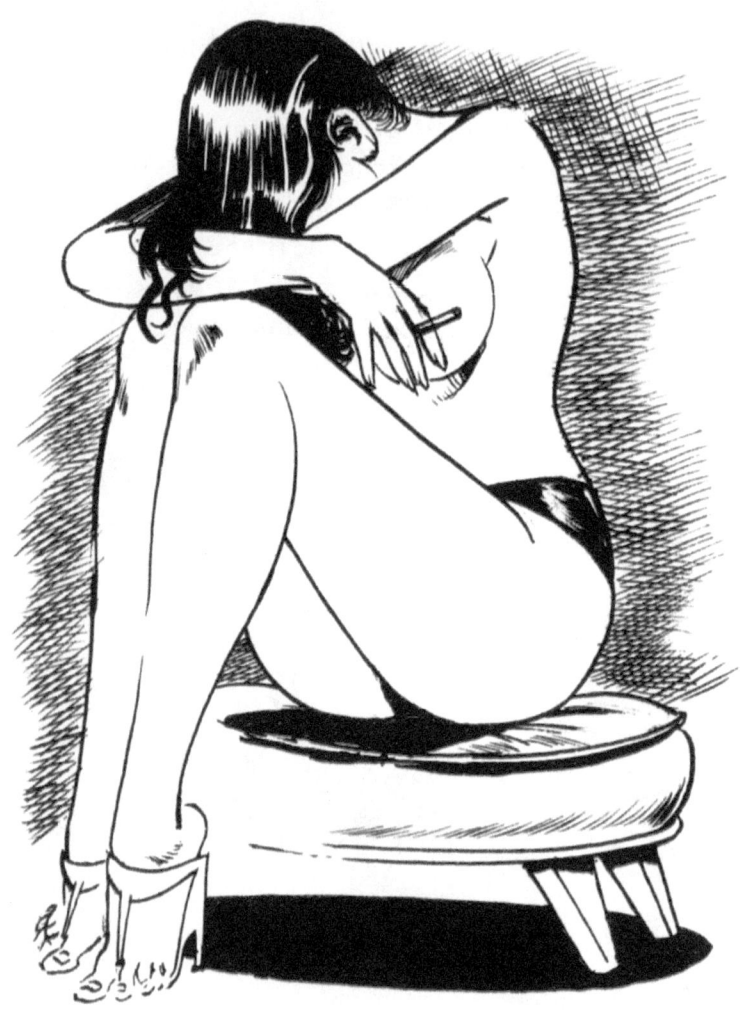

In 1962, following his split from Satellite, Stanton upended Bilbrew's position with Leonard Burtman at a time when Bilbrew seemed unchallenged as art director for Burtman's line of full-sized magazines. Why Burtman made the switch from Bilbrew—the artist who, after all, had been at his side since 1955—to Stanton remains unknown, although we can speculate that it may have been a question of Bilbrew's deteriorating professionalism. The official change of art director was noted in magazine mastheads, which went from "G. Bilbrew" in 1961 to "E. Stanton" in '62. [cviii]

To compound matters, in 1963 Stanton clearly surpassed Bilbrew technically as an artist, while previously the two had been neck-in-neck, playing out their destiny as the Lennon and McCartney of bizarre art. Stanton's high-level work for Burtman's peripheral digest-sized publications, in particular, must have thrown Bilbrew for a loop.

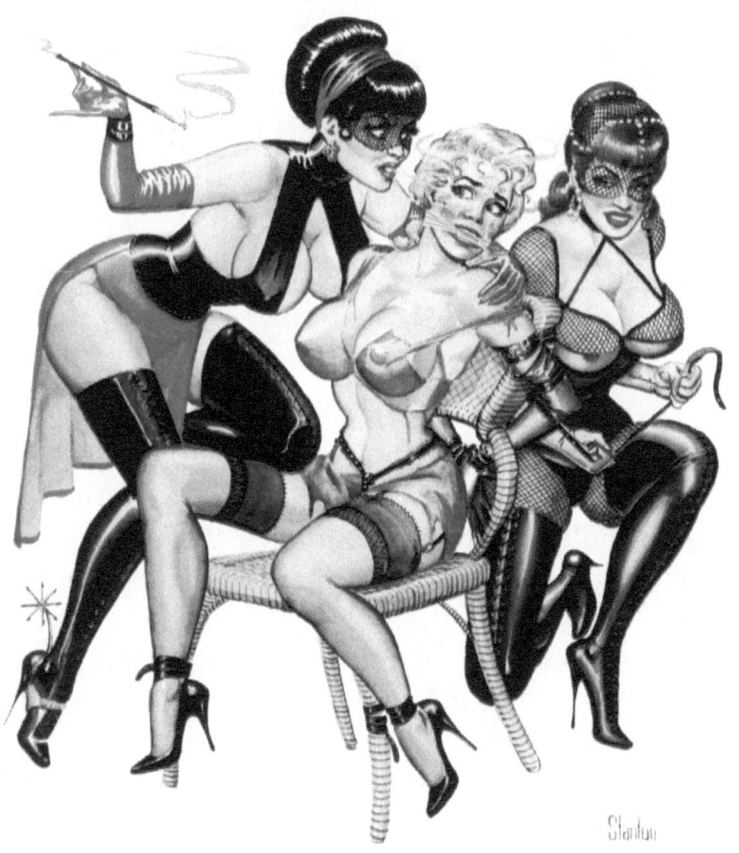

Stanton art in 1963

If Bilbrew was graced with more God-given talent, as he evidently was, then how did this bastard—Stanton—manage to outstrip him even while Stanton suffered from substance abuse problems of his own?

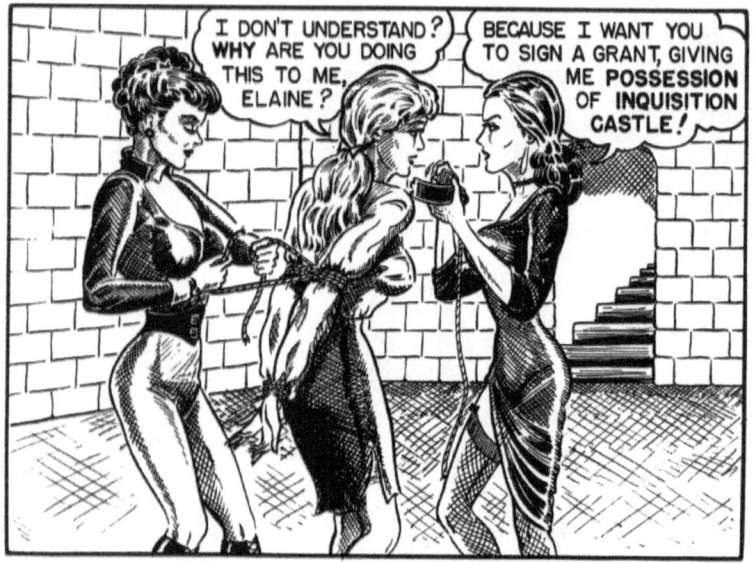

Stanton art in 1951, when he met Bilbrew

More uncertainty followed that same year as Stanley Malkin launched his new line of sexploitation paperback imprints and hired Stanton and Bilbrew as cover artists. Here again, there were indications that Bilbrew was personally struggling. Bilbrew's line—the Nitey-Nite imprint—was discontinued after four books while Stanton's line, First Niter, took off.

Hinting at greater difficulties, in '64 Bilbrew appears to have abandoned the bizarre art scene altogether, producing virtually no work—only to resurface a full year later, in '65, with various sexploitation imprints attributed to the Sturman brothers (Joe and brother Reuben, future porn czar of America), based in Ohio.[cix]

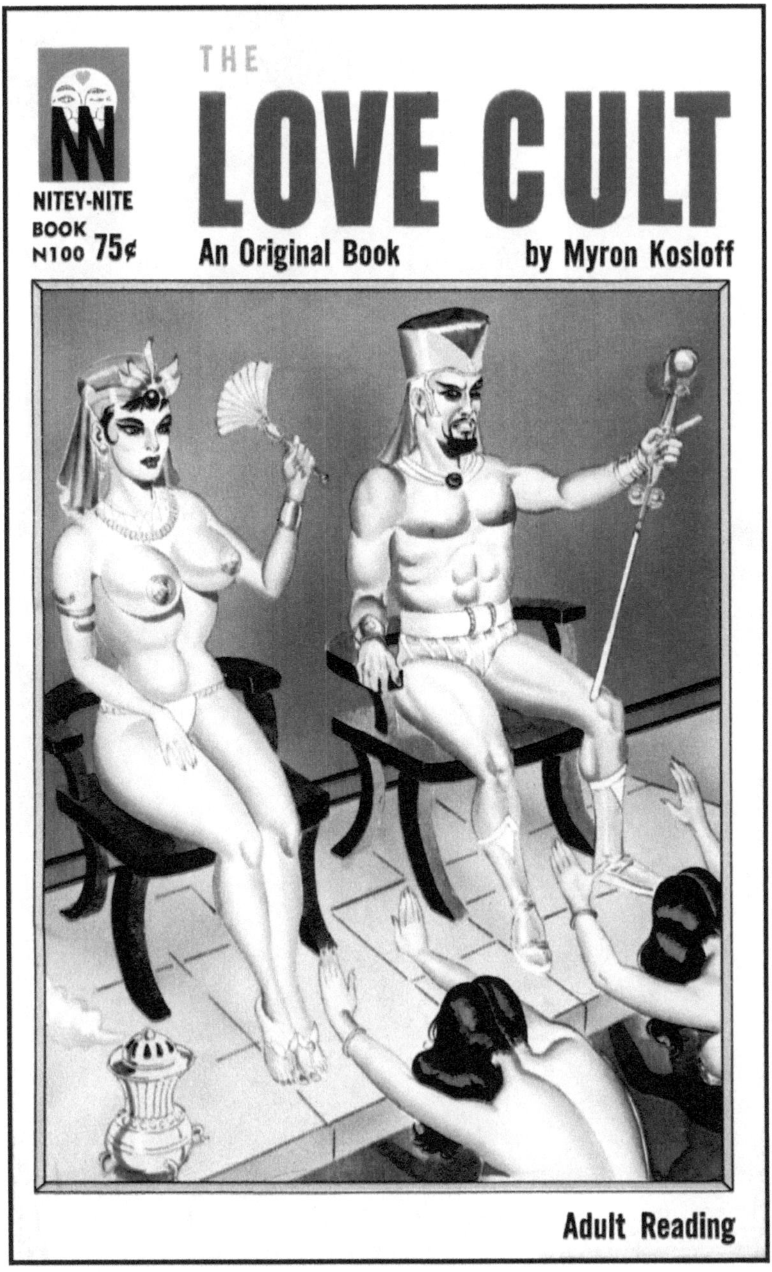

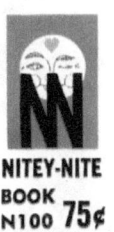

THE
LOVE CULT

NITEY-NITE
BOOK
N100 75¢

An Original Book

by Myron Kosloff

Adult Reading

The first of Bilbrew's ill-fated Nitey-Nite books

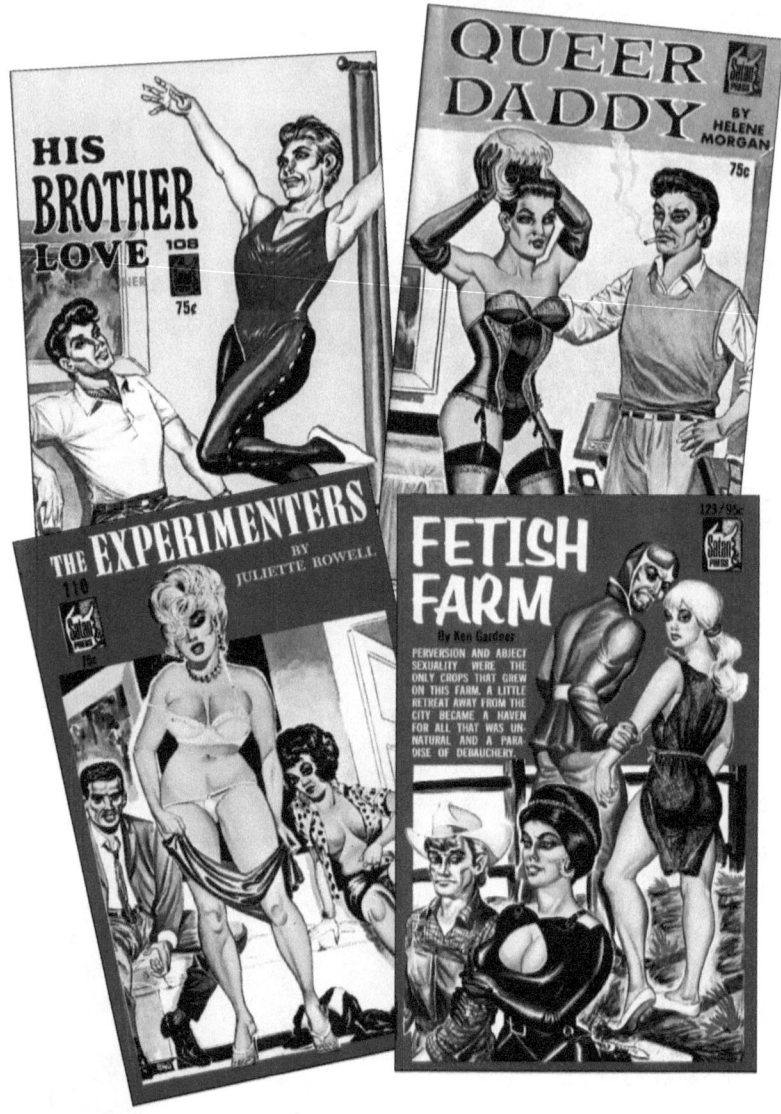

At this point, with rare exceptions, Bilbrew's once elegant fetish art devolved into what's today affectionately categorized as "vintage sleaze," and the material Bilbrew produced for Sturman's Satan Press line, among others, was the pinnacle of that.

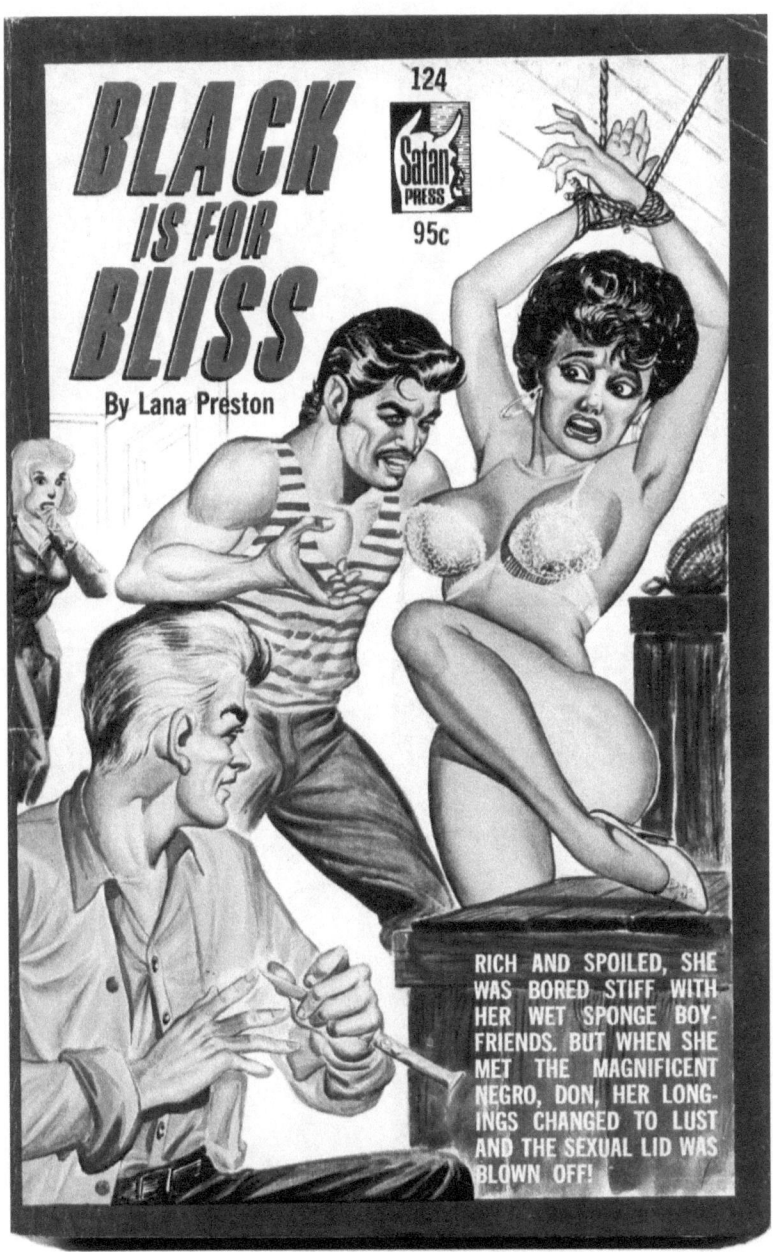

For the Sturman brothers (1966)

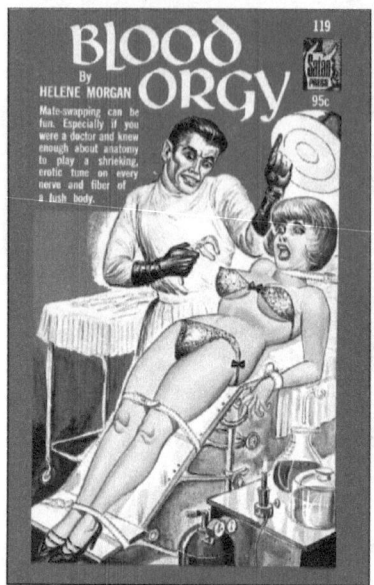

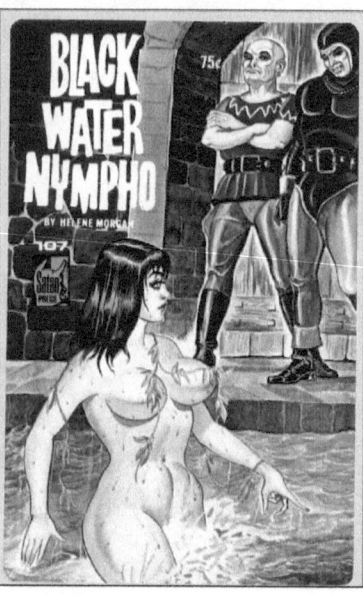

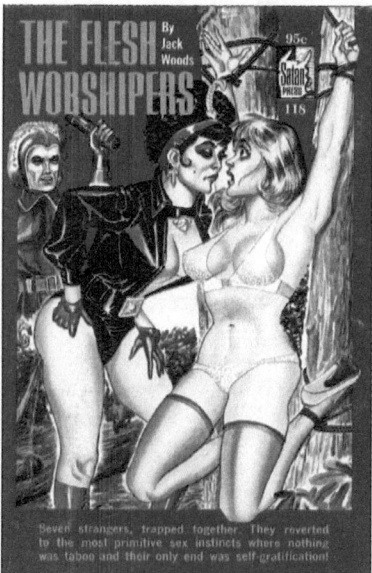

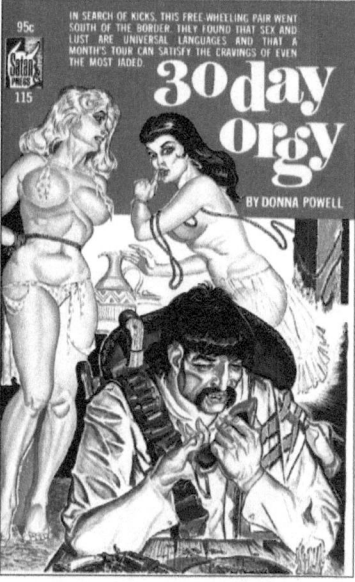

Bilbrew illustrated the full line of Satan Press books—all 26

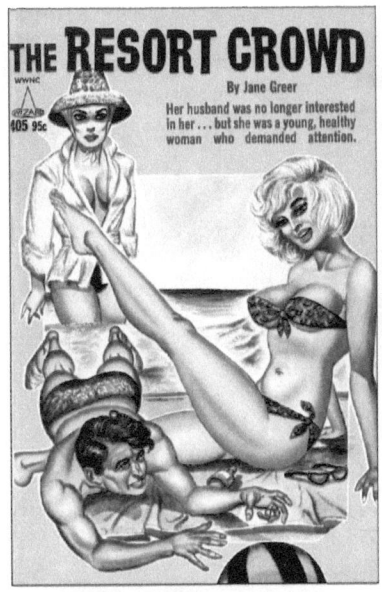
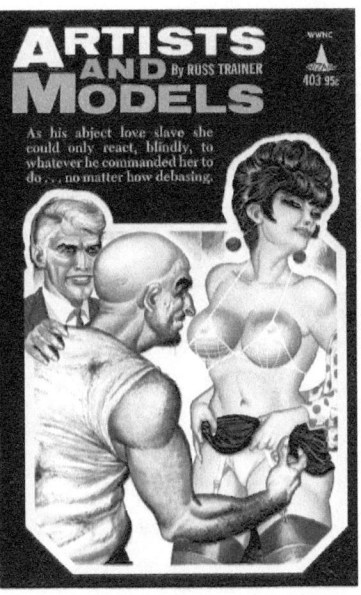
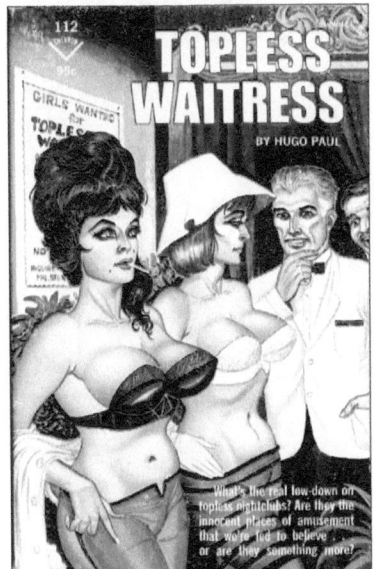
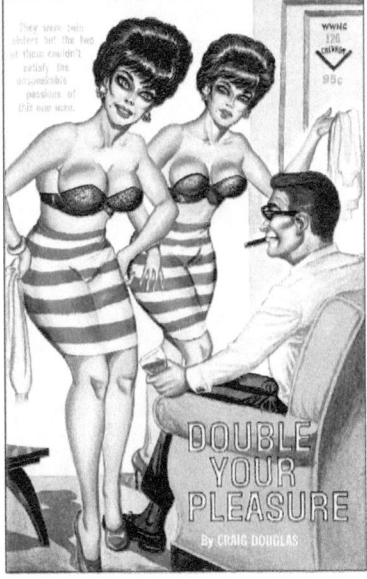

Other Sturman imprints included Crescent, Mercury, Chevron, Corsair, Wizard; Bilbrew contributed to all of them.

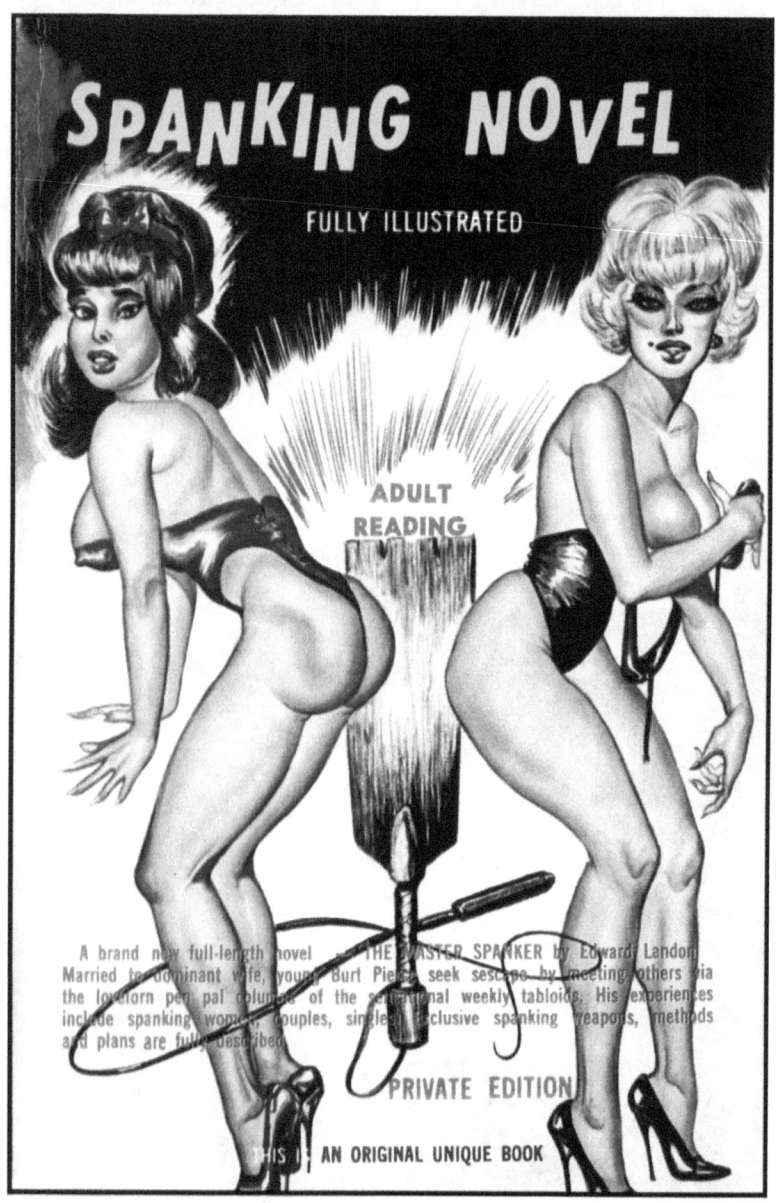

For Stanley Malkin (1966)

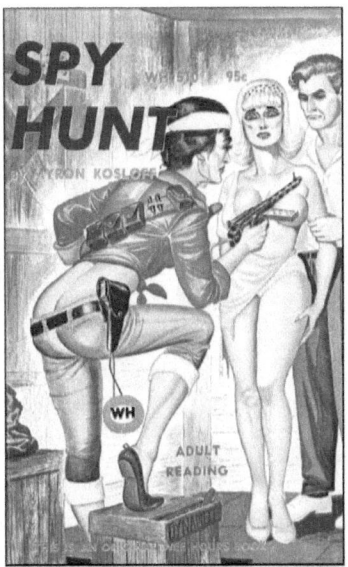
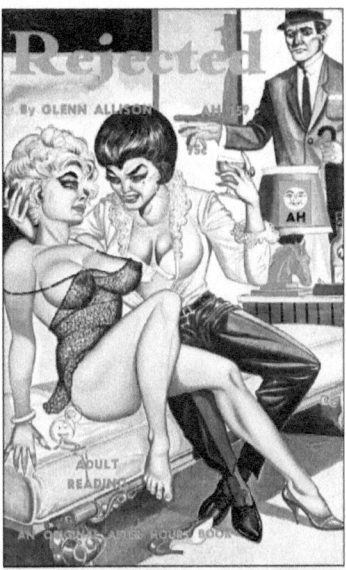
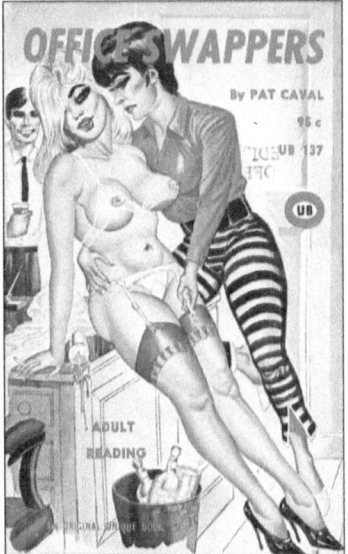
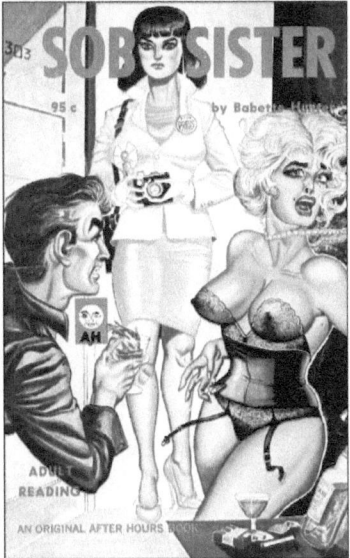

Bilbrew returned to work for Malkin[cx] and Burtman, contributing artwork here and there, but things would never be the same.

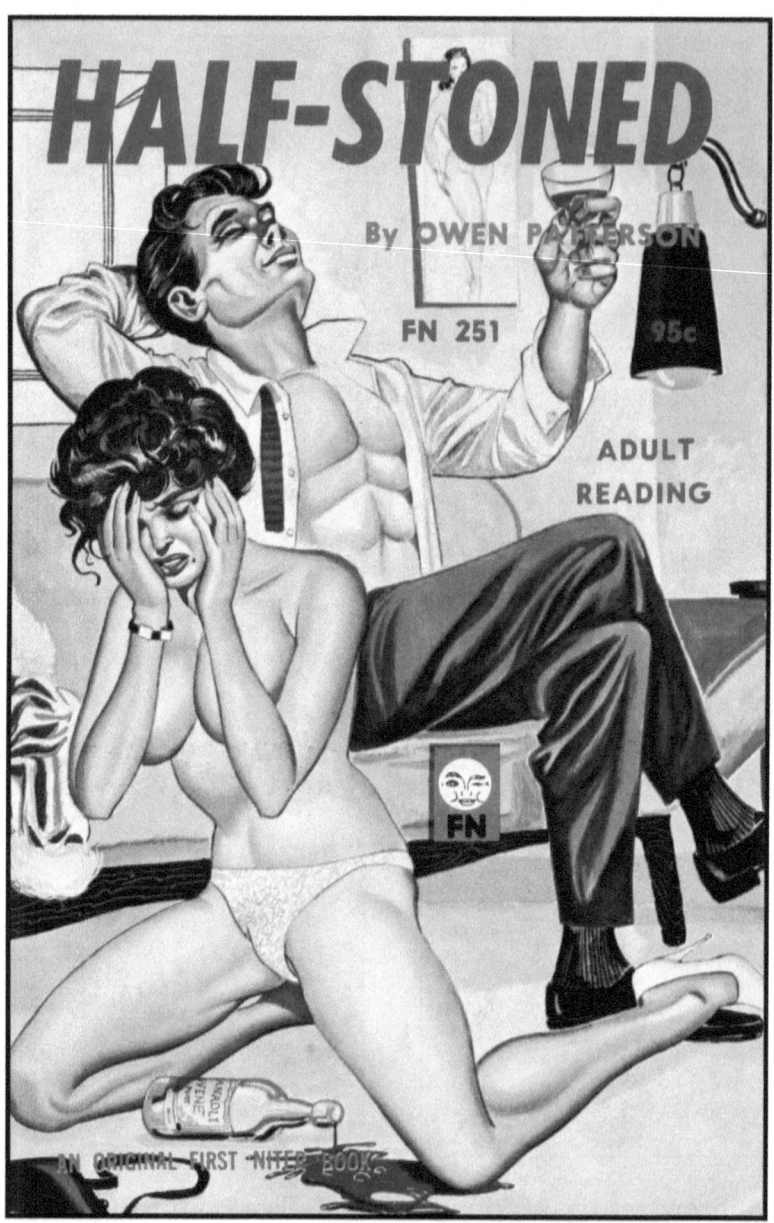

For Malkin (1967)

BILBREW

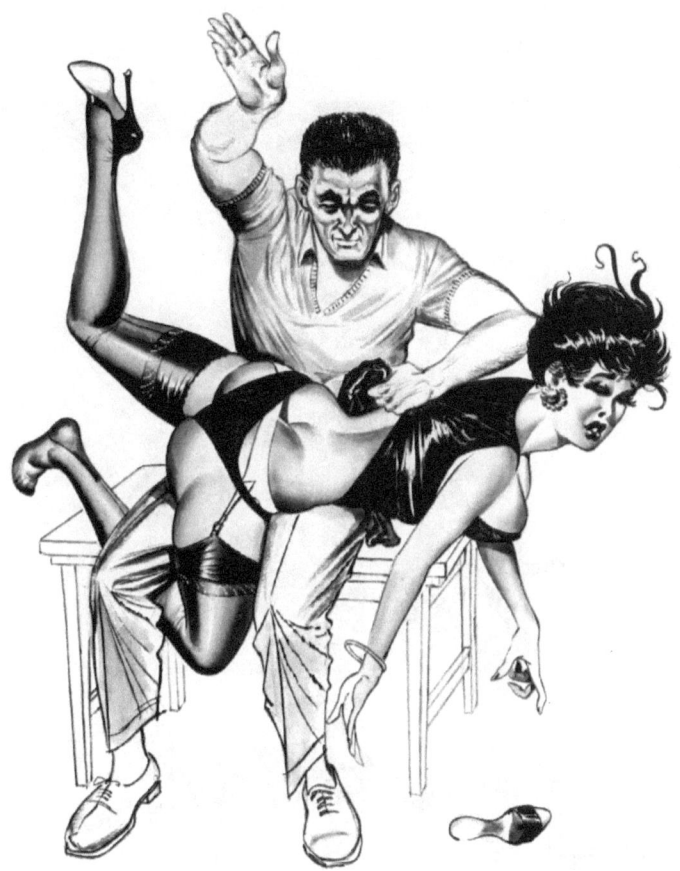

SLEAZE

There are those, of course, who might argue that the so-called "sleaze" element in Bilbrew's work was there from the beginning. And they could be right. The material Bilbrew produced under the alias Van Rod, in particular, may have crossed the line—and this dates back to the mid-1950s—even showing Bilbrew's fondness for the grotesque.

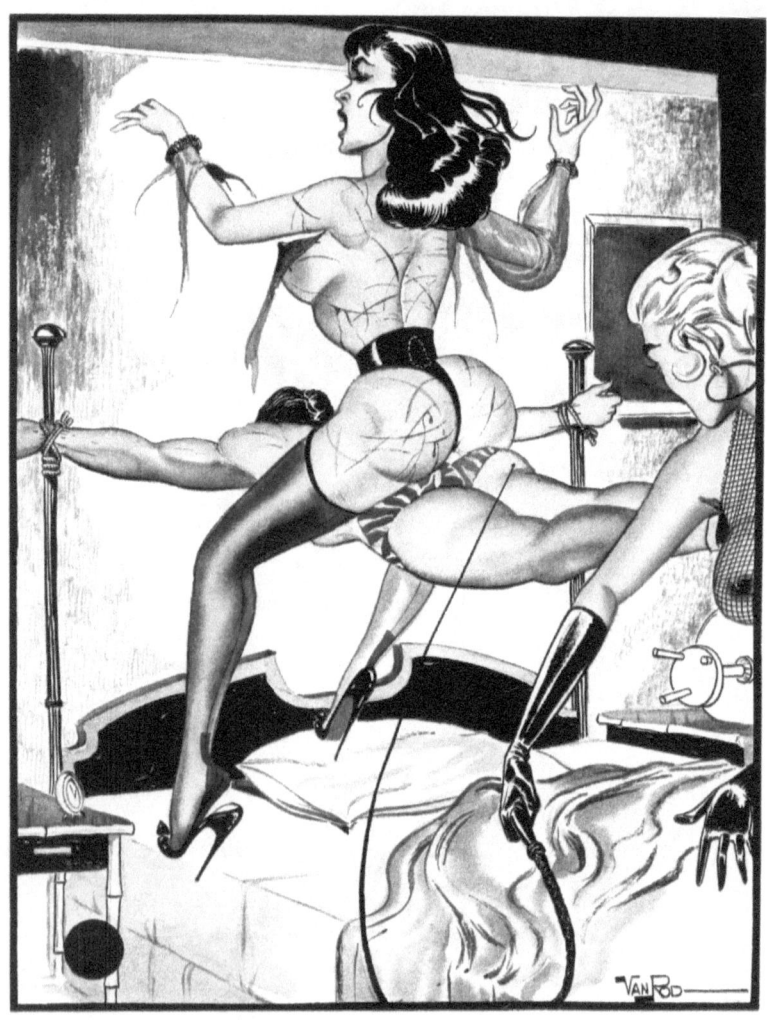

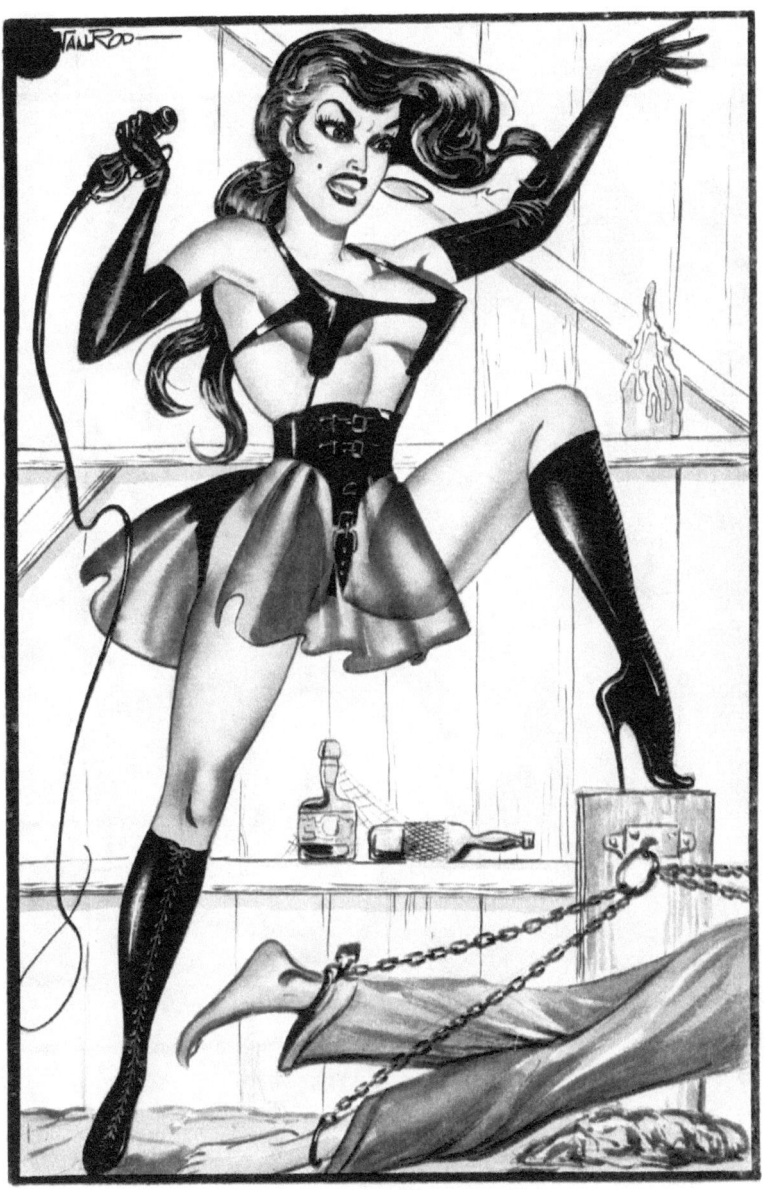

Bilbrew's proto-punk, anarchic spirit as Van Rod

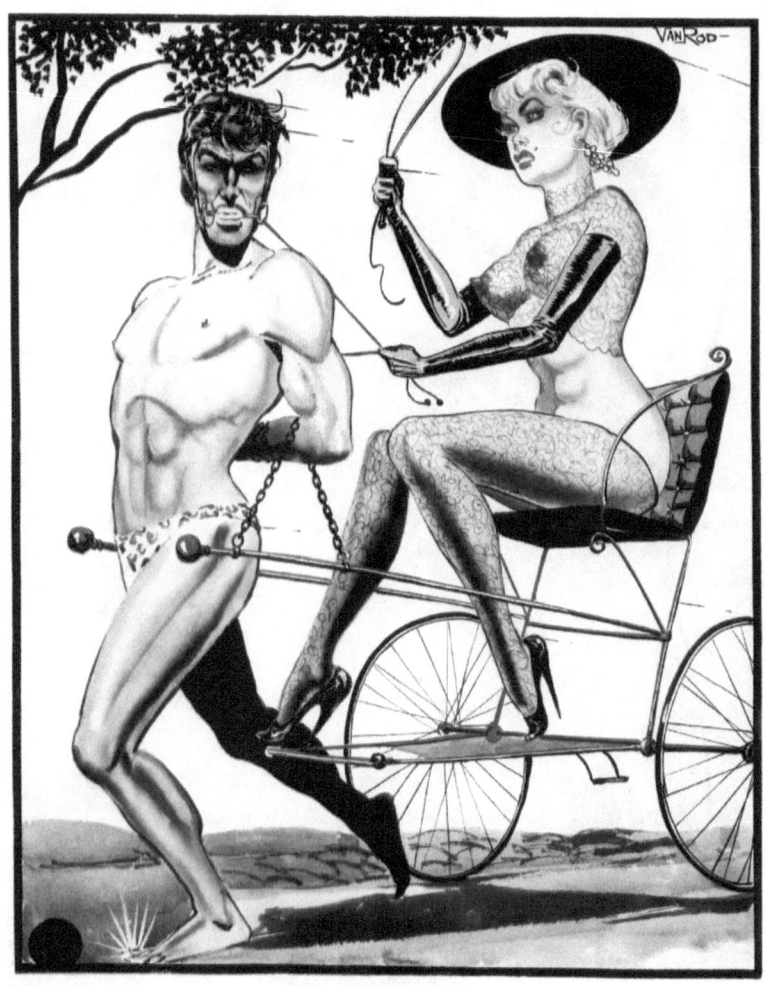

Van Rod, *The Whip Artist*

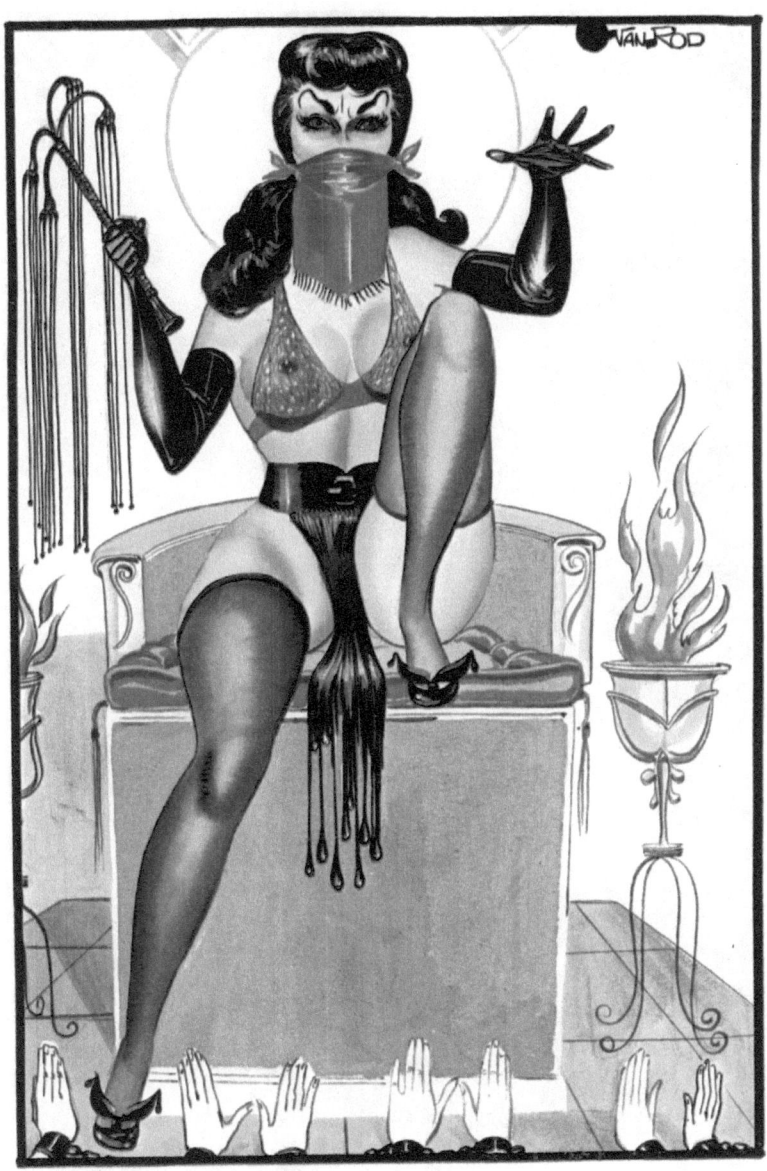

Van Rod, lost work

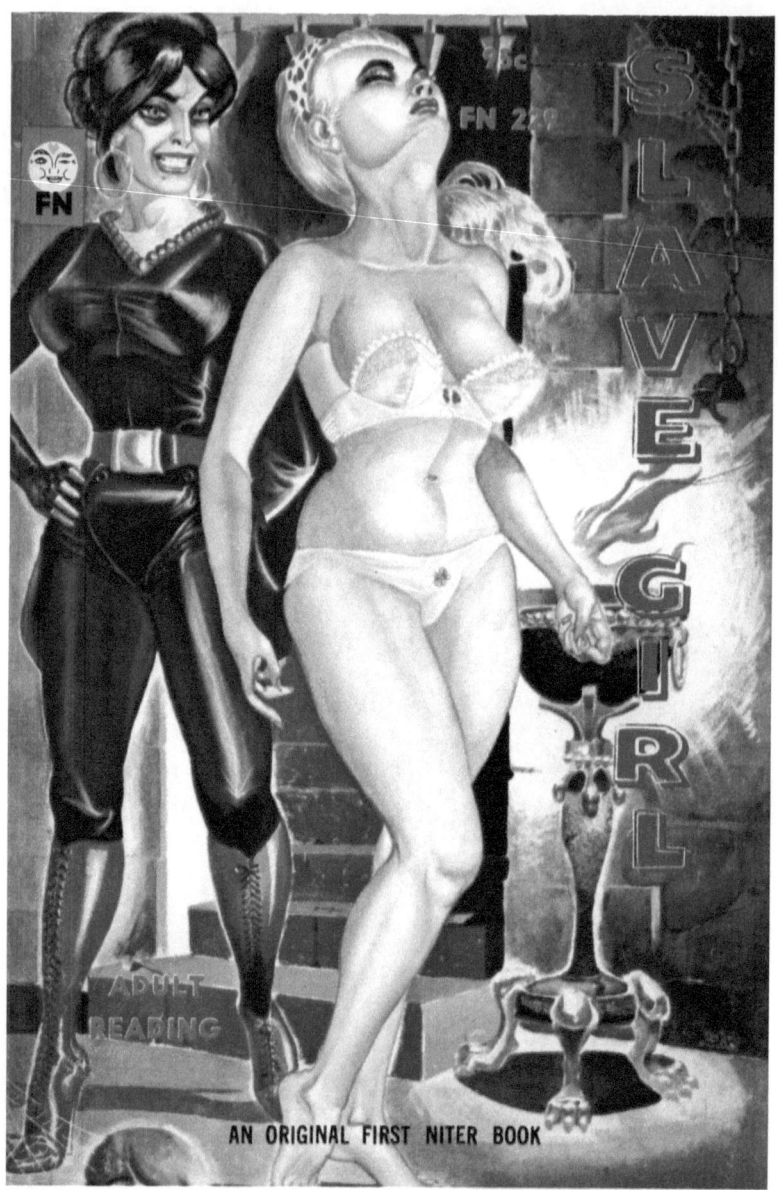

For Stanley Malkin (1966)

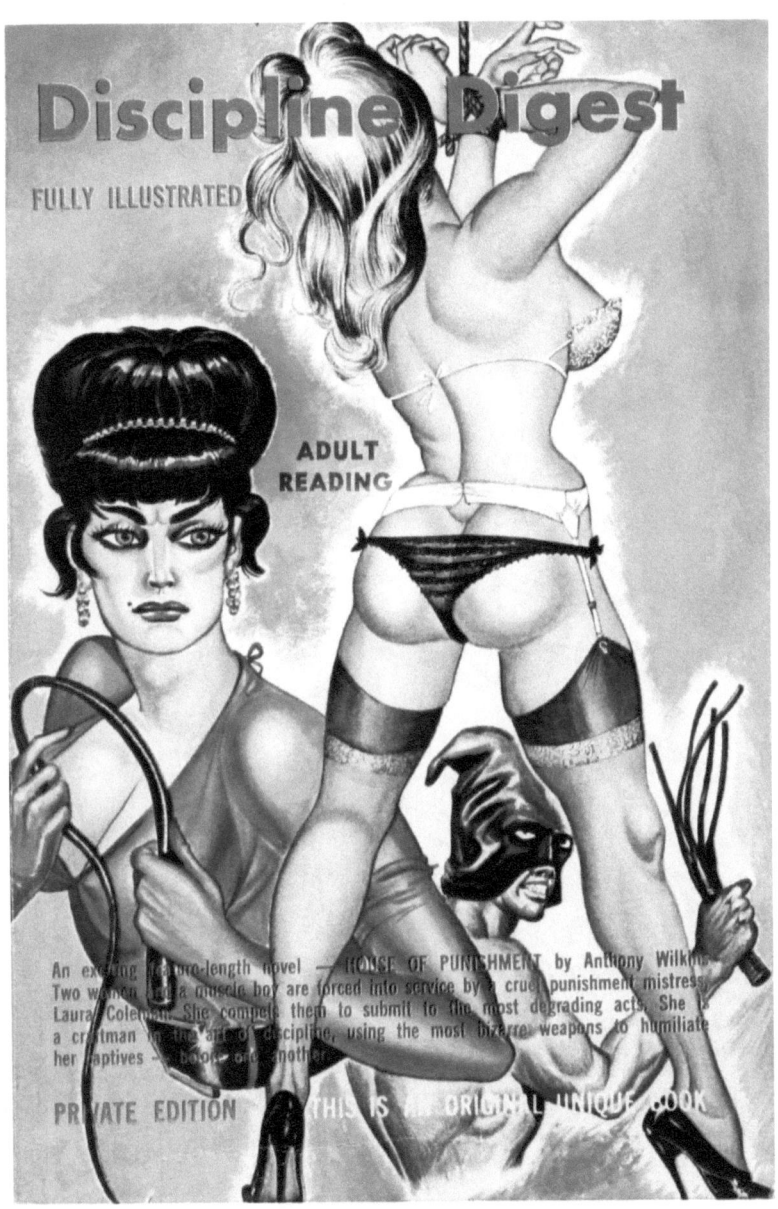

For Malkin (1966)

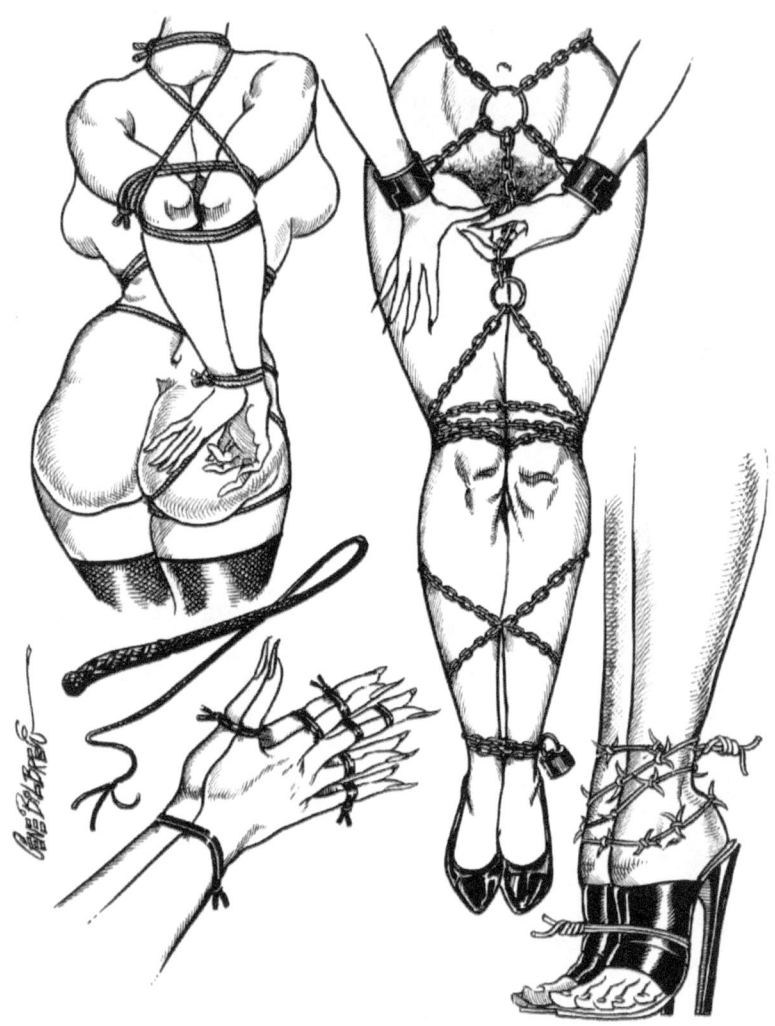

For Leonard Burtman (c. 1969)

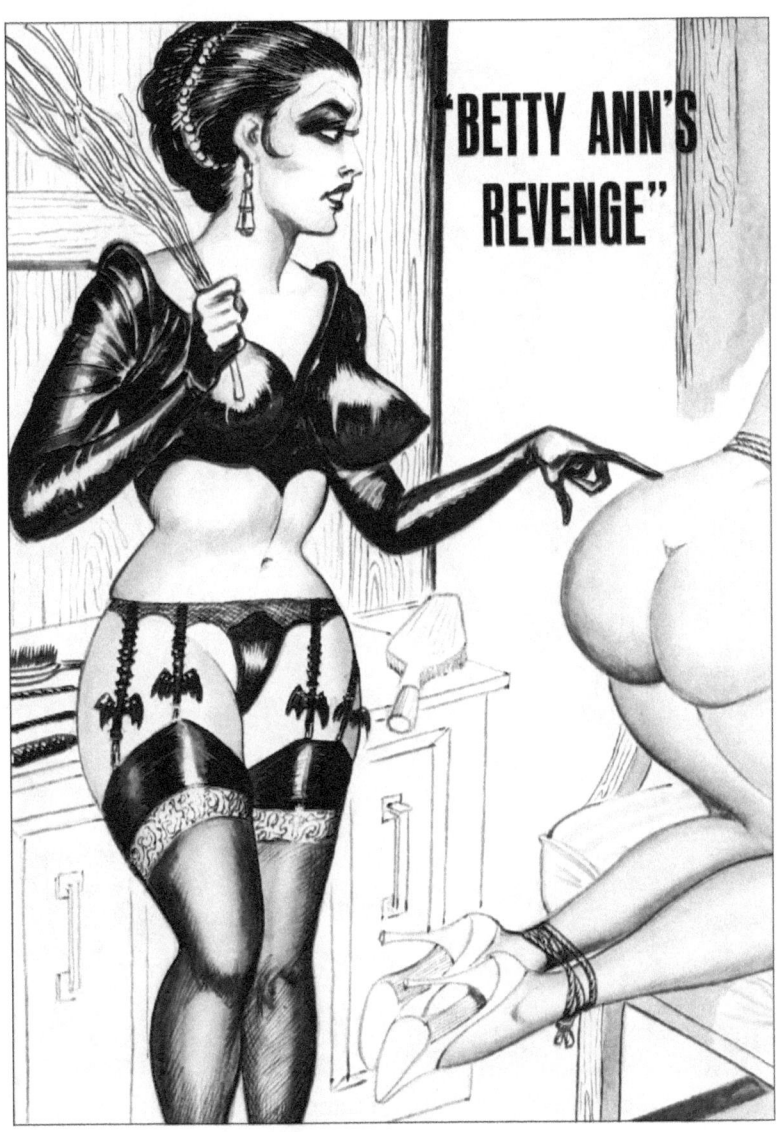

For Burtman (1968)

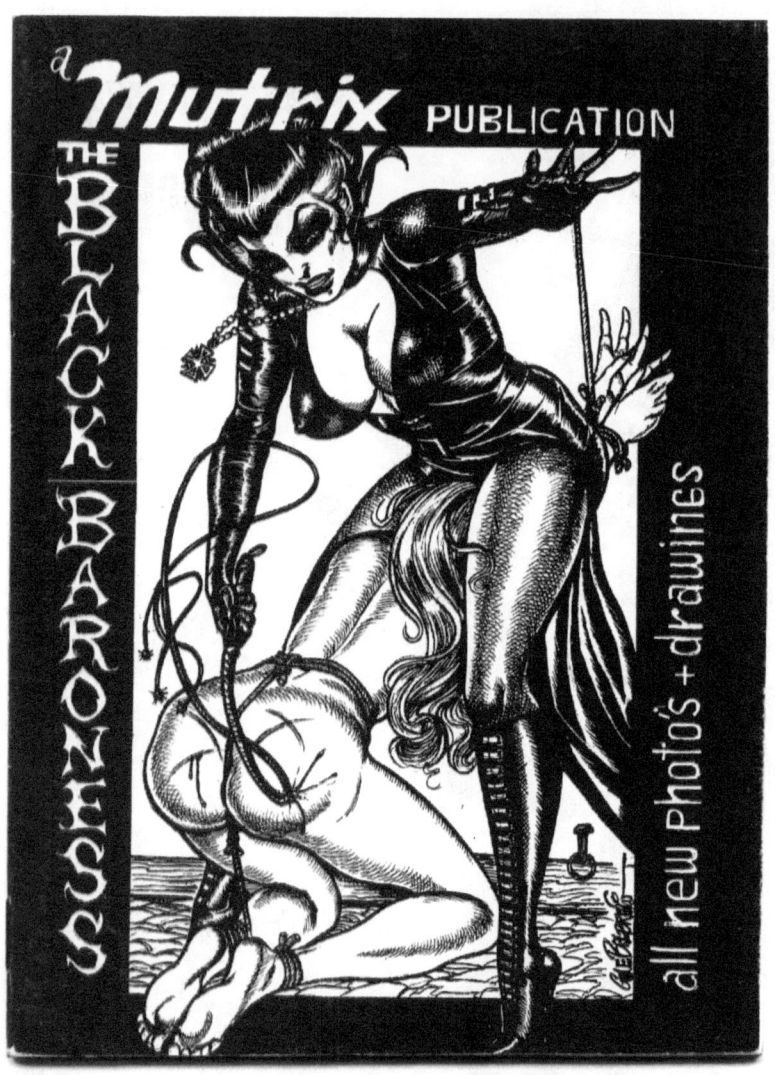

For Edward Mishkin, undated (early 1970s)

By the time we reach the 1970s, we see Van Rod's spirit is alive and well.

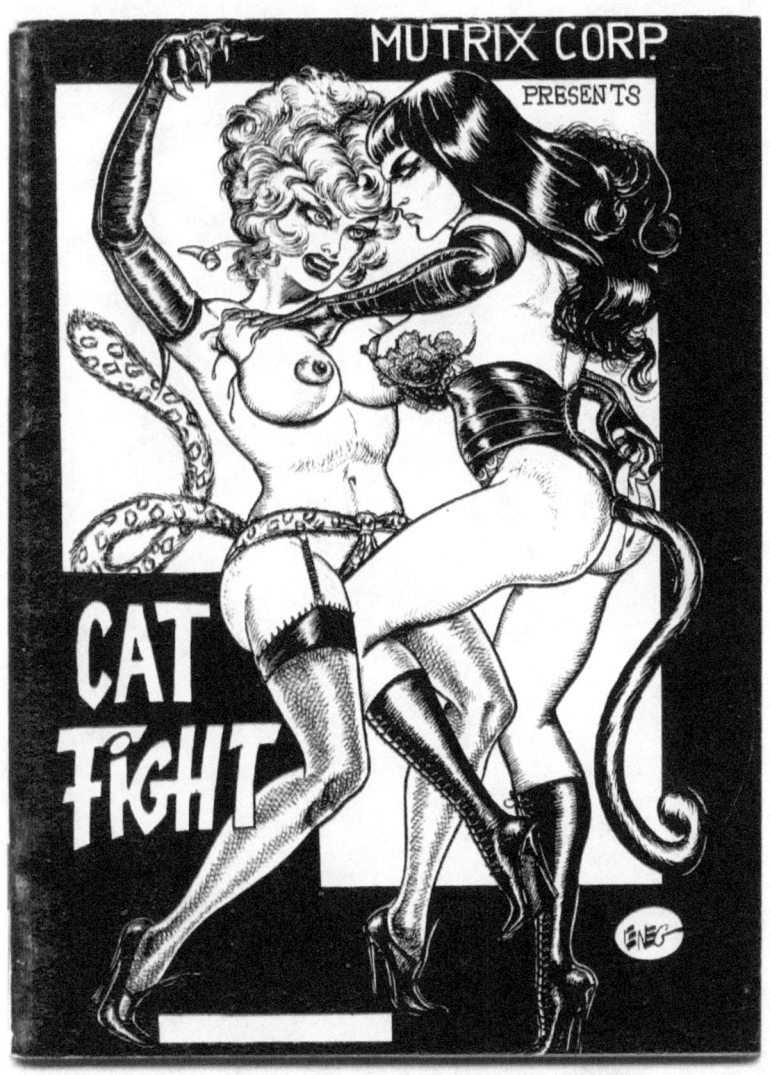

For Mishkin, undated (early 1970s)

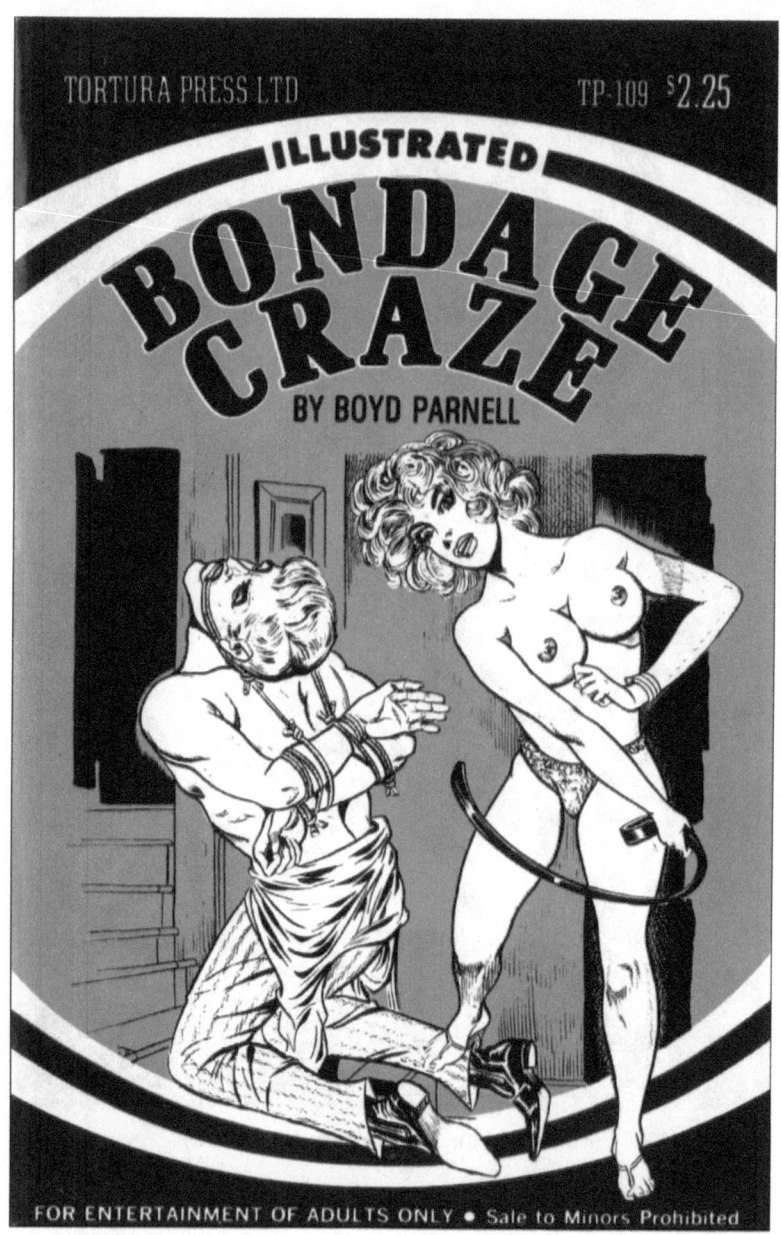

For Hilbarth Inc./Tortura Press, Ltd. (1971)

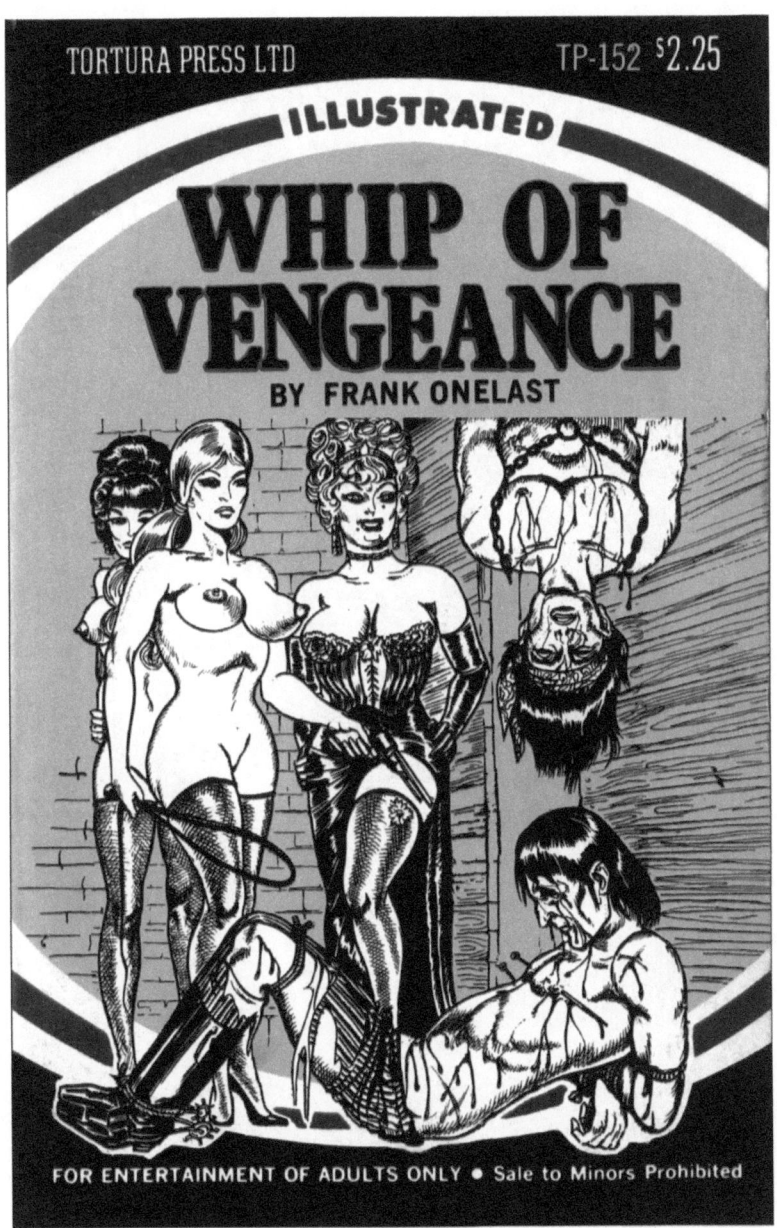

For Hilbarth Inc./Tortura Press, Ltd. (1972)

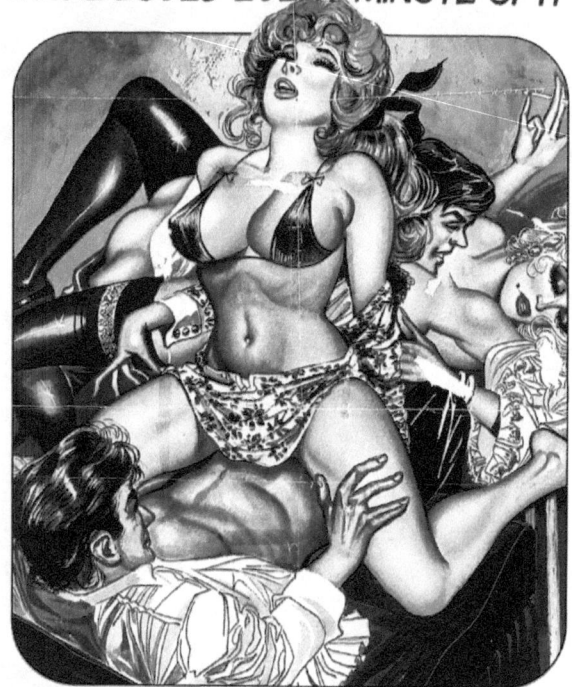

BILBREW IN THE XXX '70s

The end of the sexploitation/softcore era hit fetish artists hard. Fetish art was never overtly about sex, and now with the arrival of hardcore porn, both Bilbrew and Stanton found themselves further marginalized. What's more, as several major US court decisions [cxi] now made it safe to produce fetish art, there seemed a horde of new artists—inspired by Bilbrew and Stanton—willing to work for peanuts. Bill Ward, former artist of glamour girls and mild sexploitation gag comics, was among them; sometime in 1972, he became the leading artist for Leonard Burtman.

Stanton reacted by starting his own niche mail order business, which relied on private commissions, while Bilbrew spiraled into further decline, taking any sleazy art job he could get. Bilbrew's main patron at the time was Edward Mishkin who had served his time in prison and was now back to running his adult bookshops, at this point clearly in league with the mob. [cxii] Wholesale Book Corp. was now his primary office-warehouse while Candor Books Inc. served as his central mail order business. [cxiii] By then, Mishkin was publishing his "Mutrix" booklets, derived from the remnants of Irving Klaw's decimated "Nutrix" business, which Mishkin had purchased from Paula Klaw c. 1970. [cxiv] More and more, Mishkin churned out trans-themed material, which seemed to be most in demand at the time.

Although these were only semi-serious efforts on the part of everyone involved—as underscored by the frivolous titles of the booklets—occasionally Bilbrew delivered good work.

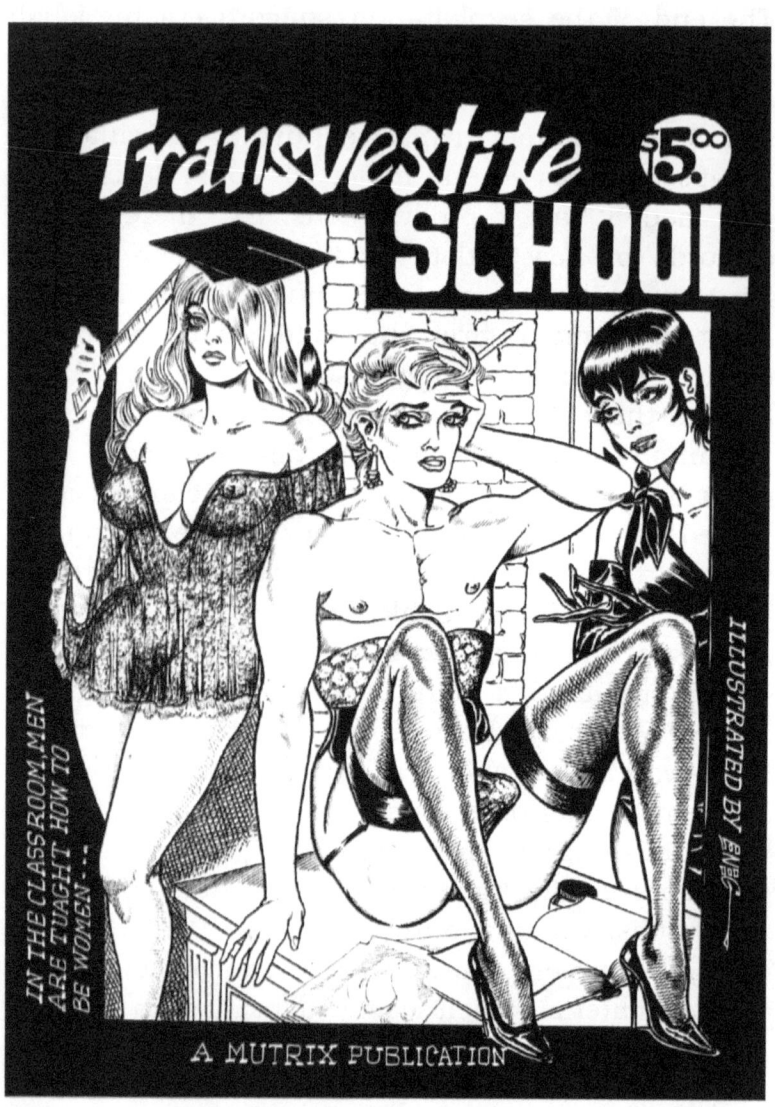

For Mishkin, undated (early 1970s)

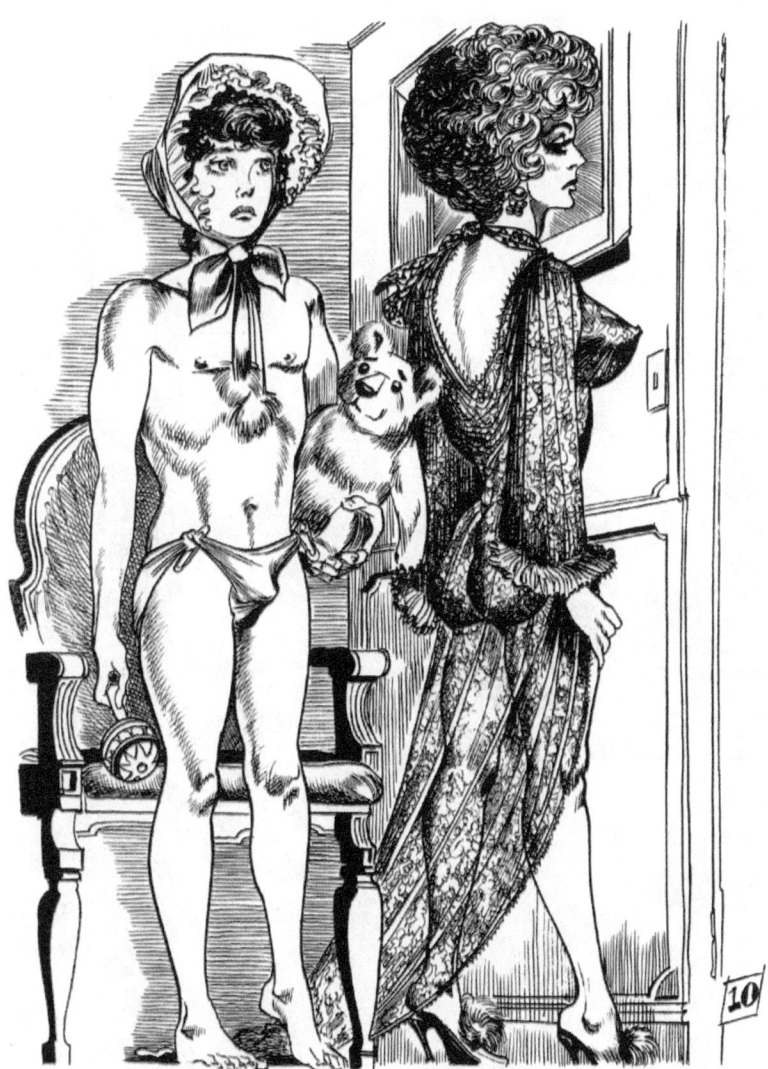

For Mishkin, from *Panty-Waist Male* (early 1970s)

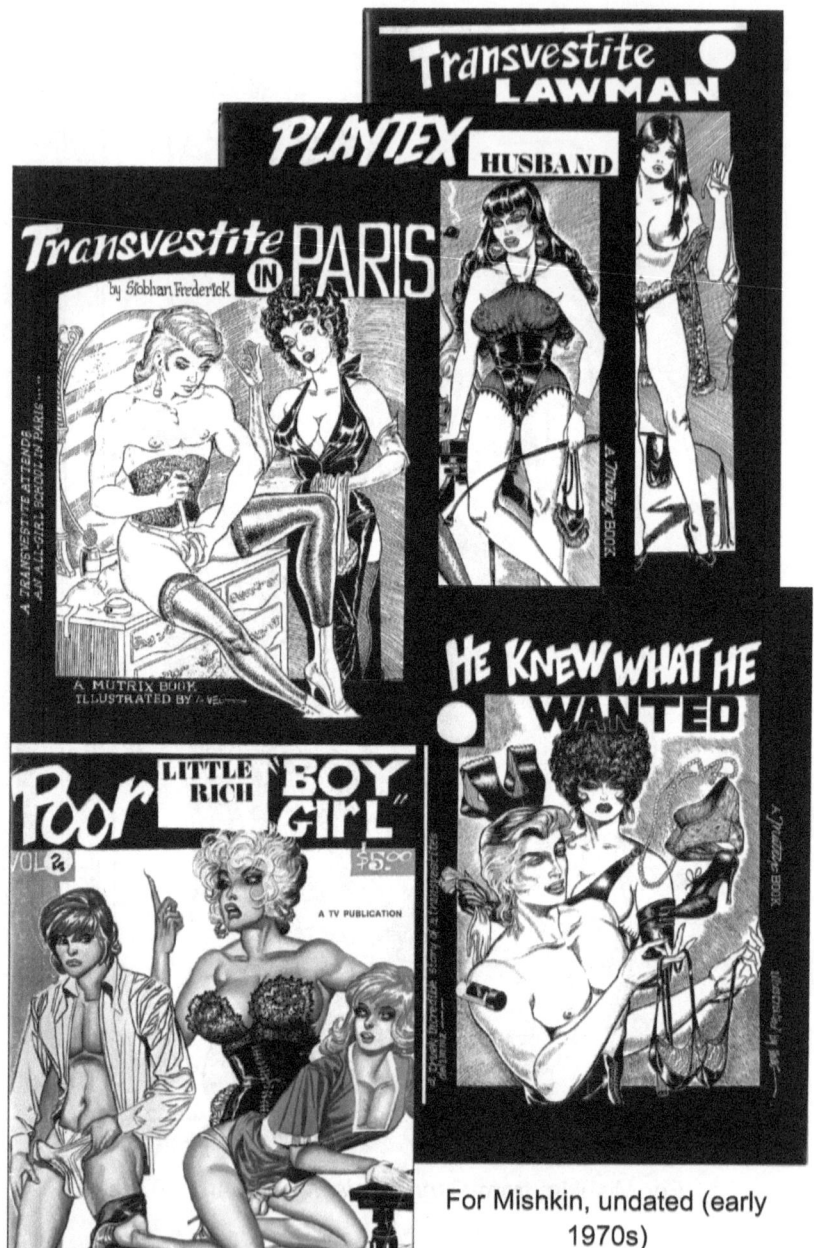

For Mishkin, undated (early 1970s)

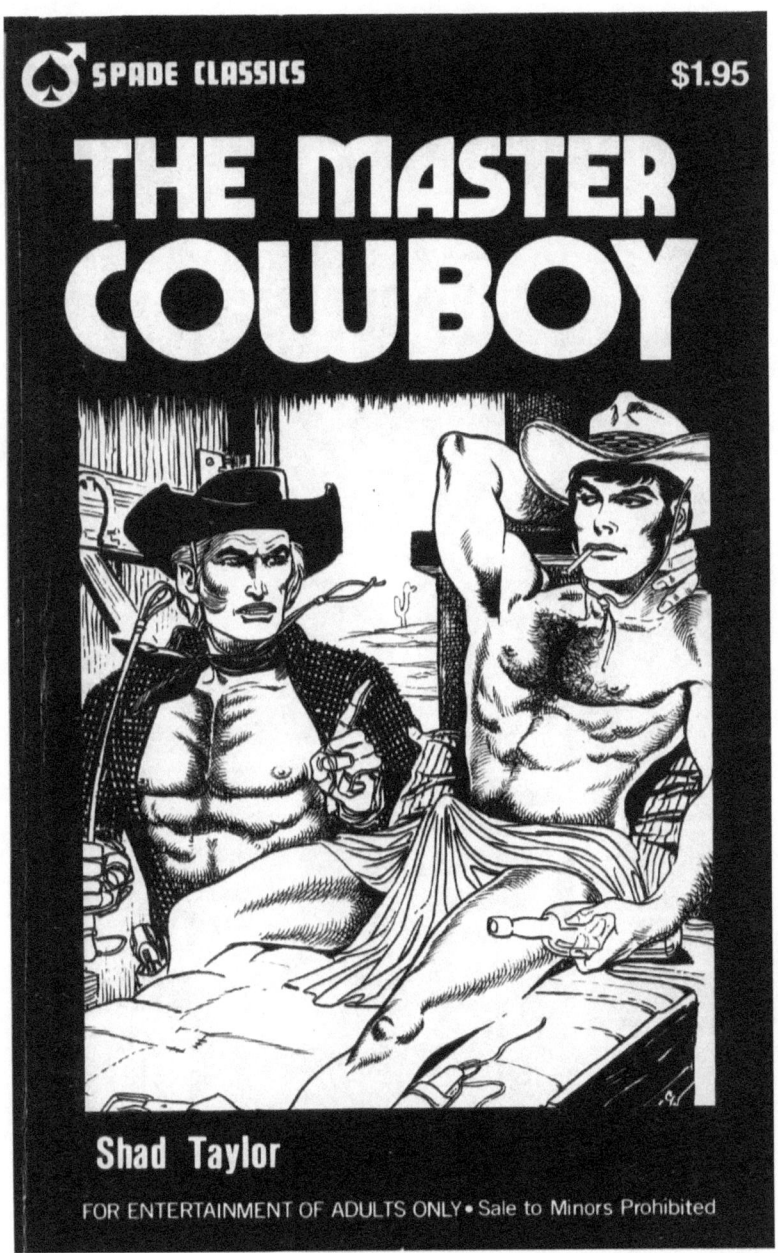

For Star Distributors (1972). Among Bilbrew's last line of books

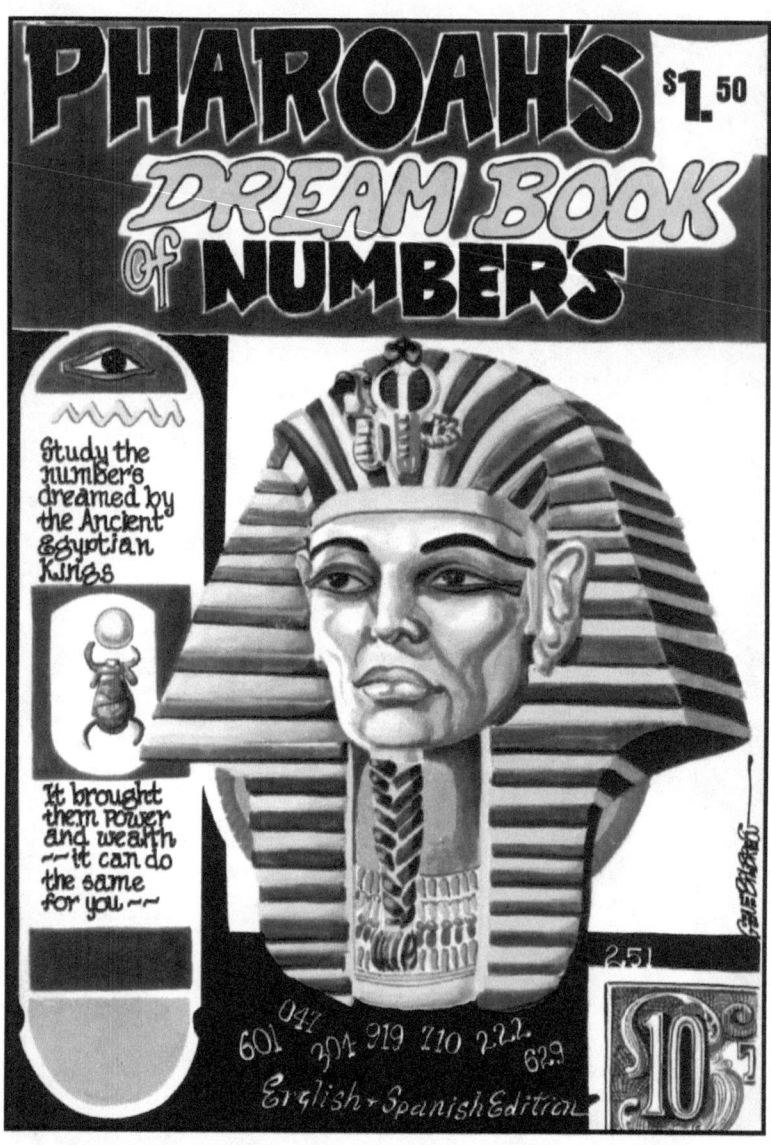

For Mishkin. Among Bilbrew's final efforts: his Dream Books

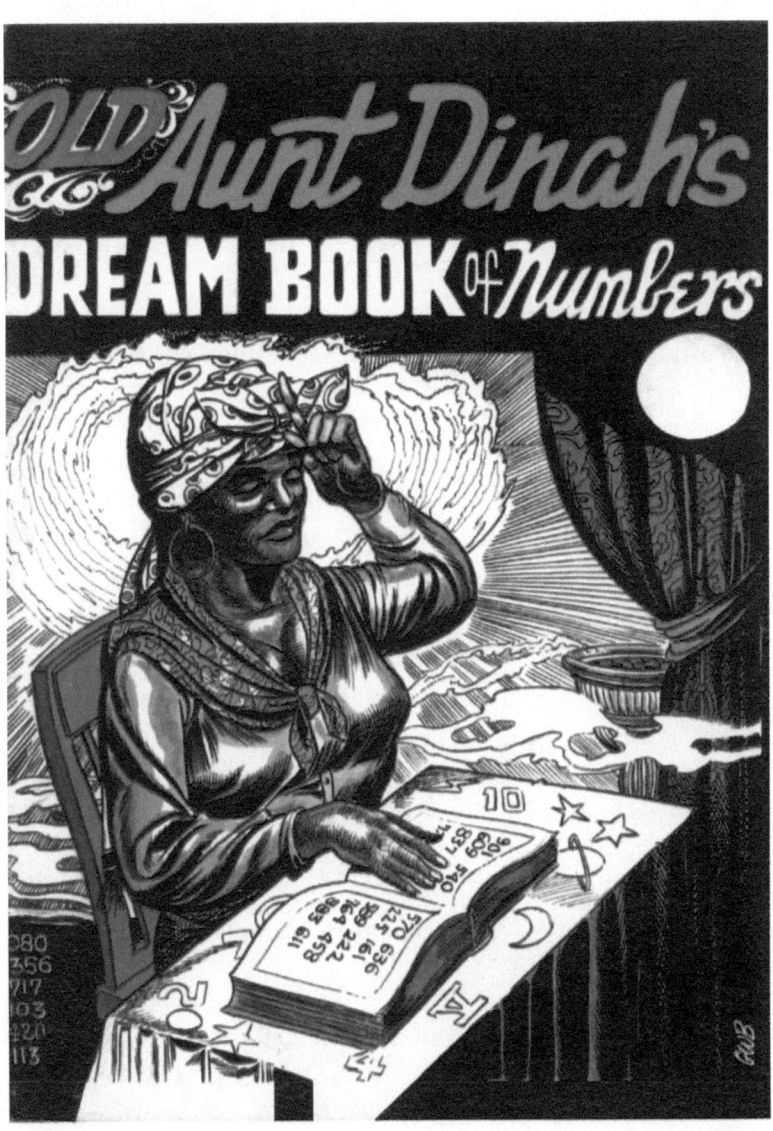

For Mishkin. (Note rare signed initials for his full name: "GWB")

Bilbrew worked for various other mob-controlled publishers/packagers, like Tortura Press/Hilbarth, Inc.[cxv] and Star Distributors (Spade Classics, Cathay Library and other imprints [cxvi]) where his friend Bill Alexander was art director, but it wasn't long before Bilbrew, struggling to keep it together, found himself living in the back of one of Mishkin's stores.

In a phone interview, publisher J.B. Rund vividly recalled seeing Bilbrew's pathetic living quarters at the office-warehouse known as Wholesale Book Corp:

> You're in a big room with books on the floor, remainders ... and in the back of the room, there was this addition—a plywood room. It had three sides with the back obviously the back of the room. It had a padlock on it and painted on the door was "Gene Bilbrew, Art Director." What was in that room? I don't know. It was pretty small; it may have been just a bed... This was on 21st Street. 'Cause he [Mishkin/Wholesale Book Corp.] subsequently moved around the corner to 20th Street and Broadway—902 Broadway.[cxvii]

Rund also shared an interesting account of Bilbrew's passing:

> At the local Flea Market, I met someone by the name of Jeffrey Goodman, who wrote a lot of porno in the '70s. Among others, he wrote many of the *Bizarre Library* and *Dr. Lamb* paperbacks [for which Bilbrew produced some covers]. He also wrote for Mishkin, mainly

transvestite stuff and one or two of the Dream Books. He told me that Bilbrew actually died on the premises of Mishkin's Wholesale Books [902 Broadway] and that his body was moved to the back of one of the Times Square Bookshops. This information came directly from Mishkin's lips. As to the Why, well, obviously, Mishkin certainly didn't want the police sniffing around his main place of business. According to Goodman, there was a huge safe with a lot of undeclared cash in it. [cxviii]

According to the Department of Veterans Affairs, Bilbrew's death date was May 23, 1974. He was about one month short of 51 years old. [cxix]

What did Bilbrew die of? Was it a heroin overdose as widely rumored on the Internet? Or did his body just give out after years of abuse? Or was it simply poverty? Or heartbreak? No one knows. As Stanton later recalled, "Eneg got so involved in drugs and alcohol his work began to deteriorate. When he died Eddie Mishkin was putting him up in the backroom of one of his stores. He was doing drawings there and he died there." [cxx]

If Bilbrew's lifeless body was moved to another location by Mishkin rather than simply discarded (as Mishkin had friends who might take care of that sort of business), then can we assume the body was removed by the City of New York? Was he disposed of as an indigent? Were his remains taken to the place known as Potter's Field, as was customary, where he was buried in a nameless grave?

To date, no grave marker for Gene Bilbrew has been identified. In short, he simply vanished—without fanfare or tears.[cxxi] At the time of his death, he received no memorial or obituary in any publication of merit and, as yet, has still to receive his due. To the art community at large, he remains an aberration, at best a marginal artist connected to a dark and troubling subgenre of art, whose value remains in question.

An outsider among outsiders, he was cast from one limbo into another, where to this day he remains.

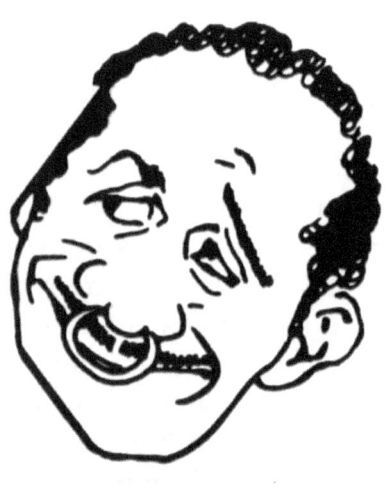

In 1975, drawing from memory, Stanton produced a septum-ringed caricature of a middle-aged Bilbrew for the cover of the *Bizarre Comix* series published by Bélier Press. Stanton's image was likely closer to how Bilbrew appeared in real life just around the time when the artist— perhaps with a premonition of his own death—produced a romanticized, youthful, curiously detailed illustration of himself (opposite).[cxxii]

We might imagine that this was how Bilbrew— former vocal group singer, pioneering rebel of bizarre art—wanted to be remembered.

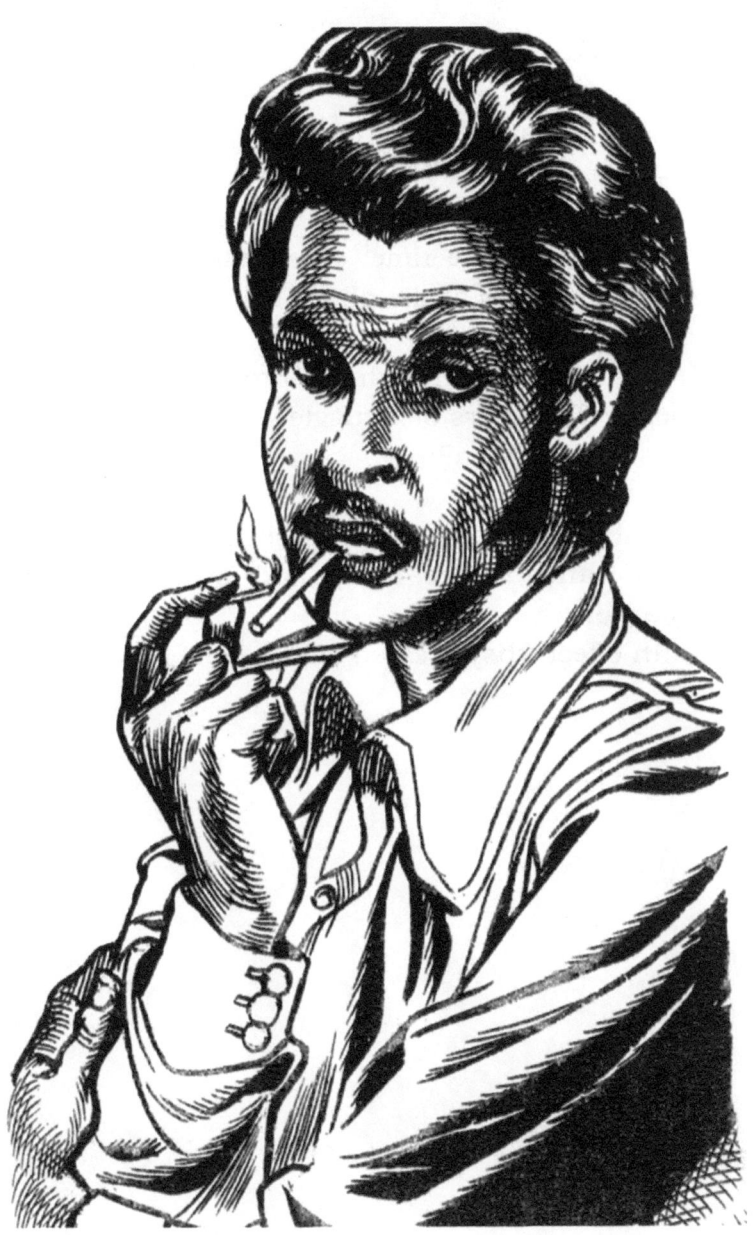

EPILOGUE

So what was Eric Stanton's reaction to Bilbrew's death?

According to Stanton's widow, Britt, who was with him at the time, when Stanton heard the news, he stood at the phone and cried. "Eric loved Eneg," she recalled.

What went through Stanton's mind at that point? The years of struggle with Klaw, Burtman, Mishkin, Malkin?

Regrets?

There were only two American fetish artists of importance in the 1950s and '60s: Bilbrew and Stanton.

In effect, they created each other.

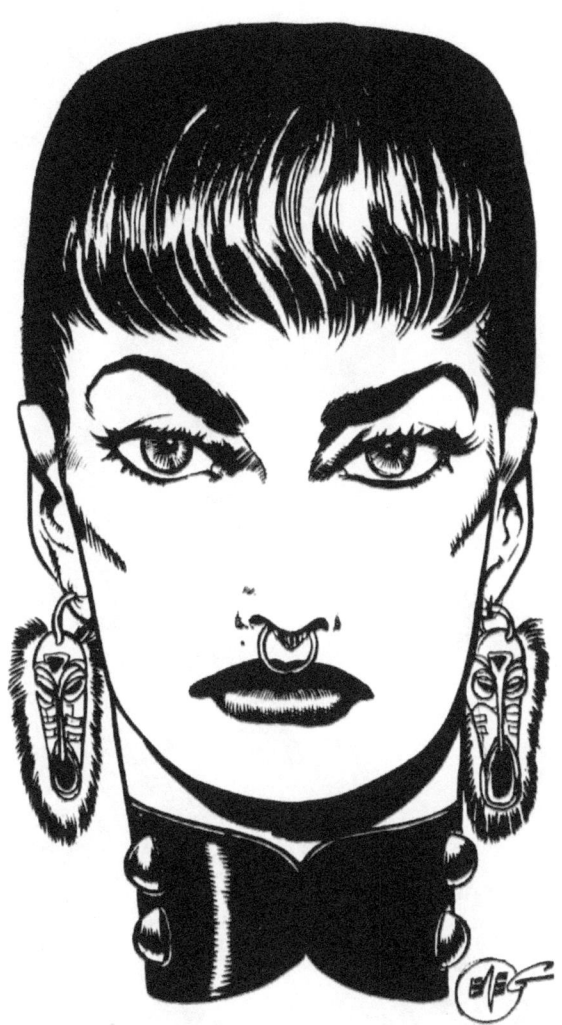

Afterword

When I was doing research for my book, *Eric Stanton & the History of the Bizarre Underground*, I found this image, among others, pinned to the wall of Stanton's basement office in Connecticut—not fully understanding its significance. As for other Bilbrew pieces that were in his office? See the following pages. Eric Stanton passed away in March 1999.

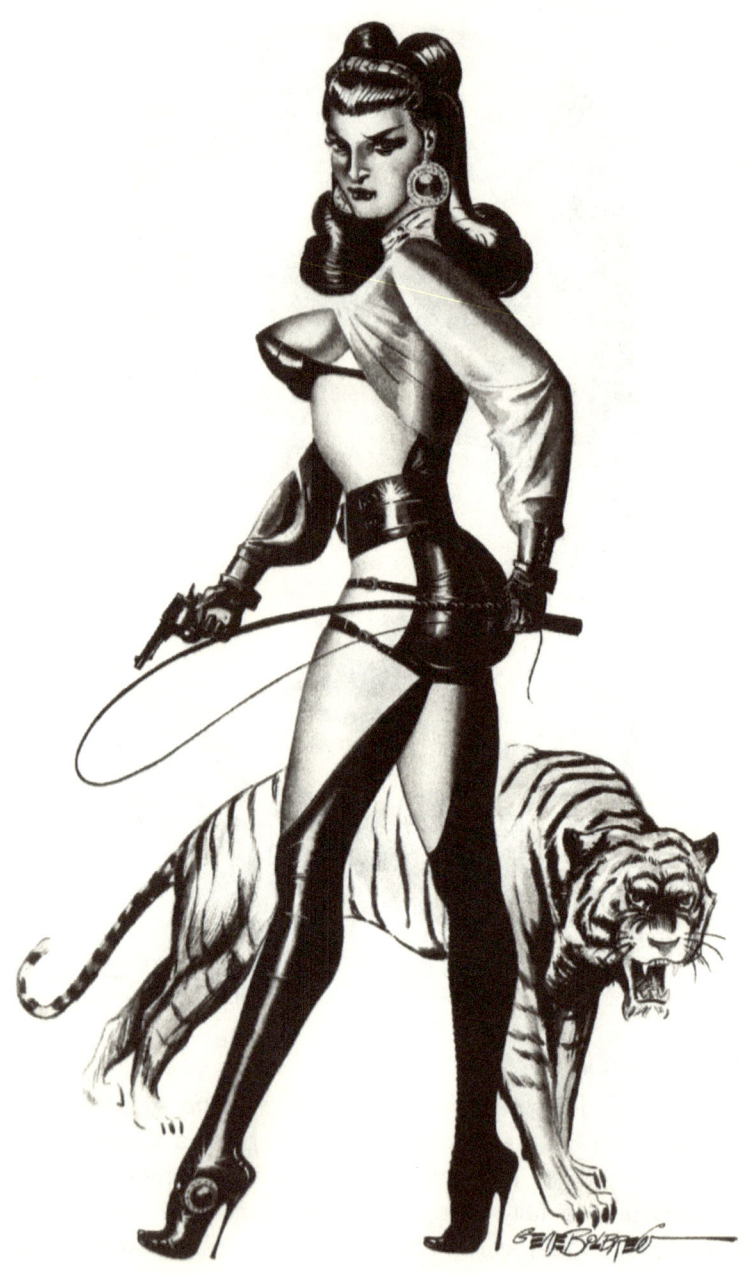

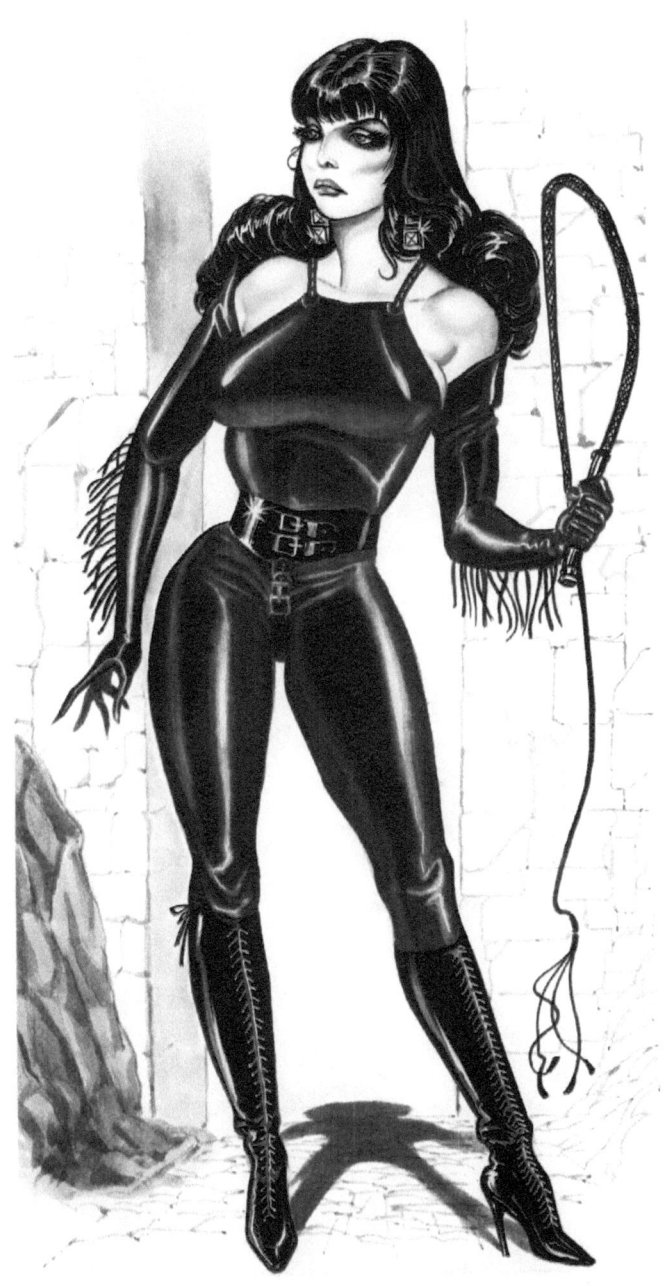

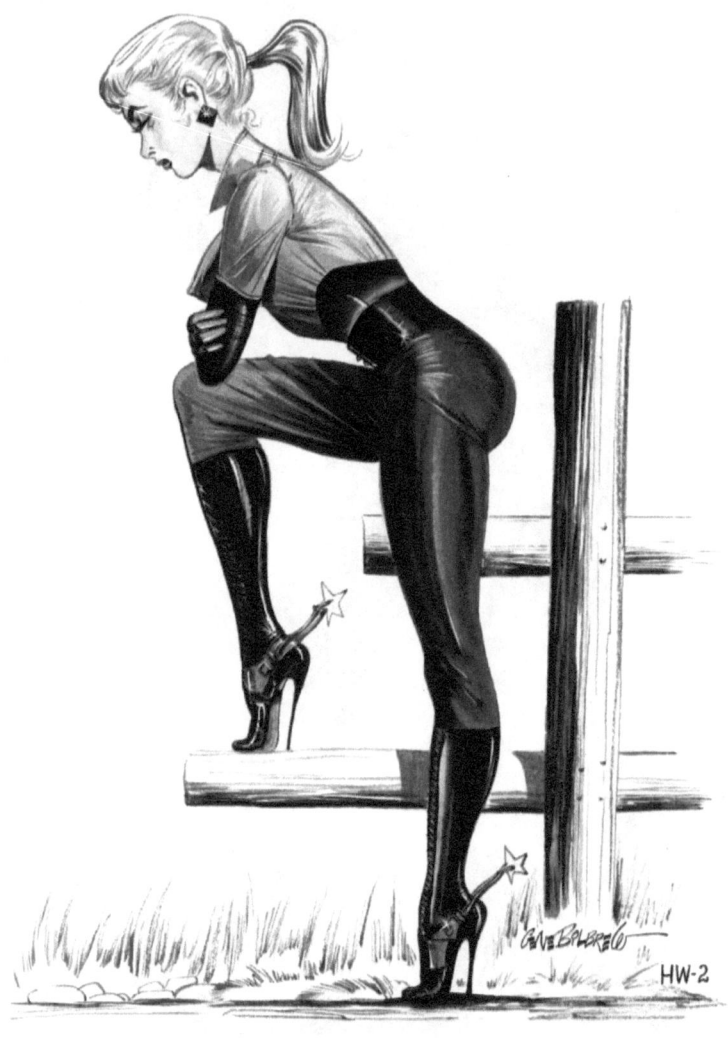

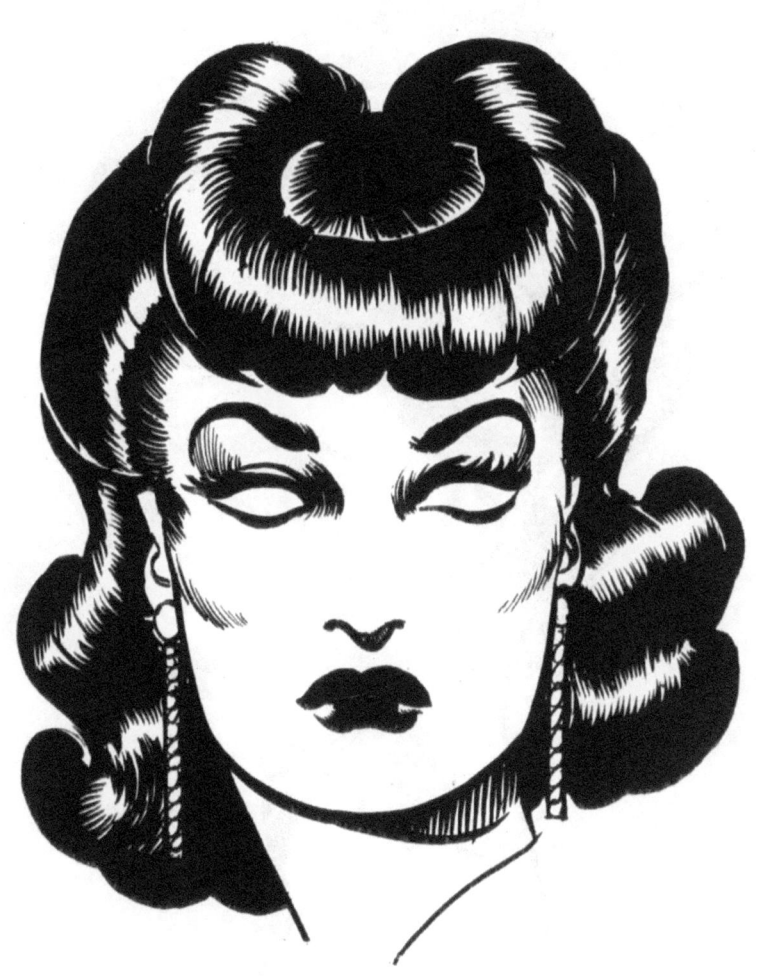

"The Exotique"

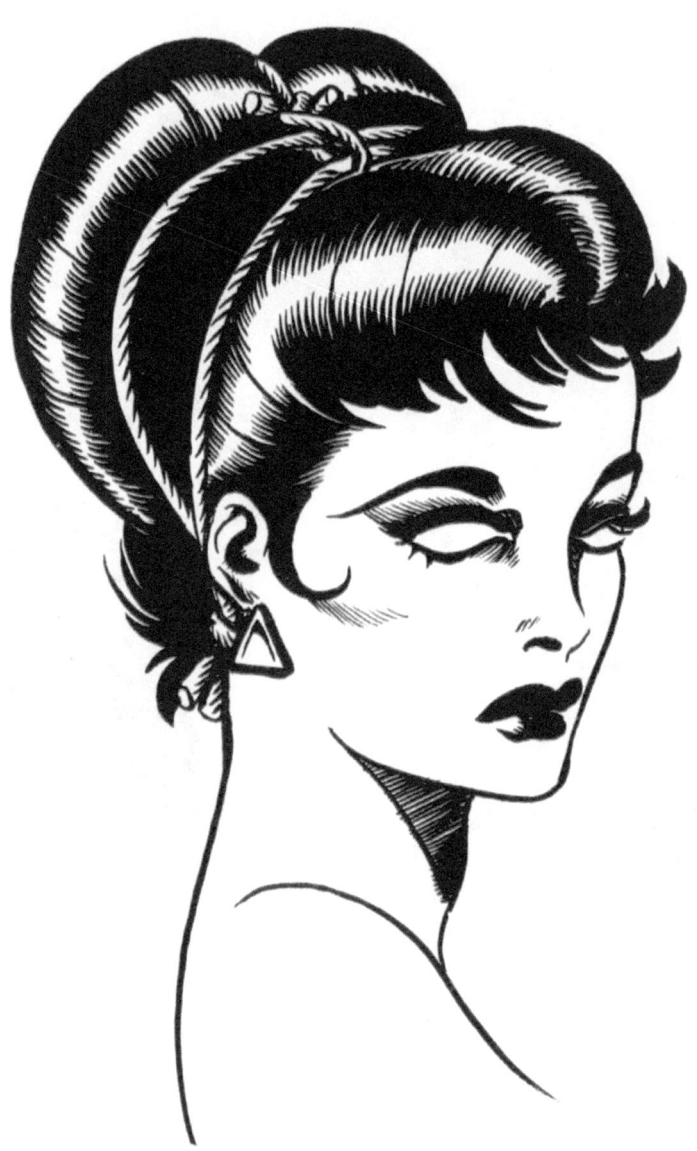

"The Peppermint Twist"

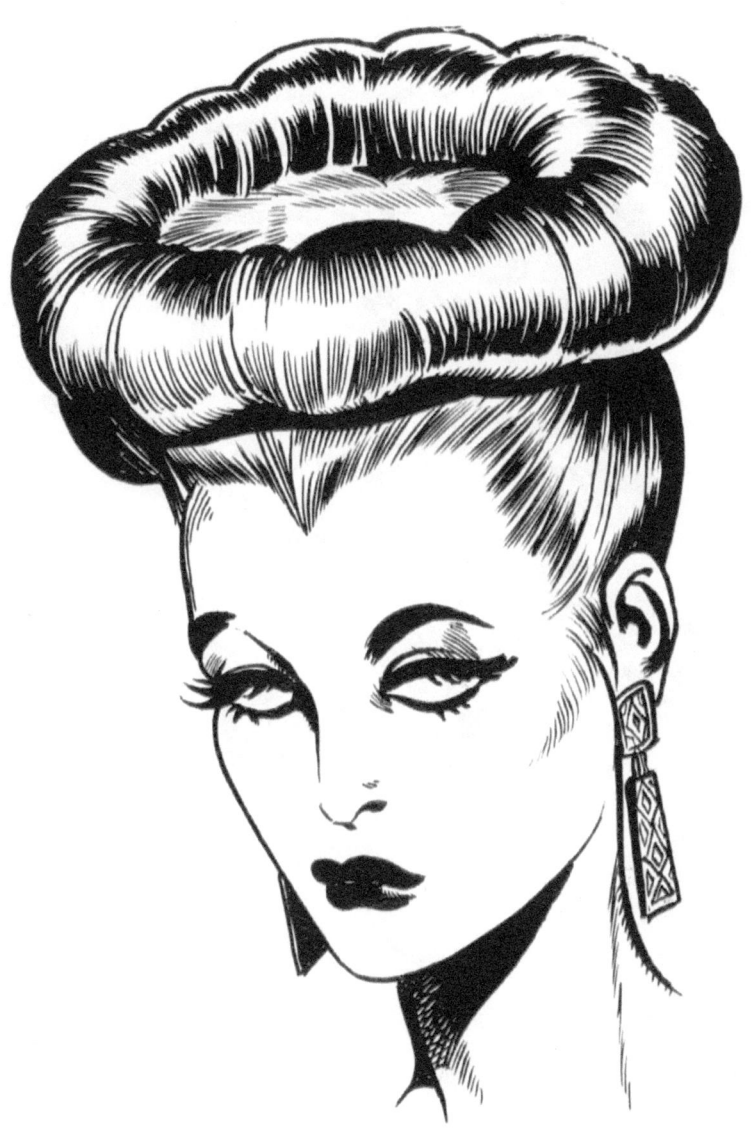

"The Dominatrice"

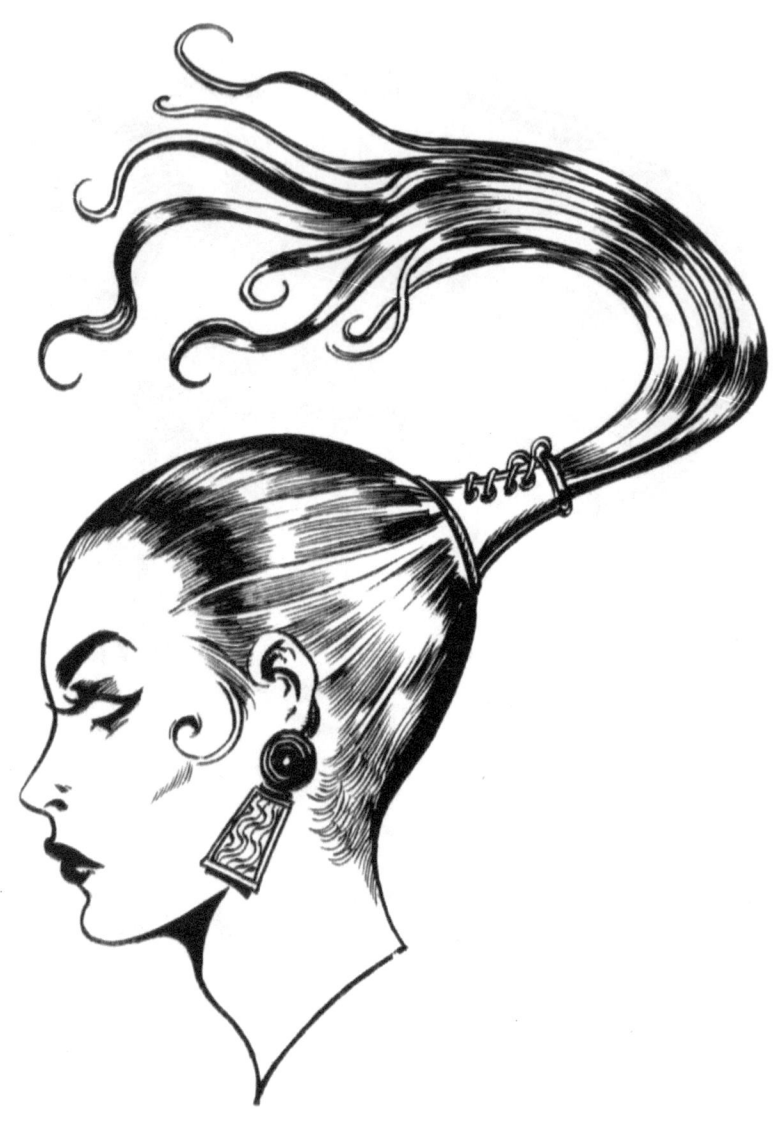

'The Minx''

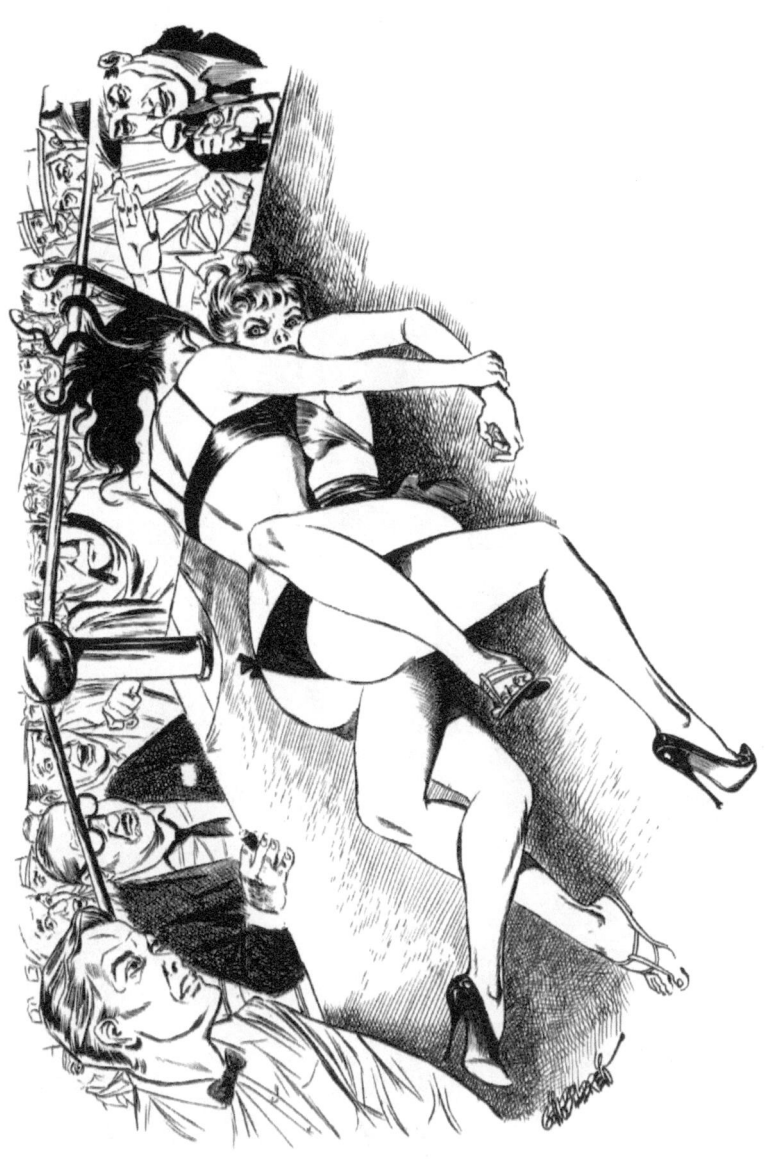

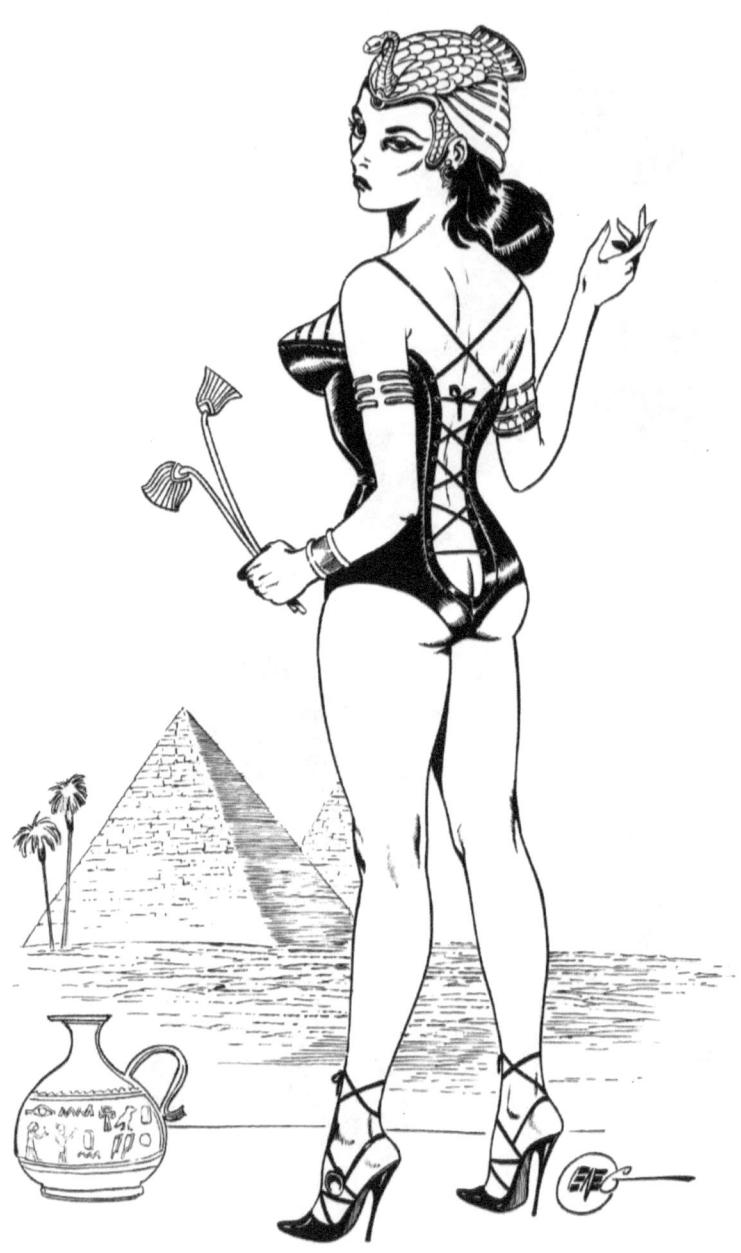

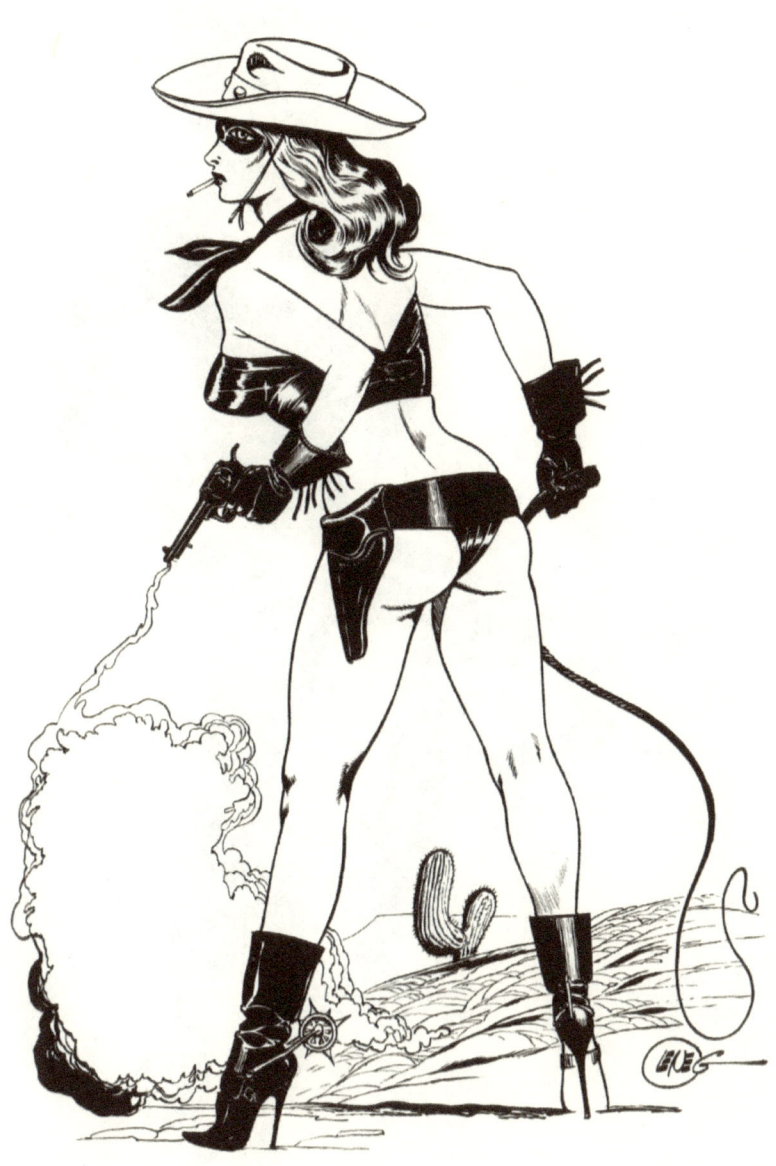

255

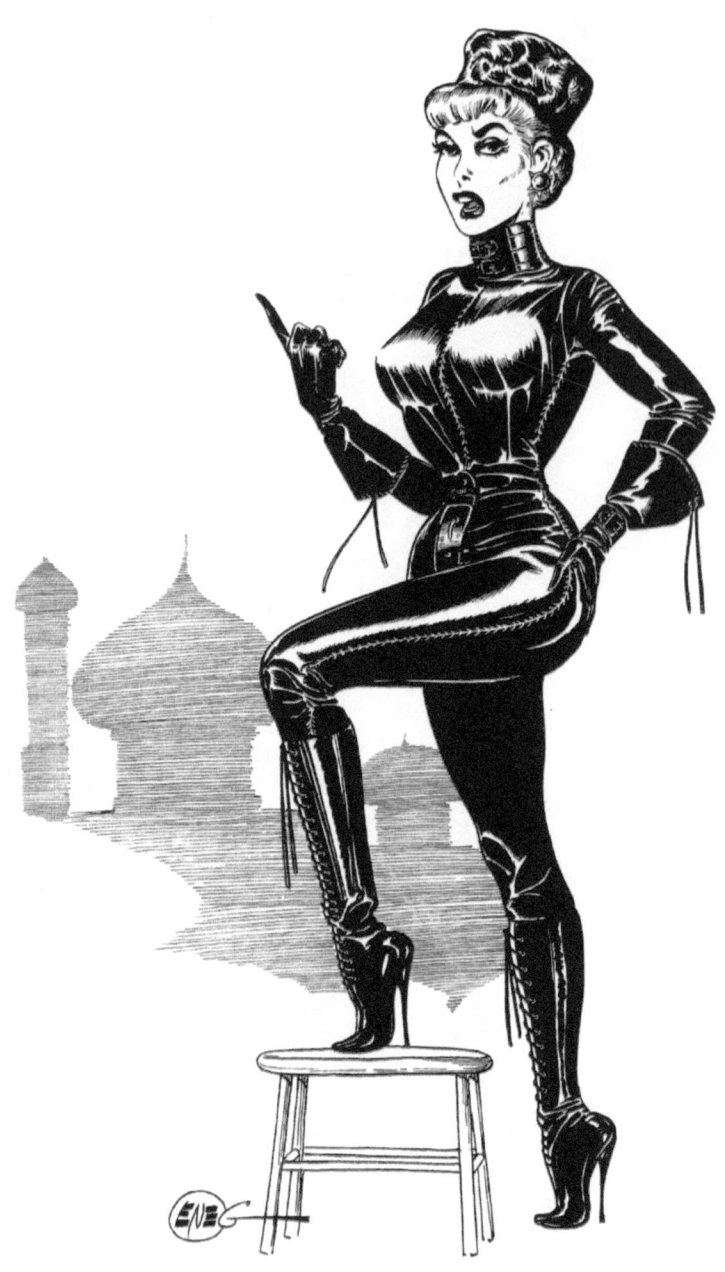

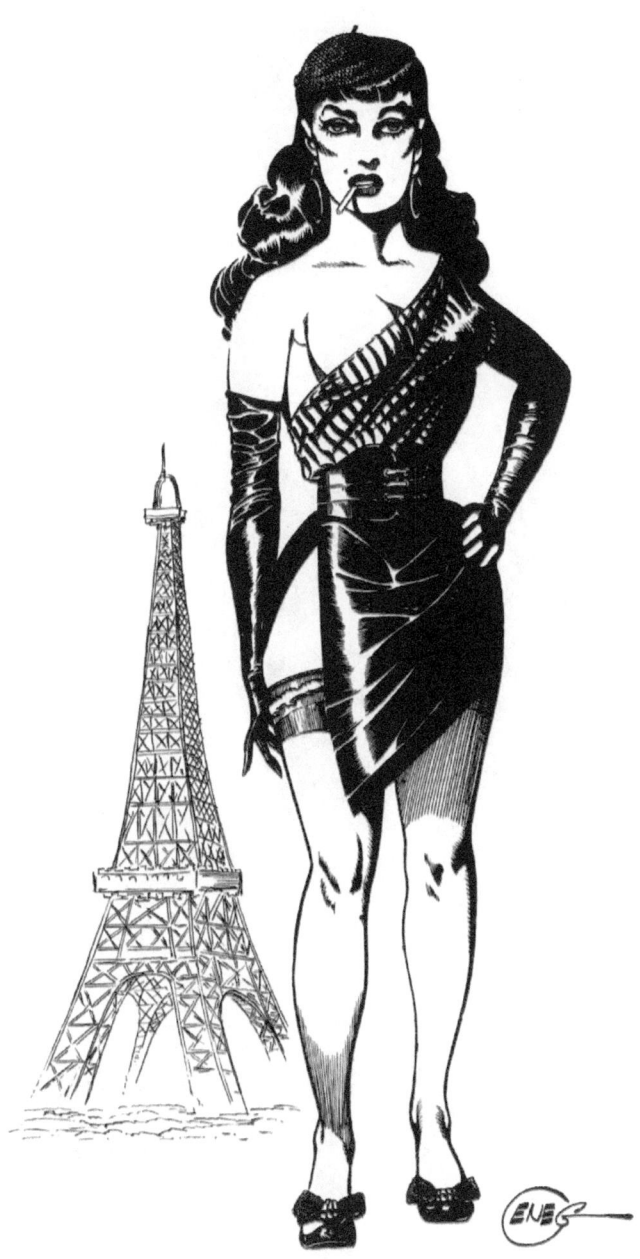

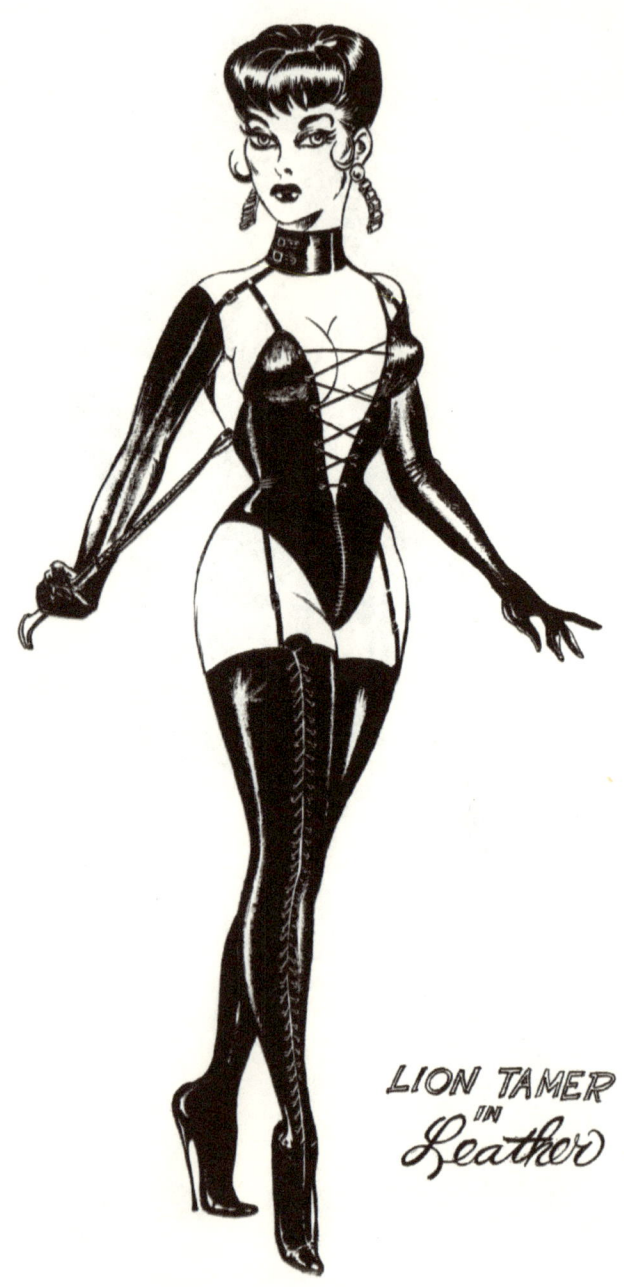

LION TAMER *in* Leather

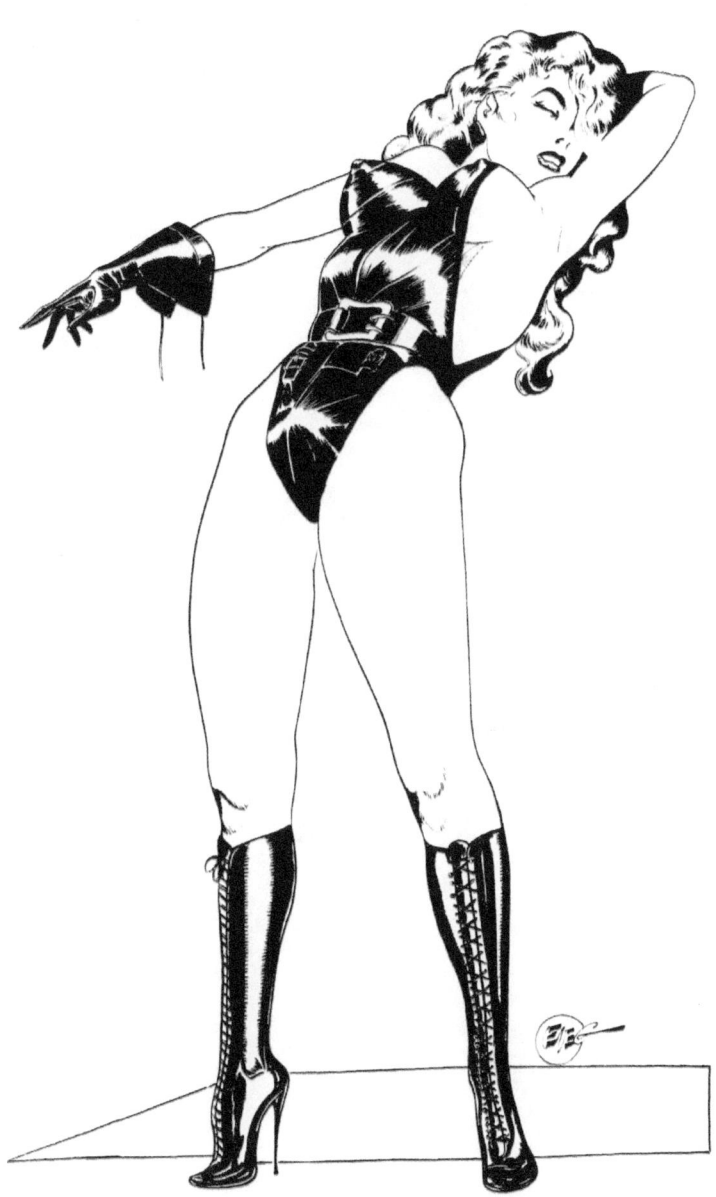

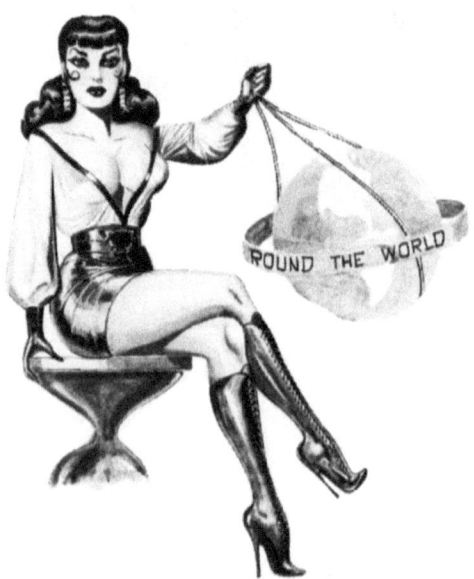

FIN

ABOUT THE AUTHOR

Richard Pérez Seves is the author of *Eric Stanton & the History of the Bizarre Underground* and the curator/author of *Charles Guyette: Godfather of American Fetish Art*, and *Jackie Miller Recollection: A Tribute in Photos,* as well as two novels about bohemia. His work has been translated into Italian, Korean, and Turkish. Among other things, he has contributed to the *New York Times.*

Another important aspect of his work has been the restoration of alternative and underground art, including long-overlooked, fetish art classics such as *The Return of Gwendoline, Sweeter Gwen, Bound To Please, Bondage Enthusiasts Bound in Leather,* and *Brutal Punishment for Captive Girls.* Currently his books are available in 12 countries: Germany, UK, US, Canada, France, Australia, Italy, Spain, Japan, Poland, Sweden, and the Netherlands.

For more, go to: FetHistory.com

৬৬

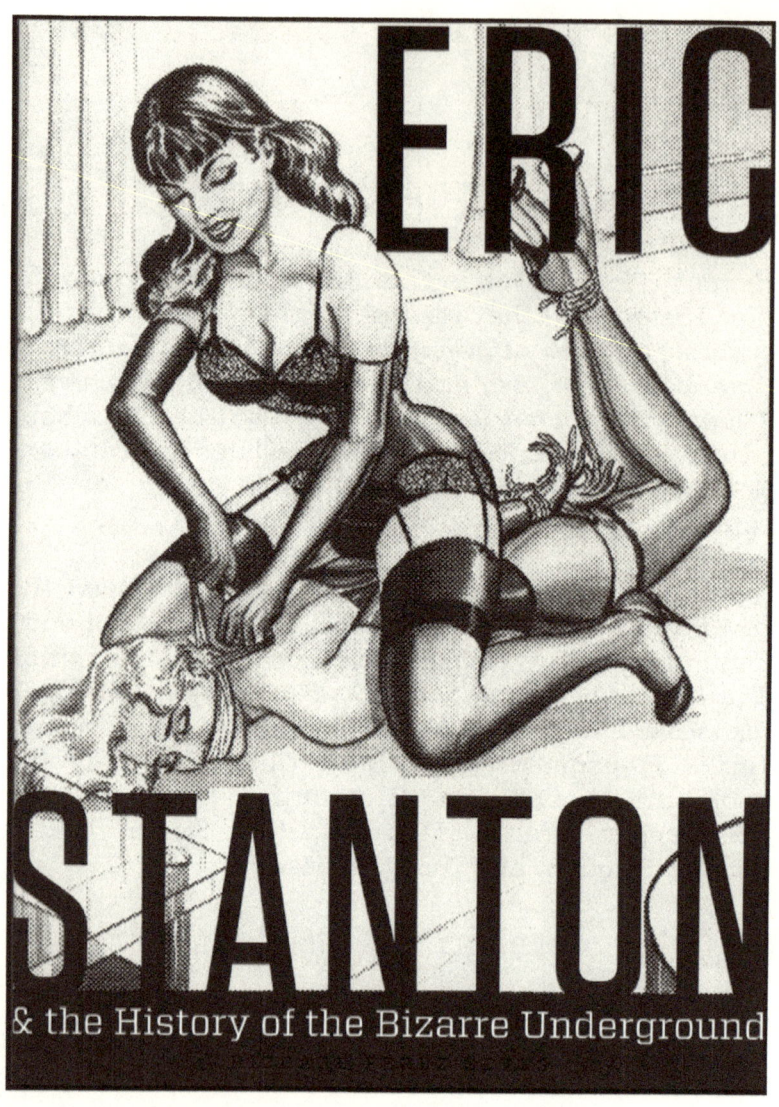

Available now! On Amazon/
FetHistory.com

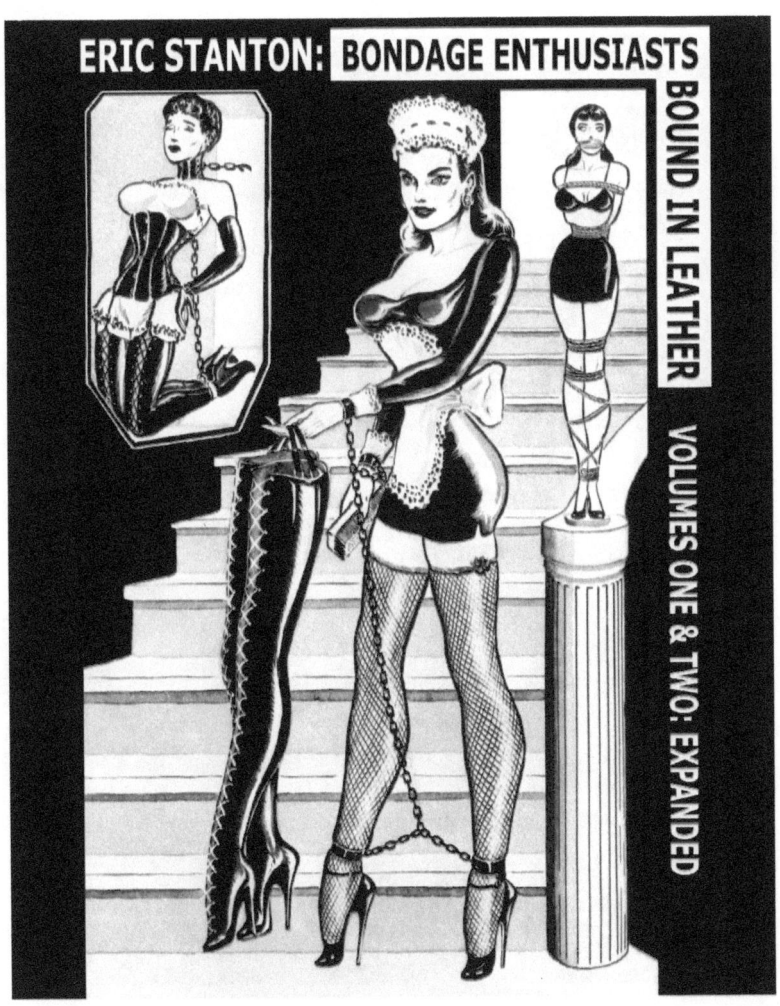

Available now! On Amazon/
FetHistory.com

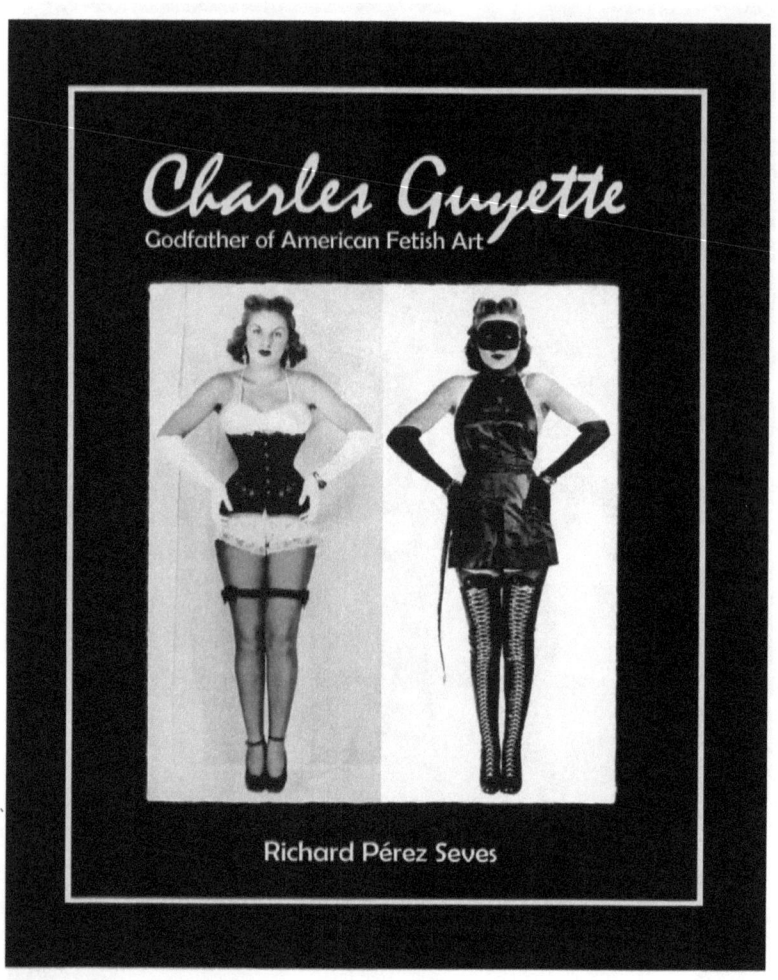

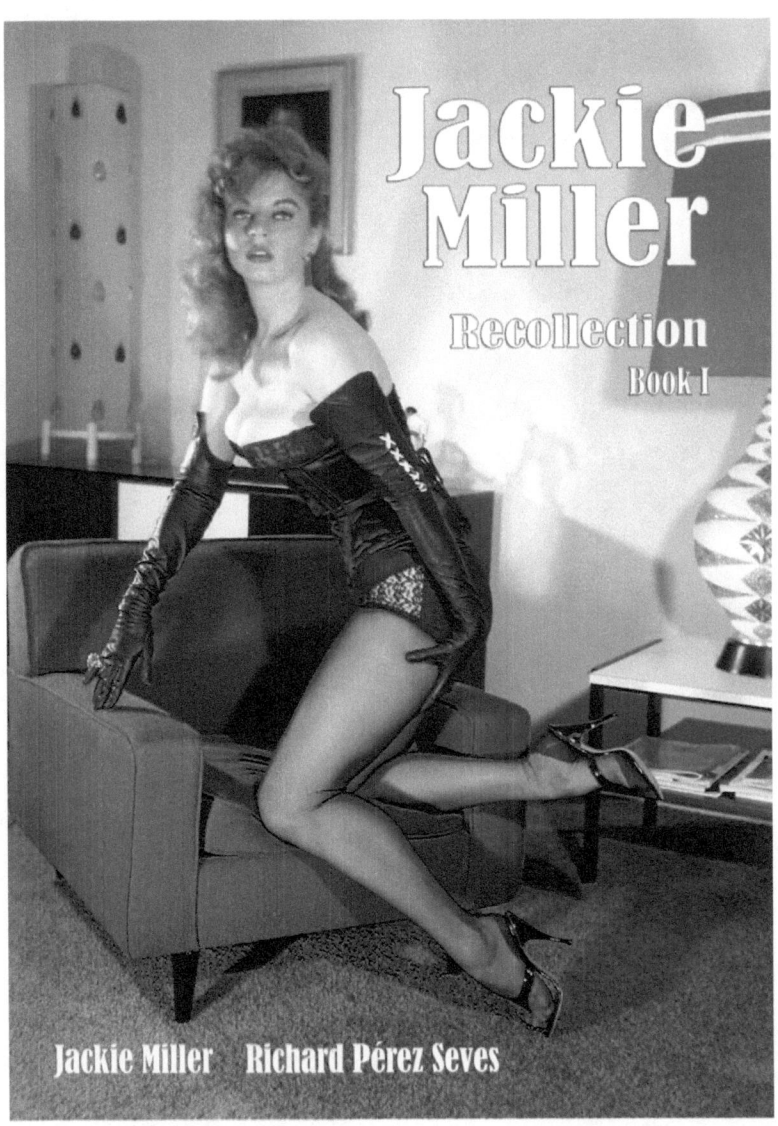

Available now! On Amazon/
FetHistory.com

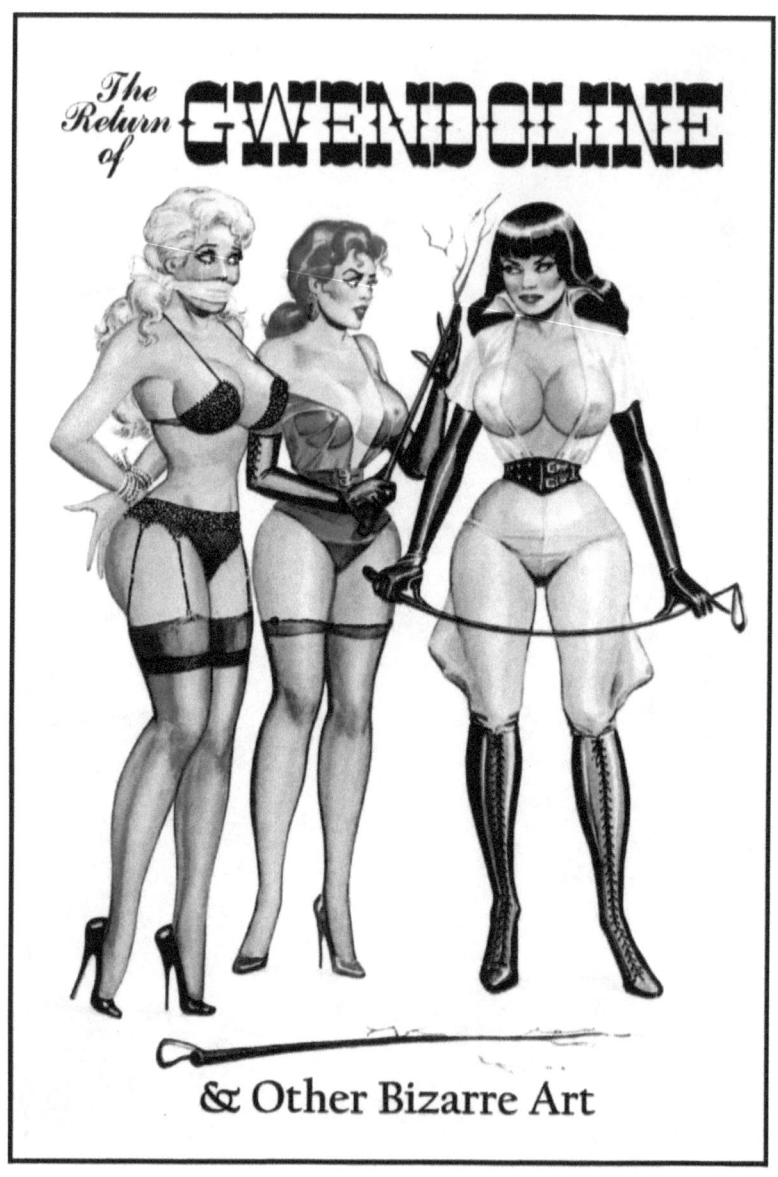

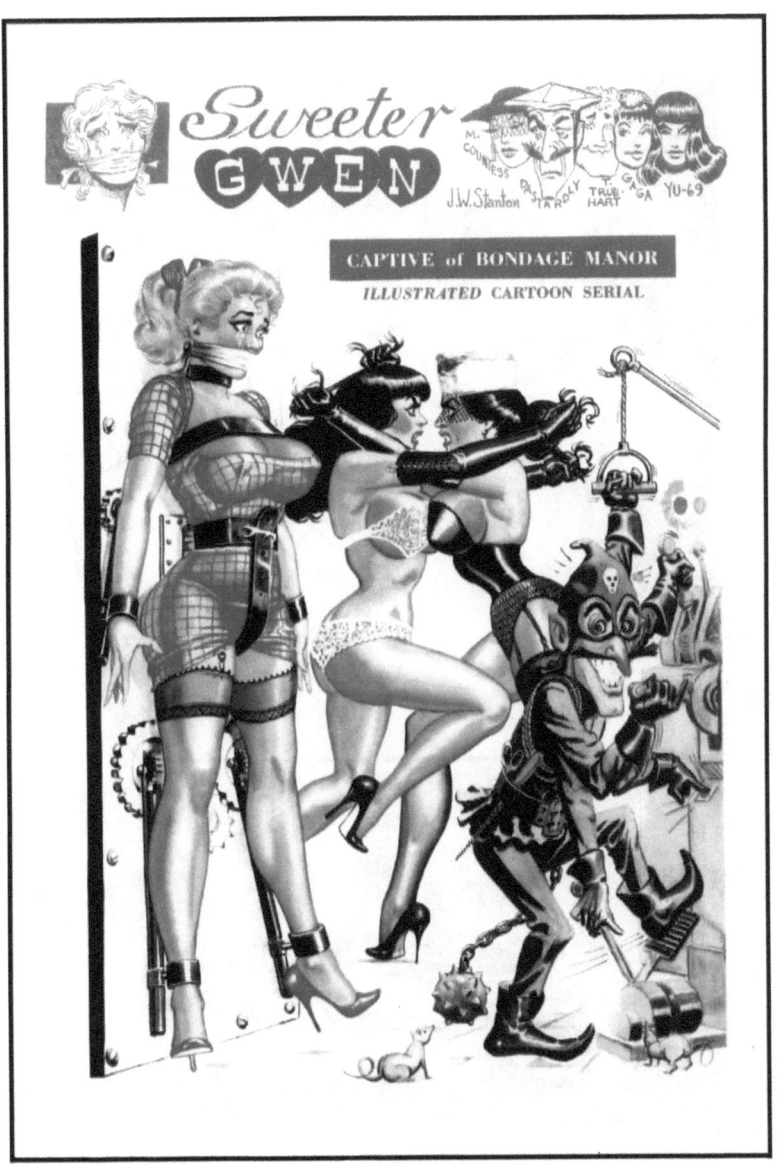

Available now! On Amazon/
FetHistory.com

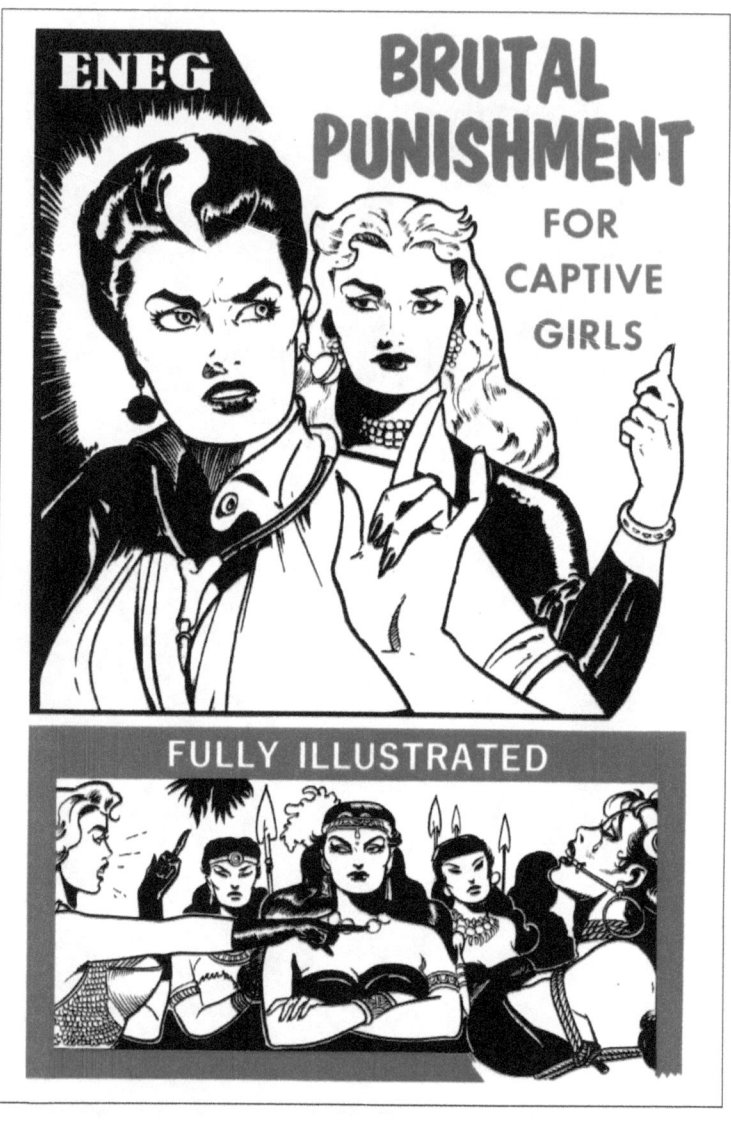

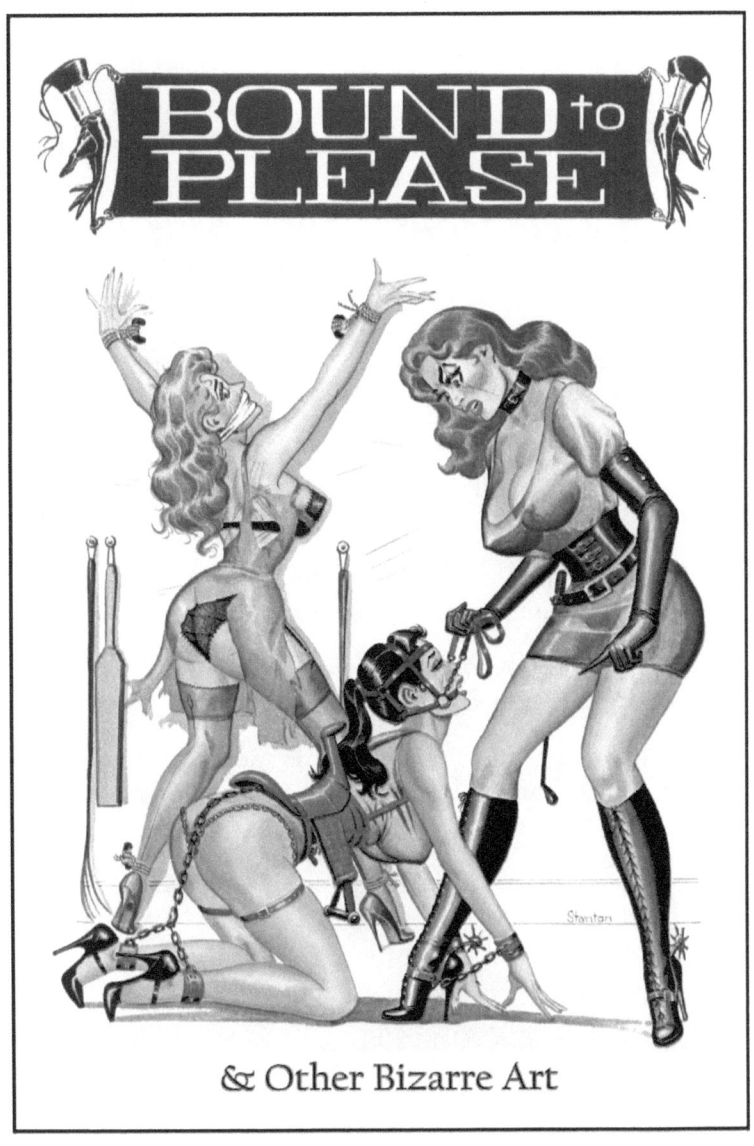

NOTES

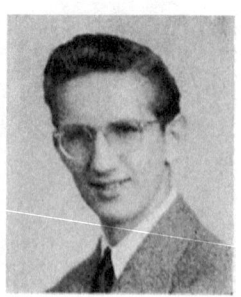

Yes, Gene was one of the students in Jerry Robinson's class.

SD.

Steve Ditko's 2012 note to the author

Known Addresses of Gene Bilbrew

- 1930 (age 6): 1280 E. 47th Street, Los Angeles CA. 90011 (see map on pg. 9)

- 1940 (age 15, according to the census): 1226 1/2 East 52 Street, Los Angeles, CA 90011 (see pg. 9)

- 1943 (age 19, still living with his mother, according to his draft card): 1230 East 52 Street, Los Angeles, CA 90011 (see pg. 9)

- 1951 (age 28, listed in the Brooklyn telephone directory under Bilbrew's name): 464 Flushing Ave, Brooklyn, NY 11205

- 1953 (age 30, listed in the Manhattan directory): 112 W 45 Street, NYC 11205

- 1960 (age 37, stated at Edward Mishkin's trial): 201 West 87th Street, NYC 10024

- 1970s (c. age 50): 48 East 21st Street & 902 Broadway, NYC 10010 (The two bookstore addresses for Mishkin's "Wholesale Books")

---

[i] *Encyclopedia of Black Comics* by Sheena C. Howard: The book description on Amazon.com:
https://www.amazon.com/dp/1682751015

[ii] Alexander, as "Ander," is associated with four Irving Klaw titles: *Peggy's Distress on the Planet Venus* (1952/53), *Castle of Terror* (1952/53), *Belle of the Plains* (1953), and *Return Visit to Fetterland* (1959: a Nutrix booklet).

[iii] William Alexander art discography:
https://www.discogs.com/artist/2678518-William-Alexander-3

[iv] Verified using the 1930 and 1940 US Federal Census Reports, along with Bilbrew's surviving military records.

[v] "...for sheer numbers, no school in Los Angeles turned out more renowned musicians than Jefferson High School in the Central-Alameda neighborhood. Don Cherry, Dexter Gordon, Art Farmer, Ernie Royal, Jackie Kelso, Ginger Smock, Bill Douglass, O.C. Smith, Roy Ayers, and Horace Tapscott are just a few of the gifted musicians..." : *Los Angeles' Citywide Historic Context Statement*, pg. 167:
http://preservation.lacity.org/sites/default/files/SurveyLA_AfricanAm ericanHCS_09252017.pdf

[vi] California Department of Public Health, courtesy of www.vitalsearch-worldwide.com.

[vii] In the 1930 census report, Omri's occupation is listed as janitor; in 1940 as a porter in a retail clothing store. On his military registration card, he wrote "Desmonds," a once famous department store whose building remains a historical landmark in Los Angeles. Omri would survive the death of his wife, Carrie, and son, Gene, and die 11 Feb 1988, at the ripe age of 97.

[viii] This according to J.B. Rund. If this is so, it was Thomas Jefferson High School, located at 1319 East 41st Street; Bilbrew's house, at age 15, was located at 1226 1/2 East 52 Street.

[ix] According to military papers, under "marital status," Bilbrew wrote "single, with dependents" ... a rumor circulating on the Internet is that

his son's name was "Bennie," born 26 June 1938, which would make Gene Bilbrew 14 years old—or three days away from 15 (as Bilbrew was born June 29). Another rumor is that Bilbrew had a second child, at some point. In either case, the mother remains unknown.

^x According to military papers, "United States World War II Army Enlistment Records, 1938-1946," database, *FamilySearch* (https://familysearch.org/ark:/61903/1:1:K85Q-T3Z : 5 December 2014), Gene W Bilbrew, enlisted 18 May 1943, Los Angeles, California, United States; citing "Electronic Army Serial Number Merged File, ca. 1938-1946," database, *The National Archives: Access to Archival Databases (AAD)* (http://aad.archives.gov : National Archives and Records Administration, 2002); NARA NAID 126323, National Archives at College Park, Maryland.

^{xi} While Bilbrew's U.S. Department of Veterans Affairs BIRLS Death File shows "18 May 1943" as his enlistment date in the Army, his surviving military registration card shows "date of registration" as "JUN 30 1942" on the back (see image). That is the day he registered for Selected Service, as required by law.

^{xii} "Medical Disposition: Under the provisions of section II, AR 615-360, and later, AR 615-361, issued on 4 November 1944, the neuropsychiatrist was frequently appointed as a member of the board of medical officers generally referred to as the "CDD (certificate of disability for discharge) Board." Even more frequently, however, he presented neuropsychiatric cases before this board which determined whether disposition would be accomplished by medical discharge. A major involvement of the psychiatrist with this board was the determination of the line of duty relative to disposition and commitment of psychotic patients. Those cases of psychosis whose line-of-duty status was determined to be "yes" after prior presentation before the "600-500 Board" (pg. 476) offered little difficulty in disposition except 483.": http://history.amedd.army.mil/booksdocs/wwii/NeuropsychiatryinW WIIVolI/chapter16.htm. Also see: https://history.amedd.army.mil/booksdocs/wwii/NeuropsychiatryinW WIIVolI/chapter9.htm

xiii It's unknown if Bilbrew staged a psychological breakdown to avoid active duty (as was somewhat common), or if he had genuine psychological issues. CDD (certificate of disability for discharge) applies specifically to the army, where he enlisted on 18 May 1943. By 27 August 1943, he was discharged.

xiv *Bizarre Comix* v. 2, 1975, Belier Press. J.B. Rund historical introduction.

xv Jessie Mae Brown, "What's Doing In The Younger Set," *The California Eagle*, 30 Sept 1943.

xvi *The California Eagle*, 30 Sept 1943: "The Mellow Tones, a fast-rising quartet, lent their talents to the Jr NAACP jamboree dance last Saturday night at the Alpha. The mellow cats came on solidly with the ever popular "Coming in on a Wing and a Prayer," and "Straighten Up and Fly Right."

xvii *Detroit Free Press*, 24 thru 27 Nov 1944.

xviii *The California Eagle*, 9 Jun 1938.

xix *California Eagle*, 19 Dec 1946: "Gene Price, first baritone with 'The Basin Street Boys….'"

xx *Arkansas State Press* (Little Rock, Arkansas), 31 May 1946.

xxi Gibson would achieve enduring fame with the Red Caps. Gibson and his original Basin Street Boys migrated to Lost Angeles in 1937: Jay Warner, *American Singing Groups: A History from 1940s to Today* (Milwaukee: Hal Leonard, 2006), pg. 12.

xxii *The Billboard*, 9 April 1949, pg. 46: full notice reads: "Ormonde Wilson, leader of the disbanded Basin Street Boys, responsible for the "I Sold My Heart to the Junk Man" record click last year, joined his step-brother, Steve Gibson in the latter's Five Red Caps, currently at Chubby's in nearby Collingswood, N. J."

xxiii *The Pittsburgh Courier*, 15 Mar 1947.

xxiv "Price" was the name of his brother-in-law, Ernest B. Price who married Frances Muriel in 1939.

xxv A.C. Bilbrew's husband was Ralph Richard Bilbrew, brother of Omri Watson Bilbrew, Gene's father. Although Ralph's name appears spelled as "Ralf" on the 1900 census report (with a different birth year than later reported by Ralph Richard Bilbrew), both are tied to Cherry Brooks, the family contact that appears listed on both their World War II military registration cards. Cherry Brooks at 1328 E. 27th Street, was their sister; she also appears on the 1900 census report.

xxvi A. C. Bilbrew was so highly considered that she would eventually have a library named after her: http://www.colapublib.org/history/willowbrook/faq.html#q1

xxvii Conversely, Kitty Jean Bilbrew, A.C. Bilbrew's daughter—coincidentally born the same year as Gene—would gain exposure through her mother to launch her own singing career, gaining celebrity under the name "Kitty White."

xxviii *The Pittsburgh Courier*, 20 Apr 1946.

xxix Hal Leonard, *American Singing Groups: A History from 1940s to Today,* 13. Also see: *Los Angeles Sentinel;* 3 Apr 1947: "..."I Sold My Heart to the Junk Man" is creating a sensation on the nation's record boxes, and is rated among the top ten in the coin machine operator's annual platter popularity poll." Also see: *The Cash Box*, 21 Oct 1946: "Burning the Jukes in Harlem" ("The Ten Top Tunes Netting Heaviest Play Compiled From Reports Submitted Weekly To The Cash Box By Leading Music Operators in New York City's Harlem."), where "I Sold My Heart to the Junkman" placed at the top—at number one.

xxx They also shared a record (two sides) with Judy Carol, in 1946: http://doowopheaven.blogspot.com/2014/03/the-basin-street-boys-2.html. *The Billboard* 14 Dec. 1946 (pg. 13) reviews an early television appearance via station W6XYZ (Paramount): "Seg opened with honeyed harmonizing by Basin Street Boys... Basin Street Boys were brought back for an encore. Lad's pic slowly faded into test pattern, their toned-down singing serving as background for Lane's closing commentary."

ˣˣˣⁱ At least twenty artists have covered the song: https://secondhandsongs.com/work/50820/versions; in 1974, Bruce Springsteen also covered it in live performance.

ˣˣˣⁱⁱ In 1946 and '47, Gene Bilbrew and Ormonde Wilson copyrighted their own songs ("Voot Nay Ion The Vot Nay" and "Ain't Got No Loot"), but it didn't seem to matter. The songs failed to chart.

ˣˣˣⁱⁱⁱ

https://archive.org/details/catalogofcopyrig315libr?q=%22Ormonde+Wilson%22

ˣˣˣⁱᵛ *Herald and News* (Klamath Falls, Oregon) 9 May 1947.

ˣˣˣᵛ *The California Eagle*, 14 Oct 1948, "Gene Price Now On His Own As Featured Act"

ˣˣˣᵛⁱ *The California Eagle*, Oct 1948, but the actual day, unfortunately, has been cropped off in the scan of the newspaper.

ˣˣˣᵛⁱⁱ The first example of Ormonde putting his name first appears in the *Pottstown Mercury* (Pottstown, PA.) 18 Sept 1948.

ˣˣˣᵛⁱⁱⁱ *The Plain Speaker* (Hazleton, Pa.) 17 Oct 1949.

ˣˣˣⁱˣ *Standard Sentinel* (Hazleton, Pa.) 21 Oct 1949; also see: *Wilmington Morning News* (Wilmington, Delaware), 6 Dec 1944.

ˣˡ *The Berkshire Eagle* (Pittsfield, Mass), 8 Nov 1949.

ˣˡⁱ "Three Ebonaires": *The Berkshire Eagle* (Pittsfield, Mass), 11 Nov 1949; "Jay Johnson...": *The Bristol Daily Courier* (Bristol, PA), 16 Dec 1949.

ˣˡⁱⁱ *The Bristol Daily Courier* (Bristol, PA), 17 Dec 1949.

ˣˡⁱⁱⁱ The phone number was ULstr 2-5350; the address 464 Flushing Ave, Brooklyn. In 1951, it was listed in the Brooklyn telephone directory under Bilbrew's name; in 1952, listed under "Roszetta Davis." See: (1951) https://archive.org/details/brooklynnewyorkc1951newy and

(1952) https://archive.org/details/brooklynnewyorkc1952newy

[xliv] *The New York Age* (New York, NY) 27 Dec 1952.

[xlv] His address: 112 W45 Street: 1953 Manhattan phonebook. *U.S. City Directories, 1822-1995*. In an FBI report dated from Oct. 1959, Bilbrew is still listed at that address.

[xlvi] singing in nightclubs: *The Journal News* (White Plains, NY), 21 Dec 1962; appearing on TV: *The New York Age* (New York, New York), 11 Sep 1954; also: The Jack Parr Show: *The Freehold Transcript and The Monmouth Inquirer*, 20 Oct 1960; hosting an R&B radio show: *The New York Age* (New York, New York), 9 Oct 1954; romantically linked to Sammy Davis Jr.: *Jet* magazine, 7 Oct 1954, 46; give birth to a daughter: *The New York Age* (New York, NY) 26 Mar 1955. Also: *Daily News* 1 May 1960.

[xlvii] Bilbrew did produce art for a digest-sized publication titled "Hampered Hercules" c. 1961 for Satellite Publishing Co. Could this be what Alexander was recalling?

[xlviii] Beth Kleber, archivist for the School of Visual Arts, in an email to the author: 25 April 2018 "…he was at SVA (then C&I) in 1950 (don't know if he started in summer or fall). Our registrar doesn't have any information beyond that."

[xlix] Jules Feiffer in an email to the author: 29 July 2012. The final Clifford comic drawn by Feiffer, dated 31 Dec. 1950, also appears as part of *Clifford* collection published by Fantagraphics Books in 1988.

[l] Jules Feiffer in an email to the author: 27 April 2018.

[li] Rund, *Bizarre Comix* v. 2, 1975, introduction.

[lii] Ibid.

[liii] Andelman, *Will Eisner: A Spirited Life*, pg. 103.

[liv] A recently covered installment of *Clifford*, bears the pub. date of 29 June 1952.

[lv] http://www.svaarchives.org/timeline.html

[lvi] Stanton and Steve Ditko both relied on the GI Bill to pay for art school; however, Bilbrew's quick discharge from the military may have denied him this option. Considering he was released for psychiatric reasons, it is possible that he claimed disability benefits.

[lvii] http://www.svaarchives.org/timeline.html

[lviii] Even into the 1970s, we can see Hogarth's overemphasis on muscularity in Bilbrew's depiction of women (giving rise to the Internet rumor that Bilbrew sometimes used Times Square transvestites as models).

[lix] In a 2012 note to the author, Ditko distinctly remembered Bilbrew from that class in reply to my question (going as far as to cross out the name "Eugene" to pencil in "Gene.") "Stephen John Ditko" appears on his Veteran Compensation Application, 6 May 1950. Source: Pennsylvania (State). World War II Veterans Compensation Applications, circa 1950s. Records of the Department of Military and Veterans Affairs, Record Group 19, Series 19.92 (877 cartons). Pennsylvania Historical and Museum Commission, Harrisburg, Pennsylvania.

[lx] That year, he had legally changed his last name from "Stanzoni" to "Stanten." See: Richard Pérez Seves, *Eric Stanton & the History of the Bizarre Underground* (Atglen, Schiffer, 2018), pgs. 37, 38. Much later he would adopt the name "Eric," which he combined with his Klaw artist's name "Stanton;" but "Eric Stanton" was never his legal name.

[lxi] Rund, *Bizarre Comix* v. 2, 1975, introduction.

[lxii] Pérez Seves, *Eric Stanton & the History of the Bizarre Underground*, pgs. 35, 44.

[lxiii] Ibid.

[lxiv] Ibid.

[lxv] Ibid., pg. 45.

[lxvi] Rund, *Bizarre Comix* v. 2, 1975, introduction.

[lxvii] Nine chapter serials by the end of 1951: *Battling Women, Fighting Femmes, Juanita Lady Wrestler, Dawn's Fighting Adventures, Dawn Battles the Amazons, Jill Undercover Girl, Poor Pamela, Diana's Ordeal, Perils of Diana.*

[lxviii] R.Q. Harmon, "A Conversation with Eric Stanton," *Bondage Life* v. 1 n. 3, August 1978, pg. 26.

[lxix] These are completion dates, although Klaw sold chapter/episode installments earlier.

[lxx] Starting in the late 1950s, Klaw condensed various earlier chapter serials into 5x7" Nutrix booklets.

[lxxi] "late '50s booklets" would be those published under the Nutrix publishing imprint, which Klaw established in New Jersey circa 1958. Although the Nutrix era lasted from 1958 to 1964, Eneg's Nutrix material is dated from 1959 to 1962.

[lxxii] Harmony Book Shop 112 West 49th St., shows Mishkin on the paperwork: #4770, 19 Feb. 1946. Mishkin's first arrest for bookmaking is noted in a newspaper article: "3 Found Guilty in Bookmaking," Long Island Daily Press, 21 Nov. 1936.

[lxxiii] Pérez Seves, *Eric Stanton & the History of the Bizarre Underground*, pg. 72.

[lxxiv] Shapiro also served in a "mentor" capacity for Leonard Burtman, according to one FBI report, dated 21 March 1960. And Mishkin and Burtman were also business associates, likely meeting through Shapiro, who had known Burtman since c. 1953 (according to the same FBI report).

[lxxv] These were "petticoat punishment" tales. "Petticoat punishment, also known as forced feminization, petticoating or pinaforing and sometimes abbreviated PP, is a kind of roleplay or fantasy that revolves around a male being dressed as a girl in front of his mother, sisters, or in some cases, girls of his own age whom he had offended

by his boorish behavior. It is a kind of forced cross-dressing for punishment, a form of psychological punishment.": https://spankingart.org/wiki/Petticoat_punishment

lxxvi Bilbrew might have seen the name of the cover of *Le Dominateur ou l'école des vierges*, which was illustrated by French art pioneer, Carlo. "Aimé Van Rod," specialized in corporal punishment. "'Aimé' means 'to love' and Rod means rod." More here: https://spankingart.org/wiki/Aim%C3%A9_Van_Rod

lxxvii Bilbrew's most referenced serials as "Gilbert" are Adventures in Petticoats, Memoirs From a Pink Mirror, and Panty Raiders—all with 48 illustrations.

lxxviii again, *Bizarre Life* #11.

lxxix incorporated 26 Oct. 1954; dissolved 28 June 1957.

lxxx These weren't themes that interested Irving Klaw at the time, and Stanton was exclusively a Klaw artist then.

lxxxi People v. Mishkin, 26 Misc.2d 152 (1960).

lxxxii Special thanks to J.B. Rund for sharing a transcript of Bilbrew's court appearance.

lxxxiii Once Bilbrew mentioned another Mishkin shop: Main Stem Book Store, which was on 49th Street.

lxxxiv Pgs. 539, 540 of the printed transcript: People v. Mishkin, 26 Misc.2d 152 (1960). The exchange that follows is edited for narrative flow.

lxxxv Paul Niloc was a pseudonym of Harry Roskolenko: https://library.syr.edu/digital/guides/r/roskolenko_h.htm

lxxxvi In the late 1950s, *Handsome Abductor* would republished by Mishkin under the title *Devil Doll*, with a memorable Bilbrew cover.

lxxxvii The artwork inserts in these publications were placed by hand, so the order of images could be different—or additional images added:

whatever was at hand. "Sham" publishing imprints were unregistered business imprints.

[lxxxviii] FBI report dated 13 November 1957, pg.5: with the California Institute of technology "as a member of the research staff in the development of telemetering devices for the atom bomb..."

[lxxxix] In the 1940s, Burtman was arrested three times. The first time for theft (stealing government property) while employed as a radio technician; source: *Riverside Daily Press*, 22 November 1944. The second time for draft evasion. The third time for transporting stolen property, in conjunction with writing bad checks; FBI report dated 13 November 1957, pg. 15, 16. Burtman served a year in prison: FBI report dated 11 October 1957, pg. 13.

[xc] Burtman's FBI files petitioned (by me) through FOIA (The Freedom of Information Act).

[xci] FBI report dated 16 September 1959.

[xcii] FBI report dated 21 March 1960.

[xciii] It would cease to exist as a publishing imprint, but the company ("Kaysey Sales") would carry on as Burtman's principal mail order business in the early 1960s.

[xciv] Original issues of *Fads and Fancies* are typically dated c. 1950, and the Burtman versions (issues #1,2,3,4,5,6) were offered for sale in 1957 (issue #20 of *Exotique*), featuring different covers.

[xcv] Fantasia issues 11 – 16, 18, 19.

[xcvi] Information courtesy of Jim Linderman

[xcvii] Bilbrew's artwork for the dust jacket is primitive enough to be from 1951, but there's a question regarding the photo of Bettie Page, which appears to be dated later. Pigalle Imports, a Burtman/Himmel company, later sold it via mail order.

[xcviii] FBI memo dated 4 Dec. 1957, lists *Slave-Mistress* (Stanton cover), *The Forbidden Path* (Bilbrew), *Woman of Evil* (Stanton), *Virgins Come*

High (Stanton), Pushover (Bilbrew), *Celeste* (Bilbrew), *Come On Girls* (Bilbrew and Stanton).

xcix *Exotica* issue #1, which became a rebooted, full-size magazine.

c "Devil Doll" was a strip advertised for the magazine *Diabolique*, though this particular strip evidently first appeared in *Santana* #3, 1962. By then, *Diabolique* was discontinued.

ci Only the Peerless Sales comics, "Lydia" and "Dark Conquest" seem to address white privilege directly.

cii This according to Stanton's widow, Britt. For more on Peerless Sales, see Pérez Seves, *Eric Stanton & the History of the Bizarre Underground*, pgs. 89 – 92.

ciii Eric Kroll, *The Art of Eric Stanton: For The Man Who Knows His Place*, pg. 9.

civ Ibid.

cv According to what Stanton told J.B. Rund.

cvi Eric Kroll, *The Art of Eric Stanton: For The Man Who Knows His Place*, pg. 11, 12.

cvii According to J. B. Rund, *Island of Captive Girls* was produced between Dec. 1952 and Aug. 1953.

cviii This is visible in magazines like *Orbit* and *Nocturne*.

cix Bilbrew evidently connected with the Sturman brothers in '63, producing the first two covers for their "Exotik" book line. For a first-hand account regarding the Sturman brothers, see "Me and the Kingpin" by Mike Resnick: http://novelspot.net/node/1519 ; also included in the paperback collection of author essays, *Resnick at Large*. Crescent, Mercury, Chevron, Satan Press among the imprints. Also see: http://www.vintagesleaze.com/catalogs-evs-crescent.htm

cx contributing to his line of paperbacks: First Niter, After Hours, Wee Hours, and Unique Books.

[cxi] The major decision that, more or less, paved the way for the rest was "Massachusetts vs. Memoirs of a Woman of Pleasure": (a.k.a. "the U.S. Supreme Court's Fanny Hill decision"); see Robert V. Bienvenu II, The Development of Sadomasochism as a Cultural Style in the Twentieth-Century United States (PhD diss., Indiana University, 1998), 205; also, Stephen J. Gertz, "West Coast Blue," Sin-a-rama (Los Angeles: Feral House, 2005), 27.

[cxii] "DeCurtis helped organized crime get its hooks into Mishkin's Wholesale Books...": R. Thomas Collins Jr., Newswalker: A Story for Sweeney, 107; also see "Mobsters Skim New York City Sex Industry Profits," The New York Times, 27 July 1977.

[cxiii] "Candor Books Inc....": the mail-order business was established in late 1970, according to a 1971 Candor Books Inc. bulletin/supplement. It shared a Madison Square Station P.O. box, recalling Gargoyle Sales Corp. The same box numbers as Gargoyle but scrambled.

[cxiv] Paula Klaw offered to sell the surviving offset-litho films and copyrights of her late brother's Nutrix booklets to Edward Mishkin...: source is J.B. Rund, who heard it directly from Paula Klaw and Edward Mishkin, whose shops Rund used to frequent in the 1970s. The "M" of Mutrix alluded to the "M" of Mishkin.

[cxv] Tortura Press/Hilbarth, Inc. was distributed by "Regent House," the mail order side of Parliament News, Inc. and Milton Luros, who had ties to organized crime. In those days, the distributor usually ran the show, providing the funding for any publisher/editor wanting a "package deal." Star Distributors was connected to the Gambino crime family through Robert DiBernardo, who a business partner.

[cxvi] The list of Star imprints that Bilbrew contributed to includes: Special Collection, Euro Classic(s), Free Press Library, Peacock, Club, Female Slave Series, Harding File, Dr. Lamb Library, MP Series.

[cxvii] J.B. Rund interview by author: 17 August 2012.

[cxviii] "At the local Flea Market, I met someone by the name of Jeffrey Goodman...": J.B. Rund email to the author, 10 August 2013.

[cxix] U.S., Department of Veterans Affairs BIRLS Death File, 1850-2010

[cxx] Eric Kroll, *The Art of Eric Stanton: For The Man Who Knows His Place, pgs.* 8, 9.

[cxxi] No trace of Bilbrew in the city or state of New York, nor was there a military funeral.

[cxxii] For the Mutrix booklet, *Catfight*, see page 227.

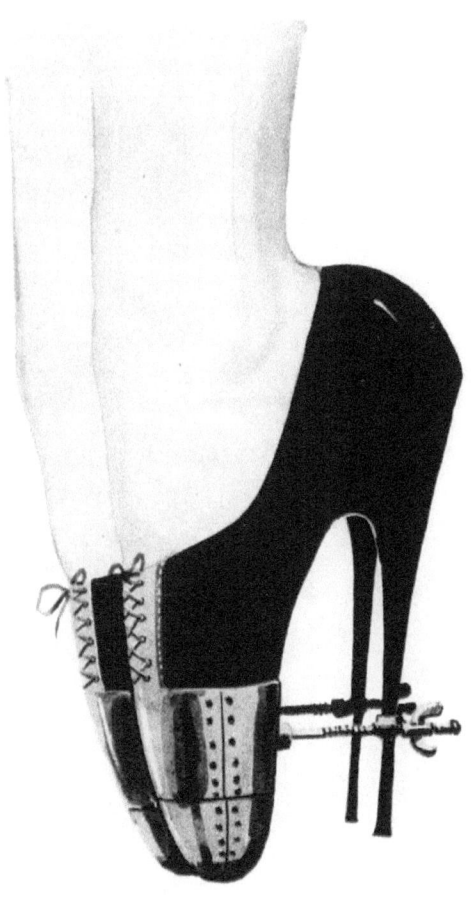

www.ingramcontent.com/pod-product-compliance
Lightning Source LLC
Chambersburg PA
CBHW020731180526
45163CB00001B/186